Feminist Practice
in the 21st Century

Feminist Practice

in the 21st Century

NAN VAN DEN BERGH, EDITOR

NASW PRESS

National Association of Social Workers
Washington, DC

Jay J. Cayner, ACSW, LSW, *President*
Robert H. Cohen, JD, ACSW, *Executive Director*

First impression, September 1995
Second impression, October 1997

Linda Beebe, *Executive Editor*
Nancy Winchester, *Editorial Services Director*
Patricia D. Wolf, Wolf Publications, Inc., *Project Manager*
Annette R. Hansen, *Copy Editor*
Ronald W. Wolf, Wolf Publications, Inc., *Copy Editor*
Susan Harris, *Proofreader*
Susan Nedrow, *Proofreader*
Bernice Eisen, *Indexer*

Library of Congress Cataloging-in-Publication data

Feminist practice in the 21st century / Nan Van Den Bergh, editor.
     p.   cm.
     Includes bibliographical references (p.   ) and index.
     ISBN 0-87101-244-8
     1. Social service–Philosophy. 2. Feminist theory. I. Nan, Van
Den Bergh.
HV40.F38   1995
361'.0082–dc20   95-16016
                                               CIP

Printed in the United States of America

Contents

Foreword

The National Association of Social Workers (NASW) has a history of addressing women's issues in the context of public policy, social work practice, and association processes and procedures. For example, NASW established the National Committee on Women's Issues (NCOWI) as a bylaws-mandated committee in 1975. As one of the three "equity" committees of the association, together with the National Committee on Racial and Ethnic Diversity and the National Committee on Lesbian and Gay Issues, NCOWI develops affirmative action initiatives and monitors plans and goals, ensures that women's issues are addressed in NASW programs and policies, and encourages chapter committees on women's issues. The committee's broader mission, however, is to promote women's leadership in the profession, to promote pay equity in the profession, and to combat discrimination in the profession and in society.

NASW's current policy statement on women's issues, which the 1987 Delegate Assembly (NASW, 1994) approved to supersede the 1977 policy, calls for action in five areas: (1) human rights, (2) civil rights, (3) economic rights, (4) political rights, and (5) professional issues. When the 1996 Delegate Assembly convenes, delegates will consider a revision, which is likely to voice the continuing economic inequities and other discrimination that women face in today's society.

Society's discrimination against women is echoed in the social work profession, even though the profession is principally female. In 1991, when the NASW membership totaled 134,240, 77.3 percent of the NASW members reporting gender were female (Gibelman & Schervish, 1993). When Gibelman and Schervish (1995) analyzed the labor force data for NASW's 1991 membership, they found that the mean salaries for women were 84 percent of the mean salaries for men. Men continue to dominate leadership positions. The Council on Social Work Education's (CSWE's) 1994 directory of schools of social work listed 62 men and 51 women as deans or directors of master of social work programs and 192 men and 190 women for baccalaureate programs. In managing its progressive affirmative action program, NASW consistently has difficulty meeting goals, not for racial and ethnic diversity, but for women, in member leadership.

In their introduction to *Feminist Visions,* Van Den Bergh and Cooper (1986) noted the irony in this incongruency:

> *Social work is supposed to share many of the fundamental concerns of feminism, particularly the relationship between individual and community, between individually and socially defined needs as well as the concern with human dignity and the right to self determination. Social work, like feminism, is theoretically committed to improving the quality of life for all people.* (p. 3)

Van Den Bergh and Cooper then identified five feminist principles as particularly relevant to social work education and practice, which they used as the framework for their book. Those five principles include

- eliminating false dichotomies and artificial separations
- reconceptualizing power
- valuing process equally with product
- validity of renaming
- the personal is political.

Since the book was published, thousands of students have learned from the strong theoretical and conceptual chapters in *Feminist Visions.*

NASW Press committee leadership and staff are very pleased to publish its sequel, *Feminist Practice in the 21st Century,* which we believe will enhance the profession's capacity for effective practice with women and advance the leadership of women in the profession. Eighteen excellent chapters address feminist practice within methods, fields of practice, and special populations. We hope that faculty, students, practitioners, and policy developers will find the compilation extraordinarily useful.

Linda Beebe
Executive Editor

Council of Social Work Education. (1994). *Directory of colleges and universities with accredited social work degree programs.* Alexandria, VA: Author.

Gibelman, M., & Schervish, P. (1993). *Who we are: The social work labor force as reflected in the NASW membership.* Washington, DC: NASW Press.

Gibelman, M., & Schervish, P. (1995). Pay equity in social work: Not! *Social Work, 40,* 622–629.

National Association of Social Workers. (1994). Women's issues. In *Social work speaks: NASW policy statements* (3rd ed., pp. 268–269). Washington, DC: NASW Press.

Van Den Bergh, N., & Cooper, L. (1986). Introduction. In *Feminist visions for social work*. Silver Spring, MD: National Association of Social Workers.

Acknowledgments

First, I want to extend my sincere appreciation to all contributors. They have been exceedingly patient during the process of bringing this book to fruition. Unfortunately, significant stressors experienced during the past two years—including the downsizing of the program I directed at the University of California at Los Angeles, a relocation to the South and the accompanying culture shock, as well as various vicissitudes and vagaries associated with undertaking a new academic position—stretched the "manageability" of my life and delayed the publication of this volume. Hence, please accept my amends, contributors, and know that I value the creativity and effort expended in your contributions to this volume.

To Linda Beebe, Nancy Winchester, Patricia Wolf, and other NASW Press staff, I extend my gratitude for your support and assistance. Readers should know that with a relatively small staff, the NASW Press does a superb job in the publication and dissemination of books that advance the knowledge base of our profession. Pay your NASW membership dues! More than 50 percent of that relatively low yearly fee supports local NASW endeavors; the balance provides operating expenses for the organization that voices our professional missions and advocates for our causes.

To feminist social work practitioners and academics who have offered definitions of feminist practice and its applications within the literature during the past 30 years, I extend my gratitude for the contributions you have made. In preparation for my chapter in this book, I reviewed feminist social work literature published since the mid-1970s. Because it has been somewhat hazardous to publish as a feminist, I commend your courage, insight, and perseverance in advancing our cause.

I also want to acknowledge those individuals, overwhelmingly women, who have taken risks and made stands in a variety of contexts, to voice women's realities and to advocate to remediate the oppressive life conditions that women and their dependents disproportionately experience, including violence, impoverishment, poor health care, substandard housing, inadequate educational opportunities, and other oppressive life conditions. This book is dedicated to you . . . for your help in envisioning and voicing feminist concerns, so as to bring women from margin to center.

—*Nan Van Den Bergh*

Feminist Social Work Practice
Where Have We Been . . .
Where Are We Going?

Nan Van Den Bergh

It was, at first, important that you
    See us
So we spoke of Vision.

And now
    you must Hear us
As we are not the same,
    nor do we have similar
    stories, beliefs, needs.

But, we have
    Standpoints
From which we Know,
    So
Do not tell us what is True
    or ask for the Proof.

We are a web of interconnected
    Meanings,
Diverse but interdependent,
    and Spirited
To resist being silenced and invisible.*

---

*When I thought about a way to open this chapter and synthesize all that I wanted to impart, I realized that one of my own clients was affecting this process. A woman with whom I am working is just now, in midlife, developing her creative abilities and has shared both her poetry and prose with me. As I reflected on what I wished to say in this chapter, a poem came to mind. I believe that creative thought is the interconnection of the intersubjective, reflexive, and co-creative process that my client and I experience.

While compiling this book, I experienced a dizzying perception, to quote Jane Flax (1990), that "something was happening" (p. 3) in terms of describing feminism and its impact on the world. To that extent, I experienced concern as to whether the project I was undertaking, editing an anthology on feminist social work practice, might be seen as "epistemologically incorrect." You may ask, "What does that mean?" *Epistemology* is the study of knowledge and knowledge-generating processes. *Feminism* is a conceptual framework and mode of analysis that has analyzed the status of women (and other disempowered groups), cross-culturally and historically to explain dynamics and conditions undergirding disparities in sociocultural status and power between majority and minority populations (Van Den Bergh & Cooper, 1986, 1987). Consequently, feminism can be considered an epistemological framework. The relevance of under-scoring feminism as an epistemology is that an evolving kind of Kuhnian scientific revolution (Kuhn, 1970), called "post-modernism," has been wielding an increasingly significant impact on extant knowledge in the social sciences, natural sciences, arts and humanities, and on feminism and social work. Postmodernism might be considered as a harbinger of change in altering what is consid-ered to be truth, because it questions basic precepts about what con-stitutes knowledge as well as processes associated with the scientific method and logical positivism.

Basically, *postmodernism* is a reaction to modernist traditions dat-ing from the 17th century Enlightenment movement. The Enlight-enment sought to remediate medieval strictures against inquiry and distortions of reality, such as earth being the center of the universe. To be deemed as truth, the scientific method was created, establish-ing that knowledge needed to be acquired by logical, rational, and empirical processes. Despite the value the Enlightenment has served, its logical positivist tradition has generated some unfortunate out-comes. For example, truth became dichotomized or split; that is to say, knowledge was categorized and placed in a hierarchy of right versus wrong. Because those who "created" knowledge were over-represented by privileged members of society, perceptions of reality based on marginalized people (that is, women, ethnic minorities, and poor people) tended to be overlooked and excluded (Nicholson, 1990). Hence, postmodernism has questioned established knowl-edge. Its proponents have been seeking to reconstruct truth based on deconstructing grand theory through a process of looking for who and what was excluded. Then, knowledge can be recon-structed by bringing voices of disempowered people from mar-gin to center.

Because social work is an applied social science and feminism serves as an epistemological framework with applied value in suggesting the need for structural social change, postmodernism has been causing reverberations in the foundations of knowledge in both fields. Assumptions associated with postmodernism will be elaborated subsequently, but the premise that underpinned the compilation of this book (that is, to describe feminist social work's applicability for contemporary and future practice) could be viewed as epistemologically dystonic with postmodernism. Postmodernism questions the veracity of grand theory or propositions concerning reality that are to be generalized and ubiquitously applied.

Consequently, I was faced with an intellectual dilemma. How could I edit a state-of-the-art volume on feminist social work practice that described "how to do it" if such an approach, based on theorizing and generalizing, was being increasingly questioned as an inappropriate epistemological process? As noted previously, my desire had been to edit an anthology true to feminist precepts as well as being helpful in applying feminist analysis to social work methods, fields of practice, and interventions with special populations. My request to contributors had been that they were to indicate what would be feminist about the method, practice domain, or approach of which they wrote. After reflecting on contributors' chapters, as well as the burgeoning literature related to postmodernism's influence on feminism (Butler & Scott, 1992; Flax, 1990; Nicholson, 1990) as well as social work theory, pedagogy and practice(Doll, 1989; Laird, 1993; Pardeck, Murphy, & Choi, 1994; Payne, 1991), I believe that I have been able to resolve my "intellectual vertigo" in a way that honors assumptions associated with feminism, social work practice, and postmodernism. Having qualified my process in editing this volume, I now undertake an explication of postmodernism to ground the subsequent description of its impact on ideas related to feminist social work practice.

POSTMODERN ASSUMPTIONS ABOUT KNOWLEDGE CREATION: IMPLICATIONS FOR FEMINISM AND SOCIAL WORK

Postmodernism (as an epistemological framework) opposes the construction of grand theory based on the assumption of underlying structures and truths (Featherstone & Fawcett, 1994; Nuccio & Sands, 1992; Sands & Nuccio, 1992). Paradigms of that ilk, within the social sciences, include most of the knowledge that has been borrowed to inform social work practice (Compton & Galaway, 1994), including systems and ecological theories; ego psychology, object relations, self psychology, and cognitive or behavioral theories; learning theories; psychological and moral development paradigms (Erikson, 1950; Kohlberg, 1981); determinist frameworks (that is, biological or cultural determinism); and political or economic models of societal relations, such as Marxism.

Questioning essential truths and underlying structures

Logical positivism, or modernism bases knowledge construction on *structuralism*, the discernment of underlying structures that have meaning that is fixed and universal. *Logocentrism* is a belief inherent within positivism that reality and truth are imbued with a fixed, rational, and logical order based on innate, deterministic, essentialist traits (Sands & Nuccio, 1992). Truths, established through positivist processes are assumed to delineate *essentialism*; that is, unequivocal and universal understandings that can create dichotomized and hierarchical categories of right and wrong (Featherstone & Fawcett, 1994). Essentialist properties are often based on assumptions of biological determinism (intrinsic biologically based qualities that determine behavior) or, more loosely, human nature. Hence, people are seen as defined by a fixed set of attributes that are conceptualized as innately physical, intellectual, or emotional (Stanley & Wise, 1993).

Essentialist thinking, for example, underpins the bifurcation of gender-associated traits that are at the etiology of assumptions concerning what is masculine, as diametrically opposite (and superior) to what is feminine. As an example of how this dichotomization of feminine and masculine traits plays out, modernist thinking dichotomizes humans as comprising a mind and a body only. Blatantly absent from this rendition of human components are emotion and spirit. In opposition to this narrow and split perspective, feminist analysis has depicted human "beingness" as multifaceted, an interconnection of mind, body, spirit, and emotion. To this extent, the pervasive tendency in Western medicine to dissect and prescribe is antithetical to a feminist purview of health care, which supports prevention and a wholistic treatment approach.

Related to modernist gender role structures and essentialist traits has been the association of body with women (and nature), whereas the mind has been associated with men. Furthermore, gender-associated dichotimization is exhibited by description of the rational aspects of the mind as male and the emotional aspects as female (Stanley & Wise, 1993). This very split in the modernist gender dichotimization of the mind may serve as the foundation for negative attitudes toward mental illness and psychotherapy (that is, to display emotions; to experience debilitating depression, anxiety, or psychosis; or to engage in psychotherapy that depicts one as out of control, weak, and not strong.) Stereotypically, those descriptors would be seen as more feminine than masculine, and henceforth, qualitatively evaluated as negative. Research in the 1970s showed that stereotypically feminine traits were associated with depictions of a less mature adult, whereas traits associated with masculinity were synonymous with descriptors of a psychologically mature adult (Broverman, Broverman, & Clark, 1970).

The dichotimization of gender-associated traits suggests the etiology of the philosophy of mind over matter. As to the implications of this philosophy when applied to the material world, consider the relationship between the desecration of the natural environment, and adherence to the modernist technological desire to control Mother Nature (Griffin, 1993).

Partnerships rather than domination
Another example of the dangers that could be attributed to gender-associated bifurcated thinking is described by Eisler (1987) in her historical/anthropological tract on cultural transformation theory. Within this model, which should be considered modernist in the sense that it is presented as a grand theory, there are two basic types of societies: dominator and partnership. Within dominator societies, stratification and inequality exist if one group is ranked as superior to others. Partnership societies, however, have social relations built on the principle of linking, rather than ranking. In this latter model, diversity between social groups based on gender, ethnicity, age, and sexual orientation would not be equated with inferiority or superiority. Eisler's theory proposes that the original direction of human cultural evolution was toward partnership societies; however, after a period of chaos and almost total cultural disruption (during the prehistory of Western civilization), a fundamental social shift occurred. Societies that had worshipped the life-generating and nurturing powers of the universe (associated with female forces), symbolized by the chalice, were decimated by "prehistoric... invaders." The latter social groupings adorated the "lethal power of the Blade" (Eisler, 1987, p. xvii) manifested by the ability to take, rather than to give life. Thus, through the threat of violence, domination was established and enforced.

Eisler's provocative historical and anthropological exposé suggests that the kind of cultural climate associated with patriarchy (and the dominion of masculinity over femininity) is built on social relationships characterized by domination, conquest, and control and the derision of values associated with caring, partnership, and concern with collective welfare. The implications of this analysis for social work should be obvious. For our profession to be successful in our change-inducing missions, social work would be most optimized by practicing within a cultural context supportive of our cardinal values (Compton & Galaway, 1994), including the validation of human dignity and worth, as well as undertaking caretaking toward others and concern with the collective welfare. Similarly, to both prevent and remediate client problems, social work practice should ascribe partnership as the motto for our relationship-building endeavors, regardless of the size of the client system. Within our profession, the extent to which there remain feuds between direct and indirect service proponents, clinical service providers and community organizers, or the perceived correct versus incorrect approach to pedagogy or practice encourages relational dynamics whereby domination and competition are pervasive.

I believe it is incumbent on social work practitioners and educators to model community-building "partnership" behaviors as opposed to engaging in battles with each other, a clear regression to dominator social relationships. What is needed is an end to the modernist tendency to establish truth via processes of categorization and hierarchization, which engenders such dichotomizes as right versus wrong, correct versus incorrect, and winners versus losers. All of our professional missions can be accomplished by placing greater emphasis on voicing the social gospel of caring and demonstrating that belief through behaviors that model partnership and coalition-building. Consequently, to ensure a social context supportive of social policies and services that promote collective well-being, it is critical to oppose the kind of dichotimization inherent in sex role stereotyping and the splitting and hierarchization of human worth, demonstrated through power over social relationships.

The potential value of establishing partnership professional relationships is not a new concept within the area of feminist practice. Social work feminist practice literature has placed considerable emphasis on the need to establish equality in the therapeutic relationship (Bricker-Jenkins & Hooyman, 1984, 1986; Collins, 1986; Doninelli & McLeod, 1989; Lundy, 1993; Nes & Iadicola, 1989; Van Den Bergh & Cooper, 1987). One might think of this as analogous to the postmodern conceptualization of treatment as a partnership endeavor between client and practitioner. Although ideas pursuant to the co-creation of meaning between practitioner and client were not voiced within earlier feminist practice literature, that assumption could be considered implicit within "equality of the therapeutic relationship" assumptions. The latter belief is associated with a pervasive theme within the early feminist literature on remediating power imbalances within relationships. That issue was born out of concern with sexual politics and the disadvantaged status of women in society relative to men.

"Partnership" as descriptive of a feminist practice treatment relationship is actually a more valid assumption than "equality" between a social worker and his or her clients. The latter belief is naive, according to some African American feminist practitioners, because clients, having experienced the multiple impacts of race, class, and gender, will not approach a treatment provider assuming a relationship of equality exists. The therapist has obviously experienced some "privilege" to be within a professional role (Greene, 1994; Lewis & Kissman, 1989). However, despite their demographic differences, clients and practitioners with diverse backgrounds can arrive at co-created understandings as to client needs and directions to pursue in solving problems by ensuring that an ethic of partnership strengthens their professional relationship.

Local rather than universal truths

As opposed to the modernist practice of establishing "truth" through the discovery of ubiquitous and essential underlying intrinsic structures, postmodernism suggests that knowledge is "local" in nature. Such an assumption is based on the belief that knowledge should be created through a partnership, rather than a dominator, model. Positivist knowledge-building is constructed through the categorization and hierarchization of information, which creates a dichotomy of expert and nonexpert between the researcher and his or her subjects. Such relationships objectify those being studied; as such, an inherent domination occurs within the research relationship. The dominator model of knowledge generation is questioned within postmodernism. Rather than being an end in and of itself, knowledge becomes a process (Weick, 1993) of generating co-created meanings through participant engagement in discourse. The social scientist and his or her informants become co-researchers in ascertaining themes within life experiences and their meanings, as they might portend trends in social reality. Within the knowledge-generation process, participants engage in mutual dialogue and reflection; their knowledge-building process also includes reflexivity and intersubjectivity. As a result, "reality" becomes linguistically created through shared perceptions of truth and interpretations of the meaning of those truths, based on life experiences (Pardeck et al., 1994). As opposed to presenting knowledge within tomes built from the discovery of underlying essential traits and structures, knowledge is espoused through narratives ("stories"), where truth is based on an individual's perceptions of reality and its meanings, which are contextually based.

Establishing "community" meanings

The local nature of knowledge creation in a postmodern perspective suggests implications for the focus of social work interventions. A postmodern practice venue should be community based, with community not being defined by demographic or geographic terms. Rather, a community could be conceptualized as a domain where certain assumptions about reality are acknowledged to have validity; a term useful in describing this kind of community is lebenswelt. The translation of that term is lifeworld and, used within the context of a community, it means a grouping of individuals who perceive reality in a similar fashion. Hence, within a lebenswelt there is a web of "meanings" created and sustained through collective linguistic understandings (Pardeck et al., 1994). This postmodern purview suggests that practitioners be aware of how a client's cultural context affects all aspects of problem assessment and remediation. Through the "community-based" practice relationships, clients can take on an "expert" role by supplying the interpretive context for determination of a presenting problem's nature and the best intervention approach.

I believe there is great import for feminist social work practice in the incorporation of this postmodern practice *lebenswelt* concept in terms of being able to coalesce critical masses around issues of feminist and social work concern. In general, rather than trying to create social change via a unifocus endeavor, such as passage of the Equal Rights Amendment, the potential for more broad-based support of social issues could be accrued through organizing efforts focused on problems that have cross-sectional impact in terms of the demographic diversity of people affected by them. For example, addictions are feminist issues (Van Den Bergh, 1991) based on their negative impact on families and individuals, which cuts across gender, ethnic, and class lines. A feminist *lebenswelt* experience was facilitated by the Center for Substance Abuse Prevention in the spring of 1994, whereby feminist researchers, practitioners, and educators from around the country convened in Washington, DC, to co-create "meanings" related to the impact of substance abuse on women's lives. Through this gathering of individuals with diverse backgrounds, it was possible to create a community of women who desired to establish a common cause around ways to organize, advocate, and take action to reduce the negative impact of alcoholism and drug abuse. One outcome of that *lebenswelt* experience was the creation of a Women's Network on Substance Abuse. The network was created with the purpose of undertaking information dissemination and support for garnering prevention and treatment resources. It is hoped that another outcome of this women's network would be a national Women's Recovery Day, which would raise community consciousness pursuant to the need for expanded women's addiction prevention and intervention programs. The point to be underscored here is the value in creating "communities of understanding" comprised of individuals who have similar perceptions of reality through their life experience and who use their co-created knowledge to affect social change.

Deconstructing and reconstructing knowledge
An assumption of postmodernism associated with a repudiation of essentialism and structuralism is that there are diverse ways of knowing (Belenky, Clinchy, Goldberger, & Tarule, 1986) that can be formulated by deconstructing "grand theory" and reconstructing broader and more-inclusive perceptions of reality. Deconstruction entails uncovering knowledge "phallacies" by recovering repressed or marginalized knowledge. When deconstructing, one looks at the assumptions and constructs included within a particular explanatory framework in relation to social, economic, and political realities. For example, what assumptions exist about women? Are assumptions about women based on beliefs that women are innately dependent, biologically predestined to need protection and considered unfit or unfulfilled unless married? Processes of deconstruction allow biases to be uncovered; you look for who has not been included and what has not been articulated in the explanation of some phenomenon. Nuccio and Sands (1992) have offered compelling descriptions of deconstruction and its utility for social work policy analysis based on using postmodern feminist theory to deconstruct fallacies of poverty. Readers are referred to their work to acquire a fuller understanding of how one can deconstruct analyses relevant to social work. In essence, through the deconstruction process, biased knowledge can be altered by reconstructing truth through inclusion of the voices of disempowered people. Knowledge that had previously been marginalized can then be centered (hooks, 1984). As a result, that which is known is broadened, expanded, enriched, and deepened by allowing the voices of disempowered people to be articulated.

The above-noted assumption is based on the premise that disempowered people have "double knowledge." Not only are they aware of what is ostensibly true according to the majority culture's perception of reality, they understand additional truths based on their experiences as minority people (Butler, 1992; hooks, 1989; Weick, 1993). There have been authors within social work who have used a similar analogy, albeit applying different terminology. For example, as applied to ethnic populations, Norton (1978) coined the concept "dual perspective" to explain how people of color can have more than one perception of reality based on the potential disparities between the truths articulated in their micro environment compared with assumptions emanating from the macro environment.

Social work's person-in-environment (PIE) and ecological perspectives seem syntonic with the postmodern precept that "truth" is a function of one's ontological experience. An *ontology* is a theory of reality or "being" (Stanley & Wise, 1993). We might construe a kind of postmodern ontology inherent within the PIE/ecological "many-layered" purview used in assessing and remediating client problems. That is, social work's professional perspective as to the ontology of client problems is that they are contextually based in the client's history and "life space."

In fact, postmodern approaches to treatment suggest that practitioners assist clients in conceptualizing problems as "paralyzing narratives" (that is, stories that limit possibilities). Hence, treatment solutions are engendered by externalizing the problem. *Externalizing* entails depicting the problem as outside of the client, in the sense of being external, or separate from, client strengths and capabilities. This perspective can free clients from self-pejorative beliefs that can be disempowering. For example, a manic-depressive client's illness could be redefined as overenthusiasm. A practitioner could then render assistance in co-creating with the client action plans to self-monitor overenthusiasm tendencies (White, 1992). In externalizing the problem, client strengths are drawn on, and negative distortions of one's capabilities can be thwarted. By using this narrative approach to treatment, practitioners engage in questioning, with their clients, whether the client's "storying" about himself or herself is a representative fit with the client's actual life experiences. Solutions accrue within client and practitioner co-construction of new narratives that are less negatively defining and less distant from the client's life experiences (Laird, 1995a; White & Epston, 1990).

As a feminist practitioner, I have found the "restorying" of client experiences to be extremely valuable in deterring the impact of client negative self-valuations acquired through internalized pejorative stereotypes and based on one's demographics or life experiences. For example, some gay male clients I have worked with have had a sense of diminished self-efficacy based on internalizing societal stereotypes of gay men as "weak." When we examine their life experiences as gay men through restorying episodes when they have demonstrated pride in their sexual orientation, they can rescript themselves as courageous and strong. This allows for a new self-narrative to be brought from the margin to the center of their life story in terms of identifying positive traits and behaviors they can ascribe to themselves.

In a related vein, female adult incest survivors can have an internalized sense of being a victim. This self-deprecatory story can deter the development of a woman's motivation to take charge of her life and to self-actualize. By restorying instances in which a female client demonstrated courage, conviction, and strength through overcoming obstacles such as going back to school, standing up to workplace harassment, or protecting her children from abusive partners, such women can rewrite their life narratives from a perspective of empowerment. Both of these examples serve to underscore the treatment value accruing from deconstructing and then reconstructing client life experiences so as to rewrite self-narratives with a more empowering meaning.

Socially constructing knowledge

A postmodern assumption inherent within undertaking processes of knowledge deconstruction and reconstruction is that reality is socially constructed; the concept applied to that notion is social constructivism (Laird, 1995b). Actually, feminists have been proposing analyses that are social constructivist in their intonation, such as "the personal is political," since the beginning of the second wave of the women's movement in the 1960s. Consequently, as I began to delve into the postmodern literature my first thought was "This is not new thinking...We (feminists) figured that out 30 years ago!" For example, the feminist process of consciousness-raising entails knowledge-building through social constructivist means. From the early days of the feminist movement, women gathered in groups to share their experiences and to "speak bitterness." By engaging in dialogue with each other, they were able to redefine their identities, realize their strengths, and analyze their disempowered status. This enabled women to engage in personal and political acts with the goal of affecting individual and social change, hence, the etiology of the "personal is political" adage (Van Den Bergh & Cooper, 1986, 1987).

Other civil rights movements of the 1960s and 1970s also gave voice to the need for minority populations to "name" their own reality. Minority is used here, in the sociological sense, to indicate populations experiencing discrimination based on sociocultural, economic, and political power inequities (Allport, 1954). Activists with the Black Power, Chicano, and Native American movements, disability activists, and participants within the gay rights movement have sought to define their own realities and, sometimes, to alter referents and nomenclature. For example, the term "African American" is currently preferred by many people who had previously identified themselves as "Black." Some disability activists have chosen to rename themselves as "differently abled." As another example, gay rights' activism has engendered an epistemological contribution known as "queer theory" that is grounded in ontological and political reflections of lesbians, bisexuals, transsexuals, and gay men . All of the above examples serve to add credence to the poststructuralist assumption that knowledge is socially constructed, or otherwise stated, "reality is in the eyes of the beholder." To name one's reality and use language that is more representative of one's life experiences can be an "empowering" experience (Van Den Bergh, 1987).

Awareness of the empowerment potential inherent in building knowledge through a social constructivist approach strengthened questioning by feminists and other civil right's activists (during the 1960s and 1970s) as to the validity and reliability of much extant social sciences knowledge. Those voices of dissent called for a "rewriting" of history and a reconstruction of social sciences "truth." This was because knowledge frequently espoused as generalizable had been normed primarily on white male samples. An outcome of such activism within academia was the establishment of programs of women's studies, ethnic studies, gay and lesbian studies, and commensurably, the publication of journals that sought to give voice to previously excluded knowledge. Hence, within social work, the journal *Affilia* (which deals with feminist issues and social work practice) was actualized by efforts of feminist social workers who sought to ensure that a scholarly journal would exist providing opportunities to bring feminist social work thought from margin to center.

As a related example, mandates by the Council on Social Work Education pursuant to curricular inclusion of knowledge on women, gay men and lesbians, people from racial and ethnic groups, and poor people exhibit a kind of social constructivist belief within social work education. The function of those "minority" standards is to ensure that our profession's educational foundation is inclusive of knowledge dealing with marginalized groups. We hope such standards preclude a professional knowledge tyranny within social work, because populations typically written out of history and the social sciences are those that our profession has a historical and ethical mandate to empower. For example, social workers must be familiar with the varying social problems that disproportionately affect women, such as poverty and violence, as well as assumptions related to feminist practice, because most social services recipients are women and their children (Wetzel, 1976, 1986).

The inextricable link between knowledge and power
Eluded to within the above social constructivist discussion is the postmodern premise that knowledge and power are inextricably linked; therefore, the forces that "rule" society control what is "known" and what is "true" (Butler, 1992; Doll, 1989; Laird, 1993; Pardeck et al., 1994; Singer, 1992). This view is particularly associated with Foucault (1978) an "elder pundit" of postmodernism who maintained that there is no possibility for knowledge creation outside of societal power structures. What is deemed truth is a function of who has power. As such, Foucault believed that voices of the "disempowered" have been systematically silenced through "expert" knowledge systems (Featherstone & Fawcett, 1994).

As social workers, we need to ask the extent to which the practice models and the theories that guide our interventions have been derived by listening to the voices of our clients. Claims that social welfare programs are ineffective and casework approaches have not proven their efficacy may be a function of methodological myopia within the theories and models on which our service delivery systems and approaches have been based. For example, to what extent have the voices of Aid to Families with Dependent Children recipients been listened to pursuant to the impact of income maintenance programs on their everyday lives? Similarly, have "voices of experience" been heard in the design and delivery of addiction prevention and intervention approaches?

Biases may exist in the ability to design and assess the effectiveness of social programs and interventions because we may be blinded by the privilege inherent in being a professional, regardless of our demographics or personal backgrounds. Swigonski (1993, 1994), a feminist social work researcher, found through study she has undertaken that "privilege is invisible to those who hold it" (Swigonski, 1993). The implications of this finding should be obvious. As social workers we are likely affected by an endemic myopia inherent in becoming professional that distances us from clients' everyday lives and oppressive realities. Consequently, it would behoove us in the interest of being effective and ethical practitioners to "inform" our program designs and interventions with knowledge based in the life experiences of our clients. It is presumptuous to think that we can theorize ways to design service delivery systems if we have not based our assumptions in the storied life experiences of potential service recipients. To be rid of this potential professional myopia, we should, as a matter of course, ask ourselves, "To what extent am I being guided by client perspectives on problem etiology and solution potentialities?"

As a case in point, the most significant amount of research funded by the National Institute on Drug Abuse related to female addicts has studied pregnant and postpartum women. Deconstructing this reality leads one to assume that federally funded research priorities related to female addicts seem specified to their role as "breeders and feeders." Only recently have studies that examine the sociocultural factors associated with the etiology of female drug abuse such as childhood neglect and abuse, incest, rape, and domestic violence been funded. Additionally, I find it extraordinary that although women constitute two-thirds of the population receiving psychotropic medications yearly (Prather & Minkow, 1991) and have a 3:1 prevalence ratio in depressive disorders, compared with men, the overwhelming majority of psychopharmacological research on antidepressant medications has been undertaken with male subjects. The reason why female subjects have been excluded from such research is based on the rationale that it would be very difficult to rigorously control for the effect of hormonal fluctuations associated with the menstrual cycle. Hence, because men do not have periods or become pregnant, they are presumed "safer" to study.

Within both of the examples described above, women were either "invisible" or their status as "subjects" was based on a very circumscribed perspective of "women's realities." The point is that science undertaken with all the elegance of positivist traditions, if based on pejorative and diminutive stereotypes or biases, does not serve in advancing "knowledge" about those who are studied. Rather, such methodologies perpetuate assumptions that strengthen and perpetuate institutionalized discriminatory practices.

As a remediation of the authoritarian knowledge creation process endemic to logical positivism, the social constructivist approach is based on sharing perceptions of reality and its meanings through processes of mutual discourse rather than through a subject–object relationship. Consequently, the pursuit of knowledge is a process rather than an end in itself. Rather than being external, objective, and neutral, the social constructivist researcher sees himself or herself as engaged within a discovery process built on mutuality, dialogue, reflexion, and intersubjectivity. Because human "knowing" is shaped by cultural, societal, and psychic forces, there is no such thing as "objective reality" or seeing something as it really is. The knower influences what is known and how it is known. As a result, the value-free perspective associated with logical positivism is impossible. Values influence every aspect of the research process from the questions that are asked to the analysis of results.

Inherent within the social constructivist approach to creating knowledge is the belief that truths are located within individuals' perceptions of their reality. To that extent, knowledge does not lie outside oneself; each person can become a knowledge creator, and this can be an empowering experience (Weick, 1993). To underscore this point, it has been suggested that the appropriate context for research activities should be everyday life (Swigonski, 1994). In studying the realities of marginalized people, it becomes possible to see how the public world, and its institutions, structures everyday private lives. As an example, a researcher might ask female youths about the impact of strictures surrounding access to birth control and about the precautions they take when engaging in sex. Similarly, one might speak with women in homeless shelters to determine how eligibility criteria for income and housing assistance affected becoming homeless.

The construction of knowledge grounded in life experiences, particularly of disempowered people, carries the potential for a more representative depiction of "truth." Additionally, through use of a knowledge-building process facilitated by collaboration between researchers and their informants, knowledge creation can be empowering for all those involved in the co-creation endeavor.

VOICING STANDPOINTS

As previously noted, the primary feminist criticism of logical positivism as the mainstream scientific approach to knowledge creation is that it has been, too often, "malestream" (Stanley & Wise, 1983). Because the logical positivist approach is based on assimilationist (value free and neutral) as well as alienating (separate from) assumptions and methodologies, the social world experienced from women's standpoint has frequently been ignored and silenced. Aspects of a postmodern approach, with its emphasis on validating locale-specific knowledge creation, has the potential to be more inclusive of "women's ways of knowing."

The astute reader, however, may have considered that despite the many virtues of postmodernism, there are some endemic aspects to that epistemological perspective that would not be synchronistic with feminism or social work. This is because feminist epistemology and our profession have a "political" nature, whereas, in many regards, postmodernism is apolitical. When postmodernism's locality rather than generality focus is taken to its ultimate conclusion, the outcome is not one supportive of articulating ubiquitous truths from which advocacy and activism are undertaken. Hence, there are postmodern feminists who believe it is a disservice to women to espouse statements regarding "women's oppression" and "women's realities." Such feminists believe that each woman, situated in her own time and place, constructs her own reality (Davis, 1993). Additionally, postmodern feminists believe that searching for commonalities among women provides ammunition for oppressors, in the sense of categorizing women. Grouping according to assumed commonalities is seen as regressing back to the kind of essentialist assumptions that strengthen sex role stereotypes. Some postmodern feminists believe that subscribing to a generalized description of "women's reality" means embracing a "place" that has been imposed on women (subordination) that contributes to women's objectification. "Purist" postmodern theorists view all perspectives equally and hold none as absolute standards. All categories are deconstructed, including that of "women"; this obviously means that one cannot speak of "women's oppression" in the collective sense. A woman could describe oppression only through her individual life experience.

Consequently, there is a tension, of sorts, in reconciling postmodernism with feminism and with social work. Both our profession and the women's movement have historically sought to remediate oppressive conditions for marginalized groups by generalizing about the extent and degree women and disempowered people have been disadvantaged. Such advocacy is requisite for engendering the kind of constituency building requisite within the social policy creation process.

Historically, feminism has sought to bring women into focus and to give them voice. In other words, gender has been the organizing theme around which both the women's suffrage movement and feminism's "second wave" have coalesced. It is salient to mention, having just noted women's suffrage, that 1995 marks the 75th anniversary of women having the right to vote; this is not a very long time. That fact, in and of itself, suggests that securing civil rights requires generalizing about disempowered groups so as to mobilize support and influence the political process. For example, to underscore the reality that gender remains a significant predictor of socioeconomic inequality, the following facts are shared related to the status of women:

- Although women perform two-thirds of the world's work, they receive only 5 percent of the world's income and own only 1 percent of the world's land.

- In the United States, every seven minutes a woman is raped, and every 18 seconds a woman is battered.

- By the year 2000, women and their children will make up almost all of this country's poverty population (Allen, 1989).

Based on recognition of the dangers incumbent to generalizing, as admonished by postmodern theorists, while recognizing the need to establish bases for voicing, advocating, and undertaking activism to remediate the kinds of "women's realities" eluded to in the above data, feminist standpoints have emerged as an epistemological/on tological perspective from which to undertake research and knowledge-generation processes. *Standpoints* are truths or knowledge created through awarenesses of reality gleaned from particular social locations. The concept of standpoint assumes that all people see the world from the place in which they are situated socioculturally. What is considered to be real depends on one's standpoint and is grounded in experiences related to one's position within the sociocultural topography (Davis, 1993; Stanley & Wise, 1983, 1990; Swigonski, 1994).

For feminist standpoint theorists, it is gender that grounds the reality of women's lives. To that extent, women's victimization experiences via incest, domestic violence, and rape, in addition to their marginalized economic status and other discriminatory realities, provide the opportunity to create standpoints for the analysis of oppression based on gender. Where this perspective differs from earlier feminist analysis is in the standpoint emphasis on multiplicity and diversity within women's experiences. As opposed to proposing a unilateral feminist standpoint, there are multiplicities (that is, African American women's standpoints, lesbian standpoints, Latina standpoints, and older women's standpoints). Hence, there is no a priori placement of varying female ontological perspectives into a more correct versus less correct hierarchy. Each feminist standpoint has epistemological validity as each has ontological validity because all standpoints are contextually grounded within specific women's realities.

An interesting variation on feminist standpoint terminology is suggested by Stanley and Wise (1993) who have coined the term "fractured foundationalism" (p. 200). By the use of this term they mean that standpoints are women's truths that speak to the existence of different and overlapping but not coterminous material realities.

UTILITY OF STANDPOINTS

Employing standpoint perspectives can have great value for informing feminist social work research and practice. First, the logical positivist approach based on assumptions of an objective and value-free inquiry is antithetical to both feminism's and social work's historical legacy as being value-driven. For example, endemic to the social work education process is student immersion within the value base of our profession, which includes respect for client self-determination, belief in the dignity and worth of individuals, affirming client strengths, and validating client individuality and uniqueness (Hepworth & Larsen, 1993). Those values are consonant with feminism and several feminist social workers have written on the complementary perspectives between our profession and feminism (Browne, 1994; Collins, 1986; Dore, 1994; Hyde, 1987; Jimenez & Rice, 1990; Lundy, 1993; Wetzel, 1986). The question then becomes, "Why has there been such resistance to incorporation of feminist analyses within social work?" This resistance is particularly odd given that social work clients are overwhelmingly female and most social workers are women. That paradox has been explained by the pervasive sexism and extant sexual politics within our profession whereby those who have occupied positions of authority in our field have been overwhelmingly men (Simon, 1988).

Besides a values complementarity between feminism and social work, our practice frames of reference (that is, ecological and person-in-environment) are synchronistic with the feminist adage "the personal is political." Those feminist and social work conceptual frameworks speak to the need for us to view client problems contextually to be cognizant of how sociocultural and political realties affect their etiology.

On the other hand, "elegance" in positivist research design requires decontextualizing by controlling for the effects of history as well as environmental and sociocultural factors. Furthermore, the function of positivist research is to make inferences about people as a result of generalizing from group trends. Also, positivist conceptions of "good science" are those devoid of the researcher's influence on a study in terms of his or her values, demographics, or the process by which he or she engages with her respondents.

Compared with positivist research traditions, which have been highly valued in our profession (as a way to give us legitimacy as social scientists), research undertaken from a feminist standpoint attempts to decipher how social structures contribute to the problems that clients experience. Research that begins in the everyday life experiences of clients will inherently be grounded in cultural diversity; hence, knowledge distortions based on stereotypes can be decreased. In comparison to positivism, the goals of standpoint research are explicitly political, that is, to transform social structures and to promote client empowerment. Those goals are accomplished by employing methodologies that facilitate consciousness raising and critical thinking on the part of the researcher and the subjects (Swigonski, 1993). Inherent within standpoint research are the following processes:

- selecting issues for investigation that are based on problems associated with the everyday lives of marginalized people

- assisting subjects who are members of oppressed groups to develop critical consciousness about the impact of public structures on their private lives and personal problems (this can be facilitated through the use of focus groups)

- advancing the subjects' causes by ensuring that study results are used to remediate problems

- adopting a reflexive role as the researcher by reflecting on the impact of oneself on the research process.

It should be clear that standpoint research is value based as opposed to value free. For example, inherent in this research approach is the belief that individuals who have lived through experiences are more credible than those who have read or thought about them (Swigonski, 1994). This premise resonates for me as a social work educator and practitioner. I have always appreciated the enrichment brought to the classroom through older students, in particular, sharing life experiences that underscore pedagogical points being addressed. It is my impression that our profession has had an implicit, if not explicit concurrence with this standpoint, as reflected in some schools of social work admissions' policies that suggest the value of work experience before graduate school education. I have often felt that valuing life experience has given our profession a reality base potentially greater than that which exists for psychology or psychiatry.

Another value associated with standpoint research is that the knowing process should be guided by an ethic of caring and responsibility (Swigonski, 1994). Studying realities that affect women's lives so intimately and profoundly as, for example, incest or sexual assault, demonstrate empathy and unconditional positive regard for one's respondents. Having interviewed women who have been sexually victimized as youths or as adults, I assure you that their stories have never been recounted in a dispassionate fashion. Such narratives typically evoke anger, grief, shame or self-doubt, guilt, and anxiety. It seems to me unconscionable that a researcher could interact with his or her respondents and not demonstrate empathy for the women who have endured such painful stories.

Related to the feminist standpoint principle concerning the responsibilities of the researcher, it seems imperative that having been made privy to narratives of marginalized people, we must bear witness to those stories by sharing them with policy makers. I believe the primary responsibility of social work researchers should not be to aggrandize themselves through grant receipt; rather, our priority should be to share research findings with people in administrative and political roles who exercise control over resources and opportunities. Networking and building relationships with individuals outside of social work is critical, or else we end up "preaching to the converted." I am an ardent believer in the need to garner research funding from a variety of sources not typically used by social work, such as the Department of Defense, the Department of Labor, the National Institute on Drug Abuse, the National Institute on Alcoholism and Alcohol Abuse, Center for Substance Abuse Prevention, Center for Substance Abuse Treatment, and the Department of Housing and Urban Development. Despite the current federal retrenchment environment, it seems there is some willingness to fund research dealing with women's realities that is undertaken with a feminist standpoint perspective.

WHY FEMINIST STANDPOINTS?

It should now be clear that feminist standpoint perspectives have definite utility for informing feminist social work practice because they are consonant with both feminism's and social work's value-based and contextual perspectives for analyzing client problems and conceptualizing solutions. Additionally, using feminist standpoints is consistent with similar historical and political themes within our profession and feminism related to engendering methodologies effective in actualizing social and personal change. After immersion in several bodies of literature addressing feminist postmodernism, feminist postmodern pedagogy, psychotherapy, and postmodern social work education and practice, I concluded that there seem to be certain feminist standpoints that have particular applicability in informing our professional practice, both currently and in the future. The standpoints that stood out to me portray action as well as values and represent what social work is as a profession, that is, the operationalization of activism and caring on behalf of client advocacy and empowerment.

Social work is a value-based profession with a unique history, compared with the other "helping professions," in social change, organizing, and engagement in change-facilitating behaviors on behalf of clients. Additionally, I have always felt that our profession articulates a social gospel and covenant of caring for the promotion of collective well-being. Despite the postmodern admonition related to creating underlying structures, it seems imperative that social work practice be guided by "essential" principles. Without guiding ethics, values, and assumptions, something akin to a practice anarchy could accrue. Similarly, when considering social work with disempowered populations, it becomes critical to articulate the essential inequities experienced by members of such groups.

Given that, a caveat related to articulating standpoints is that they are dynamic, not static, and evolve and change according to the temper of the times. It is incumbent, then, to reflect on the social realities that engender the problems clients are experiencing in their everyday lives. Such an examination of contemporary and future social issues can then serve as the context for articulating feminist standpoints to inform social work practice.

We are just a few years away from a new century in which the kinds of problems our profession confronts will include ensuring the delivery of social services for an increasingly heterogeneous population that is older and more ethnically diverse than at any previous time in this country's history. Additionally, poverty, illiteracy, and homelessness will increase in a sociocultural environment adverse to expanding social services expenditures based on recessionary macroeconomics and a reactionary political climate. Violence, crime, and addiction increase in an unfortunate direct association. Families, an ever-expanding number of which are headed by females, are beleaguered by trying to provide the affiliative and instrumental tasks that society, historically, has assumed to be the family's role. Although most of these problems have been extant during the history of this profession, the challenges we face now, I believe, are greater, because there seems to be a diminishment in societal concern with developing caring communities and promoting collective well-being. This is floridly apparent with the Republican "Contract with America," which Gloria Steinhem has euphemistically termed the "Contract on America." The most critical component of the contract is a plan to reduce the national debt, and this will be achieved, in great part, through a reduction in social services expenditures.

Consequently, our contemporary society, despite the fact that we are in a post-Industrial age, may be experiencing the abject perversity associated with what sociologist Max Weber (1958) named "gesellschaft," which he predicted to be an outcome of industrialization. That term depicts a societal milieu replete with widespread feelings of isolation, atomization and "anomie." *Anomie* was used by Emile Durkheim (1951) to describe a state of disconnectedness that he associated with propensities for suicide. One might consider the increasing prevalence of addictions and violence as indicative of a kind of societal suicide. Weber named the dialectic of gesellschaft to be gemeinschaft, which describes societies undergirded by an ethic of caring, operationalized by undertaking actions to promote collective well-being to ensure the ongoing viability of the community. Therefore, although we are a gesellschaft-like culture, faced with myriad social problems that could be remediated by gemeinschaft-like actions such as the implementation of social policies providing nationalized health care, child care, elder care, educational opportunity equality, a guaranteed minimum income, and so forth, we lack broad-based covenants of caring.

A lack of caring and community-building supports may be explained by the diminished value afforded caretaking functions in general. Despite postmodern feminist scholars eschewing essentialist arguments that equate women's status with women's purported traits and qualities, many feminist social work scholars believe our contemporary crisis in caring is based on a pervasive societal undervaluing of caretaking (Browne, 1994; Freedberg, 1993; Meyer, 1990; see also the chapters by Martinez-Brawley & Zorita and Van Soest in this book). Feminists believe that the devaluation of caretaking functions is based on caring being associated with feminine traits and women's work. Browne (1994) described the double standard that exists in regard to caretaking and how it affects women economically. Although women are expected to be family caretakers and are viewed pejoratively if not in conformity with those expectations (see Abramovitz in this book), by adhering to that role, they are disadvantaged economically. That is, by not participating within the *paid* labor force women experience greater impoverishment, particularly in their senior years, because of a lack in pension receipt and reduced social security benefits. As a result of this financial inequity based on a caretaking double standard, some feminists have proposed the implementation of a social wage system; this concept is discussed within this book in the chapter by Martinez-Brawley and Zorita.

There is a long-standing historical and cultural derision of female-associated caring and relational traits that has allowed for dynamics of partnership to be subordinate to forces of domination. In view of this deleterious trend, Meyer (1990) maintained that there needs to be a societal revaluing of caring, that would be manifested by caretaking functions no longer being seen as *primarily* a female or family responsibility. The concept of the larger community assuming caretaking responsibility for its citizenry is neither a new nor radical idea. Consider the kibbutz of Israel and the children's allowances provided by the Canadian government as just two examples of how Western cultures have created societal institutions to ensure collective well-being.

Consequently, during a historical period whereby increasing diversity and expanding social problems speak to the need to be proactive in connecting, caring, and building community, our profession can gain an advantage by using feminist standpoints to inform our practice. The question, of course, becomes, "What are the feminist standpoints that should be used?"

WHICH FEMINIST STANDPOINTS?

In my literature review, I kept a running record of concepts used, descriptively, when the construct feminism was addressed. I observed through my content analysis of those themes that there seemed to be a qualitative difference in terms of feminist principles delineated in earlier practice literature compared with themes used in the more recent past. For example, my collaborator and I, in *Feminist Visions for Social Work* (Van Den Bergh & Cooper, 1986) distilled five principles we felt had authenticity in describing feminist ideology, as it had emerged to that point in time: (1) eliminating false dichotomies, (2) valuing process equally to product, (3) renaming one's reality, (4) reconceptualizing power and (5) believing the personal is political. By no means exhaustive, those five principles encapsulate what might be considered empowerment themes. That is, because feminism's second wave arose, temporally, with other civil rights movements of the 1960s, early feminist ideology underscored the need to be seen, counted, represented and given access to rights, resources, and opportunities. Hence, it may be appropriate to consider those earlier feminist principles as imparting a message of "see us...we are a critical mass...give us the rights to be who we are."

However, a review of feminist and feminist postmodern literature within the more recent past seems to impart a different message. It appeared to me that more current literature voiced four standpoints: (1) knowing, (2) connecting, (3) caring, and (4) diversity (see Table 1). Those standpoints articulate an awareness of the multiplicity of women's experiences and hence the diversity of their ways of knowing. Additionally, these standpoints represent concern with relatedness and being connected on both interpersonal and community levels. My interpretation of what these newer feminist standpoints are saying is "hear us... and know us for who we are, in our differences and similarities...we value connection and caring."

Table 1

Themes Associated with Feminist Standpoints

KNOWING

Narratives and stories

Contextual and co–created

Deconstruct and reconstruct

Discourse and dialogue; negotiate meaning

Relativity and local meanings

Reflexive, intersubjective, and immersion

Ambiguities, juxtapositions, contradictions, and shifts

Knowledge as process, not product

Knowledge within; not knowledge without

CONNECTING

Web; network of complexity

Holistic, interconnected, interdependent, and spiritual

Communuity, commonality, communality, coalitions, and coexistence

Collaborative, communicative, participative, and engaging

Think globally, act locally

CARING

Mutuality and interdependence

Concern and empathy

Morality and responsiblity

MULTIPLICITY

Diversity and differences

Pluralism and nonduality

Voices and visions

To me, those feminist standpoints have considerable value in being incorporated within social work practice, so that we can be responsive to the problems in everyday living that affect our clients currently and in the future. A practice informed by listening to many ways of knowing, centered and located within diverse client life experiences and co-created through relationships that are reflexive and intersubjective, can provide a context for caring, connecting, partnering, and community building. That, very simply, may be how we move out of the problem and into the solution.

REFERENCES

Allen, J. (1989). Women who beget women must thwart major sophisms. In A. Garry & M. Pearslall (Eds.), *Women, knowledge and reality: Explorations in feminist philosophy.* Boston: Unwin Hyman.

Allport, G. (1954). *The nature of prejudice.* Reading, MA: Addison-Wesley.

Belenky, M., Clinchy, J., Goldberger, N., & Tarule, J. (1986). *Women's ways of knowing.* New York: Basic Books.

Bricker-Jenkins, M., & Hooyman, N. (1984). *Feminist practice project: Summary of pretest findings.* Unpublished manuscript sponsored by NCOWI under auspices of NASW. Silver Spring, MD: National Association of Social Workers.

Bricker-Jenkins, M., & Hooyman, N. (Eds.). (1986). *Not for women only.* Silver Spring, MD: National Association of Social Workers.

Broverman, I., Broverman, D., & Clark, F. (1970). Sex role stereotypes and clinical judgements of mental health. *Journal of Consulting and Clinical Psychology, 34*(1), 1–7.

Browne, C. (1994). Feminist theory and social work: A vision for practice with older women. *Journal of Applied Social Sciences, 18*(1), 5–16.

Butler, J. (1992). Contingent foundations: Feminism and the question of postmodernism. In J. Butler & L. Singer (Eds.), *Feminists theorize the political* (pp. 3–21). Boston: Routledge & Kegan Paul.

Butler, J., & Scott, J. (Eds.). (1992). *Feminists theorize the political.* Boston: Routledge & Kegan Paul.

Collins, B. (1986). Defining feminist social work. *Social Work, 31,* 214–219.

Compton, B., & Galaway, B. (1994). *Social work processes.* Monterey, CA: Brooks/Cole.

Davis, L. (1993). Feminism and constructivism: Teaching social work practice with women. In. J. Laird (Ed.), *Revisioning social work education: A social constructionist approach* (pp. 147–163). New York: Haworth Press.

Doll, W. (1989). Foundations for a post-modern curriculum. *Journal of Curriculum Studies, 21*(3), 243–253.

Doninelli, L., & McLeod, E. (1989). *Feminist social work.* London: Macmillan.

Dore, M. (1994). Feminist pedagogy and the teaching of social work practice. *Journal of Social Work Education, 30*(1), 97–106.

Durkheim, E. (1951). *Suicide.* New York: Free Press.

Erikson, E. (1950). *Childhood and society.* New York: W. W. Norton.

Eisler, R. (1987). *The chalice and the blade.* San Francisco: Harper & Row.

Featherstone, B., & Fawcett, B. (1994, July). *Oh no! Not more "isms": Feminism, postmodernism and poststructuralism and social work education.* Paper presented at the 27th International Association of Schools of Social Work Congress, Amsterdam.

Flax, J. (1990). *Thinking fragments: Psychoanalysis, feminism and postmodernism in the contemporary west.* Berkeley: University of California Press.

Foucault, M. (1978). *The archaeology of knowledge.* London: Tavistock.

Freedberg, S. (1993). The feminine ethic of care and the professionalization of social work. *Social Work, 38,* 535–540.

Greene, B. (1994). Diversity and difference: Race and feminist psychotherapy. In M. Mirkin (Ed.), *Women in context: Toward a feminist reconstruction of psychotherapy* (pp. 333–351). New York: Guilford Press.

Griffin, S. (1993, March). *Ecosystems: A model for feminist practice.* Paper presented for the Tulane University Women's Studies program, New Orleans.

Hepworth, D., & Larsen, J. (1993). *Direct social work practice.* Monterey, CA: Brooks/Cole.

hooks, b. (1984). *Feminist theory: From margin to center.* Boston: South End Press.

hooks, b. (1989). *Talking back: Thinking feminist, thinking black.* Boston: South End Press.

Hyde, C. (1987, March). *The inclusion of a feminist agenda in community organization curricula.* Paper presented at the Council on Social Work Education Annual Program Meeting, St. Louis.

Jimenez, M., & Rice, S. (1990). Popular advice to women: A feminist perspective. *Affilia, 5*(3), 8–26.

Kohlberg, L. (1981). *The philosophy of moral development.* San Francisco: Harper & Row.

Kuhn, T. (1970). *The structure of scientific revolutions.* Chicago: University of Chicago Press.

Laird, J. (1995a, March). Family-centered practice in the postmodern era. *Families in Society: The Journal of Contemporary Human Services, 76*(3), 150–160.

Laird, J. (1995b, March). *Ideas for a postmodern/feminist approach to practice.* Paper presented at the Council on Social Work Education Annual Program Meeting, San Diego, CA.

Laird, J. (1993). Introduction. In J. Laird (Ed.), *Revisioning social work education* (pp. 1–10). New York: Haworth Press.

Lewis, E., & Kissman, K. (1989). Factors linking ethnic-sensitive and feminist social work practice with African-American women. *Arete, 14*(2), 23–31.

Lundy, M. (1993). Explicitness: The unspoken mandate of feminist social work. *Affilia, 8*(2), 184–199.

Meyer, C. (1990, November). *What is feminist about feminist social work?* Paper presented at Social Work '90: NASW's Annual Meeting of the Profession, Boston.

Nes, J., & Iadicola, P. (1989) Toward a definition of feminist social work: A comparison of liberal, radical and socialist models. *Social Work, 34,* 12–21.

Nicholson, L. (1990). Introduction. In L. Nicholson (Ed.), *Feminism/postmodernism* (pp.1-18). Boston: Routledge & Kegan Paul.

Norton, D. (1978). *The dual perspective: Inclusion of ethnic minority content in the social work curriculum.* New York: Council on Social Work Education.

Nuccio, K., & Sands, R. (1992). Using postmodern feminist theory to deconstruct "phallacies" of poverty. *Affilia, 7*(4), 26–49.

Pardeck, J., Murphy, J., & Choi, J. (1994). Some implications of postmodernism for social work practice. *Social Work, 39,* 343–346.

Payne, M. (1991). *Modern social work theory.* Chicago: Lyceum Books.

Prather, J., & Minkow, N. (1991). Prescription for despair: Women and psychotropic drugs. In N. Van Den Bergh (Ed.) *Feminist perspectives on addictions* (pp. 87–100). New York: Springer.

Sands, R., & Nuccio, K. (1992). Postmodern feminist theory and social work. *Social Work, 37,* 489–494.

Simon, B. (1988). Social work responds to the women's movement. *Affilia, 3*(4), 60–68.

Singer, L. (1992). Feminism and postmodernism. In J. Butler & J. Scott (Eds.), *Feminists theorize the political* (pp. 464–475). Boston: Routledge & Kegan Paul.

Stanley, L., & Wise, S. (1993). *Breaking out again.* London: Routledge & Kegan Paul.

Stanley, L., & Wise, S. (1990). Method, methodology and epistemology in feminist research processes. In L. Stanley (Ed.), *Feminist praxis: Research, theory, and epistemology in feminist sociology* (pp. 20–60). Boston: Routledge & Kegan Paul.

Stanley, L., & Wise, S. (1983). *Breaking out.* Boston: Routledge & Kegan Paul.

Swigonski, M. (1994). The logic of feminist standpoint theory for social work research. *Social Work, 39,* 387–393.

Swigonski, M. (1993). Feminist standpoint theory and the questions of social work research. *Affilia, 8*(2), 171–183.

Van Den Bergh, N. (1991). Having eaten the apple: A feminist perspective on addictions. In N. Van Den Bergh (Ed.), *Feminist perspectives on addictions* (pp. 3–30). New York: Springer.

Van Den Bergh, N. (1987). Renaming: Vehicle for empowerment. In J. Penfield (Ed.), *Women and language in transition* (pp.130–136). Old Westbury, NY: SUNY Press.

Van Den Bergh, N., & Cooper, L. (1986). Introduction. In N. Van Den Bergh & L. Cooper (Eds.), *Feminist visions for social work* (pp. 1–28). Silver Spring, MD: National Association of Social Work.

Van Den Bergh, N., & Cooper, L. (1987). Feminist social work practice. In A. Minahan (Ed.-in-Chief), *Encyclopedia of social work* (18th ed., Vol. 1, pp. 610–618). Silver Spring, MD: National Association of Social Workers.

Weber, M. (1958). *The Protestant ethic and the spirit of Capitalism.* New York: Charles Scribner's & Sons.

Weick, A. (1993). Reconstructing social work education. In J. Laird (Ed.), *Revisioning social work education: A social constructivist approach* (pp.11–30). New York: Haworth Press.

White, M. (1992). Deconstruction and therapy. In D. Epston & M. White (Eds.), *Experience, contradiction, narrative and imagination.* Adelaide, South Australia: Dutwich Center Publishers.

White, M., & Epston, D. (1990). *Narrative means to therapeutic ends.* New York: W. W. Norton.

Wetzel, J. W. (1986, March). A feminist world view conceptual framework. *Social Casework, 67,* 166–173.

Wetzel, J. W. (1976). Interaction of feminism and social work in America. *Social Casework, 57*(4), 227–236.

Methods

1

Feminist Clinical Social Work in the 21st Century

Helen Land

The challenges of feminist clinical social work practice in the 21st century are complex and multifaceted. Resources remain scant, and the intersection of sociopolitical, economic, health, and psychological stressors culminate in a troubling set of client problems. Domestic violence is rapidly increasing: Reports of wife abuse, child abuse, and incest have never been higher. We see an aging society with limited resources for employment opportunity and health care, especially for frail elderly people. Women of color and other vulnerable groups are more represented in the changing face of acquired immune deficiency syndrome (AIDS). Increased immigration from Third World countries results in populations at risk for poverty, poor health care, and lack of educational opportunity. Increased heterogeneity in the workforce, as engendered by these changes, often results in workplace stress. Women are overworked, underpaid, and undersupported by our social programs. Burgeoning pressures on family life, as it is diversely defined, include fewer resources for children; greater caregiving responsibilities for aging, ill, and disabled family members; and consequent role overload and stress. The family structure in the United States is no longer represented by the conjoint spousal unit in which the mother stays at home to care for children. Stepfamilies, extended families, multigenerational families, homosexual families, joint employment of spouses, and single parenthood are common family scenarios. Families have grown in complexity but often must survive on limited financial, social, and emotional resources.

Many of these societal problems translate into particular social and psychological problems for women, leaving them at risk for physical and mental health problems. Women commonly are seen in health and mental health clinics with depression; eating disorders; substance abuse problems; anxiety and its somatic complaints; and a multitude of medical conditions, including AIDS, cancer, and hypertension. Although reform in health care is promising, managed health care often leaves the client short of a complete service plan.

How do feminist approaches to clinical social work define intervention in these problems? What makes intervention feminist in orientation? And what about the intervention is particular to social work? Such social and psychological problems are formidable, yet approaches to problem solving are rooted in the historical values of social work, many of which were enunciated by those developing the profession. Although we must view them within their historical context, many early leaders in the field could be called feminists because they began to define problems, often family problems, and the concerns of women as being borne from societal forces interacting with interpersonal and psychological issues. Early visionaries such as Jane Addams attempted to provide social support services to aid in the acculturation process for immigrants (Fisher, 1971). Mary Richmond (1917) conceived of problems as requiring a social diagnosis where it was important to examine family interactions and family ecology. She was particularly concerned with deserted wives and women who were mentally ill (Perlman, 1971). Bertha Reynolds (Hollis, 1971) brought a perspective based in the precepts of socialism, and Gordon Hamilton (1951) constructed a close link among social casework, social welfare services, the economic factors of families in distress, and social action and advocacy (Hollis, 1970, 1971). These were women concerned with developing approaches to stem day-to-day problems that are strikingly similar to those faced by clinical social workers in the 21st century: the feminization of poverty, family discord, few social resources for immigrant groups, poor health care, and children at risk.

Clearly, our foremothers who helped define the profession of social work were much concerned with disenfranchised groups and women's issues. Adding a structural–social component to problem definition, these women conceived of problem evolution differently from other professions of their day, and they developed a stance on problem resolution that collided with other fields. In fact, Abraham Flexner (1915), at the 1915 National Conference on Charities and Corrections, questioned the validity of social work as a profession because it lacked individual responsibility and educationally communicable techniques.

These early feminist pioneers planted the seeds for the cardinal principles of clinical social work as we know them today: the biopsychosocial approach, the person-in-situation paradigm, and empowerment practice. Much in the same way that our foremothers were questioned about the contribution of their developing field, feminist practitioners today are questioned about what constitutes feminist theory and feminist clinical practice. Many of the root principles of feminist practice can be traced to the constructs developed by these women who defined clinical social work practice, that is, practice designed to provide direct, diagnostic, preventive, developmental, supportive, and rehabilitative services to individuals, families, and groups whose functioning is threatened or adversely affected by social and psychological stress or health impairment (Meyer, 1983).

COMPONENTS OF FEMINIST CLINICAL SOCIAL WORK
Feminist clinical social work can be described as a philosophy of psychotherapeutic intervention rather than a perspective set of techniques. Clinical social workers who practice from a feminist philosophy may practice from a variety of theoretical orientations, including cognitive–behavioral, psychodynamic (Chodorow, 1978; Eichenbaum & Orbach, 1983; Gould, 1984; Jordan & Surrey, 1986), psychosocial (Ruderman, 1986), problem solving, family systems (Ault-Riche, 1986; Luepnitz, 1988; Robbins, 1983), constructivist (Neimeyer, 1993), or interpersonal approaches, and they may use a variety of treatment modalities (individual, couple, family, or group). However, although feminist clinical social work may be reflective of a hybrid, there exists a body of theory and core principles that inform practice.

Theory stems from the Greek word meaning to look or see. Feminist therapy has its origins in the civil rights and women's liberation movement of the 1960s. At that time, consciousness-raising groups evolved whose purpose was akin to many empowerment-oriented self-help groups today. Women began to understand that through talking with one another and sharing experiences, feelings, thoughts, and behaviors, they could frequently begin to make sense of what often seemed to be an oppressive, stigmatizing, limited, and disabling outcome. New life paradigms were born during the turmoil of the early women's movement. Women began to understand that each woman's experience was not unique but had common ground with the experiences of other women. Women began to achieve new understandings of their experiences and recognized that internalizing the patriarchal mentality and structured gender-based role sets of society often resulted in a negative self-identity, self-doubt, and few choices for change. Through these groups and through other methods of exchange, feminist theory evolved.

Feminist theories articulate varied ways of seeing (or asking questions) and of understanding women's lives and experiences, the nature of inequality between the sexes, and the structuring of gender. Such theories have emerged from and are tied to movements to stem the oppression and disenfranchisement of women. Much of feminist theory centers on the connection among gender, privilege, social class, culture, sexuality, and the concept of self. Clinical feminist social work has blended many of the social work theories such as the person-in-situation paradigm, the biopsychosocial approach to treatment, and the ecological framework (Meyer, 1983) with feminist theories.

Validating the Social Context

Primary to the values of many feminist clinical social workers is close attention to the effects of the social context on the difficulties of the client as they are jointly assessed by client and practitioner. Such a stance is not new to social work; however, here attention is given to environmental pressures, gender roles, and gender-based discrimination that affects the client's experience, including identity formation, cognitive structure, and patterns of interpersonal behavior (Brodsky, 1980; Day, 1992; Rawlings & Carter, 1977). Feminist therapists hold that theories of human behavior must be understood within the broader social context. Our interpretations of behavior must attend to the impact of external realities on internal and subconscious processes (Brown & Brodsky, 1992). For example, many feminist practitioners believe that when women have common signs and symptoms of depression, there may be a reason for such a reaction; hence, the symptoms should be validated rather than labeled as a deviant reaction to an ambiguous set of circumstances. Depression may result from any number of factors including environmental inequity, interpersonal stress, cognitive schema, and intrapsychic issues. Whatever the etiology, depression often has a legitimate basis and should be recognized as a valid reaction. Subsequently, factors fostering the depression may be investigated by the client and therapist to alleviate the immobilizing condition. Thus, gender-related issues, particularly issues of equity, are given consideration in the assessment of the client's problems.

Revaluing Positions Enacted by Women

Many feminist practitioners feel that mainstream psychotherapies have benefited the dominant people in our society, namely white heterosexual men. As a result, that which is conceived as being normative and valuable tends toward those stances and activities that have been assumed by men. For example, striving toward upward mobility in a competitive manner is often valued because these behaviors are reflective of the white male experience. Conversely, enacting behaviors that are often performed by women, such as compromising, cooperating, seeking consensus, providing nurturing to others, and caregiving (including working in the service-oriented fields) are often devalued, ostensibly because they reflect a female experience (Freedberg, 1993; Hare-Mustin & Maracek, 1988). These behaviors and service roles are vitally important to the well-being of society; they often result in positive behavioral outcomes and should be valued (Morrison Dore, 1994).

Recognizing Difference in Male and Female Experience

Carol Gilligan's (1982) insightful research on the different courses of human development in male and female children is one example of theory that suggests men and women often have different experiences, yet one should not be overvalued and the other undervalued. Before Gilligan's research, little attention had been paid to female developmental life. Theorists assumed that all development reflected the experience of the male child with his parent figures. Gilligan elucidated the differences in relationship patterns that female children have with parent figures in our society and how their subsequent socialization and consequent behavioral actions may take different courses than those of their male counterparts. Because female children are socially permitted to have more intimate contact, especially with their mothers, for longer periods in their life, they are socialized to behavior patterns that reflect parenting concerns such as greater concern for the well-being of others, nurturing, cooperation, and collaborative problem solving. Many feminist theorists purport that developmental theories assume a gender-blind stance and suggest that the emotional worlds of men and women are the same. Central to feminist discourse is the position that to understand the internal psychic structure of women, and women's concepts of self, the effect of external and oppressive structures on women's psychological development must be acknowledged. This knowledge may then assist clinicians in understanding how the therapeutic relationship can address women's needs (Day, 1992).

Rebalancing Perceptions of Normality and Deviance

A parallel feminist corollary is that behavior which is conceived as being dysfunctional or deviant by our society often reflects behavior of less-privileged groups, such as women, people of color, poor people, older people, and gay men and lesbians. For example, feminist psychotherapists have attempted to block the diagnostic category in the *Diagnostic and Statistical Handbook of Mental Disorders* (American Psychiatric Association, 1994) of self-defeating personality disorder because they feel it defines a segment of our society as pathological. There is no attempt, they point out, to create a category for dominating personality disorder, a behavior that could be conceived as being disordered and is seen with greater frequency in men. Hence, many feminist practitioners point to the need to balance, especially within the professional psychotherapeutic community, normality and deviance and to include the experiences and perceptions of women and people from all ethnic, racial, class, sexual orientation, age, and religious groups.

Inclusive Stance
An inclusive stance mandates reexamination of our Anglocentric assumptions. For example, the strength of the kinship system among women in many African American and Latin cultures provides social support that buffers stress and increases well-being. However, such a family structure may be interpreted from an Anglocentric stance as signifying an enmeshed, collusive family system. These suppositions must be redefined because much value, such as the support offered through the female kinship system, may be lost or excluded.

Attention to Power Dynamics in the Therapeutic Relationship
Another precept of feminist clinical practice theory involves the attention to power dynamics in the therapeutic relationship. Developing an egalitarian clinical relationship is a desired goal. Social work has historically noted the importance of client self-determination in the problem-solving process. This precept elaborates the value of client–clinician equity. Many feminist clinicians believe that the historical asymmetry in the psychotherapeutic relationship between therapist and client is inimical to the goals of feminist clinical social work practice. Empowerment models (Levine et al., 1993; Solomon, 1976) that seek to harness client strength in self-advocacy and problem solving, the use of connectedness within self-psychology (Kohut, 1977), and constructivist and narrative approaches (Neimeyer, 1993; Saari, 1986) that define, at the vortex of therapy, the client's meaning and definition of the conflict are examples of rebalancing the relationship between clinician and client and renewing equity within it.

Recognizing How the Personal Is Political
Feminist practitioners often acknowledge in their work with clients the ways that the personal issues clients work with are political in nature and may reflect power inequities in relationships with others. Sexual harassment is an obvious example. A female worker who is sexually harassed by her male superior is evading more than sexual aggression. Implicit in the overture is a power component that places her at risk for job loss or demotion if she does not comply. The

political context in which the sexual advance occurs must be recognized and resolved.

Many times, the components of the political context are multifaceted, covert in nature, and defined by those in power as problems residing within the individual rather than in the system. For example, an immigrant woman is told by her boss that she is not allowed to speak about personal issues or in her native language to coworkers while on the job. Such a stance, situated within its political context, results in an inability and immobility for women workers to communicate with each other, to become more assertive, or to organize and voice their concerns about work, family pressures, and other needs. Subsequently, these women may experience work stress, depression, and anomie. Given this scenario, feminist clinicians might help clients speak with one another, organize for the common cause, and recognize and vocalize how their personal issues are enacted within a political context. Hence, problems may be resolved more equitably.

Deconstructive Stance

Feminist clinicians often look to assess how culture-bound definitions of right and wrong as well as appropriate and inappropriate behaviors require reexamination and reconceptualization. The deconstructive stance (Derrida, 1976) in feminist theory is helpful in clinical practice. Many feminist clinicians believe that to gain recognition as professionals, the male-dominated world asks women to become "honorary males" intellectually and interpersonally. Often, conceptual barriers in clinical theory are based in existing male-oriented language and, often, language defines experience (McCannell, 1986). Hence, what is given power, what is seen as devalued or dysfunctional, what is recognized as valuable, and what is included in history making often reflects the patriarchal position. Perhaps this reason explains the attention of feminists to sexist language that often echoes the patriarchy in which it was born. The deconstructive clinical stance seeks to take apart and reexamine the structure of language and experience, within the dominant culture, so as to stem the effects of privilege.

Partnering Stance

Traditional psychotherapy eschews the practice of therapist self-disclosure, except in rare instances. Many feminist clinicians believe that their clients may learn from the clinician's experience as a woman living in a male-dominated society; hence, elements of self-disclosure, especially in situations where the personal is political, are used with greater frequency in feminist clinical practice.

Inclusive Scholarship

There is a trend among feminist social work clinicians to rely on a variety of scholarly traditions including quantitative and qualitative methods and postpositivist scholarship. Moreover, many feminist scholars challenge the traditional assumption that science is objective; hence, feminist scholars see the need for inclusive research agendas and seek to critically analyze and uncover androcentric bias both in lines of inquiry and in methodology (Lott, 1985). Feminist clinical practice has been the impetus for developing lines of scholarship that seek to explain how culture constructs gender and scholarship on the formidable exigencies that women face in our society, such as the sequelae of personal violence and sexual assault, depression, eating disorders, and anxiety reactions. In contrast to knowledge that flows from the quantitatively empirical to the clinical, valuing a variety of scholarly traditions and noting the knowledge-building interplay between feminist clinical practice and feminist scholarship is a key principle in feminist clinical social work.

Challenging Reductionistic Models

Although feminists value behaviors traditionally enacted by women, the division between male and female behavioral traits such as the woman being the social and emotional caretaker and the man assuming the instrumental role is often eschewed by feminist clinical practitioners. Reductionistic models that seek to codify gender-based behaviors are seen as limiting and nonproductive for both genders. Attending to a balance between autonomy and relationship competence, for both genders, is a key component of feminist clinical practice.

Empowerment Practice

Feminist clinical practice is empowerment practice, although the means for psychotherapeutic growth may vary among feminist clinicians. Within this tradition, therapeutic goals for clients are generated cooperatively between clinician and client, and the focus is often on empowering the client to change the social, interpersonal, and political environments that have an impact on well-being rather than on helping the client adjust to an oppressive social context. Hence, feminist clinicians value a number of goals for clients that may include intrapsychic, interpersonal, and behavioral change and a changed perspective on the sociocultural aspects that affect life in whatever context clients live (Brown & Liss-Levinson, 1981). The modalities used to achieve these goals may include individual counseling, couple or family therapy, and group experiences for women. Group counseling remains a valued tradition within feminist clinical work because of the therapeutic and empowering effects of group cohesion and support, universality, and the corrective emotional experience gained in group settings.

Myth of Value-Free Psychotherapy

Many feminist clinical social workers reject the myth of value-free psychotherapy. By making their biases explicit, feminist clinicians facilitate client ownership of their values and choices. This stance is regarded as an important part of the empowerment process, and client problem solving is seen as a cooperative relationship in which both client and clinician perspectives are equally valued, although they are inevitably different in nature (Brown & Brodsky, 1992).

CHALLENGES OF THE 21ST CENTURY

How will feminist clinical social work practice meet the needs of clients in the 21st century? Many feminist practitioners believe that the principles of feminist clinical practice will become generalized throughout the psychotherapeutic community. Because of the proliferation of health maintenance organizations and managed health care, clients will by necessity become more consumer oriented, and clinicians will need to make their approaches and values known to clients as they shop for a more defined product.

With the increasing ethnic–cultural–racial diversity of clients seen by clinical social workers, the principle of recognizing, understanding, valuing, and using nondominant cultural values in the therapeutic process will become primary. Building on the historical commitment of social work to understanding the client within the situation, feminist clinical social workers and others will need to become even more conversant in how the social environment is affected by and transacts with the client's perceptions. Inclusion ideology has always been a tenet of feminist practice; however, in reality, feminist therapy and theory research to date have been largely dominated by middle-class white women (Brown, 1990; Brown & Root, 1990b; Kanuha, 1990).

Feminist clinical social workers must continue to extend themselves outside the mainstream. Just as our views of human behavior have been influenced by a patriarchal society, our views of women's development have been influenced by the experience of white individuals. This state suggests that we must continue to assess dominant norms and to incorporate nondominant ones as a means of enlarging our comprehension of women's experiences from nondominant groups. We must enlarge the paradigm to include attention to gender-relational development across cultural and class groups (Palladino & Stephenson, 1990). In other psychotherapeutic fields, feminist theory development is beginning to emerge on a multicultural basis (Boyd, 1990; Bradshaw, 1990; Brown & Root, 1990a; Ho, 1990; Kanuha, 1990; Sears, 1990). These new perspectives will continue to foster theory growth and clinical interventions. Their traditions also will be of importance to white women and society as a whole.

In the 21st century, feminist clinical social workers will need to continue to pursue knowledge building in the area of feminist theory. One difficulty in this pursuit is that many scholars of theory have been trained in the dominant culture; it is difficult to perceive outside the intellectual culture that has formed our worldview. As Daly (1983) and Johnson (1987) purported, the language and culture of patriarchy are imbued within us. It is difficult to foresee a feminist perspective that is not an amalgam of influences of other theories. A goal, therefore, is to create human behavior that is feminist in nature. Subsequently, human psychic hurting and its alleviation will be understood from a feminist orientation. This goal suggests that we must draw on multiple methodologies and ways of knowing, as we have begun to do (Ballou, 1990; Belenky, Clinchy, Goldberger, & Tarule, 1986).

We must continue the exchange among clinical practice, research, and scholarship if we are to continue to be informed from the grassroots up. Several institutes have already been established in this direction, including the Stone Center on Personality and Relational Development (Jordan, Surrey, & Kaplan, 1983); the Women's Therapy Centre Institute, which treats eating disorders and fosters growth in mother–daughter relationships (Eichenbaum & Orbach, 1983); and the Feminist Therapy Institute (Rave & Larsen, 1990). As centers of learning develop and become a part of the institutional history of feminist theory and therapy, these approaches gain greater stability and validity. What is generated by feminist scholars and clinicians becomes part of mainstream clinical intervention, a goal of many feminist practitioners.

Yet another direction for feminist clinical social work points to health and medical concerns. Feminist scholars have had a historical interest in women's reproductive health, infertility, menstruation, and menopause and health behavior centered around these issues (Sayette & Mayne, 1990). Particular attention has been directed to choice in and ownership of reproductive health. Feminist clinical scholars must now turn their attention to other health issues of women, including the prevention of and care of people with chronic diseases and illnesses such as AIDS and caregiving issues for women who often provide the only care for significant others in their lives (Land, 1992). Stress, coping, and support among female formal and informal caregivers of all cultural backgrounds should be targets for a primary academic and clinical agenda.

Moreover, children and family issues would be well served by greater feminist analysis of problems and their solutions (Walker & Edwall, 1987). Although feminist scholars were among the first to speak out about sexual abuse of children and adult incest survivors, little attention has been devoted to developing nonsexist methods of child development or work with children in their family context. We must seek to understand how institutions such as residential treatment facilities and schools have fostered gender inequality, and we must remediate their extant inequities (Kerr, 1992).

With respect to new populations, feminist treatment has tended to have been conceived as a paradigm applicable for women only. Although the origins of feminist therapy centered on issues particular to adult women, feminist therapists have always practiced with a variety of populations. In the future we need to see an expansion of inclusiveness in feminist practice with diverse populations. The problems of women are problems of the world, and what is good scholarship and practice for women is good for the whole of society. Such a view encompasses values of the uniqueness of the individual; egalitarianism among genders, races, and cultures; nurturing; relationship; and family responsibility. These are values that would benefit society as a whole (Wetzel, 1986).

Because feminists value an inclusive stance and elucidate the needs of diverse populations, feminist clinical theory should address the interactive concerns and realities of men, children, families, people of color, gay men and lesbians, older people, and individuals with physical disabilities. For example, practitioners with a feminist perspective could offer a valuable stance for men who batter, because often these men have been victimized in their youth (Bograd, 1984). The cultural pairing of masculinity with dominance, power, and violence is oppressive for everyone. This work has begun to emerge and should be fostered (Ganley, 1988; Sonkin, Martin, & Walker, 1985).

In addition, feminist family therapy will see a growth of interest based on need in the 21st century. To date, feminist family theorists have begun to critique existing theories of family development, function, and dysfunction, stating that although feminism and systemic practice have traditionally been seen as two incompatible standpoints, they can be conceptualized as two parallel traditions. Both work toward understanding the intersubjective experience that makes up the interpersonal field. Both have analogous concerns that include problems of confronting and combating power misallocation, issues of hierarchy, and the process–product debate (Goldner, 1991). Feminist revisions of family treatment need to be addressed in the future to eliminate hierarchical models and generate more egalitarian and culturally diverse representations of family life.

Because they are important to the future of feminist clinical social work, standards for education and training will need to include a feminist, multicultural perspective at all levels of social work education and licensing for clinical social workers (Morrison Dore, 1994). Feminist clinical practice is ready for greater formalization of standards. Feminist clinical social work is no longer for believers only but has become part of the mainstream because it represents an emphasis on human rights and inclusion. For example, topics such as the sexual exploitation of therapy clients, sexual harassment in the workplace, and domestic violence are now considered part of the essential knowledge base for practitioners, ethics committees, and academicians. We need to recognize that it is not feminist scholarship that has moved into the mainstream; rather, feminists have acted as a part of the conscience of ethical social work practice, helping move mainstream thought away from destructive paradigms toward new ones that are influenced by feminist thought.

Because feminist scholarship has a history of only about 25 years, what is available as practice models and research, scholarship, and teaching methods is still developing. The 21st century will see a demand for knowledge production; hence, the need to foster and promote feminist scholars and practitioners is compelling.

CONCLUSION

The role of feminist clinical social workers in the 21st century will be multifaceted and generative. We will continue creating a more egalitarian stance in the clinical world, reminding the field that gender is a cardinal construct that requires attention in theory, practice, research, and scholarship. Attention to gender and issues of power are areas that cannot be minimized. We will continue to change theories that inhibit the growth of women and men of all ages and cultures because the assumption underlying both feminism and social work values is that people realize their full potential through effective social functioning (Collins, 1986). We will make continued efforts to generate feminist theory by taking an inclusive stance in theory building and drawing on the experiences of people of color and those who have not been marginated in our society. We will set a scholarly agenda that values reciprocity in the learning process between clinical practice and quantitative, qualitative, and postpositivist approaches. We will build on the work of our foremothers in their efforts to forge a practice that attends to the needs of those in society who are often overlooked and dismissed. Their needs for service are often a result of environmental inequities, family stress, and psychological conflicts emblematic of the biopsychosocial precept that defines social work practice. In addition, feminist clinical social workers will examine policy and practice agendas within our field as both traditions develop within a shared sociopolitical context (McCannell, 1986). If we are to be true to our historical roots, we must realize for our clients an active understanding of the person-in-environment perspective that frames the solutions to personal problems within social work (Hagen & Davis, 1992). If these goals are not realized, not only will our future clients be denied a service they deserve, but also our culture as a whole will be diminished by the gap in information that is so desperately needed for the functioning of a just society.

REFERENCES

Ault-Riche, M. (Ed). (1986). *Women and family therapy.* Rockville, MD: Aspen Systems.

American Psychiatric Association. (1994). *Diagnostic and statistical manual of mental disorders* (4th ed.). Washington, DC: Author.

Ballou, M. (1990). Approaching a feminist-principled paradigm in the construction of a personality theory. In L. S. Brown and M.P.P. Root (Eds.), *Diversity and complexity in feminist therapy* (pp. 23–40). New York: Haworth Press.

Belenky, M., Clinchy, B., Goldberger, N., & Tarule, J. (1986). *Women's ways of knowing.* New York: Basic Books.

Bograd, M. (1984). Family systems approaches to wife-battering: A feminist critique. *American Journal of Orthopsychiatry, 54,* 558–568.

Boyd, J. A. (1990). Ethnic and cultural diversity: Keys to power. In L. S. Brown and M.P.P. Root (Eds.), *Diversity and complexity in feminist therapy* (pp. 151–168). New York: Haworth Press.

Bradshaw, C. K. (1990). A Japanese view of dependency: What can *amae* psychology contribute to feminist therapy? In L. S. Brown and M.P.P. Root (Eds.), *Diversity and complexity in feminist therapy* (pp. 67–87). New York: Haworth Press.

Brodsky, A. (1980). A decade of feminist influence on psychotherapy. *Psychology of Women Quarterly, 4,* 331–344.

Brown, L. S. (1990). The meaning of a multicultural perspective for theory building in feminist therapy. In L. S. Brown and M.P.P. Root (Eds.), *Diversity and complexity in feminist therapy* (pp. 1–22). New York: Haworth Press.

Brown, L. S., & Brodsky, A. M. (1992). The future of feminist therapy. *Psychotherapy, 29,* 51–57.

Brown, L. S., & Liss-Levinson, N. (1981). Feminist therapy, I. In R. Corsini (Ed.), *Handbook of innovative psychotherapies* (pp. 299–314). New York: John Wiley & Sons.

Brown, L. S., & Root, M.P.P. (1990a). *Diversity and complexity in feminist therapy.* New York: Haworth Press.

Brown, L. S., & Root, M.P.P. (1990b). Introduction. In L. S. Brown & M.P.P. Root (Eds.), *Diversity and complexity in feminist therapy* (pp. i–xiii). New York: Haworth Press.

Chodorow, N. (1978). *The reproduction of mothering.* Berkeley: University of California Press.

Collins, B. (1986). Defining feminist social work. *Social Work, 31,* 214–219.

Daly, M. (1983). *Pure lust: Elemental feminist philosophy.* Boston: Beacon Press.

Day, L. (1992). Counseling for women: The contribution of feminist theory and practice. *Counseling Psychology Quarterly, 5,* 373–384.

Derrida, J. (1976). *Of grammatology* (G. C. Spivak, Trans.). Baltimore: Johns Hopkins University Press.

Eichenbaum, L., & Orbach, S. (1983). *Understanding women: A basic feminist psychoanalytic view.* New York: Basic Books.

Fisher, J. (1971). Jane Addams. In R. Morris (Ed.-In-Chief), *Encyclopedia of social work* (17th ed., pp. 8–10). New York: National Association of Social Workers.

Flexner, S. (1915). Is social work a profession? *Proceedings of the National Conference on Charities and Corrections,* 576–590.

Freedberg, A. (1993). The feminine ethic of care and the professionalization of social work. *Social Work, 38,* 535–541.

Ganley, A. L. (1988). Feminist therapy with male clients. In M. A. Dutton-Douglas and L.E.A. Walker (Eds.), *Feminist psychotherapies:*

Integration of feminist and psychotherapeutic systems (pp. 186–205). Norwood, NJ: Ablex.

Gilligan, C. (1982). *In a different voice.* Cambridge, MA: Harvard University Press.

Goldner, V. (1991). Feminism and systemic practice: Two critical traditions in transition. *Journal of Strategic and Systems Therapy, 10,* 118–126.

Gould, K. (1984). Original works of Freud on women: Social work references. *Social Casework, 65,* 94–101.

Hagen, J., & Davis, L. (1992). Working with women: Building a policy and practice agenda. *Social Work, 37,* 495–502.

Hamilton, G. (1951). *Theory and practice of social casework.* New York: Columbia University Press.

Hare-Mustin, R., & Maracek, J. (1988). The meaning of difference: Gender theory, post modernism and psychology. *American Psychologist, 43,* 455–464.

Ho, C. K. (1990). An analysis of domestic violence in Asian–American communities: A multicultural approach to counseling. In L. S. Brown & M.P.P. Root (Eds.), *Diversity and complexity in feminist therapy* (pp. 129–150). New York: Haworth Press.

Hollis, F. (1970). The psychosocial approach to the practice of casework. In R. Roberts & R. Nee (Eds.), *Theories of social casework* (pp. 33–75). Chicago: University of Chicago Press.

Hollis, F. (1971). Social casework: The psychosocial approach. In R. Morris (Ed.), *Encyclopedia of social work* (16th ed., pp. 1217–1226). New York: National Association of Social Workers.

Johnson, S. (1987). *Going out of our minds: The metaphysics of liberation.* Freedom, CA: Crossing Press.

Jordan, J., & Surrey, J. L. (1986). Self in relation: A theory of women's development. In T. Bernay & D. W. Cantor (Eds.), *The psychology of today's woman: The psychoanalytic vision* (pp. 81–104). Cambridge, MA: Harvard University Press.

Jordan, J., Surrey, J., & Kaplan, A. G. (1983). *Women and empathy, work in progress.* Wellesley, MA: Stone Center for Working Papers Series.

Kanuha, V. (1990). The need for an integrated analysis of oppression in feminist therapy ethics. In H. Lerman and N. Porter

(Eds.), *Feminist ethics and psychotherapy* (pp. 24–36). New York: Springer.

Kerr, V. (1992). Feminism on the front lines: The effects of backlash. Feminist perspectives in child and youth care practice [Special issue]. *Journal of Child and Youth Care, 7,* 1–10.

Kohut, H. (1977). *The restoration of the self.* New York: International Universities Press.

Land, H. (Ed.). (1992). *AIDS: A complete guide to psychosocial intervention.* Milwaukee: Families International Press.

Levine, O., Britton, P., James, T., Jackson, A., Hobfoll, S., & Lavin, J. (1993). The empowerment of women: A key for HIV prevention. *Journal of Community Psychology, 21,* 320–334.

Lott, B. (1985). The potential enrichment of social/personality psychology through feminist research and vice versa. *American Psychologist, 40,* 155–164.

Luepnitz, D. A. (1988). *The family interpreted: Feminist theory in clinical practice.* New York: Basic Books.

McCannell, K. (1986). Family politics, family policy and family practice: A feminist perspective. Women and mental health [Special issue]. *Canadian Journal of Community Mental Health, 5,* 61–71.

Meyer, C. (1983). *Clinical social work in the eco-systemic perspective.* New York: Columbia University Press.

Morrison Dore, M. (1994). Feminist pedagogy and the teaching of social work practice. *Journal of Social Work Education, 30,* 97–106.

Neimeyer, R. (1993). An appraisal of constructivist psychotherapies. *Journal of Consulting and Clinical Psychology, 61,* 221–234.

Palladino, D., & Stephenson, Y. (1990). Perceptions of the sexual self: Their impact on relationships between lesbian and heterosexual women. In L. S. Brown & M.P.P. Root (Eds.), *Diversity and complexity in feminist therapy* (pp. 231–254). New York: Haworth Press.

Perlman, H. (1971). Social casework, the problem-solving approach. In R. Morris (Ed.), *Encyclopedia of social work* (16th ed., pp. 1206–1216). New York: National Association of Social Workers.

Rave, E. J., & Larsen, C. (1990). Development of the code: The feminist process. In H. Lerman & N. Porter (Eds.), *Feminist ethics and psychotherapy* (pp. 14–23). New York: Springer.

Rawlings, E., & Carter, D. (Eds.). (1977). *Psychotherapy for women: Treatment toward equality.* Springfield, IL: Charles C Thomas.

Reynolds, B. C. (1975). *Social work and social living: Explorations in philosophy and practice.* Washington, DC: National Association of Social Workers. (Original work published 1951)

Richmond, M. (1917). *Social diagnosis.* New York: Russell Sage Foundation.

Robbins, J. (1983). A legacy of weakness: Unresolved issues in the mother–daughter arrangement in a patriarchal culture [Special issue]. *Women Changing Therapy, 2,* 41–50.

Ruderman, E. (1986). Gender-related themes of women psychotherapists in their treatment of women patients: The creative and reparative use of countertransference as a mutual growth experience. *Clinical Social Work Journal, 14,* 103–126.

Saari, C. (1986). *Clinical social work treatment: How does it work?* New York: Gardner Press.

Sayette, M. A., & Mayne, T. J. (1990). Survey of current clinical and research trends in clinical psychology. *American Psychologist, 45,* 1263–1266.

Sears, V. L. (1990). On being an "only one." In H. Lerman & N. Porter (Eds.), *Feminist ethics and psychotherapy* (pp. 102–105). New York: Springer.

Solomon, B. (1976). *Black empowerment.* New York: Columbia University Press.

Sonkin, D. J., Martin, D., & Walker, L.E.A. (1985). *The male batterer: A treatment approach.* New York: Springer.

Surrey, J. (1985). Self in relation: A theory of women's development. In *Works in progress.* Wellesley, MA: Stone Center Works in Progress Series.

Walker, L.E.A., & Edwall, G. E. (1987). Domestic violence and determination of visitation and child custody in divorce. In D. J. Sonkin (Ed.), *Domestic violence on trial* (pp. 127–154). New York: Springer.

Wetzel, J. (1986). A feminist world view conceptual framework. *Social Casework, 67,* 166–173.

2

Family-Centered Practice
Feminist, Constructionist, and Cultural Perspectives

Joan Laird

Feminism came late to family therapy. A number of phenomena account for this delay, not the least of which is that family therapy from the early 1950s was dominated by a number of "fathers" or "masters" who established major models or "schools" of family therapy and who had free rein in shaping the prevailing discourse for three decades. Both women and social workers have been invisible in this history-making process, even though both were centrally involved in the historical development of the field.

A second reason for the delay concerns the theory itself and, predominantly, the notion of "system." Whether grounded in general systems, cybernetics, or structural or biological theories, the family was examined holistically and mechanistically. What was of interest was how parts of families were organized into some more or less coherent whole and how these parts worked together. Problems or dysfunctions were not located inside people or viewed as defects in personality. Rather, they were seen as relational, operating at the interfaces and communications between people or levels in the family system. Problems were seen as a result of faulty family structure, inappropriate boundaries, and alliances (Minuchin, 1974); as faulty organization or hierarchy (Haley, 1987); as part of family rule systems or the "family game" (Selvini Palazzoli, Boscolo, Cecchin, & Prata, 1978); or as a matter of insufficient intergenerational differentiation (Bowen, 1978). Family therapists could comfortably believe that they were avoiding the distressing individual-blaming and mother-blaming patterns so predominant in individual psychological models. We forgot it was in the family that many of the early radical feminists located the major forces of patriarchy.

> *We were so intrigued by what was going on inside of families or within their immediate environments that we failed to place families themselves in an historical and sociopolitical context. We didn't notice . . . we were assuming Western cultural models of the family, normative models for family life and relationships, models that were not only ethnocentric, sexist, and heterosexist but that failed to accurately describe the growing pluralism of family forms in this society.* (Laird, 1993a, p. 83)

Feminist family therapists, however, gradually began to realize that although family theorists were presuming the equality of the sexes within the family, families were replicating the unequal gender arrangements in the larger social world. Once again, mothers, who often had less power in the family system, were being blamed for marital and child problems as well as for behaving according to traditional gender role expectations. Those behaviors, as Goldner (1985) pointed out, were the product of a historical process some 200 years in the making. The mother who had been taught to dedicate her life to her family, living for and serving husband and children, was now being told she was overinvolved or fusing, unwilling to allow her children to differentiate. Family therapy often became a matter of strategizing about how to free children from their "overinvolved" and "enmeshing" mothers and how to strengthen the role of the peripheral father, as therapists failed to notice that this historical, traditional family pattern, with its highly gender-specific roles, was still favored in social legislation and social discourse.

The traditional nuclear family remained the central model for family theorizing, even though large numbers of women were working outside the home, many were raising children alone, and others were living in innovative family forms. Few noted the social arrangements that had circumscribed opportunities for both women and men. Furthermore, rarely did the family therapist write about battered women, marital rape, and the sexual abuse of children, which are social and family problems that most dramatically attest to the inequality, oppression, and subjugation of women. When they did pay attention, therapists tended to see such phenomena as "systemic," with each actor in the family provoking and reacting to the others, all playing their parts in the family drama. Another analysis found "structural" problems such as inappropriate boundaries between parents and children. Power inequalities were largely invisible in prevailing family theory, which was dominated by Bateson's (1972) notion that power was not located in persons but in systems.

Hare-Mustin (1978) is credited with launching the feminist critique in family therapy. This, and other early efforts, went largely unnoticed; the feminist critique did not gain major momentum until the mid-1980s when a deluge of articles, chapters, books, speeches, and workshops appeared (Ault-Riche, 1986; Braverman, 1988; Goldner, 1985, 1988; Goodrich, Rampage, Ellman, & Halstead, 1988; Hare-Mustin, 1986, 1987; Lerner, 1988; Luepnitz, 1988; McGoldrick, Anderson, & Walsh, 1989; Walters, Carter, Papp, & Silverstein, 1988). In 1984 Monica McGoldrick, Carol Anderson, and Froma Walsh invited some 50 prominent women family therapists to meet together for four days of dialogue at Stonehenge, Connecticut. This gathering of women, repeated two years later, provoked a good deal of anxiety among male leaders in the field and also enabled women to collaborate, offer each other mutual support and mentoring, and strategize about how to bring to the surface and remedy the gender inequities in family theory and practice and in the professional field itself—in the journals, at the major conferences, and in training centers (Laird, 1986).

This movement-within-a-movement is still lively, healthy, and, with the introduction of postmodern thinking and growing interest in cultural metaphors for practice, represents the most exciting and challenging development in family therapy today. In this chapter I address three themes in family-centered practice: (1) feminist perspectives, (2) the implications of taking a social constructionist stance, and (3) the strengthening of cultural metaphors for practice. These themes do not always fit comfortably together; thus, points of tension and critique are highlighted.

These perspectives—the feminist, the constructionist, and the cultural—are illustrated clinically with an example of a lesbian family. One might look at any type of family, because the three perspectives are relevant to all families. The lesbian family offers a good example for exploration. It has been virtually ignored in the family therapy literature, even in feminist family therapy analyses, and few mental health professionals have taken either a postmodern or a cultural stance in trying to understand the lesbian couple or family.

FEMINIST PERSPECTIVE FOR FAMILY–CENTERED PRACTICE

There is a living diversity among feminists in family therapy because women (and a few men) differing in age, sexual orientation, ethnicity, race, and political stance define feminism and feminist practice in various ways and have differing goals. Some stress a sensitivity to issues of gender in work with families; others have more proactively begun to develop feminist models for practice; and still others see their primary mission in family therapy as women centered. The members of the latter group define themselves as advocates for women and actively work to dismantle hierarchies of power in families, in mental health professions and agencies, and in the larger society. Furthermore, feminist clinicians have often been trained in different models of practice that can provide different translations of feminist convictions into practice.

Feminist family therapists seem to agree that "neutrality" in relation to gender issues is not feasible. Walters et al. (1988) formed the Women's Family Therapy Project in the early 1980s and were central in bringing feminist ideas to family therapy. They argued that there was no such thing as gender neutrality in system thinking. Neutrality "means leaving the prevailing patriarchal assumptions implicit, unchallenged, and in place" (p. 18). McGoldrick et al. (1989) agreed, stating that

> *attention to the unequal positions of women and men in our society is necessary for all family therapists. A therapist who is not aware of the gender inequities embedded in our culture and conscious of the need to change this imbalance is contributing to the problems of families and couples attempting to survive in a new and complicated world. A therapist who fails to respond to a family's presentation of their problems with a framework that takes into account the inequities of the culture, and who attempts to maintain a so-called "neutrality" vis-à-vis the family, is necessarily doing sexist family therapy.* (p. 12)

Reflecting differences in feminist theory and women's studies, feminist family therapists position themselves differently in how they understand the concept of gender. Some lean toward the humanistic paradigms fostered in the work of Nancy Chodorow, Carol Gilligan, Jean Baker Miller, and others who have built on their theories (for example, the self-in-relation theorists at the Stone Center, Wellesley College). They tend to highlight gender differences and press for greater understanding and valuing of women's ways of knowing—in caring and in relationships. For example, Walters et al., (1988) demonstrated sensitivity to male–female power differences that they believe are an outcome of societal sex role socialization. These power differentials, then, are replicated in the family. They defined feminism as

> *a humanistic framework or world view concerned with the roles, rules, and functions that organize male–female interactions. Feminism seeks to include the experience of women in all formulations of human experience, and to eliminate the dominance of male assumptions. Feminism does not blame individual men for the patriarchal social system that exists, but seeks to understand and change the socialization process*

that keeps men and women thinking and acting within a sexist, male-dominated framework. (p. 17)

Among other things, they stressed that clinicians must affirm the values and behaviors characteristic of women, such as connectedness, nurturing, and emotionality, as well as supporting the possibilities for women outside marriage and the family. This kind of stance argues for women's "difference."

Hare-Mustin (1986), on the other hand, argued that we must be careful to neither exaggerate (the alpha error) nor minimize (the beta error) the differences between men and women. She argued that psychodynamic approaches tend to exaggerate gender differences, whereas systemic approaches ignore them. Hare-Mustin questioned the idealization of so-called women's attributes such as relatedness, arguing that neither these qualities nor qualities such as autonomy—supposedly characteristic of men—are essential aspects of male or female nature. They are false dichotomies, depending on power and status in the family and in other social contexts. Furthermore, they imply that it is women's special role to nurture others. Hare-Mustin has advocated more attention to the constraints that the family and other social contexts place on men and women in achieving both autonomy and relatedness.

Whatever the subtleties of difference in feminist philosophy, there are no simple agreed-on prescriptions, formulas, or models for feminist family-centered practice. McGoldrick et al. (1989) resisted proposing certain techniques or strategies, because the development of gender-sensitive therapy is "going to take us all working together for many years—or probably, more accurately, many generations" (p. 12). Goodrich et al. (1988) proposed that any therapy, feminist family therapy included, is a moral endeavor; "respect" is the primary defining feature. Goodrich and colleagues outlined their thoughts about problem analysis and practice guidelines in feminist family therapy. In terms of problem analysis, the practitioner needs to ask the following questions:

1. *How are gender stereotypes affecting the allocation of labor, power, and rewards in this family?*

2. *How do the stereotypes and the consequent allocations of labor, power, and rewards interact with the presenting problem?*

3. *What do family members believe about the masculinity and femininity of labor, power, desires, worth, values, and entitlement, as well as the way they are distributed?*

4. *What solutions have been closed off to the family because of their uncritical acceptance of sexist values?*

5. *Given the answers to questions 1 to 4, what will the family be likely to expect from the therapist, given her or his gender? Where shall a practitioner expect therapeutic relationship difficulties? Where can he or she make the easiest dent in customary client expectations? Where will [the therapist] feel the most vulnerable to their expectations?*

6. *What other pressures, wishes, and relationships are involved in shaping clients' problems and their solution attempts in addition to gender role stereotypes (understanding that all these other factors will be mediated by their gender role stereotypes)?* (pp. 23–24)

Feminist family therapy practice includes, according to Goodrich et al. (1988),

(1) using self in the therapy as a model of human behavior not so constrained by gender stereotypes, (2) creating a process in which the use of such skills as validation, empowerment, and demystification increases their sense of having options for themselves and develops greater reciprocity among family members, (3) developing an analysis of gender roles in the family, (4) using this analysis to guide interactions with the family in ways that both challenge and free them from constricted, stereotypical patterns of behavior, and (5) drawing techniques from a variety of extant family therapy approaches, with full awareness of the gender consequences of these techniques. (p. 28)

Although these principles can inform practice, in many situations more-decisive, action-oriented approaches are needed. The most controversial and difficult of issues concerns how feminist family theory and therapy ideas can inform practice with families in which women or children have been subjected to abuse by men—battering, marital rape, verbal abuse, or physical or sexual abuse of children—while possibly remaining in danger or vulnerable. Can family therapists work with these families? Family therapists have been faulted for failing to attend to the power differentials in violent families and for inadequately attending to the need for women to be protected and supported. Certainly many women in abusive relationships or in families where children have been sexually violated struggle to maintain and rehabilitate their families; in such cases, it is crucial that their male partners participate in the change efforts—at times separately as well as with the family. A number of feminist family therapists have addressed these issues and have pioneered family approaches to work with families that have suffered violence (Durrant

& White, 1990; Goldner, Penn, Sheinberg, & Walker, 1990; Trepper & Barrett, 1989; Yllo & Bograd, 1988). In all of these efforts, there is careful attention to vulnerability, safety, protection, responsibility, power differentials, gender differences, and the possibilities for more flexibility in gender ideologies and practices.

Feminist family-centered social workers often need to move beyond the boundaries of the individual case, to the courts, schools, and other community institutions, to bear witness to and advocate for the special needs of women and families.

POSTMODERNISM AND SOCIAL CONSTRUCTION

Overlapping with feminist critique and informed by it (although feminist contributions have been rendered invisible and devalued across most disciplines) is postmodernism, another metaperspective. The postmodern era of the 1980s and 1990s is a multidisciplinary intellectual movement ushered in through the doors of literary criticism, philosophy, anthropology, linguistics, psychology, and other sources of intellectual thought. Included under this rubric are terms such as poststructuralism, deconstruction, social constructionism, and constructivism, all coming from different positions in the intellectual world.

As these ideas made their way into language, family theorists were quick to seize on them as sources of new metaphors for family theory and practice making original contributions to this exciting body of thought and practice. Seminal contributions were made by Watzlawick (1984) with the publication of *The Invented Reality,* a book that brought constructivist thinkers like Ernst von Glasersfeld to the attention of family therapists. This early work and the older work of Bateson (1972), which was largely theoretical, was followed by a number of exciting developments that have contributed to a virtual rethinking of practice with families. Hoffman (1985) urged a rethinking of power relationships in the therapeutic endeavor, and Andersen (1987, 1991), with his development of the "reflecting team," discovered a simple way of changing the power dynamics in family interviews. By making the therapist's thinking more "transparent" and open to critique, the ideas of the "expert" (clinician) were deprivileged through the introduction of multiple reflections.

White and Epston (White, 1989, 1992; White & Epston, 1990) were intellectually challenged by the work of French philosopher–historian Michel Foucault and anthropologists Victor Turner and Edward Bruner. They began to look for the literary merit in therapy, placing metaphors such as narrative, power, and social discourse at the center of clinical work. One of their most intriguing practice contributions has been the "externalizing of the problem" (p. 16). The "problem," they postulated, is often located (by mental health professionals and clients alike) either inside of people or in relationships between people, which can lead to paralyzing or handicapping stories whereby individuals blame themselves for their misfortunes. In the view of White and Epston, neither individuals nor families are "dysfunctional," that is, people have problems with a problem. This simple shift helps empower people to undermine the life constraints of what White and Epston call "problem-saturated narratives" (p. 16).

Anderson and Goolishian (1987, 1992) situated the problem "in language," arguing that problems are socially constructed in language-determined systems. They too have drawn on linguistic and anthropological ideas, reframing therapy as a collaborative model. The therapist becomes a "conversational artist" whose task is to keep the therapeutic conversation engaged such that the linguistically determined problem can "dis-solve" and a new, more potentiating narrative can take its place.

Many others from the fields of family therapy, social work, psychology, and psychiatry are expanding on the fundamental ideas of social constructionism and deconstruction to the extent that a paradigmatic shift is affecting analysis and practice in the mental health professions. Dean (1989), Dean and Fenby (1989), Goldstein (1990), Hartman (1991), Laird (1989, 1993a, 1993c), Saleebey (1992), Sands and Nuccio (1992), and Witkin (1990) represent just a few of the growing number of social work scholars who are applying postmodern–constructionist ideas, revisiting epistemology, taking a critical stance toward hegemonic thinking, and reconceptualizing ideas about power and empowerment, social work assessment, and the meanings of "problem."

CULTURAL METAPHOR FOR FAMILY–CENTERED PRACTICE

A third metaperspective becoming more central in family-centered practice is that of "culture." Increasingly, family therapists are looking to anthropology for family theory and practice metaphors. For example, McGoldrick, Pearce, and Giordano (1982) have explored cultural theory to elucidate the meanings of the ethnic identity in families. Imber-Black, Roberts, and Whiting (1988) tapped the richness of ritual to understand better the culture of families and as a powerful source of intervention. More recently, a number of family thinkers have been mining postmodern anthropological, psychological, and linguistic work on story and narrative (Anderson & Goolishian, 1992; Gergen & Kaye, 1992; Hoffman, 1992; White, 1989, 1992; White & Epston, 1990) for new ideas and are using them in the development of innovative metaphors and models for practice.

My recent work blends ideas from feminist theory, anthropology, and postmodern thought using linguistic and cultural metaphors (for example, story, myth, narrative, ritual) to explore both the gender story in families (Allen & Laird, 1990; Laird, 1988, 1989, 1992) and the lesbian story (Laird, 1993b, 1994). Cultural metaphors, which in my view come closer to the social categories human beings draw on to define and ascribe meaning to themselves, their lives, and society, hold promise for getting us closer to what White and Epston (1990) called "lived experience." These metaphors seem more people friendly and less distancing, hierarchical, and abstract than the psychological–medical deficit-describing metaphors that have dominated clinical practice in the mental health professions. The inner psychological experience is negotiated in social and cultural worlds of meaning and might be described better in those terms.

To adopt an ethnographic stance, in my view, means that the practitioner leaves behind, or brackets, prior "diagnostic" maps or understandings, whether these have come from psychodynamic, family systems, or other theoretical stances. Such prior understandings tend to conjure up what we expected to find in the first place, helping us organize ideas but at the same time deafening us to other possibilities. Where diagnostic languages may be necessary for insurance reimbursement purposes, the clinician takes a pragmatic, co-constructionist stance. This involves the clients in selecting what White calls an "experience-near" language, that is, a language that does not offend the client's self-narrative and that is as empowering as possible. Such a stance frees the clinician to "listen" for the client's meanings in new and less-encumbered ways. One's prior knowledge is not abandoned; rather, it is used to generate questions and to float ideas. But such ideas are not privileged over the ideas of any other party to the therapeutic conversation. (This is not to argue that social meanings and conventions are never privileged—as in the case where there are important legal and social conventions and rules for moral and just behavior or where there is a need for safety or protection, when the social worker may have to assume a control function. These interventions are not, however, offered as "truths" but as necessary conditions for a "just" therapy.)

Anderson and Goolishian (1992) also have conceptualized the therapist as "ethnographer," a curious learner who takes a nonexpert or "not-knowing" stance. For Anderson and Goolishian, therapy is conceptualized as a dialogic conversational process, in which new meaning and understanding are mutually evolved and always constrained by the locally negotiated rules of meaning.

The assumption of an ethnographic stance means that the practitioner looks to ordinary life experience, using the categories that anthropologists use to understand small societies. These include, in family work, the family's stories, its folklore, and its everyday and special ritual lives. The family-centered practitioner searches for the family's system of meaning and belief, its spirituality, its identities, its dominant symbols and metaphors, and its ways of organizing itself in relation to the larger sociocultural context. The process is reflexive, in the sense that it bends back on itself, with ideas and actions blending and shifting in a conversation where all parties, including the practitioner, are changed.

CAUTIONARY COMMENT

These three perspectives—the feminist, the postmodern, and the cultural—have much to offer each other. At times, however, a naive belief exists in postmodern and anthropological thinking that influences family therapy, the social sciences, and other intellectual disciplines that all knowledges, all stories, are equal. Theorists at times fail to acknowledge that personal and social narratives are intimately connected, and there is a failure to attend to the ways in which certain knowledge and certain voices are privileged while others are subjugated (Collins, 1990). As Foucault (1980) taught us, knowledge and power cannot be separated; we do not have equal access to social resources or even to social knowledge. Certain voices are repeatedly silenced, some to the point where the story cannot be voiced even to the self, as in some cases of profound trauma. For example, women's ways of knowing, speaking, and writing may be disparaged; Native American voices are not heard; and the stories of men and women who experience horrible atrocities in war are denied an arena for sharing their stories, laying fertile ground for retraumatization. Client stories are privileged or constrained by such factors as gender, age, race, sexual orientation, skin color, and social class, depending on how such factors are "storied" in the larger surround.

Some family theorists are uncomfortable with what they consider "privileged discourses," arguing that feminists privilege their own politics in their practice, superimposing a particular story on client experience, much as someone might impose a religious narrative. But, in my view, wife abuse, child sexual abuse, the inequalities spawned in the traditional "patriarchal but father-absent family"

(Luepnitz, 1988), and other ills endemic to the American family cannot be "languaged" or "storied" away.

Can one adopt both a postmodern–cultural stance and a feminist perspective? Feminism does not necessarily mean the imposition of a set of beliefs, a privileging of a particular political stance. Feminism, in my definition, is closely linked to postmodernism in that it represents an effort to understand how gender, race, class, ethnicity, and sexuality are constructed in social contexts of power, thereby dismantling hierarchies of privilege. Feminism is about locating the subjugated voice, about questioning hegemonic "knowledge" and "truths." It is about examining gendered voices and silences. Thus, feminism can inform exploration of the family's united and disparate ideas and meanings, indicating how they are shaped in relationships of power and hierarchy. It can help us to help others consider whether their own stories are potentiating or subjugating.

Furthermore, some family thinkers who locate themselves in postmodernism fail to take into account that therapy takes place in a political context in which meanings are largely informed by prevailing social discourses and arrangements of power. It is not enough to "share ideas," to construct new narratives together. The social worker is not only a curious ethnographer but also carries the obligation to bear witness to the subjugated story in the larger world and to pursue goals of social justice (Waldegrave, 1990).

THE LESBIAN FAMILY: INCORPORATING FEMINIST, POSTMODERN, AND CULTURAL METAPHORS

Until recently, the linking of "lesbian" with the idea of "family" was an oxymoron—the two ideas were mutually exclusive. Yet, the lesbian couple with or without children (unacknowledged as a form of family in the U.S. census) may be thought of as a pioneering family in this era, a family in the vanguard of experimenting with new ways to couple and to raise children (Blumstein & Schwartz, 1983). The dominant psychological–pathological metaphor in the helping professions often has blinded us to the tremendous strengths in these families, to their emerging social and cultural richness, and to the learning potential they offer for all families (Laird, 1993b).

Together, the civil rights movement, women's movement, and gay and lesbian rights movement have helped to create a context and shape a social discourse in which it is increasingly permissible for lesbians to form families openly and to insist on the right to bear, adopt, and raise children. To date, the literature suggests that lesbian couples and families, despite homophobia and economic and social oppression, are functioning as well as other couples. Furthermore, children raised in single or coparenting lesbian families, whether from former marriages, heterosexual relationships, planned birth, or adoption, are faring as well as children in heterosexual, single-mother, or married families (Patterson, 1992).

Yet, as a "problem-saturated" profession, social work knows little about the stories of these families—their everyday lives, strengths, and emerging lesbian family culture. Many of these women have been inspired by and are strongly grounded in a feminist stance that shapes their efforts to rethink how to create families that will be potentiating and that will allow for the visions of everyone concerned.

All couples must struggle with common issues such as how to share household work and parenting; balance work and family; manage finances; deal with intimacy and sexuality; and negotiate relationships with families of origin, friends, and others in the community. It is particularly challenging for the lesbian family to determine how to "story" their family—how to describe and present themselves as a family to others. Furthermore, lesbian parents must teach their children how to take care of themselves in a societal context that has little language for describing or understanding them and that may express considerable hostility toward them.

A postmodern–cultural perspective, enriched by a feminist stance, offers a strengths-oriented, nonpathologizing, potentiating way to work with lesbian couples and families (Laird, 1994). The themes of domestic roles, parenting, working, managing income, intimacy, and sexuality are explored in the following case discussion.

Lesbian families are far less vulnerable to problems emanating from the model of dichtomized, sex-segregated roles that has dominated the traditional, hierarchically organized heterosexual or patriarchal family. Typically, lesbian couples share the work of the household and paid employment, dividing responsibilities by interest and skill rather than by gender-driven ideology. Of course, today most women work outside the home, but heterosexual couples have had a more difficult time than lesbian couples learning how to share the work of household and parenting. We can guess, because depression and other symptoms in women have been linked heavily to gendered responsibilities in families (Lerner, 1988), that lesbians will be less at risk in this area. Furthermore, because most lesbians work actively and consciously to dismantle sex role ideologies in child rearing, their children seem to be more flexible, tolerant, and androgynous—that is, less susceptible to rigid sex role ideas. Nevertheless, lesbians (for the most part) have been socialized in heterosexual families in which gendered roles are taken for granted and, in that sense, will often struggle to define innovative ways of sharing household responsibility.

JANICE AND BETH

Janice (age 35, divorced and previously married for 13 years) had a 20-month-old daughter, Susan, when she met Beth. Even though Janice had worked outside the home during most of her married years in the couple's demanding business, she also had carried most of the responsibility for managing the home and parenting Susan. Raised in a family modeled in similar traditional fashion, she had both high homemaking standards and aspirations for a successful career of her own.

Beth (age 43 and a self-defined lesbian since adolescence), on the other hand, was well advanced in her hotel management career and as an adult had always supported herself. She traveled a great deal, conducted training seminars, and taught in a local business college. Although enormously skilled at carpentry and home repairs, she had little interest in homemaking and was indifferent about the state of the house. Raised by her divorced mother in an all-female family, she had been seen as the competent "son" and was thus unconstrained by notions of ideal womanhood.

Initially, Janice was thrilled to be in an intimate relationship with someone so gentle, patient, and nurturing who also was autonomous, competent, and admired in her chosen career. She felt cared for and protected in a way never experienced within her marriage. Janice also was grateful that Beth did much of the cooking, the grocery shopping, and the heavy yard work. Beth was thrilled to have a partner who was clearly so "feminine," who created and took care of a beautiful environment, while also admiring her and bringing a child into her life.

As the relationship continued and deepened, the complementary roles took a firm hold. Janice, although she worked part-time outside the home as a bookkeeper, also was trying to launch a writing and teaching career and believed she should carry most of the household and child care responsibility, because she earned less money and spent more time at home. Janice also was the family bookkeeper and, believing she should "pay her way equally," was keeping a set of books whereby her "debt" to Beth was growing weekly. The couple frequently squabbled about money. Beth could not understand why Janice would not let her do most of the supporting, whereas Janice kept telling Beth they could not live at a level suited to Beth's income but not hers. In fact, Janice had moved into Beth's home and insisted on paying "rent," so that Beth's investment was growing while Janice found she could not keep up. Gradually, as Janice found herself increasingly burdened and tired, she began to develop the same resentments that had been central in her decision to divorce her husband. Beth, on the other hand, was in a position similar to what many husbands experience in relation to their wives, not understanding what was troubling her partner. Janice was excited about her developing career in creative writing, but because she worked part of the time at home, she found herself with almost all of the home and child care responsibilities, even though the couple had some outside help with cleaning and yard work.

Beth, by contrast, worked entirely outside the home and continued to travel a great deal. She contributed to household chores only when her work schedule permitted. When the couple finally sought counseling, after six years together, Janice's resentments had grown to the point where she had withdrawn sexually, was avoiding intimacy, and was considering separation.

The social work clinician helped Janice and Beth examine how gender-linked expectations (shaped by societal and familial dichtomized gender roles and a lesbian culture that supports "butch–femme" roles) were interfering with their relationship. Janice, as she revisited the "woman" narratives in her life, came to understand how she was evaluating herself in the context of women's cultural scripts that better fit her grandmother's generation. Her grandmother had been a woman whom Janice admired but who had not worked outside the home, had suppressed any dreams of a career, and (in some ways) had been deeply discontented with her life. She channeled considerable creativity, intelligence, and energy into cooking, sewing, and interfering in the lives of her children, even after they were grown. Janice could not give herself permission to neglect the "perfect housewife" model. Beth, on the other hand, a self-styled "butch," had been freed from some of the typical constraints on women's lives. But, by meeting her mother's need for a man in the house, she had adopted some stereotypical male ways of knowing and being that clouded her sense of coparenting rights and her full participation in domestic life. Furthermore, her role as coparent received virtually no recognition in the world around her. Even though she was giving Susan advantages that had not been provided by the child's father and was involved in Susan's parenting far more than he, she felt she had no "parental" legitimacy.

The clinician was able to help the couple through an exploration of their dominant stories, rituals, and everyday experiences to envision a fully democratic, shared dream for family cultural life. For

Janice that meant letting go of some of her perfection narrative, which included inviting and helping Beth to be more involved in domestic life and parenting Susan, at the same time giving herself permission to carve out career time and enlisting Beth's help in warding off intrusion. Janice's re-authoring of her gender narrative proved an apt metaphor for giving herself permission to become an author in her own right.

Beth, despite her pride in her career achievements, often felt shut out of the closeness between Janice and Susan and the important household decisions (similar to the so-called peripheral father position common in traditional, heterosexual families). The re-authoring of the democratic couple narrative led to Beth's assumption of more responsibility for parenting Susan and for giving higher priority to household responsibilities, both of which she welcomed. In a sense, she needed to become more of an "executive" at home and a bit less of an "executive" in the corporate world. Beth made the shift by scheduling fewer trips and planning in advance, with Janice, for coverage at home.

In terms of money, Janice thought she was embracing a feminist and politically correct lesbian stance when she insisted that she contribute equally to the family's financial coffers. This stance was difficult to maintain because her own earnings were modest and child support from Susan's father was minimal and sporadic. Her belief in the dominant cultural narrative that "privileges" money and links it with power proved disempowering for her. By avoiding traditional family situations in which men typically earn more than women and carry a disproportionate burden of financial responsibility, Janice and Beth had adopted a constraining narrative that did not allow for a more egalitarian relationship in which each partner could contribute according to her abilities and needs.

Finally, this was a couple who, for various reasons, were not public about their lesbianism. They were open about their commitment and caring for each other, had established connections to their respective families, and had constructed a somewhat satisfactory social life. Yet, they had never named their relationship as lesbians in public—with family, friends, or in any other context. Janice was terrified of losing custody of Susan, a realistic fear, and Beth had once been fired from a job after it was discovered that she was a lesbian. Both were afraid of family rejection. These anxieties, not without substance, were exacting all of the costs such secrecy and silence engender (Laird, 1992). Because being openly intimate was constrained, they were cut off from a social and cultural life whereby they could explore more varied cultural visions and share their joys and struggles with others. Susan, too, did not know how to "explain" her unusual family to her friends or teachers.

The clinical work involved a close exploration of the symbols, rituals, and legacies Janice and Beth wished to carry on from their own families and those they wished to leave behind. This couple had to give themselves permission to explore fully the meaning of becoming a lesbian family. This definition of family meant their right to shape a family culture that would express their meanings and values and link them to a larger cultural world, much as people form linkages through shared ethnic heritage or religious affiliation. Janice and Beth were encouraged to make connections with the lesbian community in the city where they lived. The worker suggested readings and introduced them to the stories of other lesbian couples and to the history of lesbian experience and culture-making in society. Janice and Beth began to watch videos and to discuss the few lesbian films available, searching for and evaluating the stories, cultural symbols, and rituals available in the larger world. Their difficulty in claiming legitimacy for their family meant that they had paid insufficient attention to their family ritual and weren't expressing their unique family "vision" nearly as much as the culture handed down in their heterosexually organized families. They joined a lesbian mothers group, which proved to be enormously helpful as they learned how other couples had struggled with similar issues and were designing creative solutions. They began to experiment with "coming out" to their families and trusted friends. In the process, a context was created in which eight-year-old Susan could ask questions and talk about her uncertainties related to her "different" family. Intimacy and sexuality, originally such positives in the relationship, became self-correcting as Janice's resentments faded and the couple began to more comfortably "own" their definition of family. They began to consider having another child, this time in the context of the lesbian relationship.

Instead of seeing themselves as a "deviant" family, they began to restory themselves as "pioneers" in developing a family form where children might thrive and reach their full potential unconstrained by gender stereotypes. Such a family would be well-adapted to survive in a world where gender wars are being fiercely waged and women find themselves alone, poor, exhausted, or worse yet, in danger of being beaten, raped, or killed.

In sum, lesbian couples and families bring all of the same issues and concerns to clinical work as any family, usually overlaid with the burden of being negatively defined and unsupported in the community around them. Such couples and families are not monolithic—

they cross all of the same ethnic, social class, age, and other boundaries as any family. Thus, we need no special models of practice. What works well with most families will work well with lesbian families and vice versa.

Lesbian families, like all families, will be best served by practice approaches that are gender sensitive and that expose and dismantle subjugating narratives for women, men, and same-sex families. Furthermore, lesbian families will be best served by practitioners who value and respect lesbians as members of a cultural group in the making.

Lesbians and gay men may be one of the last groups in our society for which it is still socially and linguistically acceptable to openly abrogate their civil rights. It is our obligation, as social workers, to move beyond the "case," to bear witness publicly to the strengths and the needs of these families and to work for more socially just responses in the courts and legislatures.

CONCLUSION

This chapter blends together three metaperspectives for a postmodern family-centered practice: feminist, social constructionist, and cultural. Among other things, this positioning suggests a moving toward strength rather than pathology, a greater sharing of power between worker and client, a privileging of the client narrative, a search for the subjugated story, an exploration and dismantling of gender hierarchies, and a focus on experience near cultural categories of meaning. Central to the perspective is an ethnographic stance for the worker, that is, a stance that abandons prior categories of meaning or preconceptions to free up the clinician to listen to the family's own meanings in less-encumbered ways.

REFERENCES

Allen, J., & Laird, J. (1990). Men and story: Constructing new narratives in therapy. *Journal of Feminist Family Therapy, 2*(3/4), 75–100.

Andersen, T. (1987). The reflecting team: Dialogue and meta-dialogue in clinical work. *Family Process, 26,* 415–428.

Andersen, T. (1991). *The reflecting team: Dialogues and dialogues about the dialogues.* New York: W. W. Norton.

Anderson, H., & Goolishian, H. (1987). Human systems as linguistic systems: Preliminary and evolving ideas about the implications for clinical theory. *Family Process, 27,* 371–394.

Anderson, H., & Goolishian, H. (1992). The client is the expert: A not-knowing approach to therapy. In S. McNamee & K. J. Gergen (Eds.), *Therapy as social construction* (pp. 25–39). Newbury Park, CA: Sage Publications.

Ault-Riche, M. (1986). *Women and family therapy.* Rockville, MD: Aspen Systems.

Bateson, G. (1972). *Steps to an ecology of mind.* New York: Random House.

Blumstein, P., & Schwartz, P. (1983). *American couples: Money, work, sex.* New York: William Morrow.

Bowen, M. (1978). *Family therapy in clinical practice.* New York: Jason Aronson.

Braverman, L. (Ed.). (1988). *Women, feminism, and family therapy.* New York: Haworth Press.

Collins, P. (1990). *Black feminist thought: Knowledge, consciousness, and the politics of empowerment.* London: HarperCollins.

Dean, R. (1989). Ways of knowing in clinical practice. *Clinical Social Work Journal, 17*(2), 116–127.

Dean, R., & Fenby, B. (1989). Exploring epistemologies: Social work action as a reflection of philosophical assumptions. *Journal of Social Work Education, 25*(1), 45–64.

Durrant, M., & White, C. (Eds.). (1990). *Ideas for therapy with sexual abuse.* Adelaide, Australia: Dulwich Centre Publications.

Foucault, M. (1980). *Power/knowledge: Selected interviews and other writings.* New York: Pantheon Press.

Gergen, K. J., & Kaye, J. (1992). Beyond narrative in the negotiation of therapeutic meaning. In S. McNamee and K. J. Gergen (Eds.), *Therapy as social construction* (pp. 166–185). Newbury Park, CA: Sage Publications.

Goldner, V. (1985). Feminism and family therapy. *Family Process, 24,* 31–47.

Goldner, V. (1988). Generation and gender: Normative and covert hierarchies. *Family Process, 27,* 17–31.

Goldner, V., Penn, P., Sheinberg, M., & Walker, G. (1990). Love and violence: Gender paradoxes in volatile attachments. *Family Process, 29,* 343–364.

Goldstein, H. (1990). The knowledge base of social work practice. *Families in Society, 71*(4), 32–43.

Goodrich, T. J., Rampage, C., Ellman, B., & Halstead, K. (1988). *Feminist family therapy: A casebook.* New York: W. W. Norton.

Haley, J. (1987). *Problem-solving therapy* (2nd ed.). San Francisco: Jossey-Bass.

Hare-Mustin, R. (1978). A feminist approach to family therapy. *Family Process, 17*, 181–194.

Hare-Mustin, R. (1986). Autonomy and gender: Some questions for therapists. *Psychotherapy, 23*, 205–212.

Hare-Mustin, R. (1987). The problem of gender in family therapy theory. *Family Process, 26*, 15–27.

Hartman, A. (1991). Words create worlds [Editorial]. *Social Work, 36*, 275–276.

Hoffman, L. (1985). Beyond power and control: Toward a "second order" family systems therapy. *Family Systems Medicine, 3*, 381–396.

Hoffman, L. (1992). A reflexive stance for family therapy. In S. McNamee & K. J. Gergen (Eds.), *Therapy as social construction* (pp. 7–24). Newbury Park, CA: Sage Publications.

Imber-Black, E., Roberts, J., & Whiting, R. (Eds.). (1988). *Rituals in families and family therapy.* New York: W. W. Norton.

Laird, J. (1986). Women, family therapists, and other mythical beasts. *American Family Therapy Association Newsletter, 25*, 32, 35.

Laird, J. (1988). Women and ritual in family therapy. In E. Imber-Black, J. Roberts, & R. Whiting (Eds.), *Rituals in families and family therapy.* New York: W. W. Norton.

Laird, J. (1989). Women and stories: Restorying women's self-constructions. In M. McGoldrick, C. Anderson, & F. Walsh (Eds.), *Women in families: A framework for family therapy* (pp. 427–450). New York: W. W. Norton.

Laird, J. (1992). Women's secrets—Women's silences. In E. Imber-Black (Ed.), *Secrets in families and in family therapy* (pp. 243–267). New York: W. W. Norton.

Laird, J. (1993a). Family-centered practice: Cultural and constructionist reflections. In J. Laird (Ed.), *Revisioning social work education: A social constructionist approach* (pp. 77–109). New York: Haworth Press.

Laird, J. (1993b). Lesbian and gay families. In F. Walsh (Ed.), *Normal family processes* (2nd ed.). New York: Guilford Press.

Laird, J. (1993c). *Revisioning social work education: A social constructionist approach.* New York: Haworth Press.

Laird, J. (1994). Lesbian couples and families: A cultural perspective. In M. P. Mirkin (Ed.), *Treating women in their social contexts: A feminist reconstruction.* New York: Guilford Press.

Lerner, H. (1988). *Women in therapy.* New York. Jason Aronson.

Luepnitz, D. (1988). *The family interpreted: Feminist theory in clinical practice.* New York: Basic Books.

McGoldrick, M., Anderson, C., & Walsh, F. (1989). *Women in families: A framework for family therapy.* New York: W. W. Norton.

McGoldrick, M., Pearce, J., & Giordano, J. (1982). *Ethnicity and family therapy.* New York: Guilford Press.

Minuchin, S. (1974). *Families and family therapy.* Cambridge, MA: Harvard University Press.

Patterson, C. (1992). Children of lesbian and gay parents. *Child Development, 63,* 1025–1042.

Saleebey, D. (Ed.). (1992). *The strengths perspective in social work practice.* New York: Longman.

Sands, R., & Nuccio, K. (1992). Postmodern feminist theory and social work. *Social Work, 37,* 489–494.

Selvini Palazzoli, M., Boscolo, L., Cecchin, G., & Prata, G. (1978). *Paradox and counterparadox.* Northvale, NJ: Jason Aronson.

Trepper, T., & Barrett, M. J. (1989). *Systemic treatment of incest: A therapy handbook.* New York: Brunner/Mazel.

Waldegrave, C. (1990). Social justice and family therapy. *Dulwich Family Centre Newsletter, 1,* 5–47.

Walters, M., Carter, B., Papp, P., & Silverstein, O. (1988). *The invisible web: Gender patterns in family relationships.* New York: Guilford Press.

Watzlawick, P. (1984). *The invented reality.* New York: W. W. Norton.

White, M. (1989). *Selected papers.* Adelaide, Australia: Dulwich Centre Publications.

White, M. (1992). Deconstruction and therapy. In D. Epston & M. White (Eds.), *Experience, contradiction, narrative & imagination: Selected papers of David Epston and Michael White, 1989–1991.* Adelaide, Australia: Dulwich Centre Publications.

White, M., & Epston, D. (1990). *Narrative means to therapeutic ends.* New York: W. W. Norton.

Witkin, S. (1990). The implications of social constructionism for social work education. *Journal of Teaching in Social Work, 4*(2), 37–48.

Yllo, K., & Bograd, M. (1988). *Feminist perspectives on wife abuse.* Newbury Park, CA: Sage Publications.

3

Sources and Visions for Feminist Group Work

Reflective Processes, Social Justice, Diversity, and Connection

Charles D. Garvin and Beth Glover Reed

Participating and providing leadership within a small-group context is a fundamental "staple" of being a social worker, in all settings, in all jobs. Social workers in human services and community organizations work with clients, their family members, community representatives, and other human services colleagues in many kinds of groups. In fact, much of life is spent in groups, both in the "public" spheres (for example, workplace, government, or commerce) and those considered "private" (for example, the family, peer groups, or neighborhoods). Skills in facilitating and participating in groups of various kinds have always been important in maneuvering through life and being an effective social worker.

In this chapter we assert that developing and sustaining high-quality groups are likely to be increasingly important in the 21st century and that feminist principles and processes used within groups of various kinds will be essential tools in groups of the future. In fact, groups are a wonderful medium for the application of feminist principles. Many features of modern feminism and feminist practice were developed in group settings, and social group work and feminist practice share historical roots. In some ways, contemporary social group work models and feminist principles are similar and compatible, but feminist approaches also add additional elements and are critical of and would transform others.

Throughout this chapter we describe key elements and dimensions for the application of feminist thought and principles within group contexts and intersect some of the literature on feminist thought and practices with concepts and writings about social group work. We summarize ways that work in groups has contributed to developing feminist theory and practice, note some important contributions that women have made to the development of group-based practice within social work, and discuss some feminist themes that thread through the history of social group work. Then, we continue the integrative effort begun by Lewis (1992) with a critique of the compatibility of feminism with four commonly accepted models for group work practice, using six dimensions within group work, and summarize key aspects of feminist group work. Finally, we explicate ways in which these applications can help meet the challenges of the 21st century.

We define *feminist practice* as the action of developing, applying, reexamining, and revising feminist principles, which the practitioner also can use as guidelines for assessing and reflecting on practice. We use feminist principles but within a group context. Note that these principles are drawn from many "types" of feminism, they are not mutually exclusive, others might cluster them differently, and different forms of feminism emphasize some principles more than others and often use them differently (Reed & Garvin, 1993). Feminist thought continues to evolve, and the multiple feminisms that exist as this is written are at different stages of development, articulation, elaboration, reformulation, and transformation (Donovan, 1985; Ferguson, 1993; Tong, 1989).

These evolutions are one reason that we intend not to proscribe a particular model or create standards for making judgments about the "correctness" of feminist group practice. We also believe that feminist principles can be used in many ways, depending on key characteristics of the group such as size, goals, composition, theoretical orientation of worker, and setting. In addition, the growing literature on how class, race, ethnicity, sexual orientation, and other factors are linked to societal inequalities intersects with and changes our understanding of gender-based inequities and gendering processes (Brown & Root, 1990; Collins, 1990). We need dimensions that can catalyze further development and assessment and provide a framework for examining one's theories, actions, and aspects of the group simultaneously for the ways they reflect gendered assumptions and create gendered thoughts and interactions. We believe that groups may be the ideal setting for such reflections, because group processes can greatly enhance the "vision" of the practitioner and the theorist, once norms are established for open exploration within a supportive environment.

BACKGROUND AND HISTORY: FEMINISM, GROUP WORK, AND SOCIAL WORK

In the modern women's movement, small groups of women, often structured collectively, were instrumental in generating multiple forms of feminist thought and theory and designed and implemented major feminist social change strategies and other forms of practice. In addition to the overt goals of the groups, which usually included a sharing of experiences and analyses that led to personal social changes, members also experimented with alternative leadership styles and structures. At that time, a number of practice-focused publications articulated how to conduct feminist meetings and consciousness-raising groups and raised cautions about the skills and balance needed in effective groups. Men, concerned about the application of feminism to men's lives, also worked extensively in groups. Feminist thought continues to be shaped by work occurring in group contexts. For instance, in a recent book on feminist theory, Ferguson (1993) alluded several times to discussion within a group constituted to explore feminist theory.

Despite the centrality of group-based practices within so many fields of social work and of group-based experiences in the development of many areas of feminism, the literature on practice and theory for practice includes few examples of the application of feminist approaches within group practice of various types. Brodsky (1973) discussed ways that consciousness-raising groups could be a model for therapy with women. Wyckoff (1977) and others (Lerman, 1974; Mander & Rush, 1974) stated that work in groups with other women was a critical ingredient of feminist work with women. The first books and articles that applied feminist principles explicitly to social work practice (Bricker-Jenkins & Hooyman, 1986; Burden & Gottlieb, 1987; Van Den Bergh & Cooper, 1986), however, mentioned work in groups only occasionally. In 1983 we (Reed & Garvin, 1983) we edited a special issue of *Social Work with Groups* that focused on gender, but neither we nor Brody (1987) focused on principles for the practice of feminist groups. Butler & Wintram (1991) described in detail a feminist method for conducting groups for women. Trimble (1986) discussed feminist groups with a subgroup of men, and Lewis (1992) explored the potential for "several facets of feminist theory . . . to focus social group work practice with vulnerable populations more precisely" (p. 271).

Within social work, unlike other disciplines and professions, the first people to develop and discuss group work practice were dynamic and dedicated women. These women did not describe themselves as feminist theorists, but their experiences as women and their work with women certainly informed their ideas about working with groups, as did their concern about overcoming oppression as an important goal of practice. Many of their views were probably informed by earlier feminist thought, and they anticipated and paralleled many contemporary views about feminist group work practice. The major contexts for early social group work practice were settlements and the Young Women's Christian Association (YWCA) (Reid, 1981). Lewis (1992) noted that both settings provided opportunities for supportive communities of women to be concerned about the public or political realm with an emphasis on social justice.

One of the most famous settlement house organizers was Jane Addams of Hull House in Chicago. Addams identified early with social work by accepting the presidency of the National Conference of Charities and Corrections in 1910 and later by supporting its name change in 1917 to the National Conference of Social Work. Addams operated in group contexts of many kinds, and her work and writings emphasize many feminist ideas. She reconceptualized work with constituents as work with "members" rather than "clients," similar to the concern of modern feminists with the ways that language both reflects and shapes unrecognized gendering (shaped by gender-related assumptions, processes, and structures), power imbalances, and cultural assumptions. She also understood individuals within their social conditions, in ways similar to the current principle of "the personal is political." Addams was awarded the Nobel Peace Prize in 1931 and served as president of the Women's Peace Party and the Women's International Peace Congress (later renamed the Women's International League for Peace and Freedom). Concern about peace continues to be an ongoing focus within feminist thought and activism, reflecting both feminist values and the principle of challenging dichotomous thinking (of "friends" or "enemies," for instance) and working toward connectedness and wholeness.

The woman, however, who is recognized by contemporary authorities as contributing as much if not more than anyone else to the conceptualization of social work with groups is Grace Coyle. In her first professional days, she worked as a settlement worker and then at the Industrial Women's Department of the YWCA. In this division of the YWCA, the focus was on safe working conditions, improved pay, union organizing, and efforts to change systemic conditions for women "without the protections of family or husband" (Lewis, 1992, p. 275). Coyle stressed such principles as the need for the worker to consider simultaneously the activities of the group; the social relationships among the members; and the wholeness of each person incorporating her or his body, mind, and emotions. She also stressed the idea that growth of individuals must be toward identifying with the good of the social whole and, thus, to using their capacities for social ends beyond themselves (Coyle, 1948). Again we see parallels to current feminist principles, linking the personal (micro) with the political (macro), respecting various levels of human connectedness, and attending carefully to processes (how things are accomplished) as well as to outcomes (what is accomplished).

Gertrude Wilson was another highly influential group work pioneer. She was a renowned group work teacher, practitioner, and writer for many years and wrote with her close associate Gladys Ryland the influential text *Social Group Work Practice* (1949). In an article portraying her view of the history of group work, Wilson (1976) described her activities as an industrial secretary in the YWCA and her appreciation of the unity of personal growth and social responsibility as follows:

> *Economic, social and religious adjustment of women and girls to the life of today is the general field of the Young Women's Christian Association. . . . Education of women and girls in industry leads to personal development and participation in activities within their own group and in the community. . . . The solution of individual and sometimes personal problems of girls in the club has come in for special emphasis . . . such as (a) difficulties in spending wages wisely and (b) personal problems when one is in love.* (pp. 16–17)

Although the context and language of this quote reflects the time in which it was written, Wilson anticipated modern feminism in her concern about the overall development of girls and women, their economic well-being, the quality of their relationships, and the link between personal and community (political) spheres.

A historical note does not do justice to the many women who played important roles in the evolution of social work with groups, but we need to mention two more. Clara Kaiser (1930) published a set of records to exemplify group work practice, an example of the strong commitment of these group work pioneers to ground their theories and concepts in practice experience and to reflect on their experiences to continue to develop "theory." Current feminist principles describe such iterative and reflective processes as "praxis." And

Neva Boyd contributed to group workers' understanding of creative activity (Boyd, 1935). Early in group work theorizing, Boyd saw the importance of using a variety of media and methods along with verbal activity to enhance human development, anticipating current feminist work on valuing and building on multiple forms of knowing, learning, and doing (Belenky, Clinchy, Goldberger, & Taruli, 1986).

Unfortunately, as has been the case among many concerned about women, these group work pioneers were also products of their time with respect to racism. They did not resist, and even justified, the emerging pattern of residential segregation of people of color and were more sensitive to the needs of European migrants than the needs of African American people who were moving in large numbers from rural to urban environments (Berman-Rossi & Miller, 1994).

FEMINIST THOUGHT AND THE STATE OF KNOWLEDGE ABOUT GENDER, FEMINISM, AND GROUPS

A major principle in all feminist practice is to work from feminist values and theory and to apply the developing knowledge on women, differences among women, gender, and gendered processes to create a just world. Evaluating the sources, adequacy, and context of available knowledge is important if a practitioner is to understand the strengths and limitations of the current literature on gender and groups. The 21st century is likely to present complex ethical dilemmas, new challenges, and technologies with great potential for harm or benefit, depending on how and by whom they are applied. Thus, evaluating relevant sources of knowledge and skills and understanding how this knowledge has evolved are important ongoing tasks for a feminist practitioner. Evaluating the impact of culture, ethnicity, sexual orientation, and other factors associated with oppressive dynamics within this culture also is important if a practitioner is to understand the strengths and limitations of the literature on gender and groups. The following are some examples of theory and research relevant for group work in which a feminist critique or feminist perspective is in different stages of development.

Initiation of a feminist critique usually requires some awareness that existing models of theory and of practice are not sufficient or are deficient or biased in some respect. Work of this type includes the many early critiques of personality theories, models for individual and social change, and assumptions about health and mental health. Specific to group work are Kanter's (1977) review and critique of groups used in staff development concerning their adequacy for women and early feminist papers that criticized the patriarchy's use of power and hierarchy (Ferguson, 1984).

Common in the earlier stages of critique of theory and practice and the development of revisions were studies of women in comparison with men or in comparison to models developed from the study of men or studies in which gender had not been examined. For instance, a study by Aries (1977) described different dynamics, structures, and topics of discussion in groups of women compared with gender-balanced groups or all-men groups. Social workers also initiated examinations of the effects of group gender and race composition (Carlock & Martin, 1977; Davis, 1980, 1981) and the effects of the gender of therapist–leader and gender-related themes in groups (see Reed, 1981, for a summary). Examinations of all-women groups began to define ways in which group development may diverge from what had been presented earlier as universal patterns (Hagen, 1983), and descriptions of all-men groups also delineated special leadership and development issues in these groups (Stein, 1983). Some research (Tower, 1979) suggested that patterns of unequal participation by women and men within gender-balanced groups were difficult to change, even with training and observation. Moreover, members often misperceived small patterns of change as much larger than they were, probably because these patterns deviated from their usual frame of reference. These distortions in perceptions meant that members, both female and male, no longer noticed the imbalances and thus saw no need to keep working to change them.

Another type of feminist work develops alternative theories and approaches that challenge earlier assumptions that either ignored gender or contributed to limiting stereotypes. These new formulations then can guide new research and models of practice. With regard to small groups, two important literature reviews (Lockheed & Hall, 1976; Meeker & Weitzel-O'Neill, 1985) applied the theoretical framework of inferred status characteristics to "explain" the multiple studies of gender differences in behavior within groups (for example, people with less power act in more feminine ways; those with more power act in ways usually associated with men). Previously, masculine (for example, assertive or focused on task) and feminine (for example, socioemotional) behaviors had been interpreted as the natural results of biological predispositions or the influence of social roles. Status perspectives added power and its effects to our understanding of behaviors between women and men and presented new possibilities for change.

Yet another type of feminist work emphasizes women's experiences and "standpoints" as the center of focus rather than "in the margins." Some of the previous studies grew from women's efforts to understand their own experiences in groups or as group leaders. Works that focus on particular subgroups of women are appearing (Boston Lesbian Psychologies Collective, 1987). Authors such as Butler and Wintram (1991) are beginning to focus especially on women's needs and experiences within groups.

As more alternative bodies of knowledge are developed, we must turn our attention to the ways that earlier models and theories based on work by men, with men, or from a male-shaped perspective must be transformed to incorporate the new knowledge and perspectives; reflect the experiences of both women and men; and acknowledge the impact of discrimination, power imbalances, privilege, and different cultures. Transformative work on gender, small-group theory, and group work practice is not well developed, although Ridgeway (1992) has taken steps in that direction and de Chant (1993) has sought to broaden and change our understanding of the assumptions that underlie psychodynamic strategies for individual and group change. de Chant has also presented alternatives to gendered group processes, communication patterns, and interpersonal dynamics, focusing primarily on psychodynamic group practice. Ridgeway stresses the need to identify the microstructures that continually re-create patterns of privilege and processes of devaluing within small groups, even when individuals within a group are trying to identify and confront patterns of inequity.

Another form of doing feminism "deconstructs" the notion of any unifying theory and challenges any effort to generalize or define collective experiences. This type of work is less developed within small-group theory, although application of discourse analysis (Tannen, 1990) within small groups could move in this direction. These approaches are represented within the principles we apply, however, by those that focus on attention to processes and those concerned with the use and construction of language (for example, renaming our concepts and experiences and examining the ways words and nonverbal interactions construct and reconstruct meaning, relationships, and inequalities).

Finally, as scholarship and practice become more attuned to the intersections among different forms of oppression and contributors to identity and group membership, the development of theories and practice models often must juxtapose different approaches with each other and cycle and zigzag through various processes and steps multiple times. For instance, both the race and the gender of group leaders change the nature of the experience for members (Brower, Garvin, Hobson, Reed, & Reed, 1987), and the subjective experience of balanced-group composition differs substantially between African American and Euro-American members (Davis, 1980). We need to explore the implications of these findings for group work theory and practice.

FEMINIST CRITIQUE OF CURRENT GROUP WORK MODELS

This section presents a feminist model of group work and discusses current models of group work practice in the light of this model. Because of the complexity of this discussion, we use Table 3-1 to list and condense these comparisons. One problem we face in this critique is that there is no clear consensus regarding a typology of models of group work. An often-cited early attempt to categorize models is the work of Papell and Rothman (1966). These writers identified three models that they termed (1) "social goals," (2) "remedial," and (3) "reciprocal." In a summary of Papell and Rothman's categories, Middleman and Goldberg (1987) wrote

> *The social goals model, which they elaborated, draws on the work of several early theorists including Coyle (1948), Wilson and Ryland (1949), Phillips (1957), and Kaiser (1958). This model aimed to influence groups toward democratic values, social conscience, and social action for the "common good"; to encourage socialization; and to enhance individual growth, development, and learning. The remedial model, formulated by Vinter (1959), was grounded in psychoanalytic concepts, ego psychology, and social role theory and used the group to alter and reinforce individual behavior change. The reciprocal model, conceptualized by Schwartz (1961), was based on social systems theory and field theory. It directed the worker to mediate the engagement of individual and society as each reached toward the other for mutual self-fulfillment. This model introduced the terms "contract" and "mutual aid" into the vocabulary of social group workers.* (p. 715)

Despite these differences, the 18th edition of the *Encyclopedia of Social Work* contained a single article on social group work practice (Middleman & Goldberg, 1987) that notes the overlaps and convergences occurring. The authors referred to a "mainstream" model combining elements from a variety of writers and defined approaches as mainstream if they incorporated the following ideas:

> 1. *The work of the practitioner must include attention to helping the group members gain a sense of each other and their groupness.*
>
> 2. *The work of the practitioner must focus on helping members develop a system of mutual aid.*

Table 3-1

Feminist critique of group work models: Implications for a feminist model

ASPECT OF GROUP WORK	SOCIAL GOALS MODEL	REMEDIAL MODEL	RECIPROCAL MODEL	TASK-GROUP MODEL	FEMINIST MODEL
Purpose	To help individual fulfill social change roles CONTRIBUTES TO FEMINIST IDEAS ON THE "POLITICAL" *Lack of explicit attention to gender issues*	To help individual improve in social functioning CONTRIBUTES TO WAYS IN WHICH SELF-EFFICACY AND, THEREFORE, EMPOWERMENT CAN BE ENHANCED *Lack of explicit attention to gender issues as well as power transactions between individual and environment: "the personal is political"*	To help individual and social system to negotiate in such ways as to meet each other's needs RELATES TO THE CONCEPT THAT THE PERSONAL AND THE POLITICAL ARE NOT SEPARABLE *Lack of explicit attention to gender issues*	To help groups to accomplish a task, produce a product, or carry out a mandate. CAN HELP GROUPS TO CARRY OUT POLITICAL OBJECTIVES *Lack of gender analysis; lack of attention to needs of individual members and to relationships among members*	All of the preceding but with an emphasis on identifying gender issues and rectifying power imbalance between men and women so that men and women interact without constraints imposed by sexist values; relationship between individual and social not seen as a dichotomy; empowerment.
Change target	Individual social action skills; change in social situation CONTRIBUTES TO FEMINIST FOCUS ON OPPRESSIVE	Individual social functioning; aspect of group related to members' social functioning	More authentic interaction between and among individuals and systems CONTRIBUTES THE IDEA	Often aspects of systems outside the group; may be a product of benefit to whole group. TARGET IS CONSISTENT	Individual, group, agency, environment-focus on those aspects that promote oppression related to gender; enhance

	FORCES IN THE ENVIRONMENT *Lack of explicit attention to gender issues, especially those related to power*	DOES CONTRIBUTE THE BASIC IDEA THAT CHANGES IN BOTH THE INDIVIDUAL AND THE ENVIRONMENT CAN BE SOUGHT *Lack of focus on power issues related to gender as well as to the concerns brought by the individual to the group. Also, cognitive aspects of functioning given greater emphasis than in many behavioral approaches*	OF THE RECIPROCITY BETWEEN INDIVIDUAL AND ENVIRONMENTAL CHANGE *Lack of focus on how these interactions reflect gender and gender-related power dynamics*	WITH POLITICAL OBJECTIVES OF FEMINISM. *Target does not reflect relationships among members or increased gender consciousness of members*	members' consciousness of oppression and options for resisting this. Strong emphasis placed on the social change target; less distinction between therapeutic and social action groups.
Theory of change	Small group theory, social action theories CONTRIBUTES THE IDEA THAT BOTH GROUP AND SOCIAL ACTION THEORIES SHOULD BE USED	Psychoanalytic and behavioral theories, small group theories, organizational theories CONTRIBUTES A BROAD SENSE OF THE	Social systems theories, small group theories, negotiation and conflict theories CONTRIBUTES THE IDEA THAT THEORIES SHOULD BE CHOSEN THAT FIT	Small group theories, especially those dealing with problem solving, decision making, task accomplishment, and leadership. USEFUL FOR ACCOM-	All of the preceding theories as reconstructed in the light of contemporary feminist theory; the relationship between the individual and the social not viewed

continued

Table 3-1 continued

		RELEVANT THEORIES	WITH SYSTEMIC CONCEPTS	PLISHING POLITICAL PURPOSES	
	These theories are not examined and critiqued in the light of sexist and other gender-related dynamics	*These theories are not examined and critiqued in the light of sexist and other gender-related dynamics*	*These theories are not examined and critiqued in the light of sexist and other gender-related dynamics*	*Not examined and critiqued in the light of sexist and other gender-related dynamics*	as a dichotomy but stages in a process. Role theory is helpful in understanding many gender-related issues.
Role of practitioner	Facilitate the ways members develop a mutual aid system THE EMPHASIS ON HOW THE PRACTITIONER HELPS BUILD A MUTUAL AID SYSTEM IMPORTANT FOR FEMINIST PRACTICE *Does not emphasize helping members engage in gender role analysis*	Utilize means of influence to modify individual, group, and environmental conditions TECHNOLOGIES FOR BOTH INDIVIDUAL AND SYSTEM CHANGES USEFUL IN FEMINIST PRACTICE *Although values are considered targets, there is no emphasis on the worker's feminist values or worker's own change-oriented activities; approach may be interpreted in a way*	Tune in to feelings and needs of members; develop mutual aid system; challenge forces that block change; mediate between system levels; lend a "vision" of what life can be. THE IDEAS AS TO HOW PRACTITIONER RELATES TO BOTH INDIVIDUAL AND SYSTEM IMPORTANT FOR FEMINIST PRACTICE *Major component missing is the worker's emphasis on gender role analysis and the worker's own*	Often the "staffer" for the group; works with indigenous leadership; secures resources for group; responsible for agenda and record keeping. THE FACULTATIVE ROLE OF THE STAFF PERSON MIGHT BE USEFUL IN SOME FEMINIST TASK GROUPS. *Major component missing is the worker's emphasis on gender role analysis and the worker's own investment in working against oppression.*	Compatible with many reciprocal ideas such as tuning in, expressing one's own values (especially gender-related ones) but supportive of member's values; working to eliminate hierarchy between worker and members; worker also striving for a nonoppressive society; help members engage in sex role analysis; demystifies all approaches taken.

continued

		that emphasizes hierarchy between worker and members	*investment in working against oppression*		
Role of member	Expected to work with other group members to create social change SOCIAL CHANGE ROLES OF MEMBERS IMPORTANT FOR FEMINIST PRACTICE Expectation that changes related to oppression will be emphasized is lacking	Expected to develop individual goals and work to attain goals as well as help other members to attain theirs. EXPECTATION THAT MEMBERS WILL FORM INDIVIDUAL GOALS IS APPROPRIATE FOR FEMINIST PRACTICE *Members are not asked to work toward goals in ways that recognize their relationships to issues of gender oppression; they are not asked to work to eliminate hierarchical relationships within and outside of the group*	Expected to focus on work, to help to create a mutual aid system, and to develop authentic relationships with other members; also expected to interact with other members as well as other systems outside the group to discover a common ground and work to maintain it. EXPECTATION THAT MEMBER'S ROLE EXTENDS TO BOTH SELF AND SYSTEM IS IMPORTANT IN FEMINIST PRACTICE *Does not emphasize members' responsibility to understand and work to modify oppressive circumstances, especially those related to gender*	Expected to focus on accomplishing the group's task and to contribute one's skills to this end; may require filling leadership roles. IN FEMINIST GROUPS MEMBERS ALSO EXPECTED TO WORK TO ACCOMPLISH TASKS CHOSEN BY GROUP *Does not emphasize member's responsibility to modify oppressive circumstances especially those related to gender and to be supportive to other members*	Expected to deal with issues related to oppression and sexism and to develop an understanding of how one's own issues relate to these. Expected to support other members during as well as outside of meetings. Explore how the personal and the political interact; focus on changing both personal and environmental barriers to overcoming oppression

Table 3-1 continued

Kind of group process				
Problem solving and decision making; program processes; social action processes ALL OF THESE PROCESSES RELEVANT FOR FEMINIST PRACTICE *Many aspects of mutual aid to overcome oppression not emphasized*	Problem solving and decision making; program processes; other group processes so as to modify task and social-emotional conditions so as to be conducive to individual goal attainment. ALL OF THESE PROCESSES RELEVANT TO FEMINIST PRACTICE *Mutual processes to identify and overcome gender oppression not emphasized*	Sharing data, dialectical process; entering taboo areas; all in the same boat; mutual support; individual problem solving; rehearsal; strength in numbers; mutual demand ALL OF THESE PROCESSES RELEVANT TO FEMINIST PRACTICE *The relationship of these processes to gender oppression not emphasized; otherwise compatible with feminist principles*	Problem solving and decision making, negotiation, determining division of labor THESE ARE USEFUL PROCESSES IN ACCOMPLISHING THE POLITICAL ROLE OF THE FEMINIST GROUP *The relationship of these processes to gender oppression not emphasized; processes for establishing mutual aid and individual consciousness not included*	Share data especially as related to gender experience, dialectical processes as these help members appreciate and use "difference" in order to arrive at creative solutions; remove taboos related to discussing gender and power issues; recognize how all in same boat refers to gender; mutual support to confront sexism; mutual demand to accept responsibility for one's actions; decision making around issues of how one wishes to lead one's life; strength in numbers especially important for oppressed people

Note: Ways in which the model is consistent with a feminist model are presented in small capital letters and ways in which it is inconsistent with a feminist model are presented in italics.

3. *The practitioner should enable the group to increase its autonomy so that it can continue as a self-help and mutual support group after the worker either withdraws completely or changes to the role of consultant or sponsor.*

4. *The practitioner helps the members reexperience their groupness at the point of termination.* (pp. 721–722)

Our feminist approach to social work with groups does not reject any of the ideas posed by Middleman and Goldberg but adds elements that are not simply derivative of the ideas noted above. In this chapter, we use the Papell and Rothman typology as the most parsimonious one as well as one that we believe represents differing approaches to group work practice that still exist in social work, typically in groups created for individual member enhancement. We have found it necessary, however, to add a fourth approach, which we call a "task group." Task groups are formed to accomplish some task that is external to the group such as creating a set of recommendations for an organization or working toward social change in a community. Such groups include boards and committees of agencies, community organizations, and legislative bodies.

We decided to add the task group category for two reasons: (1) A feminist approach to group work should be one that can be used with any type of group, not only one formed for individual enhancement. (2) Feminist principles do not support a dichotomy between groups formed for individual enhancement and social change; all groups are seen as having both of these purposes that are inseparable in feminist thinking, although some groups may emphasize one set of purposes more than the other. The literature on task groups also can contribute a great deal to the accomplishment of the political purposes of feminist-oriented groups.

Dimensions of Feminist Model

We identified six possible dimensions to frame our feminist model of group work and compare it with other models. We describe these dimensions below and apply the principles of our feminist model with each. Examine Table 3-1 to see how we contrast this feminist model with the other four.

1. *Purpose.* For what kinds of issues or problems is group work used? The feminist model supports the premise present in several of the other models that the purpose of group work is to help individuals and social systems (including the group and the systems outside the group) negotiate to meet each other's needs. The feminist model has the additional purpose of helping members identify

gender issues and rectifying power imbalances between men and women so that both men and women act without constraints imposed by sexist values. This requires that a major purpose be the empowerment of members and attention to gendering processes.

2. *Change target.* What will change with respect to group members and their environments if members participate in group work? In a feminist model, the targets, depending on the situation, can be the individual, group, agency, or larger environment. The focus is on those aspects of all these entities that promote or allow oppression related to gender. A target within the belief system of individuals as well as within the norms of multiperson systems is consciousness of oppression and options for resisting or eliminating oppressive forces and those that facilitate privilege.

3. *Theory of change.* Why are the methods of group work expected to work the way they do? A feminist model will draw on many contemporary theories such as social system theories, role theories (especially as these deal with gender roles), small-group theories, and oppression and conflict theories. All theories, however, must be critiqued and reconstructed in light of contemporary feminist theories.

4. *Role of practitioner.* What are practitioners expected to do? How are they expected to do it? A feminist model will be drawn heavily from the reciprocal model, especially as that model uses such processes as tuning in, expressing one's own values (especially gender-related ones) while being supportive of members' values, and working to eliminate hierarchy between worker and members. The worker must also strive for a nonoppressive society in ways that are visible to members, help members engage in gender role analysis, and help make usually unrecognized processes more visible so they are subject to change. The worker should seek to demystify any approaches taken.

5. *Role of member.* What is the member of a social work group expected to do? A feminist model indicates that members are expected to deal with issues related to oppression and sexism and to seek an understanding of how personal, interpersonal, group, organizational, and societal issues relate to these. Members are expected to provide support to one another during as well as outside meetings, although because many women have been socialized to be caretakers, women also may need to work on recognizing and addressing or asking for attention to their own needs—without guilt. Members also should explore how the personal

and the political interact and as a result of this, focus on ways to change both personal and environmental barriers to overcoming oppression.

6. *What kinds of group processes (relationship development, problem solving, activities) are expected to occur in a social work group?* A feminist model emphasizes processes in which group participants share data related to gender experiences. Another process concept has been referred to as "dialectical," which means that members are helped to appreciate and use "difference" to arrive at creative solutions and remove taboos related to discussing gender and power.

Table 3-1 compares each of the four approaches with a feminist approach on each dimension. This format cannot do justice to the full range of material written about each approach. Instead, we intend to illustrate how some of the main features of each approach relate to a feminist model and how a feminist model draws from, yet goes beyond, these approaches. We depicted this graphically. Ways in which each approach is consistent with a feminist one appear in small capitals, while those in which it is inconsistent appear in italics.

Feminist Critique of Practice

A common denominator within our discussion of these models is the absence of a consistent and recurring critique or deconstruction of the ways that various systems of thought, action, and society advantage some people and disadvantage others and create systems of language and meaning that support and obscure these inequalities. A feminist practitioner also works to critique his or her practice and practice models—the theories, meanings of language used, individual behavior, processes and practices within the group, group and member goals, and relations with the environment. This critique must attend to the ways that (1) the need for basic social and conceptual changes are obscured and reframed into individual problems and approaches or simple problems to be solved; (2) the behaviors and mechanisms within the group perpetuate inequities unless continuously monitored and challenged; and (3) other aspects of individual and group cultures and elements associated with discrimination other than gender (for example, race, ethnicity, sexual orientation, age, or class) interact with gender and affect the meaning and impact of gender.

The worker also will use, in relation to all these ideas, the concept of *praxis,* which means that all theories will be seen as evolving based on one's experience (or actions) and such actions will be guided by this evolving theory, with each used to critique and enhance the other. Even when individual change is the primary target, social injustice is considered to be a major target of as well as barrier to change; the practitioner works to recognize how other societal dimensions that construct inequities intersect with gender, and work in the group seeks to illuminate ways in which these are internalized within individuals and in group processes.

Feminist Group Example

We present an example of a feminist group that has the purpose of improving the parenting skills of members to illustrate how these abstractions might be used in a particular type of group. Such a group considers the gender and gender-related power issues that intersect with parenting and the ways that oppression can interfere with parenting and influence the need for and impact of parenting. A feminist group, whatever its other purposes, seeks to attend to the power imbalance between men and women that is manifested in the other issues on which the group focuses and the ways in which these imbalances have been internalized by individuals, shape and become re-created in their interactions, and have been incorporated into many theoretical and practice models. Thus, in our parenting group, the members examine the inequalities that might exist between parents and children who differ by gender and the gendered (and cultural) assumptions embedded in advice about parenting. With regard to other dimensions of social justice, the group members might discover that people of color in the group have children who are denied access to school opportunities because of their ethnicity. A feminist group is likely to seek some means of joining the struggle against such discrimination and, thus, the targets for change enlarge to include a particular school, a school system, or broader school system policies.

In conjunction with other goals, a feminist group also attends to creating processes to empower its members. This involves the power of members both to determine the fate of the group and to be more effective outside the group with a sense that their efforts can and will effect change. In the example of the parenting group, empowerment could include involving the members in determining what approach the group will use to help members enhance their parenting skills and who the group members will be. Through the group, members can acquire a sense that they can seek changes in other institutions in the community, such as the school, if these institutions limit their opportunity to carry out their parenting functions. They also can learn and practice skills for such change through discussions and role playing in the group; remove taboos about discussing and challenging dynamics related to gender, race, and power; and develop ways to approach concerns with each other, children, and school system officials constructively.

Note that it may be necessary that group foci and processes differ for women and for men and in different group compositions. In this parenting group, it is likely to be productive to subdivide the group by gender for all or part of some sessions (Bernardez & Stein, 1979) to bring to the surface those parenting issues that may be common for men and different for women or that vary across different couple dynamics. If groups are all of one gender, special attention may be necessary to address elements that are heightened or suppressed by the group composition. In all-women groups, for instance, one is likely to need to stress ways to bring to the surface and negotiate conflict and differences and challenge pressures for uniformity that can suppress differences (Hagen, 1983; Miner & Longino, 1987). In all-men groups, norms for cooperation and strategies for challenging hierarchies and competition are likely to be important (Stein, 1983).

FEMINIST PRINCIPLES AND CONTEXT FOR GROUP WORK IN THE 21ST CENTURY

Thus far, we have presented several different approaches to illuminate feminist issues within the practice of group work and to create a framework to support the further evolution of feminist group work models and practices. Principles for feminist group work also can help us address the critical issues likely to confront us in the 21st century and, most important, can allow us to see and address the ways in which our theories and practices can be mobilized to work toward social justice and empowerment in all types of practice.

We noted earlier the importance of working in groups in social work practice. Much policy development work requires meetings of different kinds—at a minimum to collect information, identify priorities, and gather support for the policy. Agencies have staff meetings, team meetings, case conferences, and seminars. Agency directors must attend various kinds of interagency and community meetings and meet with boards of directors. Those workers with a community focus often form and work with task forces, neighborhood organizations, coalitions, and organizing committees of different kinds. Community mobilization strategies require multiple kinds of group work. Total quality management (TQM) uses teams, group problem-solving strategies, and meetings for more-effective organizational functioning and change. All of these efforts are likely to continue into the next century, probably greatly aided by new computer and communications technologies.

Within practice directly involved with individuals and families, those concerned about empowerment, especially for women of color, believe that particular kinds of work in groups are a major staple of empowering practice (Gutierrez, 1990). Approaches derived from self-help groups are being incorporated into practitioner-facilitated groups, and self-help groups are increasingly important in many fields of practice—to provide support, education, models for change, skill-building opportunities, new ways of thinking, constructive ways to spend time, and social networks. Many elements of consciousness raising are integrated within these groups. Multiple family groups, groups for children in many types of settings, groups to facilitate surviving trauma, groups that help catalyze new learning, and groups that help people face and change compulsive behaviors are increasingly important components of practice. They are likely to continue to be important in the future, partly because they are less expensive than more worker-intensive models but mostly because behavior is strongly shaped and influenced by group life—people's connections with others—despite the strong belief in individualism in the United States. This need for connections with others and skills in developing and sustaining these connections are likely to be more important in the future.

We next describe some of the challenges that social work and the world are likely to face in the future and some of the ways in which the application of feminist principles within groups can strengthen and inform social work practice. Each challenge requires skills, perspectives, and knowledge best acquired through group interactions of various kinds; each will need to be addressed by people working together in various group contexts; and each will be responsive to the use of groups for social support, support for change, or as alternatives to traditional family forms and structures.

Ethnic and Cultural Diversity

Ethnic and cultural diversity within the United States will continue to increase; consequently, everyone will be required to develop more skills to negotiate and to empower. At the same time, ethnic identification and the potential for intergroup conflicts are likely to increase. In a world with more global connections, more ways to address ethnic and intergroup conflicts around the globe will be necessary. Gender issues and dynamics within these cultural contexts are often obscured and allow various forms of exclusion and violence against women to continue.

We are seeing destructive examples of this throughout the world today, in the former republics of the Soviet Union, in the Middle East, in Ireland, and in the inner cities and universities of the United States. Groups are trying to dominate and "cleanse" each other and blame others for their economic and social circumstances. We must find ways for disempowered groups to live and work together constructively and to recognize that privileged statuses create additional privileges and inequities.

These developments require the use of both small-group and intergroup theories and practice models within workplaces, in our neighborhoods and our families, within government, and in international relations. For instance, as diversity increases, corporations and other groups are beginning to create models and processes for multicultural organizations, although attention to oppressive power dynamics within these organizations often lags behind the development of knowledge and skills in cross-cultural communication.

Acknowledging and addressing the oppression and conflict that arise from racism and ethnic conflict while also addressing the violence perpetuated against women and those with alternative sexual orientations and other differences requires multiple areas of knowledge and many skills. Individuals and groups will need to develop stronger skills in cultural competence and communication (Green, 1982) and knowledge about gendered and ethnically shaped dynamics within and across groups. Workers need to develop and apply a high degree of ethnic and gender consciousness within their work— a continuing understanding of one's background and the effects of culture, areas of oppression, and privilege within one's life, worldview, and interactions. Skills that will be particularly important will be those that surface and address the positive and negative aspects of privilege (McIntosh, 1992).

Also required will be new ways to negotiate intergroup tensions, conflict alternatives, and creative use of conflict. Knowledge and skills that allow us to recognize, change, and transform the group and intergroup dynamics that inhibit empowerment and collaboration can best be developed and practiced within small groups of different kinds. Feminist principles particularly important for working with conflict include an emphasis on both process and product; examination of gendering, discriminatory dynamics, and processes; recognition and use of multiple ways of knowing; regular scrutiny of power dynamics; promotion of empowerment and use of alternative synergistic conceptualizations of power, rather than a win–lose, zero-sum understanding of power; and ways to integrate and balance attention to different forms of oppression and privilege.

Fighting Discrimination

As work to combat discrimination gradually removes more-blatant and obvious barriers to full participation and social justice within societies (for example, laws prohibiting participation or redlining), we are increasingly faced with more-subtle and difficult to recognize dynamics that create and re-create inequities. If we do not recognize and change these dynamics, social work practices and human services organizations will create and perpetuate discrimination and disempowering structures and practices. Addressing relationships among women, between women and men, among men, and in cultural and ethnic groups and examining the impact of micro and macro social structures and concepts will be important. Too often, social work practice has promoted social control rather than social justice; we must continue to uncover and change these conditions.

Specialization and Increases in Technology

The next century is likely to continue the rapid growth in information, knowledge, and new technology, with more pressure on people both to specialize in particular roles and in specific areas of knowledge and skills and to work closely with others with different specialties and roles. At least two aspects of these trends have implications for social group work. The first involves how to assist people in the quest to keep up with rapidly evolving bodies of knowledge and new skills and technologies. Support and learning groups of different kinds can provide opportunities both for reducing emotional stress through sharing and mutual commiseration and for exchanging tips, pooling knowledge, engaging in mutual problem solving, and providing opportunities for peer consultation and group learning.

The second aspect focuses on developing and sustaining the skills and mechanisms necessary to support effective work in teams, coalitions, and collaborations and other ways to work with others to combine skills and knowledge, coordinate activities, and acquire and process different types of information and knowledge. Interdisciplinary social work often requires collaboration to address situations that are beyond the skills and knowledge of any one discipline or profession. Individuals and families with multiple needs require that specialists from different service sectors negotiate ways to coordinate their work and create common approaches.

All of the feminist principles have some utility for these purposes but especially for those that focus on the processes of groups and the development of knowledge—praxis, interrogating language, a focus on empowering group process as a goal in addition to other group goals, and building on multiple ways of knowing and learning.

Changes in the Traditional Family

Multiple family forms are increasing, with more serial relationships and blended families, greater mobility, changing gender and work roles, multiple careers, and longer life expectancy. Families are small groups, and they perform many social and socialization functions. Complex blended families need members with skills in group facilitation, intergroup conflict, and new group formation. Shifts in gender roles through the life cycle mean that people must negotiate relationships rather than follow prescribed gender roles and learn to recognize and address how gendered role prescriptions and dynamics continue to affect families and other relationships. Some effects are useful, whereas others can be destructive, especially if their source is not recognized and individualized blame for behavior is assigned. Feminist principles applied in groups can help people develop skills for changing family forms and create alternative ways for social support in new locations or when the biological family of the individual is not a supportive environment.

Injustice and Social Problems

Many new and continuing social problems are caused or complicated by injustice. These include poverty, homelessness, acquired immune deficiency syndrome (AIDS), substance abuse, and violence. Confronting these problems will require a more sophisticated understanding of how oppression and inequities contribute to and sustain them. We also will need to create more-effective ways of building public support for interventions that address these underlying factors and stronger skills and models for intervention. Feminist principles applied within group work contexts can catalyze much of this work, because they provide many ways to recognize oppressive dynamics and processes and powerful methods to develop and transform new knowledge and practices. Recognizing bias and omissions, creating alternative language, and doing and then reflecting on that doing are ways to continue to develop empowering methods of practice and social change for social justice.

Violence

Given the levels of societal violence and some of the factors described earlier, we need more ways to incorporate attention to the effects of victimization and perpetration into practice and theory. Feminist approaches to practice in groups, including transforming language—from victim to survivor, for instance—and now to even more empowering language that focuses less on the violence and more on growth beyond the violence, have been major staples in the work against violence thus far. Feminist analyses that illuminate the processes underlying more-subtle forms of violence and intimidation, examine the climate of fear and its effects, and then help name and change these dynamics will be essential ingredients within group work practice. Groups with perpetrators can help establish and enforce expectations and behaviors that oppose violence, challenge the assumptions that justify violence, provide an arena for practice, and reinforce alternatives.

Increase in Chronic Health and Physical Conditions

Advocacy and support for those living with chronic health conditions will be necessary as new technologies allow people to live longer because a longer life increases the prevalence of chronic physical problems and major physical challenges. More and stronger support groups are one way to respond to and anticipate these needs, as is a greater array of effective self-help advocacy groups. For these, we need workers with the skills and perspectives not only to help develop and provide assistance to these groups when needed but also to enable members to develop the skills and mechanisms to create and manage these groups. Many of the feminist principles will be important in these groups for both group workers and other group members.

Environment

Deterioration of the environment and confrontations that require the world to recognize the interdependence of nations, the environment, and people will increase. Goals here include developing and maintaining peace, strengthening ecological movements, and promoting justice and human rights. Feminists have developed knowledge and approaches in each of these areas that involve deconstructing human efforts to dominate others and the environment and proposing alternative approaches that involve interdependence, cooperation, mutual respect, and concern. Planning and advocacy processes related to these issues almost always occur in small groups, and the relevant theories of peace and ecology will need to continue to evolve to anticipate and respond to changing world conditions, opportunities, and crises.

SUMMARY AND NEXT STEPS

In general, the application of feminisms to social group work has not evolved as much as some other forms of feminist practice within social work, despite the (at least partially) feminist origins of social group work. To some degree this reflects the relative lack of attention to small-group theory by feminist scholars, the relative decline of social group work as a valued method within schools of social work, and a reluctance to examine the fabric of our lives as social work practitioners. Examining our group work practice requires us to examine our assumptions not only about the frameworks of practice but also how we interact with each other and how we run our social agencies and classrooms—not just what we do behind closed doors with our clients or in grant applications or budget development. To a large degree, we agree with Lewis's (1992) assertion that too often the practice of social group work "has succumbed to the pressures of containment and management of symptoms and to the definition of participants (clients) not as equal partners and members in a common endeavor but as somehow damaged and defective beings" (p. 273). She urges that social group work reclaim its roots through the application of feminist perspectives.

Like Lewis, we believe that the application and "doing" of feminism in its various forms can provide enormous opportunities for transforming our theories, practice models, and practices in ways that can reclaim the social movement aspects of early group work practice. We have made progress in changing some of the major structural and personal barriers to empowerment and change. However, inequities persist, and gendered processes that block empowerment continue. Many of these inequities persist in forms that are subtle and therefore difficult to recognize and thus to challenge and change.

Internalized oppression and macro patterns of inequity are all mediated through interactional and group processes. Thus, strengthening our understanding of and skills in feminist group work should present us with great opportunities to study and learn how micro and macro inequalities are created and re-created and provide opportunities to develop effective ways to change them. We hope that the questions and issues generated from the intersections we have presented can stimulate and help shape explicitly feminist and multicultural approaches within social group work.

REFERENCES

Aries, E. (1977). Male-female interpersonal styles in all male, all female and mixed groups. In A. Sargent (Ed.), *Beyond sex roles* (pp. 272–299). St. Paul, MN: West Publishing.

Belenky, M. F., Clinchy, B. McV., Goldberger, N. R., & Taruli, J. M. (1986). *Women's ways of knowing: The development of self, voice, & mind.* New York: Basic Books.

Berman-Rossi, T., & Miller I. (1994). African-Americans and the Settlements during the Late Nineteenth and Early Twentieth Centuries. *Social Work with Groups, 17*(3), 77–96.

Bernardez, T., & Stein, T. S. (1979). Separating the sexes in group psychotherapy: An experiment with men's and women's groups. *International Journal of Group Psychotherapy, 29*, 493–502.

Boston Lesbian Psychologies Collective (Eds.). (1987). *Lesbian psychologies.* Urbana: University of Illinois Press.

Boyd, N. (1935). *Group work experiments in state institutions in Illinois: Proceedings, National Conference of Social Work.* New York: Columbia University Press.

Bricker-Jenkins, M., & Hooyman, N. R. (1986). *Not for women only: Social work practice for a feminist future.* Silver Spring, MD: National Association of Social Workers.

Brodsky, A. (1973). The consciousness-raising group as a model for therapy with women. *Psychotherapy: Theory, Research, and Practice, 10*, 24–29.

Brody, C. M. (Ed.). (1987). *Women's therapy groups: Paradigms of feminist treatment.* New York: Springer.

Brower, A., Garvin, C. D., Hobson, J., Reed, B. G., & Reed, H. (1987). Exploring the effects of gender and race on group behavior. In J. Lassner, K. Powell, & E. Finnegan (Eds.), *Social group work: Competence and values in practice* (pp. 129–148). New York: Haworth Press.

Brown, L. S., & Root, M.P.P. (Eds.). (1990). *Diversity and complexity in feminist therapy.* New York: Harrington Park Press.

Burden, D. S., & Gottlieb, N. (Eds.). (1987). *The woman client.* New York: Tavistock.

Butler, S., & Wintram, C. (1991). *Feminist groupwork.* Newbury Park, CA: Sage Publications.

Carlock, C. J., & Martin, P. Y. (1977). Sex composition and the intensive group experience. *Social Work, 22*, 27–32.

Collins, P. H. (1990). *Black feminist thought: Knowledge, consciousness and the politics of empowerment.* London: HarperCollins Academic.

Coyle, G. (1948). *Group work with American youth.* New York: Harper & Row.

Davis, L. E. (1980). Race and group proportions: When the majority is the psychological minority. *Group Psychotherapy, Psychodrama, and Sociometry, 33,* 179–184.

Davis, L. E. (1981). Racial issues in the training of group workers. *Journal for Specialists in Group Work, 6,* 155–160.

de Chant, B. (1993). *Women and group psychotherapy: Gender, theory and practice.* New York: Guilford Press.

Donovan, J. (1985). *Feminist theory: The intellectual traditions of American feminism.* New York: Frederick Ungar Publishing.

Ferguson, K. E. (1984). *The feminist case against bureaucracy.* Philadelphia: Temple University Press.

Ferguson, K. E. (1993). *The man question: Visions of subjectivity in feminist theory.* Berkeley: University of California Press.

Green, J. W. (1982). *Cultural awareness in the human services.* Englewood Cliffs, NJ: Prentice Hall.

Gutierrez, L. (1990). Working with women of color: An empowerment perspective. *Social Work, 35,* 149–154.

Hagen, B. H. (1983). Managing conflict in all-women groups. In B. G. Reed & C. Garvin (Eds.), *Groupwork with women/groupwork with men* (pp. 95–104). New York: Haworth Press.

Kaiser, C. (1930). *The group records of four clubs.* Cleveland: Western Reserve.

Kanter, R. M. (1977). Women in organizations: Sex roles, group dynamics, and change strategies. In A. Sargent (Ed.), *Beyond sex roles* (pp. 371–386). St. Paul, MN: West Publishing.

Lerman, H. (1974, September). *What happens in feminist therapy?* Paper presented at the meeting of the American Psychological Association, New Orleans.

Lewis, E. (1992). Regaining promise: Feminist perspectives for social group work practice. *Social Work with Groups, 15*(2/3), 271–284.

Lockheed, M. E. (1985). Sex and social influence: A meta-analysis guided by theory. In J. Berger & M. Zelditch (Eds.), *Status, rewards, and influence* (pp. 406–429). San Francisco: Jossey-Bass.

Lockheed, M. E., & Hall, K. P. (1976). Conceptualizing sex as a status characteristic: Applications toleadership training strategies. *Journal of Social Issues, 32*(3), 111–124.

Mander, A. V., & Rush, A. K. (1974). *Feminism as therapy.* New York: Random House.

McIntosh, P. (1992). White privilege and male privilege: A personal account of coming to see correspondences through work in women's studies. In M. L. Anderson & P. H. Collins (Eds.), *Race, class, and gender: An anthology* (pp. 70–81). Belmont, CA: Wadsworth Publishing.

Meeker, B. F., & Weitzel-O'Neill, P. A. (1985). Sex roles and interpersonal behavior in task-oriented groups. In J. Berger & M. Zelditch (Eds.), *Status, rewards, and influence* (pp. 379–405). San Francisco: Jossey-Bass.

Middleman, R. R., & Goldberg, G. (1987). Social work practice with groups. In A. Minahan (Ed.-in-Chief), *Encyclopedia of social work* (18th ed., Vol. 2, pp. 714–729). Silver Spring, MD: National Association of Social Workers.

Miner, V., & Longino, H. E. (1987). *Competition: A feminist taboo?* New York: Feminist Press.

Papell, C. P., & Rothman, B. (1966). Social group work models: Possession and heritage. *Journal of Education for Social Work, 2*(2), 55–77.

Reed, B. G. (1981). Gender issues in training group leaders. *Journal of Specialists in Group Work, 6*(3), 161–170.

Reed, B. G., & Garvin, C. D. (Eds.). (1983). *Groupwork with women/groupwork with men.* New York: Haworth Press.

Reed, B. G., & Garvin, C. D. (1993). Feminist thought and group psychotherapy: Feminist principles as praxis. In B. de Chant (Ed.), *Women and group psychotherapy: Gender, theory and practice.* New York: Guilford Press.

Reid, K. (1981). *From character building to social treatment: The history of the use of groups in social work.* Westport, CT: Greenwood Press.

Ridgeway, C. L. (Ed.). (1992). *Gender, interaction, and inequality.* New York: Springer-Verlag.

Stein, T. S. (1983). An overview of men's groups. In B. G. Reed & C. D. Garvin (Eds.), *Groupwork with women/groupwork with men* (pp. 149–162). New York: Haworth Press.

Tannen, D. (1990). *You just don't understand: Women and men in conversation.* New York: Ballantine Books.

Tong, R. (1989). *Feminist thought: A comprehensive introduction.* Boulder, CO: Westview Press.

Tower, B. (1979). *Communication patterns of women and men in same-sex and mixed-sex groups.* Unpublished manuscript.

Trimble, D. (1986). Confronting responsibilities: Men who batter their wives. In A. Gitterman & L. Schulman (Eds.), *Mutual aid groups and the life cycle* (pp. 229–244). Itasca, IL: F. E. Peacock.

Van Den Bergh, N., & Cooper, L. B. (Eds.). (1986) *Feminist visions for social work.* Silver Spring, MD: National Association of Social Workers.

Wilson, G. (1976). From practice to theory: A personalized history (pp. 1–44). In R. W. Roberts and H. Northen (Eds.), *Theories of social work with groups.* New York: Columbia University Press.

Wilson, G., & Ryland, G. (1949). *Social group work practice.* Boston: Houghton Mifflin.

Wyckoff, H. (1977). *Solving women's problems through awareness, action, and contact.* New York: Grove Press.

4

Feminist Administration
Style, Structure, Purpose

Roslyn H. Chernesky

Since the early 1990s there have been signs of unrest in the management field. Upset that American corporations are no longer competitive or productive and fearful that they will never regain prominence in the international market, critics are blaming both the leadership and the structure of today's organizations, claiming that neither is suitable for the times. Articles and books on the two themes advise business and industry of the kind of organizational leadership and the type of organizational structures that are needed both today and to prepare for the 21st century.

It may be only coincidental that the advice being given to American corporations has the same two fundamental characteristics of feminist administration: (1) a care-and-empower leadership style as opposed to a command-and-control approach and (2) participatory or self-managing structures such as teams, task forces, or matrices rather than rigid, hierarchical arrangements. Ironically, even though the values of corporate America and feminism are very different, they bring us to the same place today as we deliberate what effective management is.

This coming together of two different values, one feminist and the other traditionally patriarchal, is in contrast to the backlash focused on thwarting women's ideas and the progress of the past decade as described by Faludi (1991). Given that backlash, one might have expected heightened efforts to devalue women's management styles to prove that a caring approach and horizontal structures are ineffective.

Women's ways of managing are clearly at a different point today than in the past. When first addressed in the early 1970s, the issue was simply getting women into management, especially in proportion to their numbers in the social work profession. Efforts to explain why women were underrepresented in administration emphasized individual barriers and organizational obstacles to advancement. At the beginning of the 1980s, concern was centered on providing possible strategies for women to overcome the deterrents. In many instances women managers were encouraged to "pass" as male managers. Women were advised to dress like men and to refrain from acting in ways that were stereotypical of women: emotional, soft, and indecisive.

During the 1980s, focus was on demonstrating that female managers were really no different from male managers; women could perform just as well as men, and workers, even men, would accept female managers. At the close of the 1980s, the differences in administrative style between men and women that increasingly emerged, despite attempts to deny or prevent their appearance, raised questions as to whether it was necessary, or even desirable, for men and women to lead in the same way. These differences, as well as a better understanding of what the women's style had to offer, continued to attract considerable attention at the start of the 1990s. Today, although it is not universally accepted that men and women differ in their managerial styles, the idea is popular and the possibility that women may indeed be more effective managers is receiving support in wider circles.

This chapter examines what is meant by women's way of managing, or the feminist leadership style, in the context of broader management thinking. Feminist administration is defined and then today's preferred leadership style and organizational structure are evaluated, with emphasis on how they relate to the qualities women bring to administration. Examples of feminist administration in practice are offered, mindful that style and structure, albeit fundamental to feminist administration, are not sufficient. The use of a care-and-empower leadership style or a participatory management structure, even by women managers, is not necessarily a feminist approach.

WOMEN'S QUALITIES FOR MANAGEMENT

Whether women's unique qualities stem from sex-role socialization, derive from their actual life experiences, or are biologically determined, the idea that women are different and view the world differently from men is more readily accepted today (Gilligan, 1982). What are the qualities women bring to organizations that may influence their administrative approach? Only some of the thinking on this topic is summarized here.

Coining the term "the female advantage," Helgesen (1990) stressed that women bring special qualities and preparation to the workplace because of their experience in the domestic sphere. "Increasingly, motherhood is being recognized as an excellent school for managers, demanding many of the same skills: organization, pacing, the balancing of conflicting claims, teaching, guiding, leading, monitoring, handling disturbances, imparting information" (p. 31). As mothers, women are prepared to expect interruptions, to be flexible and ready to alter their schedules, to respond to the needs of others, and to change priorities constantly during the day.

Helgesen also pointed out how the nature of women's work always has been to sustain the family by doing those tasks that need to be done again and again. Satisfaction comes from the doing, from the process itself, rather than from an achievement or closure such as winning a game or a "big kill." In contrast to earlier thinking that women were at a disadvantage because girls' games did not teach them team play and the importance of winning, girls' play is now seen as providing women with the skills and attitudes useful for management. Girls' play, which emphasizes taking turns, improvising to include others, reformulating rules to fit situations, and cooperating so that everyone wins, helps women to value cooperation and relationships, to disdain complex rules and rigid structures, to reject abstract notions like winning at the expense of harmony among friends, and to be flexible and adaptable rather than relying on established rules that prescribe how to play the games.

Gilligan (1982) contrasted male and female voices and suggested that there are two ways of thinking and interpreting problems. Women are more likely to make moral choices within the context of particular situations and out of concern for specific individuals, whereas men are more likely to make moral choices on the basis of impersonal rules of fairness and rights. Women, therefore, value connectedness and relationships. Belenky, Clinchy, Goldberger, and Tarule (1989) stressed that women not only listen differently, more intensely, and more thoughtfully, but they value listening as a way of making others feel comfortable and important and of encouraging others to find their own voices and grow.

Rothschild (1987) suggested that women have been taught to listen, to be responsive to the concerns of others, to seek acceptable and equitable solutions, and to stabilize group life, especially when relevant to their role in the family. Consequently, women develop strong group skills that enable them to turn to group problem solving, consensus building, cooperative ventures, and democratic ways of operating organizations.

Grant (1988) elaborated on the qualities associated with women that can be valuable to organizations. She too believed that these qualities emanate from women's early experiences in family life as well as from their involvement in the reproductive process, the community, and economic and political structures. According to Grant, women's communication networks serve as the foundation for social interaction in most societies. Women find a means of conciliation with others instead of getting involved in confrontation. They engage in cooperative communication behavior, such as taking turns in group discussion, which deepens their attachment and connectedness. This communication style grows out of women's strong sense of concern for others and indicates the importance they afford to affiliation. Women experience, use, and view power differently from men. Power is a transforming force from within, equated with giving and caring or with nurturance and strength. Women's physicality, tied to images of birth, blood, pregnancy, lactation, and nurturance, grounds them in an earthiness and concreteness. Women's capacity for empathy and sense of connectedness to others lead them to value closeness, nurturance, and intimacy. Finally, women are able to express emotionality, vulnerability, and helplessness.

Having examined some of the qualities associated with the way women engage with others, we would expect feminist administration to reflect these qualities as well as women's experience of caring, cooperating, and being connected to others. To what extent does a feminist approach recognize, validate, and incorporate those attributes? It is now appropriate to consider how these qualities relate to characteristics attributed to feminist administration.

DEFINING FEMINIST ADMINISTRATION

There seems to be general agreement that feminist administration is based on such feminist principles as valuing women's perspectives and experiences, eliminating false dichotomies or artificial separations, empowering women, democratizing organizational structures, valuing process, and linking the personal and the political (Hooyman & Cunningham, 1986; Hyde, 1989; Kravetz & Jones, 1991; Schwartz, Gottesman, & Perlmutter, 1988; Weil, 1988).

Working Definition

Drawing on earlier formulations of feminist administration, we can identify three common elements:

1. exercise of a leadership style that is derived from women's unique qualities and that incorporates feminist principles

2. creation of nonhierarchical and collaborative organizational structures in which power is redefined and process is valued

3. commitment to improving women's lives through fundamental change and empowerment.

These three elements are useful in defining feminist administration. We can think of style, structure, and purpose as the three cornerstones of feminist administration. All three must exist to conclude that someone is a feminist administrator or that a feminist approach is being used in managing a program, a unit, or an agency. For this chapter, we define *feminist administration* as the exercise of a leadership style based on feminist values and principles that recognize, validate, and incorporate traditional feminine attributes and that use organizational structures that shift responsibility, authority, and control away from hierarchical arrangements and relationships to create workplace environments and service delivery systems that improve women's lives and empower individuals whether they are staff, volunteers, or clients.

In some ways this definition may best represent an ideal model: a goal we are working toward or a vision we are striving toward. It serves as a guiding principle, influencing decisions and actions. There are many obstacles to achieving these ends, yet each day women in all types of organizational settings are taking small steps in the right direction. It is not necessary to be in a feminist organization or to hold a management position to behave in ways consistent with this definition. Many women realize they have much further to go to meet this goal, but in trying they have successfully introduced a new way of thinking or a different approach to the way their organizations are managed—one that is based on feminist values and principles.

ELEMENTS OF FEMINIST ADMINISTRATION

Having defined feminist administration, we can compare the management style and structure that are preferred today with earlier and more traditional approaches to show how closely the essential elements of feminist administration parallel contemporary management thinking on how to manage workers and organizations. Leadership style and organizational structure are so closely related that the two are often used interchangeably. There is indeed a link between the two. A traditional leadership style, associated with men, relies on a hierarchical structure of organizations in which directives and communications flow only through formal channels and decision-making authority is concentrated at the top. As a result, workers are prevented from functioning autonomously or reaching decisions regarding their work. This style precludes fostering staff participation, empowering workers, encouraging planning from the bottom up, or using collaborative work structures.

Preferred Leadership Style

We begin with leadership style, clearly the most popular element in feminist administration and the subject given greatest attention by the management literature and by social workers concerned with women and management (Bombyk & Chernesky, 1985; Chernesky & Bombyk, 1988; Hooyman, 1991; Hooyman & Cunningham, 1986; Weil, 1986). There is a growing consensus today that the preferred leadership style is no longer the traditional autocratic or controlling approach but one that is supportive and relationship-oriented. The preferred style has actually been suggested for a number of years under different names: transforming (Burns, 1979), Beta (L. Rosener & Schwartz, 1980), change master (Kanter, 1983), high involvement (Lawler, 1986), total quality management (Deming, 1986), empowering (Block, 1987), coaching (Evered & Selman, 1989), and superleadership (Manz & Sims, 1991). All stress relationship behavior; managers maintain a personal relationship with workers by developing two-way channels of communication and providing socioemotional support. Relationship-oriented leaders "unleash the abilities" of their workers (Manz & Sims, 1991) and "focus on discovering actions that enable and empower people to contribute more fully, productively, and with less alienation" (Evered & Selman, 1989, p. 16).

A relationship-oriented style is considered more appropriate for today's organizations because they are in the midst of rapid changes and must fully use their human resources. An infusion of relationship behavior into organizations is seen as a way of making the workplace more humane. It is viewed as more organizationally beneficial, resulting in "increased employee performance and innovation flowing from enhanced commitment, motivation, and employee capability" (Manz & Sims, 1991, p. 33). A recent study (Hornstein, Heilman, Mone, & Tartell, 1987) confirmed that supportive managers were seen as more likable and more competent than directive managers. They also were thought to produce more satisfaction and better performance. Some go so far as to believe that this style holds promise as a way of overcoming the inefficiency, lack of productivity, and low worker morale that have been attributed to the traditional, overly rigid leadership style.

Gender and the Preferred Leadership Style

The traditional command-and-control leadership style that is now out of favor has long been associated with men and the masculine sex-role stereotype. It conjures up images of the cowboy, the fighting commander, the tough "leader as a striking figure on a rearing white horse, crying 'Follow me!'" (Manz & Sims, 1991, p. 18). This style reflects faith in a rational, orderly, and scientific approach to solving problems and handling situations. It also reflects a belief in a "best way" to achieve results and in "winning" as what really matters. However, it also is a way of responding to uncertainty and ambiguity by exerting control.

The preferred leadership style is associated with feminine sex-role attributes and is now generally recognized as the way women lead (Chernesky & Bombyk, 1988; Helgesen, 1990; Loden, 1985; J. B. Rosener, 1990). Paradoxically, the qualities traditionally associated with women and therefore devalued have now been elevated to assets. These qualities are being recognized as critical to the health and survival of organizations. Women managers are now being told that they no longer need to deny or suppress their caring qualities for fear they might demonstrate weakness or incompetence.

Women have been credited with having a greater capacity for being sensitive and caring with workers, exercising interpersonal skills, and making people feel a part of and involved with organizations (Helgesen, 1990; Sargent, 1981). Because women bring to their positions sensitivity and empathy toward others, they can foster a sense of belonging and inspire workers, which in turn creates an atmosphere in which people feel good about their jobs and what they do (Cohen, 1989; Hughey & Gelman, 1986). Women encourage participation, share power and information, and enhance the self-worth of others by energizing them (J. B. Rosener, 1990).

Organizations are being advised to take advantage of women and the qualities they bring. In *Newsweek* Hughey and Gelman (1986) reported that

> *considering the important contributions women managers have to offer, corporations that don't make room for the feminine style risk losing more than just some valuable executives. They may also be losing a chance to build themselves into stronger, more competitive enterprises. (p. 47)*

Grant (1988) advised readers of the journal *Organizational Dynamics:*

> *These "human resources" skills are critical in helping to stop the tide of alienation, apathy, cynicism, and low morale in organizations. . . . If organizations are to become more humane, less alienating, and more*

responsive to the individuals who work for them, they will probably need to learn to value process as well as product. . . . Thus women may indeed be the most radical force available in bringing about organizational change. (p. 62)

Harvard Business Review, considered by many to be the final word on the art of management, published J. B. Rosener's (1990) article, which claimed that "as the workforce increasingly demands participation and the economic environment increasingly requires rapid change, interactive leadership may emerge as the management style of choice for many organizations" (p. 125).

Finally, *Time* magazine (Rudolph, 1990) predicted that women's flexible and mediating approach will play a vital role in managing America's heterogeneous workforce.

Preferred Organizational Structure

How work should be structured to be most productive, effective, and efficient has dominated management thinking from the beginning. A search for the best structure led to the idealization of bureaucracy, experiments with less-hierarchical and more-flexible structures, and an appreciation that the structure of an organization must be related to the work that is done and to the organization's environment. The benefits of traditional, bureaucratic structures, which emphasize vertical levels that differentiate workers from managers, centralized authority, standardized procedures, routinized methods, and formal rules, are being increasingly questioned. There is heightened interest in bureaucracy's disadvantages: the way staff is constrained, creativity is stifled, change is difficult, and response to the environment is slow and unwieldy. Most important, there is criticism that traditional structures contribute to low morale and job dissatisfaction because of worker boredom, failure to consider worker input seriously, and the organization's incapacity to respond to worker needs (McNeely, 1992).

For the past 30 years, we have been warned of the inadequacies of bureaucracy. In 1964 Argyris claimed that bureaucracies create workers who are more childish than adult and that such behavior is incompatible with the human need to grow and develop (cited in Bennis, 1970). Bennis stated that

it is my premise that the bureaucratic form of organization is becoming less and less effective; that it is helplessly out of joint with contemporary realities; that new shapes, patterns, and models are emerging which promise drastic changes in the conduct of the corporation and of managerial practices in general. (p. 3)

There is a growing realization that the traditional hierarchical and bureaucratic structure is outdated. The preferred organizational structure today is based on a collaborative model that allows workers increased control and participation in their work and in their workplace. America's flirtation with Japanese management, quality of work life, and self-managing teams represents efforts to use nonhierarchical structures. An extensive body of literature exists on collaborative group functioning; despite variations among the models, each vests in the work group to some degree the management functions of planning, organizing, directing, and controlling work. Consequently, when the work group is given autonomy and authority and takes on its own task and decision-making functions, the manager's role is redefined. As a result, the traditional leadership characteristics associated with hierarchical organizations—control, power, status, and privilege—are removed (Finch, 1977).

Gender and the Preferred Organizational Structure

Not surprisingly, men have long been associated with the hierarchical and bureaucratic organizational structures in which rational efficiency and superior domination can be achieved through vertical patterns of control and authority (Denhardt & Perkins, 1976). This style is similar to a militaristic culture that stresses strength, loyalty, obedience, and winning (Garsombke, 1988; Harragan, 1977).

In contrast, women have been associated with alternatives to hierarchy, such as collaborative structures. In a feminist critique of bureaucracy, Ferguson (1984) proposed the need for organizations that value and embody democracy, equality, caring, and nurturance over hierarchy, inequality, and impersonality. Early radical feminists insisted on fluid, temporary structures in which process was valued as equally important to the completion of the task. Also, an emphasis was placed on consensual decision making to enhance both creativity and group solidarity (Denhardt & Perkins, 1976). Feminist organizations share many of the beliefs and practices of collectivist organizations (Ferguson, 1987; Rothschild, 1987). Feminist organizations oppose a hierarchical division of authority, instead favoring empowerment by and within the entire group. Focus is placed on the process of decision making being as valuable as the outcome, and efforts for inclusive participation and consensus decision making are undertaken. Emphasis is given to the ideal of "community" and face-to-face relations rather than formal, role-defined relationships. There is a demystification of the skills and knowledge needed to perform jobs so that tasks can be shared, rewards can be equalized, and the division of labor can be integrated rather than segregated. However, only feminist organizations reflect a feminist ideology, which includes a belief that society's sexist assumptions and practices should be challenged, services or benefits to women must be provided, and a special commitment to caring and nurturance among organizational members should exist (Martin, 1987). Table 4-1 contrasts the key characteristics of a feminist management style (similar to contemporary participatory management) with a traditional, nonfeminist approach to administration.

FEMINIST ADMINISTRATION IN PRACTICE

Despite the presence of female managers, there are few examples of feminist administration in practice. Initially its practice focused on the management of feminist organizations. In such agencies, leadership steers the organizations so that authority belongs to the collectivity, there is minimal division of labor, staff responsibilities are shared or rotated, differences in rewards are limited, decision making is shared by staff and clients, and specialized training and degrees are given minimal importance (Kravetz & Jones, 1991).

The approach described at Blackwell, a feminist agency that offers gynecological services to women, is a good example of feminist administration (Schwartz et al., 1988). From the beginning, Blackwell's leadership made an effort to recognize the importance of each worker's contribution, to keep job descriptions flexible for job rotation, and to devise mechanisms to ensure that all levels of staff could respond to issues and be involved in key decisions that affected the organization.

Examples of how women lead are appearing more frequently in business and industry (Billard, 1992; Cantor & Bernay, 1992; Hughey & Gelman, 1986; J. B. Rosener, 1990). Helgesen's (1990) interviews with four successful leaders, including Frances Hesselbein, the national executive director of the Girl Scouts, are an important contribution to understanding how organizations run by women tend to be "webs of inclusion" rather than hierarchies. The style Hesselbein describes is circular; positions are represented as circles, which are then arranged in an expanding series of orbits around the director, who is in the center. In this style Helgesen saw the analogy of female executives being connected to those around them as if by invisible strands of thread that are drawn closer and closer together around the center, like the weaving of a spider's web. This image of a web was also developed by Gilligan (1982) to describe how women structure relationships whereby the process of "interweaving" relationships becomes as valuable as the final product.

Table 4-1

Feminist and Nonfeminist Styles of Administration

Characteristic	Feminist Administration	Nonfeminist Administration
Leadership style	Beta Interactive Transforming Empowering	Alpha Command-and-control Transactive Controlling
Operating mode	Caring Nurturing Teaching Cooperative Facilitative Open Inclusive	Authoritarian Combative Directing Competitive Commanding Closed Exclusive
Organizational goals	Worker empowerment Improving lives of women	Productivity Efficiency Winning
Locus of authority	Collectivity Work group Center Expertise	Top of hierarchy Formal positions
Structures	Collaborative Horizontal Self-managing Decentralized	Hierarchical Bureaucratic Centralized Formalized
Problem-solving style	Intuitive Qualitative Contextual Consensual Participative Process-oriented Mediative	Rational Quantitative Scientific Top-down Task-oriented Negotiatory
Tasks	Flatten hierarchy Diffuse power Rotate jobs Share decision making Equalize rewards Increase worker participation	Routinize work Standardize rules Formalize relationships Stabilize structure Concentrate power Differentiate rewards

Social workers also have looked at the practice of feminist administration. Chernesky and Bombyk (1988) studied 92 female human services executives and found that 60 percent of the respondents claimed they brought to administration a concern for people, sensitivity, empathy, compassion, and a tendency to nurture others. Moreover, "their illustrations of leadership style emphasized cooperation, participation, and a nonhierarchical approach that includes, rather than excludes, as many people as possible" (p. 57). A dominant theme among the 48 women studied by Healy, Havens, and Chin (1990) was the use of managerial position as a way to empower others through sharing information and joint decision making.

Hyde's (1989) study of 50 feminist practitioners in both feminist and male-dominated organizations illustrated, in greater detail, how a feminist orientation of caring, nurturing, and valuing family and community influences approaches to issues and strategies and provides a rationale for involvement in program development and mobilization efforts. Using a case study to illustrate how staff empowerment was established through a collegial and matrix structure, Weil (1988) discussed the creation of a feminist management approach in a large public agency. Chernesky (1986) envisioned how supervision from a feminist perspective might be structured in any organizational setting.

Hooyman's (1991) personal report of her efforts to implement a feminist leadership style as dean of a social work school is especially valuable. She emphasized how she looks for ways to build on the strengths of faculty, staff, and students; to create a climate in which differences can be expressed and lead to unity rather than separation; to delegate tasks that empower others; to develop horizontal methods for sharing information and solving problems; to provide opportunities to give feedback; to support individuals' personal and familial concerns; and to encourage the formation of social networks that support personal development.

SUGGESTED PRACTICES

Despite the paucity of illustrations on the use of feminist management in mainstream organizations, the practice reed not be limited to feminist organizations, nor does it require total revamping of an organization's structure. As a guide, a list of feminist administrative practices is presented in Table 4-2. These practice examples reflect the three cornerstones of style, structure, and purpose and can be undertaken by managers in any organizational setting. Although

Table 4-2

Feminist Administrative Practices

Style

Ensure that workers handle their work-related issues

Encourage risk taking to enable workers to learn for themselves

Create a climate in which diverse opinions and experiences can be expressed and valued

Support female or feminine-associated attributes

Attend to the "person" who is a worker

Model consensus decision making

Value process as well as outcome, especially group process

Weave an organizational web that includes all workers

Transfer power and authority to those who are traditionally denied it

Encourage workers to use one another to share information, collaborate, and get feedback

Take responsibility for the continuing personal and professional growth of workers

Structure

Flatten the organizational hierarchy, establishing as few levels as possible

Define jobs so they are flexible and allow for job rotation

Create horizontal structures to foster across-the-board staff input on organizational decisions

Use alternatives to the organizational hierarchy for supervision, monitoring, and accountability

Work toward a circular organizational structure in place of the traditional hierarchical ladder

Establish self-regulating work groups as a way to organize work

Cluster tasks and activities to provide individual growth and professional development

Purpose

Establish formal policies to enable all workers to balance work and family needs

Counter prevailing reward structures that tend to penalize women and others whose contributions are devalued

Continuously address sexism and racism as well as other forms of oppression, discrimination, and inequities

Ensure that women's perspectives and experiences are valued and taken into consideration

Commit to empowering women and improving women's lives

the list may omit some practices ordinarily associated with a feminist approach, it includes many that may not typically be considered.

In general, practices related to leadership style focus on how the manager influences and motivates people, giving meaning and direction to their work. A leadership style sets a tone as to what is valued and imparts a message as to how the organization and its members will be directed. A feminist style uses a consensus and process-oriented approach for solving problems and reaching decisions, focuses on workers' growth and development, and encourages organizational actions that promote women's well-being.

Practices related to structure focus on how the work itself and the total organization will be organized to ensure that the work gets done. A feminist structure claims to use nonhierarchical arrangements, eliminate the link between authority and hierarchical position, and use a variety of flexible and self-managing work groups.

From a feminist perspective, the purpose is always to make the unique needs and situations of women as workers, clients, and constituents central to the organization, regardless of the agency's mission, mandate, or program. Practices related to purpose keep us vigilant when setting goals, designing programs, planning delivery of services, or establishing work policies to ensure that women's interests are in the forefront and that the organization is not biased against women.

Feminist managers can begin by altering their behavior and thereby sending a message about what is valued and in what direction the organization will be heading. For example, a change in how routine staff meetings are planned and conducted could be a starting point. How often do staff meetings display hierarchical control rather than open communication in which ideas are shared and opportunities for group problem solving and decision making are encouraged? If agencywide task forces were given the necessary resources, power, and authority to define and conduct their work, they could become self-managing. It may be possible to reconfigure jobs so that tasks are less rigid, activities are more flexible, and staff have the opportunity to shift among jobs. Peer supervision can be introduced so that workers use each other to learn, teach, and evaluate their practice without turning to supervisors for answers, guidance, or feedback. The day's work can be distributed in such a way that workers are able to check on their children when they return home from school without feeling guilty about it. Formal agencywide policies on flexible work hours and leave for family-related reasons can be established so that individual workers do not have to request special permission every time a family need arises.

CONCLUSION

Following through on these feminist administration practices may seem overwhelming. Because they do not represent the traditional way of managing people or organizations, skepticism and a lack of support to try them are likely. J. B. Rosener (1990) warned that no one expects that women's ways will be readily accepted, despite a growing consensus that what women can bring to organizations is desirable. Holding on to values they believe are important while working in organizations that do not appreciate these values can be lonely and difficult for women. The path can be eased, however, by taking incremental steps, albeit seemingly insignificant, and by locating support from networks of female managers.

It is important to remember that the practice examples suggested here are not only illustrations of feminist administration, they also represent a more "enlightened" management approach and are associated with today's preferred leadership style and organizational structure. Given the changes already evident in organizations and the changes that are predicted in the workforce and the workplace of the 21st century, it will be essential for organizations to be led by individuals who are comfortable with relationships, process, collaborative consensus building, and worker participation. With the increasing heterogeneity of the workforce and the increasing need for organizations to respond to workers' family needs, managers must be able to bring out the best in all workers. It is no wonder that the principles associated with feminist administration are now at the cutting edge of management technology. Although the basic tasks of tomorrow's managers will remain much the same as those of today, the methods by which those tasks are handled will determine the effectiveness of future organizations. Human services organizations must not fall behind business and industry in supporting feminist administration. A feminist approach to leadership style and structure should be prevalent when managing in the social welfare field.

However, the question raised earlier in this chapter remains. If a relationship-oriented leadership style is used and nonhierarchical organizational structures are established, is that feminist administration? Clearly, if devoid of the commitment to better women's lives and improve women's condition, we would say no. However, it is possible that the preferred structure and style, even without a commitment to assisting and valuing women, could empower women who are workers and clients. As organizations involve their workforce in collaborative problem solving and consensual decision making, it is more than likely that these efforts will lead to actions that enhance the workplace, delivery of services, and women's everyday lives.

Although we may want to use a more stringent litmus test to define feminist administration, we also want to be supportive of managerial styles and activities that counter the traditional command-and-control approach that relies on hierarchical structure. We should encourage the direction in which current management appears to be heading, moving away from hierarchical structure toward practices that are more inclusive, participative, and focused on enhancing the well-being of organizational members as well as achieving organizational goals.

REFERENCES

Belenky, M. F., Clinchy, B. M., Goldberger, N. R., & Tarule, J. M. (1989). *Women's ways of knowing*. New York: Basic Books.

Bennis, W. G. (1970). *American bureaucracy*. New Brunswick, NJ: Transaction.

Billard, M. (1992, March). Do women make better managers? *Working Woman*, pp. 68–73.

Block, P. (1987). *The empowered manager*. San Francisco: Jossey-Bass.

Bombyk, M. J., & Chernesky, R. H. (1985). Conventional cutback leadership and the quality of the workplace. *Administration in Social Work, 9*(3), 47–56.

Burns, J. M. (1979). *Leadership*. New York: Harper & Row.

Cantor, D. W., & Bernay, T. (1992). *Women in power: The secrets of leadership*. New York: Houghton Mifflin.

Chernesky, R. H. (1986). A new model of supervision. In N. Van Den Bergh & L. B. Cooper (Eds.), *Feminist visions for social work* (pp. 163–186). Silver Spring, MD: National Association of Social Workers.

Chernesky, R. H., & Bombyk, M. J. (1988). Women's ways and effective management. *Affilia, 3*(1), 48–60.

Cohen, S. S. (1989, February). Beyond macho: The power of womanly management. *Working Woman*, pp. 77–88.

Deming, W. E. (1986). *Out of the crisis*. Cambridge, MA: MIT Center for Advanced Engineering Study.

Denhardt, R. H., & Perkins, J. (1976). The coming death of administrative man. *Public Administrative Review, 38*, 379–384.

Evered, R. D., & Selman, J. C. (1989, August). Coaching and the art of management. *Organizational Dynamics, 18*(2), 16–32.

Faludi, S. (1991). *Backlash: The undeclared war against American women*. New York: Crown.

Ferguson, K. F. (1984). *The feminist case against bureaucracy*. Philadelphia: Temple University Press.

Ferguson, K. F. (1987, August). *Women, feminism and collectives*. Paper presented at the meeting of the American Sociological Association, Chicago.

Finch, F. E. (1977). Collaborative leadership in work settings. *Journal of Applied Behavioral Science, 13*(2), 292–302.

Garsombke, D. J. (1988). Organizational culture dons the mantle of militarism. *Organizational Dynamics, 17*(1), 46–56.

Gilligan, C. (1982). *In a different voice*. Cambridge, MA: Harvard University Press.

Grant, J. (1988). Women as managers: What they can offer to organizations. *Organizational Dynamics, 16*(3), 56–63.

Harragan, B. L. (1977). *Games mother never taught you*. New York: Warner Books.

Healy, L. M., Havens, C. M., & Chin, A. (1990). Preparing women for human service administration: Building on experience. *Administration in Social Work, 14*(2), 79–94.

Helgesen, S. (1990). *The female advantage: Women's ways of leadership*. New York: Doubleday.

Hooyman, N. R. (1991). Supporting practice in large-scale bureaucracies. In M. B. Jenkins, N. R. Hooyman, & N. Gottlieb (Eds.), *Feminist social work practice in clinical settings* (pp. 251–269). Newbury Park, CA: Sage Publications.

Hooyman, N. R., & Cunningham, R. (1986). An alternative administrative style. In N. Van Den Bergh & L. B. Cooper (Eds.), *Feminist visions for social work* (pp. 163–186). Silver Spring, MD: National Association of Social Workers.

Hornstein, H. A., Heilman, M. E., Mone, E., & Tartell, R. (1987). Responding to contingent leadership behavior. *Organizational Dynamics, 15*(4), 56–65.

Hughey, A., & Gelman, E. (1986, March 17). Managing the woman's way. *Newsweek*, pp. 46–47.

Hyde, C. (1989). A feminist model for macro-practice: Promises and problems. *Administration in Social Work, 13*(3/4), 145–181.

Kanter, R. M. (1983). *The change masters*. New York: Simon & Schuster.

Kravetz, D., & Jones, L. E. (1991). Supporting practice in feminist service agencies. In M. B. Jenkins, N. R. Hooyman, & N. Gottlieb (Eds.), *Feminist social work practice in clinical settings* (pp. 233–249). Newbury Park, CA: Sage Publications.

Lawler, E. E. (1986). *High-involvement management*. San Francisco: Josscy-Bass.

Loden, M. (1985). *Feminine leadership or how to succeed without being one of the boys*. New York: Times Books.

Manz, C. C., & Sims, H. P. (1991). Superleadership: Beyond the myth of heroic leadership. *Organizational Dynamics, 19*(4), 18–35.

Martin, P. Y. (1987, August). *Feminist organizations: What are they like?* Paper presented at the meeting of the American Sociological Association, Chicago.

McNeely, R. L. (1992). Job satisfaction in the public social services: Perspectives on structure, situational factors, gender, and ethnicity. In Y. Hasenfeld (Ed.), *Human services as complex organizations* (pp. 224–255). Newbury Park, CA: Sage Publications.

Rosener, J. B. (1990). Ways women lead. *Harvard Business Review, 68,* 119–125.

Rosener, L., & Schwartz, P. (1980). Women, leadership and the 1980's: What kind of leaders do we need? In *New leadership in the public interest* (pp. 25–36). New York: NOW Legal Defense & Education Fund.

Rothschild, J. (1987, August). *Do collectivist–democratic forms of organization presuppose feminism? Cooperative work structures and women's values.* Paper presented at the meeting of the American Sociological Association, Chicago.

Rudolph, B. (1990, Fall). Why can't a woman manage more like . . . a woman? *Time, 136*(19), 53.

Sargent, A. G. (1981). *The androgynous manager*. New York: American Management Communication.

Schwartz, A. Y., Gottesman, E. W., & Perlmutter, F. D. (1988). Blackwell: A case study in feminist administration. *Administration in Social Work, 12*(2), 5–15.

Weil, M. (1986, March). *Women in administration: Leadership styles and organizational cultures*. Paper presented at the Community Organization and Social Administration Symposium, Miami.

Weil, M. (1988). Creating an alternative work culture in a public service setting. *Administration in Social Work, 12*(2), 69–82.

5

The Politics of Authority
A Case Analysis of a Feminist Health Center

Cheryl Hyde

I arrived today at the Community Health Center and had the strangest beginning yet. I showed up at the clinic just before 9 A.M. to meet with the coordinator, Pam. When I walked in, I was surprised to see about 15 to 20 Latino men in the waiting room. No women. Was I in the wrong place? Immediately I went back outside and checked the address and name plate. This was it. Back inside I went, approached the receptionist and asked for Pam. While waiting for her I noticed old, comfortable furniture; posters advocating various forms of and means to revolution; condom gift baskets; and all these men speaking Spanish and looking a bit nervous. Later, after meeting Pam, I asked her what was going on. She said that the clinic was a support organization for undocumented people in the area. They offered low-cost immigration exams, necessary for gaining amnesty. The staff viewed this as an important political commitment and as a way of trying out whether they should provide services to men. After all, she said, these men are central to the lives of the women the clinic cared for and thus, could not be ignored. (From the author's field work journal, May 1988)

When it was founded in the early 1970s, the Community Health Center was a collective with a clearly articulated socialist–feminist ideology. Its membership was white, largely middle class, and university educated. By 1988 the center advanced a multicultural mission that called for 50 percent of the paid staff to be women of color, of mixed class and educational levels, and for provision of bilingual programs and materials. The center also had become a democratically managed organization with a four-tier hierarchy. This chapter analyzes the relationship between diversity and the organizational changes in authority. In particular, the conflicts between multiculturalism and collectivism are explored within the context of a feminist social-change mandate.

The topic of authority is a staple of organizational study. Authority is fundamentally an expression of political ideals, reflecting ways in which people ought to relate to one another in a given setting. In his analyses of organizational power and structure, Weber defined authority as "the power to command and the duty to obey" (Rothschild & Whitt, 1986, p. 22). Weber delineated the manifestations of authority: The ruler manifests authority through tradition, the mass-based leader through charisma, and the executive through legal and rational means. In a collective, an organizational form overlooked by Weber, all members simultaneously command and obey. The core belief of a collective is that no individual has the right to dominate another (Rothschild & Whitt, 1986).

Organizational authority can be examined along various dimensions: rules, levels of stratification, reward systems, definitions of expertise, and social relations. A shift along any of these dimensions from collective to more-bureaucratic forms is interpreted as a sign of organizational conservatism. Examples include the rise in the number of professional staff, the promulgation of standardized written policies and procedures, and specified and specialized positions.

Ideally, feminist organizational praxis emphasizes social change goals, minimization or elimination of hierarchy, inclusivity, collaboration, equalized reward structures, nurturing of social relations, and use of lay rather than professional expertise (Ahrens, 1980; Brandwein, 1981, 1987; Hyde, 1989). The creation of feminist organizations is viewed as a political act designed to advance the status of women and challenge patriarchal systems. As advanced by radical and socialist feminists, the ideal organizational form is the collective (Baker, 1986; Gould, 1979; Hyde, 1991; Riger, 1984).

Less attention has been focused on the dilemmas that arise when these values are put into practice in organizational settings. Often, organizations that are not able to incorporate or sustain most or all of these feminist values are deemed unfeminist. In perhaps the strongest articulation of this position, Ferguson (1984) argued that bureaucratic authority is essentially oppressive and patriarchal. Truly radical feminism subverts and rejects bureaucracy. Case study literature helps substantiate Ferguson's assertion with examples of feminist organizations co-opted through bureaucratic authority and its attendant characteristics (Ahrens, 1980; Ferraro, 1983; Murray, 1988; Rodriquez, 1988). By extension, collective authority, as the antithesis of bureaucratic domination, best advances the ideals of revolutionary feminist organizational praxis. Such collective entities model different and preferable means of membership relations and labor processes.

However, the problem with this approach to organizational praxis is that it reduces the definition of the feminist organization to authority and discounts other dimensions such as the kind of services offered or the diversity of membership (Baker, 1986; Harvey, 1985; Hyde, 1991, 1992; Martin, 1990). By focusing primarily on a particular kind of authority, an organization often does not critically or honestly evaluate goals and processes. Freeman's (1973) classic article, "Tyranny of Structurelessness," sounded a warning about the hidden and unacknowledged power dynamics that exist in feminist groups. In her estimation, it was not sufficient to claim a collectivist structure to avoid forms of domination. In a critique of Ferguson's work, Martin (1987) suggested that "feminists should reject idealization of feminist organizations just as they reject wholesale condemnation of bureaucracies" (p. 548). Finally, the ways in which organizational values and objectives (which could include collectivism) conflict often are not examined. These points are key to the case analysis of the Community Health Center.

RESEARCH METHODOLOGY
The data for this case analysis were collected as part of a comparative study of nine feminist movement organizations that determined what effect the New Right had on organizational change and survival (Hyde, 1991). All nine organizations (three National Organization for Women chapters, three health clinics, and three antiviolence centers) were nonprofit. They were oriented to service, advocacy, and education for the public and were viewed as feminist by their members. The organizations varied in size, type of staffing, region of the country, governance structure, age, and degree of service emphasis. All experienced New Right opposition, although the type and intensity of opposition varied during the period of the study (1977–87).

The primary data, collected during seven- to 10-day visits, consisted of organizational documents (grant proposals, meeting minutes, annual reports, budgets, correspondence, and pamphlets) and interviews with past and current members. With respect to the Community Health Center, more than 550 documents were analyzed and five women were interviewed. I kept a fieldwork journal in which observations, assessments, preliminary analysis, and personal reactions were recorded. For reasons of confidentiality, names and locations of organizations and names of members cannot be revealed.

The data gathering and analysis was guided by the process of analytic induction (Denzin, 1989; Katz, 1983). This approach is premised on systematic data analysis in which a priori propositions and emergent themes are compared and contrasted. There is continuous movement between data and competing theories as the researcher simultaneously engages in inductive and deductive analysis. Three feminist research principles initially anchored this study: (1) Knowledge is grounded in the experiences of women, (2) research benefits women, and (3) the researcher immerses herself or himself in, or exhibits empathy for, the world being studied (Harding, 1987). However, the use of analytic induction and the application of a feminist research approach proved to be more complex and messier than anticipated (Hyde, 1993).

COMMUNITY HEALTH CENTER

As with many feminist health clinics, the Community Health Center began as a small group of women who met to discuss and analyze their medical needs. By 1973 two years of meetings had evolved into an education and referral organization. Frustrated by the lack of woman-oriented health services and the conservative nature of the community's medical establishment, group members began to plan their own feminist health collective. They had limited experience in such organizational endeavors even though many of the women were active in the antiwar and feminist movements.

In 1974 the collective opened an office with education and research as the primary objectives. Members were 18 to 30 years old, white, middle class, and university educated. Some members were lesbians. A few were mothers. The women pooled $2,000 of their own savings, which with a matching grant served as seed money. In June 1974 the Community Health Center opened its first gynecological clinic—it took 16 hours to see eight women.

The founding period lasted until 1977. During this time, the center sought to stabilize its offerings and secure a place in the feminist and alternative health communities. The center lost a battle with the state regarding licensure for an abortion clinic and decided to offer abortion counseling only on a contractual basis with area providers. The center started programs such as a well-woman clinic, acupuncture, pregnancy screening, and alternative health education that still exist today.

Several important characteristics of the center emerged and solidified during this founding period. Center members publicly articulated a strong socialist–feminist analysis, exemplified in this 1975 letter to women of the Vietcong Army:

> We of the CHC, as socialist feminists, want to join with the rest of the anti-imperialist movement in the United States in expressing our great joy at your victory and our solidarity and support for your continued struggle against imperialism, sexism, racism and for the building of socialism. . . . The CHC fosters socialist ideals by offering medical care for women, meeting one of the basic needs common to all people. . . . We try to show women that the doctors in a capitalist society cannot have our interests at heart. . . . We believe in participatory medicine where in the clinics, patients perform as many medical tasks as possible and women are educated through our exams so they can help in making an accurate diagnosis of their symptoms. We call this process "self-help."

Members were adamant that this center be an expression of their political values. This intent clearly included the belief in the empowerment of oppressed groups, even though it was not reflected in the daily functioning of the center.

This socialist–feminist framework provided the philosophical rationale for collectivist authority relations. Egalitarianism was a core value put into practice among members and between service providers and consumers. The self-help approach emphasized that knowledge did not solely reside with experts or workers. Decisions were made through consensus. Small and large groups discussed issues and planned programs so that members could participate as much as possible. An important means of ensuring responsibility was through criticism–self-criticism, in which members offered themselves and others positive and negative feedback at the end of each meeting. Jobs were rotated and pay, such as it was, was equal. The collective devised a system of job contracting, a procedure that served as

> a way of assuring accountability of each woman to the collective. We as a collective decide what work we want to do. . . . The process of individual re-evaluation of our work and collective feedback about our work is an invaluable part of our collective commitment to consciously evaluate the effectiveness of the CHC and our feeling about the work we do. (March 1977 newsletter)

Collectivist authority, then, was an essential means of political expression.

This theme of reevaluation is an important one with respect to overall center functioning. In meetings and retreats, center members continuously reevaluated all aspects of the organization. For example, in 1974 members closed the center for five weeks to assess their progress. During such sessions collective members took stock of how they fulfilled educational and political goals. In this way they refueled themselves and reengaged in the social change orientation of the work.

There was, however, a downside. Such reevaluation practices interrupted the flow of services and undermined a stable consumer base. The seemingly endless meetings for reevaluation, feedback, and training translated into a high time commitment, often on a voluntary basis. This meant that an individual needed flexibility and perhaps a separate source of money to participate.

A major crisis and turning point for the center came in 1978 with the passage of a statewide antitax proposition. This law, in concert with a conservative county revenue board, resulted in dramatic fiscal damage to the center. The solution was to eliminate 12 of the 17 paid jobs. Ten members voluntarily gave up their jobs. The group failed to reach a decision on the final two layoffs using the consensus approach and went to a vote. The results were rejected, however, largely because the two members selected were the only women of color and one of them had a disability. Chastened, members returned to the consensus process and eventually two other women gave up their jobs.

This painful event signaled the fiscal vulnerability of the center. It also indicated that the decision-making process was cumbersome and perhaps arbitrary. The crisis resulted in the loss of talented members and tore the social fabric of the center because many of the women who went on self-imposed layoff could not afford to volunteer the time necessary for collective participation. Most important, the entire process, but particularly the vote, brought into sharp relief the racism and ablism (subordination of people with disabilities) in the organization. It was clear that ideological commitment to disenfranchised groups was not infused into daily practice.

Over the next few years, the collective addressed these dilemmas in three ways. First, true to form, the collective reworked its structure. Associate collective positions were introduced so individuals who were unable to make the necessary time commitment could participate in some center activities. The associates, however, never truly felt they were a part of the collective, despite invitations to join all the meetings.

Second, hiring decisions reflected a desire to bring in more women of color. The collective tried to diversify its staff using Comprehensive Employment and Training Act (CETA) funding. However, in

1981 the Reagan administration cut the CETA program. The center sought grants to underwrite bilingual and bicultural outreach programs to the local Latino population. This outreach program signaled an important decision to form better community alliances with populations of color and to provide services in those communities rather than having people come to the center. This program was the foundation for a spin-off Latino family health center.

Third, center members engaged in self-education on racism. Workshops and retreats were held to examine American racism and its manifestations in the center. A 1982 newsletter article summarized the training programs:

> *Our failure—for whatever reasons—to include and serve women of color could be translated into an unspoken priority given to white women's health care rather than health care for all women. Although none of us could accept this assumption once verbalized, acknowledging that we had created our organization meant accepting responsibility for the work we did and who we reached.*

These efforts culminated in a 1981 proposal that at least 50 percent of the paid staff should be women of color. Other priority groups would be lesbians, women with disabilities, and older women. The minutes note that "we are not doing this out of governmental obligation, think of our ideals." Yet implementation problems went unresolved. The financial situation meant that the center could not add positions to meet the goal. The few women of color on staff were funded by grant money that needed renewal every year, so their jobs were the most precarious. Most important, collective members received clear feedback that the collectivist structure was a barrier to diversity:

> *Though collective process is by nature slow. . . the implementation of our affirmative action plan was particularly tedious. After attending a few meetings, the women of color felt disgusted and alienated, and decided they could not participate any longer. They pointed out the racial/cultural style of our process: the tones and terms in which we speak. . . and the slowness—despite lengthy discussion—in making changes, which they viewed as avoiding the issues. These women felt that they did not have the time in their lives to talk for hours and make no decisions, especially when the necessary action to be taken seemed obvious to them. Increasing their frustration was the feeling that their input was being ignored. . . . Somewhat naively, we had thought that we could change who we are and who we serve without affecting how we work and how decisions are made.* (March 1982 newsletter)

The conflict between diversity and collective authority was now clearly identified. It seemed apparent that the center could not attain both. One longtime participant remembered how the women realized their lack of diversity:

We realized that everything about us was about white, middle-class women. It was the language we used, it was the structure, it was doing criticism–self-criticism. . . . There was a kind of intimacy that came from who we were and that we had shared speculum exams, shared our lives, shared our victimization as women, that wasn't necessarily the same shared experience for women of color who dealt with issues of poverty and being single parents, being farmworkers. . . . The vagueness of the structure also was difficult. A lot was implied without being said. It depended on shared lives. . . . We finally dropped the structure.

"Dropping the structure" was by no means an easy, nonconflictual, or smooth endeavor. From 1981 to 1984 the center was on the brink of dissolution. Yet the founding attributes of a socialist–feminist ideology, the capacity to reevaluate and change, the commitment to politicized services, as well as new links with the Latino community, anchored the transition.

Detailing the trials and errors of this transition is beyond the scope of this chapter. However, organizational documents reveal constant debate as the group struggled with its desire for collective authority and the reality that this form would not allow them to achieve other goals, specifically diversity. One member talked about the changes the center was going through:

Recognizing that we needed new ways of working together, we began to let go of the feelings that we knew what was right for CHC. As the 'we' of the CHC was changing, new ways of working together would emerge. Reaching this point was a breakthrough. . . . This process is changing all of our lives personally and is reconnecting us with our political goals.

Ultimately, a newly constituted community board, empowered by the collective to make decisions, fired everyone; restructured the positions, downsizing from 12 to nine paid positions because of fiscal difficulties; and hired workers for the new jobs.

Although criticized for this extreme action, the board achieved diversity in hiring. It also sent a clear message to the collective that it was using the authority granted by center members. The board articulated a new sense of ownership of the center. These shifts were summarized in a 1982 letter to the staff:

The purpose of the CHC as an organization is to serve the community–the broad spectrum of the community–it does not exist to solely serve the women who work there. . . . We as the board of directors are taking full responsibility for having made the lay-off decisions. Remember, we are not your enemy, we are a group chosen by CHC staff and volunteers to make decisions.

Over time, collective and board members reached a new understanding. Each group was represented at the other's meetings. The board agreed to use consensus and would put an issue to a vote only as a last resort. Staff gradually adjusted to a pay scale and set, not rotated, positions, although the opportunity remained to share or be trained in other jobs. In 1983 the center hired a full-time coordinator. In 1984 the center was formally referred to as a "democratically managed" organization, not a collective.

The period from 1984 to 1988 was one of stabilization. The center achieved fiscal solvency, program growth, and consistency. It was viewed as an organizational mother for the Latino family health center. Legitimacy with the Latino community soared when the center became an advocate for and service provider to undocumented workers. Volunteers remained essential, although being hired was no longer assured in light of the commitment that 50 percent of the paid staff be women of color.

Ideologically, the term "socialist–feminist" is no longer invoked. Yet the current statement of purpose reads in part that

we are dedicated to the provision of client centered, affordable, accessible, quality and culturally sensitive services. As feminists, part of our mission is the empowerment of women and the eradication of race, class, and gender oppression, homophobia and all other forms of institutionalized oppression. . . . The CHC emphasizes self-help, health education and preventative care. . . . We strive to equalize the relationship between patient and practitioner, by the use of community patient advocates and by involving the patient in her or his diagnosis and treatment.

The center broadened its ideological frame. Although collective governance no longer existed, other aspects of egalitarianism were maintained.

Longtime members still desire some of what collectivism offered. They also understand the trade-off necessary to achieve a multicultural, participatory, and solvent organization. One participant reflected on missing the collective:

My idealistic side misses what collectivity is. Spending lots of time listening, discussing, and processing. And ensuring through the collective process that everyone is heard because anyone can stop a collective decision. And I miss the intimacy involved. I think that we wouldn't have survived with it and so part of me that values what we do and that we exist and need to exist sadly says goodbye to the collective and gladly embraces what we have now.

LESSONS LEARNED

The decision, after contentious debate and careful deliberation, to give up the collective to achieve diversity was not a transformation to be taken lightly. Although the Community Health Center is by no means a traditional bureaucracy, this change could be viewed as an indicator of organizational conservatism and perhaps antithetical to feminist philosophy.

Over time, center participants created a form of authority that maximized the goals of political and social change, diversity, egalitarianism, fuller participation, and fiscal responsibility. These goals often were at odds with each other, and the changes the center made underscore the necessity of compromise. In the process the members redefined what they meant by feminist organizational praxis. The reconceptualization expanded the founding socialist–feminist ideology and included the values of inclusivity, self-education, and group feedback, which were central during the collectivist period. In addition, center members demonstrated that to be truly diverse, multiculturalism must be infused in a nonnegotiable way throughout the organization. Diversity was not treated as simply a matter of hiring, providing bilingual materials, or inserting women of color into existing structures and processes. Multicultural praxis dictated changes in staffing, ideological framework, community relations, and, most important, organizational authority.

The center now approximates what Weil (1986) termed a "women of color" framework in which the elimination of all human oppression is viewed as the primary purpose. Race, gender, and class are interconnected systems. Characteristics of this model include education and consciousness-raising about the forms of oppression, the development of alternative programs for the disempowered, and the creation of coalitions with disenfranchised groups to encourage political solidarity and socioeconomic development. Through the changes it has made, the Community Health Center has exhibited these attributes.

This reconceptualization of feminism, and the ability to put the new ideas into practice, stemmed from relinquishing collectivist authority. The demands of collectivism prevented participation by a variety of people. The often informal power displays by some members resulted in arbitrary decisions that enforced an unacknowledged elite. The lack of systematized procedures interfered with smooth service delivery. In theory, collectivist authority may be the ultimate means of achieving equality and the primary tool for dismantling bureaucratic power abuse. However, in practice, there are limitations to collectivism. This case indicates that collectives operate best under conditions of homogeneity, long-term intimacy, and extended time commitments, all of which are antithetical to multiculturalism, incorporation of new staff, and service delivery in a competitive environment.

With the elimination of collectivism, the question of whether the center is still a feminist organization remains. Members clearly believe that it is, albeit a different form of feminism than existed during its founding period. A 1987 letter from the board to the community stated that "the CHC is a feminist primary health care and education center which has been in the community for over 10 years. We are dedicated to the empowerment of all women and children." If the basic tenets of feminist praxis are considered, it seems that the center embodies most of them, particularly collaboration and inclusivity. Thus, this health center remains a feminist organization, even though it is no longer a collective.

Collectives offer exciting alternative models of authority. By their existence, these organizations demonstrate nonbureaucratic ways of interrelating through more humane mechanisms. However, a multicultural organization (one that allows for more than token involvement) challenges business as usual. The feminist movement has been justifiably criticized for its white, middle-class bias. Whereas some criticism is a result of a general lack of attention to process and product, other criticism is the result of particular forms of authority, such as the collective, that do not function well with a heterogeneous membership. When considering what feminist organizational praxis is, more attention must be paid to goals, services, the environment, and membership diversity to determine which authority structures and processes work best in that particular context.

The point is not to dichotomize authority as collective versus bureaucracy, which also constrains participation. Rather, what can be understood from the transformation of the Community Health Center is that there is a continuum between these two ideal forms of authority and that many dimensions, such as inclusivity and rules, must be taken into consideration. Center members skillfully and painfully redesigned the authority structure from collectivism to a participatory democracy to best achieve the organization's social change goal of delivery of politicized health care to all women and their loved ones.

Feminism, in its many guises, is fundamentally about the pursuit of social change. Within the realm of feminist organizational praxis, feminists must evaluate how the ways in which things are done advance an agenda for change. This is the fundamental lesson to be drawn from the Community Health Center: Social change (in this case feminist) praxis can occur within service organizations; it is not limited to protest movements and activist organizations. The center demonstrated the importance of reflexivity and creativity rather than getting locked into a dogmatic stance. In the process, the social change goal transformed from cultivating a socialist–feminist identity to enhancing diversity and inclusivity. Previously, collective governance was a primary expression of revolutionary politics. Now, the revolutionary stance rests on the explicit commitment to and execution of multicultural ideals. The center illustrated that this commitment can be achieved both within the organization and through linkages with a variety of community groups.

Given contemporary race and class relations in our society, this means of social change seems to offer great potential for radical transformation. What most threatens the status quo is oppressed groups learning to work in concert. That is the model offered by the Community Health Center.

REFERENCES

Ahrens, L. (1980). Battered women's refuge: Feminist cooperatives vs. social service institutions. In J. Ecklein (Ed.), *Community organizers* (pp. 194–201). New York: John Wiley & Sons.

Baker, A. (1986). The problem of authority in radical movement groups: A case study of lesbian–feminist organization. In T. Heller, J. Van Til, & L. Zurcher (Eds.), *Leaders and followers: Challenges for the future* (pp. 135–155). Greenwich, CT: JAI Press.

Brandwein, R. (1981). Toward the feminization of community and organization practice. *Social Development Issues, 5,* 180–193.

Brandwein, R. (1987). Women and community organization. In D. S. Burden & N. Gottlieb (Eds.), *The woman client* (pp. 111–125). New York: Tavistock.

Denzin, N. K. (1989). *The research act: A theoretical introduction to sociological methods.* Englewood Cliffs, NJ: Prentice Hall.

Ferguson, K. (1984). *The feminist case against bureaucracy.* Philadelphia: Temple University Press.

Ferraro, K. (1983). Negotiating trouble in a battered women's shelter. *Urban Life, 12,* 287–306.

Freeman, J. (1973). Tyranny of structurelessness. In A. Koedt, E. LeVine, & A. Rapone (Eds.), *Radical feminism* (pp. 285–299). New York: Quadrangle Books.

Gould, M. (1979). When women create organizations: The ideological imperatives of feminism. In D. Dunkerly & G. Salaman (Eds.), *The international yearbook of organizational studies* (pp. 237–252). London: Routledge & Kegan Paul.

Harding, S. (1987). Introduction: Is there a feminist method? In S. Harding (Ed.), *Feminism and methodology* (pp. 1–14). Bloomington: Indiana University Press.

Harvey, M. R. (1985). *Exemplary rape crisis programs: A cross-site analysis and case studies* (DHHS Publication No. ADM 85–1423). Rockville, MD: National Institute of Mental Health.

Hyde, C. A. (1989). A feminist model for macro practice. *Administration in Social Work, 13,* 145–182.

Hyde, C. A. (1991). *Did the New Right radicalize the women's movement? A study of change in feminist social movement organizations, 1977–1987.* Unpublished doctoral dissertation, University of Michigan, Ann Arbor.

Hyde, C. A. (1992). The ideational system of social movement agencies: An examination of feminist health centers. In Y. Hasenfeld (Ed.), *Human services as complex organizations* (pp. 121–144). Newbury Park, CA: Sage Publications.

Hyde, C. A. (1993). Reflections on a journey: A research story. In C. K. Riessman (Ed.), *Qualitative methods in social work* (pp. 169–189). Newbury Park, CA: Sage Publications.

Katz, J. (1983). A theory of qualitative methodology: The social system of analytical fieldwork. In R. M. Emerson (Ed.), *Contemporary field research: A collection of readings* (pp. 127–148). Boston: Little, Brown.

Martin, P. Y. (1987). A commentary on "The feminist case against bureaucracy" by Kathy Ferguson. *Women's Studies International Forum, 10,* 543–548.

Martin, P. Y. (1990). Rethinking feminist organizations. *Gender & Society, 4,* 182–206.

Murray, S. (1988). The unhappy marriage of theory and practice: An analysis of a battered women's shelter. *NWSA Journal, 1,* 75–92.

Riger, S. (1984). Vehicles for empowerment: The case of feminist movement organizations. *Prevention in Human Services, 3,* 19–43.

Rodriquez, N. (1988). Transcending bureaucracy: Feminist politics at a shelter for battered women. *Gender & Society, 2,* 214–227.

Rothschild, J., & Whitt, J. A. (1986). *The cooperative workplace: Potentials and dilemmas of organizational democracy and participation.* Cambridge, MA: Cambridge University Press.

Weil, M. (1986). Women, community and organizing. In N. Van Den Bergh & L. Cooper (Eds.), *Feminist visions of social work* (pp. 187–210). Silver Spring, MD: National Association of Social Workers.

Fields of Practice

6

The World of Work

Sheila H. Akabas

Whatever women do, they must do twice as well as men to be thought half as good. Fortunately, this is not difficult.

—Anonymous

Once made equal to man, woman becomes his superior.

—Socrates

We live in a male-oriented society, one organized by men to reflect their interests and their way of doing things. Nowhere is this more apparent than in the world of work. There are more women heading nations of the world than Fortune 500 companies, of which Katherine Graham of the *Washington Post* stands as the sole representative. It seems so obvious, once stated, that it is surprising how few of us, myself included, have a full grasp of the situation. Its very enunciation takes us by surprise. The truth is, however, that for a very long time women in the world of work have accepted men's definition of good practice and have tried to emulate it. The result has been success for a few and failure for many because a male model denies some of the basic talents and contributions of women. Women may not always be as competitive, aggressive, and rational as men, but rarely are women credited for being as collaborative, communicative, and intuitive as they are. In the process of mirroring males, women lose their self-identity, and their achievements become watered-down masculine imitations (Loden, 1985). How can women be expected to perform their best when they are busy denying their best?

It is the hypothesis here that in most work settings, including social agencies, women are well-equipped to provide leadership (Haynes, 1989). However, they have not been allowed to do so despite almost three decades of affirmative action legislation. This lack of fulfillment is an appropriate social work concern in both the policy and direct practice realms. The causes are multiple and complex. Not only do the well-recognized glass ceilings exist, but also glass walls as well, which ghettoize women and people of color into a space that limits their contributions and allows the world of work to do business as usual while denying the need for family-attentive work policies, demeaning the value of alternative contributions and harassing the people who make them, and rejecting the empowerment of working people. As a result, the world of work and its participants, both men and women, miss the productivity gains and personal satisfactions inherent in celebrating differences and mobilizing the commitment of all employees in the workplace in the interest of effective problem solving and profitable and efficient organizational activity (Akabas & Gates, 1993).

Recent developments make these losses untenable. The economic environment, with corporations becoming meaner and leaner in the face of global competition, makes maximum productivity necessary. Corporations can no longer afford to ignore the potential benefit from the fact that women may work differently, but as well or better, than men (Gilligan, 1982). The increasing diversity of the workforce (Thomas, 1991) requires a flexible response from corporate management that is more accustomed to tight control than to participative teamwork. The challenge facing the world of work is to organize the workplace so that it falls in line with feminist principles. Such a workplace harnesses the benefits of diversity and provides opportunities for empowerment to achieve both greater productivity and better service delivery.

OPPORTUNITIES PRESENTED BY A CHANGING WORKPLACE

This chapter explores that challenge in the context of the modern world of work and the projected changes in it. The discussion examines the present state of women in the workplace, followed by a historical overview of social services in that arena. It evaluates whether women's needs are met adequately by the existing service delivery system and considers the ways social work services might be delivered in the world of work if services reflected the needs of women and if a feminist approach informed the actions of providers. A case example reflects a feminist approach to the resolution of workplace problems. The chapter concludes with recommendations for social work strategies for the future.

This chapter is a plea for change. Economists have always identified the fact that the output of a society is maximized when everyone is contributing at the level of his or her marginal productivity. The way the world of work is currently organized does not allow that maximum output to be achieved. Furthermore, new conditions in the world of work—increasing labor force diversity, declining employee benefits, work and family demands that are out of sync, expanding global competition, and a growing concern for quality while preserving a focus on quantity—promise even greater pressure for a more responsive workplace. In the need for change, the agendas of social work and corporate management have much in common. Social work seeks to influence the structure and organization of the world of work so there is greater accommodation between the worker and the work environment. Managers know from consistent research findings that this is the road to increased productivity. Consider the parallels in the following examples.

Before World War II, when jobs could be broken down to their smallest tasks and work was machine paced, scientific management held sway, and employees were treated as interchangeable parts. Today's jobs, however, demand workers who are hired for their knowledge and whose jobs are often ambiguous. To perform these jobs successfully requires problem-solving skills and authority equal to responsibility. Productive workers are those who are committed to their work because they are empowered to participate in the work process (Ouchi, 1981).

Before World War II the majority of the labor force was male, white, young, and physically hardy. They constituted the group that had to be satisfied. All others were condemned to "3D" jobs—dull, dirty, and demeaning—and their supply was sufficient so that their needs could be ignored because they could be replaced easily. Today's labor force is diverse, including large numbers of women, people of color, people with disabilities, and older workers (Johnston, 1987). Employers seeking to recruit the best and the brightest, as any employer interested in maximizing efficiency must do, will have to dig into that diverse pool and meet its needs for growth, connectedness, and change.

Before World War II work demands and family needs were consistent. Husbands and fathers went out to work and brought home as much as they could earn to support the family. Today's workers must combine the demands of work with the responsibilities of family care because most families, whether a single-parent or a dual-income family, have no one at home to care for the dependent population (Tarr-Whelan & Isebsee, 1987). Workplace policy must value and attend to family needs to attract, maintain, and ensure the most productive contribution from all members of the workforce (Akabas, 1990).

The concepts of feminist practice referred to throughout this chapter—interconnectedness, appreciation of diversity, and reflection of personal needs in policy formation—are the same fundamental concepts that guide an efficient and productive 21st-century workplace. The gap between this understanding and actual practice reflects how hard it is for management, both corporate and social agency management, to release its tight control over managerial responsibilities. Yet we contend that social workers in the workplace, including the social agency, who seek to establish the principles of feminist practice have important reality forces on their side.

Both the workplace and social services delivery systems need the kind of change that would help the workplace achieve the full contribution of women and other excluded groups—the kind of change that is associated with feminist practice principles (Van Den Bergh & Cooper, 1987). We will all be better off economically, socially, and psychologically when the contributions of each person can be maximized, when workers are empowered to participate in meeting their own and each others' needs. In short, white men have as much to gain as women and people of color from a solution that optimizes the creative potential of a diverse workforce and a responsive social services delivery system. Social workers in the world of work are in an ideal position to help achieve the changes needed.

WOMEN AND THE WORLD OF WORK: THE PRESENT SITUATION

Women have always worked harder and longer hours than men, but there has been a division in assignment between men and women. Women usually were slotted to produce subsistence so that the males could hunt (a much less secure source of food than gathering) or, more recently, create and organize production (Leghorn & Parker, 1981). Only women's entry into the paid world of work in significant proportions is a recent phenomenon. Twenty-eight percent of women 14 years of age and older were in the labor force in 1940, compared with 84 percent of all men 14 or older. The labor force participation of women was largely restricted to those "unfortunate" few who had no man able to support them: single, widowed, and divorced women.

By 1991, however, after steady evolution since World War II, participation rates had changed significantly. Of all noninstitutionalized civilians 16 years of age and older, 75 percent of the men and 57 percent of the women were working. Yet women's experience in the world of work is anything but equal (Faludi, 1991). In 1989 full-time female workers had a median weekly earning of just 68 percent of that of men (even worse than the 78 percent that African American earnings represented of white earnings the same year). The earnings gap has continued unabated even though female education had surpassed the average level of male education by 1989. A situational analysis provides a ready explanation.

Ghettoization of Jobs

Although job classifications have changed over time, making historical comparison difficult, 29 percent of all women held "clerical and kindred jobs" in 1961, compared with 7 percent of all men. Somewhat comparable numbers for 1991 found "administrative support including clerical" jobs accounting for the employment of 28 percent of all women and less than 6 percent of all men. These are the jobs that Kanter (1977) defined as "office wives," women who cater to men's bidding. Alternatively, the traditionally high-paid "craftsmen, foremen, and kindred workers" jobs provided employment to 19 percent of all men and 2 percent of all women. Observers believe that these "glass walls" provide excess labor in the clerical field, keeping those earnings low, and maintain a shortage of skilled workers in crafts, producing a high level of wages there (Brown & Pechman, 1987; U.S. Bureau of the Census, 1991).

Ghettoization begins in educational institutions where the vocational training for boys leads to jobs with higher earning potential and the training for girls leads to low-paying jobs (sometimes referred to as "sticky floor" jobs because they not only provide low starting wages and low power but also lack a career ladder of promotional opportunity). Ghettoization reflects society's norms and practices that keep women workers subordinate and poor in relation to men. Ghettoization results in findings such as those from the longitudinal Framingham heart study on cardiovascular disease. Although the prevalence of cardiovascular disease among men far exceeds the rate experienced by women, the highest incidence of cardiovascular disease has been observed in female clerical workers who have children and are married to blue-collar men. The researchers, aware that having insufficient authority to equal one's responsibility has been found to cause such disease and that others have found blue-collar men, on average, to require greater subordination from their wives than men in general, interpret the findings to prove that double subordination (on the job and at home) exacts a lethal price (Akabas, 1988).

Sexual Harassment on the Job

The volume of sexual harassment charges received by the Equal Employment Opportunity Commission nearly doubled in the 1980s (Faludi, 1991). Anita Hill confirmed what most women knew—that they were being sexually harassed at the workplace. Since she has come forward, all polls have confirmed the widespread existence of harassment on the job (estimated at one out of every three employed women) and that most women remain silent, fearing job loss, lacking channels through which to register complaints, and knowing they would be ostracized and intimidated even further if they objected. Hostile climates are everywhere in the workplace.

Discrimination in Traditional Male Fields

Examples abound. It is rumored that when the military academies were ordered to accept women in 1975, one commander was asked what change he thought this would precipitate. He responded, "Nothing will change around here except the plumbing." For the Navy, at least, that was largely true until the unprecedented action in 1992 of ordering the entire Navy to "stand down," meaning it was taken out of service, to receive a day of training on sexual harassment. Nor is the social work profession exempt from criticism. In 1980 Chernesky noted, "Data have consistently confirmed that male social workers dominate the administrative positions, despite the fact that two-thirds of the members of the social work profession are women" (pp. 241–242). The situation remained unchanged years later (Dressel, 1992), but it must change—not merely for the sake of women but for the sake of efficient and responsive service delivery. Integrated services that build on the connections between people, typical of a feminist approach, can fulfill the promise of that improvement.

Lack of Provision for Caregiving

In a study of establishments with 10 or more employees in 1988, the *BLS Report on Employer Child Care Practices* (U.S. Bureau of Labor Statistics, 1988) found that only 11 percent provided any child care benefits or services, including employer-sponsored day care, assistance with child care expenses, child care information and referral services, and counseling for family-related issues. Furthermore, another Bureau of Labor Statistics study reporting on employee benefits in medium and large firms (firms with 100 or more workers) found that in 1989 only 3 percent provided paid maternity leave (U.S. Bureau of Labor Statistics, 1989). This was true even though more than half the mothers of children under six are in the workplace and it is universally understood that for them, and all parents, work and family pressures are stressful and debilitating (Akabas, 1984, 1990).

Patriarchal ideologies that see women as nurturers and men as providers have determined that caretaking is of little value. Confirming the cultural embeddedness of this idea, Hunt (1988) noted, "The present attitudes of society are such that. . . these [caring] responsibilities are almost automatically expected to belong to women. Seldom, if ever, in quantitative surveys about employment are working men asked about the care of their children or whether they have to look after sick or elderly people" (p. 151). Women have been motivated to perform this unpaid work, sometimes out of their own desires, but often because others have promoted women's guilt by identifying this work as "unfulfilled family responsibilities." This is usually a ploy used by political forces to avoid paying for (and therefore valuing) caregiving, a reflection that the society has been organized by men to promote the importance of their own contribution.

Rewarding a Male Model of Good Practice
Under the headline, "Bedside Manners Improve as More Women Enter Medicine," Angier (1992) reported in the *New York Times* that "a number of studies have found that female physicians spend significantly more time with each patient than do men. . . women interrupt their patients much less often than do men." The women are better listeners and therefore are probably better diagnosticians. This comes as news not because it is new, but because the accomplishments of women have gone relatively unnoticed. Some women, for example, Florence Nightingale, have even had to fight to make any contribution (Forster, 1984).

HISTORY AS PERSPECTIVE
The delivery of social work services in the workplace has not challenged this mainstream commitment. Early interventions that resembled social work services occurred in the 1800s as the increasing demand for mill hands caused manufacturers to recruit, in rural areas, young women who were unaccustomed to factory life. Welfare secretaries, usually women, were hired by male managers to continue the "socialization" of these young women (Popple, 1981). No similar services were deemed necessary for men. A feminist understanding of these "welfare" services would recognize that they promoted the oppression of women. Under the guise of helping them

adjust to work, the young women were "counseled" by other women to be compliant factory hands. As Kravetz (1992) stated, "Cultural ideology about women shapes women's reality and maintains female subordination by men" (p. 322).

A major moment for social work in the workplace occurred during World War II when women made up a majority of the workforce (with 10 million men in arms). Social workers were called on to arrange for day care and other family services to enable women to work unencumbered by family responsibilities. Despite the profession's commitment to social change and direct service, no evidence exists that this opportunity was fashioned into any effort to restructure the workplace in more lasting ways so that women could maintain their work roles after demobilization. The culturally derived definition that a married woman's place was in the home quickly returned and was supported by mainstream social work services once women's labor was no longer vital to industry.

Recent expansion of social work services in the world of work is represented by the geometric growth of employee assistance programs (EAPs) and their union parallel, membership assistance programs (MAPs). Despite initial roots in alcohol problems, the EAPs and MAPs of today often have a broad mission that includes an array of preventive and rehabilitative services to individuals and sometimes groups. Their mandate reflects, in part, management's increasing awareness that only a committed labor force can be sufficiently productive to allow U.S. industry to compete in a global economy. Current research confirms that commitment comes from consideration of workers' diverse needs and empowerment to allow them to pursue their abilities and interests (Ouchi, 1981; Peters & Waterman, 1982).

It is not sufficient to have social workers in the world of work, however. Once there, they need to challenge the workplace structures in the interest of meeting the needs of women workers and others who have been denied equal opportunity and attention. Sadly, social workers have been excessively cautious in response to these needs (Akabas, 1990). Although most EAP and MAP staff members might interpret their world of work experience as a basis for agreement with Gottlieb (1992) that "problems of women clients are largely determined by societal forces," the staff members have not moved to fulfill Gottlieb's vision that "services may be improved when women clients and women social workers can both act, with an increased sense of personal power, on their awareness of the political analysis of their circumstances" (p. 301).

FEMINIST APPROACH TO SOCIAL SERVICES
DELIVERY IN THE WORKPLACE

In a world where competition is the supreme value and everyone is struggling to reach the top, people are isolated from one another, usually in an hierarchical organizational structure that is focused on profit at all cost. This traditional male model for an organization makes it difficult to connect with other persons, care about their problems, value their diversity, organize for mutual support, evolve team activities, share information and value process, see power as more than a zero sum game, or explore one's personal problems and tease out their political implications. This model no longer meets the management needs of modern organizations.

However, feminist theory, concepts, and values suggest a different model. The impact of the "different voice" that Gilligan (1982) discerned among women is that they organize structures like a web, with information and communication spreading in all directions. In this ecological system everyone's power increases. Problem solving takes place in an environment that values diversity and where mutual respect breeds team-based working relationships that are characterized by inclusiveness and interconnectedness. The sharing that is possible in such a setting allows personal, private experiences to become grist for political action and public policy decisions.

In light of the needs of all workers and of the realities that confront today's management, the time is appropriate for occupational social workers to throw caution to the wind and, guided by feminist concepts, provide leadership to managers on the policy and practice level. It would be well for us to start with social agency settings. They are workplaces, but too often the needs of the workers have low priority in relation to those of the clients. Like workers everywhere, social workers' best work depends on having their needs satisfied. The time has arrived to revamp the personnel policies of social agencies so they respond to workers' needs for leave time, flexible schedules, and benefits that cover child and elder care. Job sharing might be offered to those with significant family responsibilities (Olmsted & Smith, 1985). These changes would demonstrate that management cares and is aware of the connections between work and other aspects of employees' lives.

Recruitment policies must seek out differences and agencies must help employees make connections with each other that are respectful of those differences. When new workers are added to a department, coworkers should be involved in the selection. Values that support client self-determination should be reflected in employee empowerment through more opportunities for teamwork and participative management. Performance appraisal should be a two-way process. Certainly, supervisors should evaluate their staff, but so, too, should staff provide feedback to their supervisors. By modeling exemplary managerial behavior, social agencies can achieve credibility for their advocacy for social policy changes in the larger community to achieve family leave without job loss and to increase funding and enforcement for equal opportunity initiatives as provided in Title VII of the Civil Rights Act of 1963, the Age Discrimination in Employment Act of 1967, and the Americans With Disabilities Act of 1990. Pressing for legislatively ensured conditions is vital. Elias and Purcell (1988) noted that "legislation can undermine the mechanisms which perpetuate patterns of gender inequality on two levels: it can improve women's *access* to the labour market and occupational opportunities, and it can seek to ensure the equal treatment of women and men *in* employment" (p. 218).

As suggested earlier, social workers in the world of work can derive support for their practice in the similarities between the objectives of management and of feminist principles. Management is anxious to maintain the functional capacity of its employees, and social work is interested in maintaining the functional ability of its clients. Working with an employed population, professionals have consumers with power. In trade union settings, social workers employed by the MAPs are actually employees of their clients! Services are universal because system membership—employee or union status—establishes eligibility. Because clients have jobs, prevention and early intervention is possible.

Direct service can deal with issues that surface within the functional community of work such as sexual harassment, work and family conflict, and perceived discrimination concerning promotions, issues that are of concern to working women and that can be redressed at work. Mutual aid is a way of life among coworkers, particularly in trade union settings where the nature of the organization hinges on peer cohesion. Self-help support groups can be, and have been, organized effectively around presenting problems like family substance abuse or the need for eldercare or to enhance attention to gender or ethnic networks.

Operating under either corporate or union auspices that have the resources to allocate to meeting client needs and the power to set policy, occupational social workers are well-situated to influence community practice. By their selection of services to which they refer, for example, they can influence service delivery patterns. Many alcoholism programs require a 28-day inpatient period, although nothing in existing research substantiates the belief that this model is preferable over other options. For women with children, such programs are particularly undesirable. An occupational social worker who makes numerous treatment referrals can influence inpatient alcoholism service to provide facilities to accommodate families or to provide day hospital services, options more friendly to women as clients, and probably better for all consumers. Feminist principles would also suggest advocacy in relation to benefit plans. The provision for multiple options that would be responsive to the varying needs of diverse populations would represent the fulfillment of feminist principles.

Occupational social workers might organize the same power to exert political influence on the policy level. Support from corporations and unions would certainly move the government, at all jurisdictions, to provide more resources for family-friendly day care arrangements. We all know it is not work itself but the problems work presents, such as balancing work and family demands, that make work difficult for women (Firth-Cozens & West, 1991). As Vagero (1992) confirmed, not only is the health of working women better than that of those who stay at home, but women's health improves after entry into the workplace.

Feminist concepts would expect those in the world of work to reach out more globally to embrace the needs within the community. Expressions of concern from parties in the world of work might increase attention to inadequate welfare payments that ensure that so many women and children live in poverty. Furthermore, as major payers, corporations and unions can demand an end to the dichotomous thinking that explores men's health problems and assumes that the solutions are equally relevant to women. Feminist thinking can identify that health care for women can and should be improved by specific attention to women's needs. Management support would reflect recognition that attending to women's health needs could help reduce or at least contain health care costs by overcoming the present level of ignorance and inattention concerning the way in which disease is connected to gender. In short, occupational social workers, acting on feminist principles, can make a good case to their industrial auspices for swinging their power toward improving the status of women in society through the world of work.

Case Example: New York City Fire Department

The author and colleagues were involved in an extraordinary opportunity within the New York City Fire Department to test a systemic feminist approach to organizational problem solving. To become a firefighter, one must pass a written exam and a physical endurance test. Appointees are called from a list ordered by applicants' scores on the qualifying tests. As of 1980, no woman had ever passed. In the early 1980s a group of women who had failed to qualify empowered themselves. They joined together and brought suit, claiming that the physical examination was not related to the essential functions of the job, thereby discriminating against them in violation of Title VII of the Civil Rights Act of 1964. The federal court found in their favor and ordered the department to develop and give an examination more reflective of job demands to all those women who were part of the class action suit. Forty-two women who passed the new examination and still wished to become firefighters were appointed. They were strong, determined, and of varied backgrounds, including single and married women, mothers, women of color, straight and lesbian women, high school graduates, women with master's degrees, and a lawyer. Their reasons for wanting to be firefighters were as varied as they were: It was a good job for a mother (providing five free days following two 24-hour shifts), it was a well-paid job for a high school graduate, and it was part of a crusade for women's rights. These and other reasons resembled those that motivated the department's 11,000 uniformed men to become firefighters.

Firefighter training depends heavily on mentoring. The women found no mentors. The equipment, from helmets to boots, was all designed for men and invariably was too big for the women. The training techniques stressed upper body strength (a male model) and ignored the power of the hips and lower body more typical of women's strength. The women were assigned, singly, to houses and had no support system available. The culture of the uniformed service closed ranks around its determination to rid the department of these "unacceptable recruits." From pornographic pictures on the walls to unsolicited visits by funeral salespeople, from beds filled with flour to cut tires, the climate was hostile. The women experienced stress and showed symptoms of alcoholism and depression.

Finally, a slashing incident occurred between a male and a female firefighter. The women returned to the courts, to the embarrassment of the city and the department's administration. It was then that my colleagues and I were asked by the New York City Fire Department "to develop training to help the men and women accept each other." We rejected that formulation and requested a six-month period to study the situation and design and implement a program that would improve the workplace climate for all firefighters. Anxious for more-immediate solutions, the department rejected the suggestion. Six months later the commissioner returned and granted us a mandate (Akabas, Grube, & Krauskopf, 1989).

A team was organized. Following feminist principles, we spread out to gather information. Our first step was to carry out a needs assessment, which included a survey of firefighters, 24-hour visits to firehouses, and focus group and individual interviews to determine attitudes and behavior. The findings indicated that turmoil had prevailed ever since the 42 women joined the service. The organizational culture was that of a macho fraternity, with great devotion among the men, particularly toward their housemates. Their reputation for courage was legendary and well deserved, but their ability to accept diversity barely covered the 10 percent of the "brotherhood" that was white but Protestant rather than Catholic, a characteristic of 90 percent of the members of the service. There was no acceptance in the culture for women in the workplace and hardly more for men of color. The classic myths about women were ascribed to by the men, in addition to one that defined women as incompetent to pass the test that each male firefighter had passed. In fact, numerous tests had been given over the years, and the women's test was just one more in the series.

It was clear to the team that the women would never be accepted into the existing culture, although the administration (new since the initial court case) was supportive of their right to be in the department. A change in culture became the goal. Recommendations for an intervention plan were guided by principles and concepts of feminist practice. What the department really needed was a way to appreciate diversity in its labor force and to extend its culture of connectedness to the diverse members of the uniformed force. For example, during the survey of response to women, several gay male firefighters called anonymously to describe their fear of exposure and to urge the team to undertake an effort to open the minds of their coworkers to other kinds of diversity.

The effort sought to support and empower the women who were currently firefighters while designing structures, procedures, and practices that would ensure a steady stream of new women into the department. We were guided by an understanding that the men were seriously threatened by the ability of women to do what the men had previously believed to be work that only a man could do. The men needed support and appreciation if they were to be motivated to reduce the tension within most houses that had women.

We were guided as well by an understanding that the culture needed to change to reflect a feminist understanding of how systems operate. Instead of exclusiveness, the department needed to embrace the contributions possible from a diverse membership, to become inclusive and foster interconnections between the old-timers and the newcomers. The feminist concept of caring, which included the neighborhood and community, offered a different vision than the intimacy of the male firefighters who saw their exclusive group as "us" and everyone else, including the women, as "them." The reward for inclusiveness would be stronger teams. Another reward would be greater support from the neighbors who sometimes viewed the firefighters as part of the power elite that was responsible for their disadvantaged condition and so paid them back by setting off false alarms and throwing stones at working firefighters.

It was necessary to dispel the notion that the acceptance of the women was an individual, personal decision for department personnel. In keeping with feminist theory, the personal had to be identified as political. The firefighters had to recognize that affirmative action was not a personal cause of the women but rather a public policy issue that society accepted and that the department was required to put into practice.

These new directions were made more difficult because the service was organized along strictly hierarchical lines rather than according to the "webs of inclusion" that Helgesen (1990) identified as typical of the way women relate to managerial assignment. The feminist concepts of attention to process as well as outcome and to sharing information that would improve communication among the parties helped to overcome the authoritarian quality of the setting and made cooperation feasible.

More than 30 complex recommendations were made to, and accepted by, the administration. They ranged from direct service issues to structural changes in the assignment of officers. For example, one recommendation was that a female counselor be available to the women because all members of the counseling unit were former male firefighters who were tied to the organizational culture and who lacked understanding of the way that culture made the women "sick." Recommended, as well, were physical plant and equipment changes to upgrade equipment to the best available, which was likely to be lighter and more manageable for all firefighters but of particular value to women. An ecological outlook helped clarify the role of physical space in determining the women's isolation. A structural suggestion was that the department take over maintenance and repair of firehouses. Previously, firefighters had performed that work using department funds. The result was that men felt the kind of ownership of the houses that allowed them to feel justified in barring the women.

The unequivocal support from the top administration needed to be communicated through the ranks in writing and in action. We suggested new performance appraisal standards for officers that would reward those who managed diversity well. Recognizing that the personal was political, the recommendation was made to replace the informal system, which depended on personal favors and empowered extremists, with a few specific, enforceable, and enforced rules. Most obvious was the need for establishing clear expectations concerning workplace behavior and immediate sanction for violators. This represented a complete change in style for departmental operations, directing attention to the commitment to inclusiveness.

To achieve networking and minimize the isolation women experienced, assignment of more than one woman to a house was suggested. Support systems for women, for officers of women, and for men in houses with women were established to help these key actors gain a sense of interconnectedness and develop new definitions of workplace behavior and new skills, such as mentoring and negotiating for officers, constructive confrontation for men, and assertiveness for women. A crisis team of a social worker, an officer, and a training specialist was formed. The mechanism was designed to demonstrate that the system cared about everyone and to troubleshoot situations before they became adversarial. Process was promoted as an end to a culture that focused only on outcome: Learn the task, put out the fire, save the life, and return the truck to the house. Furthermore, all recruitment advertisements, displays at the fire museum, and departmental publicity were planned to include women as part of the presentation, suggesting that diversity was valued. Extensive additions were made to all departmental training programs for new firefighters, new officers, and promotional upgrades to include a message of mutual respect (and warnings of the price for violation). In addition, in an attempt to redefine reality, specific training in diversity acceptance was carried out in each of the several hundred firehouses in the city.

In short, a review of the situation provided evidence of an inhospitable climate for people within the department. A program guided by feminist principles and goals of empowerment, mutual respect, acceptance of diversity, and connectedness of all members was designed. It moved to transform the departmental culture to make firefighting more congenial for the women and others who served, and more attractive to all, including women, who might join in the future. This piece of practice was possible because the social workers rejected the initial mandate "to help the women adjust to the fire department" and encouraged, albeit with a willing administration, undertaking of a feminist analysis, which allowed bolder steps to improve the workplace climate to follow.

By the late 1980s, significant progress was being made. A formal committee headed by the commissioner was established to monitor the effort. Plumbing contracts had been let because the plumbing in firehouses had not changed with the admission of women. However, the election of a new mayor resulted in the appointment of a less-committed fire commissioner, and the program was abandoned. The women once again returned to the courts to seek protection. The more than three years that feminist principles held sway in the operation of the department was the only time since women entered the New York City Fire Department that a court case was not initiated. Could there be a better recommendation for a feminist approach to problem solving in the world of work?

Another example of feminist practice in the world of work occurred under the leadership of the social workers who direct the MAPs in the unions of New York City. Many cases of spouse abuse were being identified. Because they were workers, the abused women and their children were not entitled to public services because most of those services in New York are reserved for welfare clients. The social services directors in unions developed a network among the union membership in which women were empowered to connect with and help other women in a sisterhood of problem solving. Other social agencies have joined this effort in a massive response from the work community opposing violence against women and supporting the design of safehouse alternatives.

STRATEGIES FOR THE FUTURE

In both situations, the fact that the client population was employed provided a base of strength from which to operate. Feminist principles became the organizing theme for harnessing the resources and power of the world of work to resolve a systemic problem that had a long history and no ready solution. Management and union auspices contributed significantly to the positive outcome by adopting strategies typical of feminist practice: empowering employees, sharing information, building teams, valuing diversity, and encouraging community.

A new conceptualization is necessary, however, if social workers in the workplace are to influence both their own practice and the systemic conditions of the world of work in the interest of women and their needs. It is insufficient to conclude that to achieve the best practice that practice must be informed by feminist values. Each practitioner must accept a responsibility for advocacy on an individual, organizational, and community level. Such action departs from the usual behavior of social workers in the workplace. We have tended to define our clients as both the individual and the organization, and this has provided a rationale for professional compromises in the pursuit of client advocacy. The reasoning proceeds that the organization will not accept a massive cultural change at this time. If we withdraw, we have no power at all. It is better to accept the organization's definition of our boundaries and to try to serve individual clients and to influence the system within those boundaries.

The result has been timidity, or what Stolz (1985) described as a "captive mentality" rather than a "master mentality." The former comes from "social conditioning," whereas the latter depends on an "inner voice" or perhaps that "different voice" that tells women they deserve more and are being treated unjustly. It is time for social workers in the workplace to respond to that inner voice. When a worker comes forward with a story of harassment, the usual response might be to help the client develop the skill to handle the harasser. Feminist theory would classify this as unacceptable. Assisting a client to develop skills to handle a harasser tends to support ongoing harassment by continuing as personal what is really a public issue. Rather, the EAP counselor receiving such a complaint might help the employee consider whether to lodge an Equal Employment Opportunity complaint and assist in the preparation and support of that complaint if the client decides to pursue such a process. Or, aware that several such incidents have occurred, a counselor could act on a feminist understanding that there is a concern for the wider community. With permission from each harassed employee, the social worker can help them form a self-help group to offer support for advocacy to change organizational policy and behavior.

Both these responses involve the social worker in advocacy that, at first glance, appears to attack the organization that employs her. But another interpretation is possible. Earlier, a case was made for the parallel between feminist and organizational interests in which the changing world of work increasingly depends on the commitment and productivity of its employees. Building a high-performance environment requires achieving team participation, respecting diversity, ensuring mutual caring, and accomplishing interconnectedness. These world of work strategies are indistinguishable from the prescription that would derive from feminist theory. Here we have a behavioral example. An organization in which harassment is not redressed is one that is sabotaging its own best interest. The harassed employee cannot maximize her productivity nor will others who are aware of the problem. The social worker who "negotiates" the continuation of harassment both denies feminist principles and undermines the organization's ability to maximize its own long-term productivity.

Over the short term, however, the "messenger" may be at risk. It is essential, therefore, that we use ourselves professionally to advocate in our communities for the kind of feminist policies and behavior we wish to establish in our workplaces. Community organizing can reach the political powers, the corporate managers, and the union leadership with information concerning the needs of women and of all workers for safe, family-sensitive workplaces in which the policies and procedures empower workers to participate and to influence the system. The effective occupational social worker needs to help employers, unions, and those who formulate public policy to recognize and facilitate responses to specific needs in such a way that action will carry messages of caring, connectedness, and empowerment. For example, most workplaces require advanced scheduling for vacation, making it impossible for employees to take a vacation day at random when a child is ill. An occupational social worker advocating for a responsive, caring workplace might encourage her employer, as did 3M in Minneapolis, to allow one-third of all vacation days to be taken without advance notice. Working parents can then be at home with ill children. Or, an occupational social worker can help an employer to encourage employee connectedness to community by recommending the establishment of a company policy that designates, as Levi Strauss does, its corporate philanthropic donations to those charities at which its employees volunteer.

Other work settings can be encouraged to serve as vehicles for support and empowerment for employees at points of major change in their lives. Facilitating networks among employees who feel different from the majority, as the EAP staff at Polaroid did for workers with learning disorders and other disabilities, can empower the employees in the network to pursue common needs. Other empowerment strategies are exemplified by companies such as Corning, which identified that employees live in an ecological system and that the company had a responsibility to help make that system compatible with the needs of the employees. Although Corning's workplace is viewed as a "global village" where diversity is valued, the company's location in a small town in upstate New York makes it difficult for some in that diverse workforce to find the services they require. To improve the environmental fit for its employees, Corning financed a barber who specialized in services to African Americans to establish a shop in town.

In each example detailed in this chapter, the actions taken fit both feminist principles and good business strategies, proving that it is possible to accommodate both. We Americans are, at heart, a decent people. It may take a while, but I have no question that the world of work will hear and respond to a feminist agenda that is presented appropriately and that is tied in to that world's primary interest of productive employees maximizing their contributions to the enterprise. It is an idea whose time has come.

REFERENCES

Age Discrimination in Employment Act of 1967, P.L. 90-202, 81 Stat. 602.

Akabas, S. H. (1984). Workers are parents, too. *Child Welfare, 63,* 387–399.

Akabas, S. H. (1988). Women, work and mental health. *Journal of Primary Prevention, 9,* 130–140.

Akabas, S. H. (1990). Essay: Reconciling the demands of work with the needs of families. *Families in Society, 71*(6), 366–371.

Akabas, S. H., & Gates, L. B. (1993). Work force diversity. In J. Klein & J. Miller (Eds.), *The American edge* (pp. 113–135). New York: McGraw-Hill.

Akabas, S. H., Grube, B., & Krauskopf, M. (1989, August). Gender integration and sexual harassment: A role for EAPs. *Employee Assistance, 2*(1), 8–15.

Americans With Disabilities Act of 1990, P.L. 101-336, 42 USCS 12101.

Angier, N. (1992, June 21). Bedside manners improve as more women enter medicine. *New York Times,* section 4, p. 18.

Brown, C., & Pechman, J. A. (Eds.). (1987). *Gender in the workplace.* Washington, DC: Brookings Institution.

Chernesky, R. (1980). Women administrators in social work. In E. Norman & A. Mancuso (Eds.), *Women's issues and social work practice* (pp. 241–262). Itasca, IL: F. E. Peacock.

Dressel, P. L. (1992). Patriarchy and social welfare work. In Y. Hasenfeld (Ed.), *Human services as complex organizations* (pp. 205–223). Newbury Park, CA: Sage Publications.

Elias, P., & Purcell, K. (1988). Women and paid work: Prospects for equality. In A. Hunt (Ed.), *Women and paid work* (pp. 196–221). London: Macmillan.

Faludi, S. (1991). *Backlash: The undeclared war against American Women.* New York: Crown.

Firth-Cozens, J., & West, M. A. (Eds.). (1991). *Women at work.* Philadelphia: Open University Press.

Forster, M. (1984). *Significant sisters: The grass roots of active feminism.* New York: Oxford University Press.

Gilligan, C. (1982). *In a different voice.* Cambridge, MA: Harvard University Press.

Gottlieb, N. (1992). Empowerment, political analyses, and services for women. In Y. Hasenfeld (Ed.), *Human services as complex organizations* (pp. 301–319). Newbury Park, CA: Sage Publications.

Haynes, K. S. (1989). *Women managers in human services.* New York: Springer.

Helgesen, S. (1990). *The female advantage.* New York: Doubleday Currency.

Hunt, A. (1988). The effects of caring for the elderly and infirm on women's employment. In A. Hunt (Ed.), *Women and paid work* (pp. 150–172). London: Macmillan.

Johnston, W. B. (1987). *Workforce 2000.* Indianapolis: Hudson Institute.

Kanter, R. M. (1977). *Men and women of the corporation.* New York: Basic Books.

Kravetz, D. (1992). Social work practice with women. In A. T. Morales & B. W. Sheafor (Eds.), *Social work: A profession of many faces* (6th ed., pp. 317–345). Boston: Allyn & Bacon.

Leghorn, L., & Parker, K. (1981). *Woman's worth.* Boston: Routledge & Kegan Paul.

Loden, M. (1985). *Feminine leadership or how to succeed in business without being one of the boys.* New York: Times Books.

Olmsted, B., & Smith, S. (1985). *The job sharing handbook.* Berkeley, CA: Ten Speed Press.

Ouchi, W. (1981). *Theory z.* Reading, MA: Addison-Wesley.

Peters, T. J., & Waterman, R. H. (1982). *In search of excellence: Lessons from America's best-run companies.* New York: Harper & Row.

Popple, P. R. (1981). Social work practice in business and industry, 1875–1930. *Social Service Review, 55*(2), 257–268.

Stolz, B. A. (1985). *Still struggling: America's low-income working women confronting the 1980s.* Lexington, MA: D. C. Heath.

Tarr-Whelan, L., & Isebsee, L. C. (Eds.). (1987). *The women's economic justice agenda.* Washington, DC: National Center for Policy Alternatives.

Thomas, R. R., Jr. (1991). *Beyond race and gender.* New York: AMACOM.

Title VII of the Civil Rights Act of 1963, 42 U.S.C. 2000E.

Title VII of the Civil Rights Act of 1964, P.L. 88-352, 78 Stat. 241.

U.S. Bureau of Labor Statistics. (1988, January). *BLS report on employer child care practices.* Washington, DC: Author.

U.S. Bureau of Labor Statistics. (1989). *Employee benefits in medium and large firms.* Washington, DC: U.S. Government Printing Office.

U.S. Bureau of the Census. (1991). *Statistical abstract of the United States.* (111th ed.). Washington, DC: Author.

Vagero, D. (1992, January). Women, work and health in Sweden. *Current Sweden,* pp. 1–8.

Van Den Bergh, N., & Cooper, L. B. (1987). Feminist social work. In A. Minahan (Ed.-in-Chief), *Encyclopedia of social work* (18th ed., Vol. 1, pp. 610–618). Silver Spring, MD: National Association of Social Workers.

7

The Place of Caring in Rural Women's Work

Emilia E. Martinez-Brawley and Paz Méndez-Bonito Zorita

In 1987 Martinez-Brawley and Durbin suggested that "the plight of the rural woman is that she occupies an even more disadvantaged position in an already disadvantaged female occupational structure" (p. 30). By all accounts, this situation still holds true in 1995. Women in rural areas are more likely than women in urban areas to rely on welfare benefits if they are heads of household, not only because pay for women is particularly low in rural areas but also because employment options are especially narrow. The demand for traditionally rural occupations in the free market for both men and women has continued to decline, so the options for paid employment are still narrow. However, from a feminist perspective that focuses on empowering women, the use of only a conventional analysis of women's economic reality may not best explain women's efforts and contributions in rural areas. The time has come to resort to a different framework of analysis that takes into account the spectrum of rural women's work, including underpaid or unpaid caring work.

It is clear that a great deal of what has been said about women's employment in rural areas is from a capitalist or free-market perspective that views work not as "any effort to satisfy want" but as "only activities which bring in a cash income" (Lewenhak, 1988, p. 15). In other words, if jobs are plentiful and well paid, the people who perform those tasks are viewed as successful or at least not occupationally deprived. This perspective, although very instrumental, might not always be empowering because it discounts unpaid work and caring work as unproductive. A free-market perspective penalizes women in general, but even more so rural women, whose survival, and that of their families and communities, depends heavily on their unremunerated care.

The prevailing framework for analysis, which totally accepts the free market as the way to measure social success and significance, is flawed. Furthermore, the free-market perspective alone might not be the most useful to guide analysis from either the social work or the feminist point of view. Collins (1986) observed the following:

> *The commonality of perspective embodied in the social worker's person-in-environment and the feminist's "personal is political" is compelling. The social work perspective necessitates movement beyond the limited either/or, psychological/sociological, inner/outer, personal/social dichotomies of the other disciplines. Social work's integrated thinking, with its ecological view of processes between the individual and the environment, is consonant with feminist thought.* (p. 216)

The ideologies of social workers and feminists support transactions that nurture individual well-being and self-determination. The free-market perspective is not enough to promote the empowerment of rural women. In a society that equates the role of worker with self-worth, rural women would certainly be at a serious disadvantage. Even if this disadvantage is only academic—for frameworks of analysis do not change reality—a different way of evaluating the position of rural women vis-à-vis the work they do might free social workers to become more effective agents of empowerment. We believe that a salient issue for women in general is the way contemporary society disregards caring work and obfuscates its contribution to the viability of communities and the workings of the free-market economy.

In this chapter we address the undervaluing of women's caring work, using the case of rural women as the unit of analysis. We also explore comparable worth and the social wage as frameworks that might better accommodate feminist and social work concerns vis-à-vis the realities of rural women.

Rural women have been empowered in their communities in many ways other than through wages. Formal and informal activities have often secured a place for those women, at least in their local societies. The equal worth and social wage perspectives might be more appropriate ways of analyzing the contributions and status of women in the country, where traditional roles are often preferred by the women themselves and where legal measures such as affirmative action, which have helped to ensure access to jobs in traditional male occupations in urban places, might not work simply because the jobs are not there. Furthermore, recent research has shown that the entry of women into many male occupations has resulted in new "resegregation" tendencies that "represent a 'one step forward and two steps back' pattern for women of our era and that the hard-fought entry into male dominated work has created the potential for new female job ghettos" that might be even less satisfying (Blum, 1991, p. 143).

In relation to rural women's work, the two traditional branches of feminism still appear to be struggling for supremacy in offering plausible alternatives. In the 1960s, liberal feminism told women that they would "be liberated when they enter[ed] the workforce on equal basis with men" (Stoper, 1991, p. 152). As Blum (1991) suggested, many women are concerned with the intrinsic job satisfaction they believe they derive from certain female-dominated professions. These women resist "the suggestion that they must change jobs to achieve higher earnings" (p. 143). On the other hand, "radical feminism. . . told women that they could be liberated only through profound changes in American culture and institutions" (Stoper, 1991, p. 152). For rural women, the process of cultural and institutional change of such magnitude leaves them alone to struggle with establishing the principle that women's work, particularly rural women's work, is done within "constrained choices" and with stressing that for many women, respect and recognition might be nearly as important as money (Blum, 1991). It might be that neither liberal feminism nor radical feminism is, in its entirety, the answer for rural women.

In this chapter we examine an alternative perspective on rural women's work, the principle of social responsibility for caring and the fallacy of wages for caring, and the implications of a new feminist analysis of women's work for both feminism and social work.

ALTERNATIVE PERSPECTIVES ON RURAL WOMEN'S WORK

Historian Kessler-Harris (1988) wrote about comparable worth theories:

> On the theory that low wages inhere in the job, which is itself sex-typed, advocates of comparable worth posit two central assumptions: first, that the free market has not worked for women, and second, that every job has an inherent value that can be compared with that of other jobs. Value, according to proponents of comparable worth, can be measured by such factors as the skill, effort, responsibility, training, and working conditions that are its requisites. Critics ridicule the notion that value inheres in jobs. The market, they suggest—the demand for labor and the available supply—determines the wage paid. If women are not paid well, it is because they have made bad choices. And if these choices are historically conditioned, why should employers be held responsible? The

language they use indicates something of the fear the idea evokes. Phrases like "the looniest idea since loony tunes" and "the feminist road to socialism" are the catchwords of the day. (pp. 238–239)

But, as Stoper proposed, a lingering serious problem hides behind these attacking remarks. "Studies have shown that the same work when identified as performed by men is consistently viewed as more valuable than when attributed to women" (Stoper, 1991, p. 153). An analysis sensitive to factors other than the market value of labor discloses useful alternative perspectives in relation to validating rural women's realities, options, or choices. One such perspective might suggest that, although rural women have consistently lacked formal lucrative employment, they have always been well-represented in the productive sector of rural society. They have always performed a wide variety of useful and meaningful jobs, whether paid, unpaid, or underpaid. These jobs were essential for personal and collective survival and well-being in rural areas. In the sense that these jobs empowered women in their social environments, even if they were not highly valued in the market, they were and are congruent with both social work and feminist perspectives.

Rural women have farmed alongside their husbands and have derived not only some income but a great deal of autonomy and empowerment from their labor (Sacks, 1983). Rural women have quilted, sewed, cooked, and minded children; they have taken care of elderly individuals, allowing them to stay at home; they have cared for and about people in their communities; they have bartered and kept villages alive through their ingenuity. Rural women have been full participants not only in the informal rural economy (Lewenhak, 1988) but also in the acts of ensuring the common good. From a communitarian perspective, rural women would score very high on the index of social responsibility and social satisfaction (Etzioni, 1992). Rural women's participation in helping has always been empowering, but in a more humanistic and interactional sense, not in the sense measured by any market figures.

Within feminist perspectives of power, power over, or "the ability to do one's will over the will of others" (Weber, 1968, p. 53), and other classic constructions of power are less important than *"personal empowerment*—the need for activity and achievement, the ability to act, to drive, to interact effectively with the environment" (Collins, 1986, p. 217). By this philosophy, rural women's labor, although informal or poorly paid, can be highly empowering and should not remain unnoticed or be devalued. A feminist perspective would argue that the work rural women do enhances not only their status as members of rural societies but also the unity of the private and the public, the individual and the communal, the wholeness of the human condition. The challenge is to attain recognition for both the social work and the feminist tenet that proposes "people best realize their humanity through effective social functioning" (Collins, 1986, p. 216).

The free market imposes value on all tasks. Its critics have indicted the dominance of mercantile principles as being in direct opposition to all social work theory, values, and tasks (Collins, 1986). What would be more empowering for women and men, they suggest, would be the "valuing of the *interdependent*, the *network*, and the *mutually beneficial*. . . . a societal valuing of the *feminine* principle: those values associated with women's traditional domestic role— nurturance, caring, mutual interdependence. And it requires a valuing of them as meaningful and applicable, not just in the private sphere of hearth and home, but in the political, economic public world" (Collins, 1986, p. 217).

An analysis sensitive to the special position of rural women would disclose that although women in rural areas may have always held low-paying or unpaid jobs, the importance of their labor has always been central to the survival and quality of life in rural communities. Some contend that putting cash value on all work is to siphon work, useful work, into a market economy that will rob people and communities of self-sufficiency and will impose on them the tyranny of work for cash (Lewenhak, 1988). Others argue that all unpaid work is already controlled by capital and serves the further accumulation of capital (Glazer, 1990). This unpaid work includes useful labor, such as cooking and raising a garden, and "useless" but necessary labor, such as self-serve shopping, waiting in line, filling in forms, waiting on the telephone, and driving to and from work (Illich, 1981). Unpaid work also includes housework, which is essential for the maintenance of the labor force, voluntary labor, and involuntary unpaid labor under the appearance of being work performed for the family (Glazer, 1990). Kessler-Harris (1988) observed the following:

> *The historian hears these arguments impatiently, for whatever the abstract models preferred by the economists, the historical record introduces the balm of experience. The market, as it functions in the daily lives of people, is not independent of the values and customs of those who participate in it. Justice, equity, fairness have not been its natural outcomes. Rather, market outcomes have been tempered by customary notions of justice or fairness. The specific forms these take have been the*

object of struggle. And just as ideas of fairness influence our response to the market, so, too, do they influence how the market works. (p. 239)

A less than idyllic vision of the capabilities of market forces to enhance rural women's condition will free rural women to focus on other and perhaps more-relevant dimensions in the process of empowerment vis-à-vis the work they do. Work that produces "use-value" such as food preparation, even if it has little or no exchange value, is not only essential for survival but also gives women some control over their destinies and those of their families. Such work gives them a real sense of efficacy and self-esteem, which has consequences for the types of transactions they will undertake in the future (Bandura, 1977).

Wage rates alone cannot be left to define the value of rural women's relationships in the family and the community. In modern societies, work can encompass many kinds of activities, some successfully regulated and valued by the free market, others undervalued or not accurately appraised when market conditions alone prevail. Therefore, it is important to establish the value of women's work (paid or unpaid) reliably on the basis of need and communal satisfaction rather than on market considerations. This valuation will be an antidote to the market manipulation of women's labor, such as stressing the importance of housework when there is a job shortage or stressing equal opportunities for women primarily when there are labor shortages, which has historically been the case (Lewenhak, 1988). On the other hand, women's knowledge that their work and time have been appropriated by capital and manipulated by government policies may help them fight against a definition of work that gives the name "work" only to paid activities or a definition of housework that is unspecified and sexually segregated.

We suggest that at least two other frameworks for analysis, comparable worth and the social wage, might help us move in this direction, albeit still within the parameters and constrictions of the prevailing economic system. Feminist proponents of comparable worth (Evans & Nelson, 1989; Kessler-Harris, 1988; Rhode, 1991; Shrage, 1988), students and proponents of the social wage (Rainwater, 1992; Rainwater, Rein, & Schwartz, 1986; Trory, 1992), and social workers can be of help to rural women in calling for nothing less than the reevaluation of women's work and the legitimization of a broad spectrum of choices. Kessler-Harris (1988) said that "in refusing to sanction gender distinctions, comparable worth raises a long line of earlier challenges to a new level. . . . Its strength lies in its potential for acting upon female traditions, for it assumes that women have a right to pursue traditional roles and to achieve equity in that pursuit" (p. 245).

Blum (1991) suggested that even successful job integration strategies "may have unintended consequences for women working within the present context" (p. 135). In a well-argued chapter in which she contrasted the possible gains and losses of extreme strategies for various groups of women, whether job integration or comparable worth, Blum proposed the use of comparable worth as a "fertile middle ground" for women to "defend traditional preferences, but at the same time also demand earnings and status on par with men's. . . . The logic of comparable worth suggests that women as social actors are neither misguided nor coerced into performing 'marginal' work; the problem is rather with a system that defines whatever work women do as marginal" (p. 135).

Other authors have also questioned principles of job integration and the "equity revolution" for women. Rainwater et al. (1986) suggested that one of the most dramatic developments of the 20th century industrial society has been the revolution of women's participation in the labor force. Trends suggest that by the end of the 20th century we should achieve sexual equity in participation rates. According to Rainwater et al.,

> this participatory revolution, in turn, it is argued, inaugurates an equity revolution characterized by a major and permanent change in the nature of the family as a social organization with repercussions not only for women's roles and their identities, but also for the roles, identities and life experiences of men and children. . .
>
> Our research, however, suggests that this 'two revolution' framework is not an accurate representation of what has happened. It treats women as a homogeneous category and does not adequately differentiate how participation rates among different types of women have changed over time. It fails to distinguish the degree of women's attachment to work and the impact of their work on the economic well-being of the family. Proponents of this theory fail to recognize the deeply imbedded structural obstacles to relational equity. (pp. 58–59)

In recognizing the merits of the work women and other members of society do for the collective, proponents of a type of social wage would argue that if we are to introduce greater equity in the free-market economy, we should minimally entertain the notion of a wage, paid by government, to remunerate the work done on behalf of the collective. Under such conditions, the work women do at home, caring for children or elders, as volunteers in the community, or as stewards of the most basic social institutions, would be assessed in terms of its value for society and given a social wage. The term social wage has been used in many ways, ranging from "social protection programs which are designed to supplement the income of working parents" (Rainwater, 1992) to other broader proposals that go beyond family support programs specifically tied to children. It is in the latter, broad sense, that the term is being used here. For example, we would include allowances paid to those who care for elderly or disabled persons, such as those existing in Great Britain or Scandinavia.

These different perspectives on the value of labor provide alternatives, albeit still limited ones, for framing the discussion about women, particularly rural women, and work. Yet, however limited, these alternative ways of framing the discussion are more sensitive to the subtle dimensions that must be taken into account to appreciate not just the commercial but the social significance of what women do.

CARING AS SOCIAL RESPONSIBILITY

Most caring, whether paid or unpaid, public or private, professional or vernacular, is done by women. More than 75 percent of caregivers in the United States are women (Noddings, 1991). A great deal of caring work is unpaid or poorly paid. Caring is central to women's experience and cuts across cultures, social classes, and levels of technological development achieved by a society. In examining rural women's status in their communities from a perspective of liberation and realistic economic opportunities, caring offers itself as an ideal locus of discourse.

First, the extensive and almost recalcitrant involvement of rural women in caring activities and their unwillingness to relinquish these activities challenge the experiences of urban feminists who have identified the work of caring as an impediment to women competing in traditionally male fields and becoming economically independent. Hacker (1990) observed that although farm women perform a variety of jobs that require a great deal of physical strength, such as tending livestock, shoveling manure, repairing farming implements, and other tasks traditionally associated with men, they distance themselves as much as they can from feminism. On the other hand, urban feminists are equally baffled by the adhesion of rural women to the traditional roles of wife and mother.

Second, caring has recently received central attention as a constituent of the ethical self, which cannot simply be discarded on the road to personal liberation (Mayeroff, 1971; Noddings, 1984, 1991).

Yet, caring as an ingredient of the ethical self can be and has been used as an instrument for oppression and denial of the caregiver's dignity and worth.

The contradiction between feminist aspirations and rural women's attachment to caring and to traditional women's roles and the potential for exploitation of the caregiver are a challenge to feminism and social work. That challenge is an invitation to integrate rural women's experience into a more textured and variegated feminist outlook. To do so, we must recognize caring as central to the feminist vision rather than as a hindrance to female self-fulfillment.

To incorporate caring into the feminist analysis, however, we must move beyond merely claiming it; we must watch for the exploitation of those who care. An adequate posture on women's caring will not be reached if feminism, in an effort to project an image of unity among all women—urban and rural, poor and nonpoor, from industrialized and nonindustrialized countries—glosses over its own bourgeois origin and the inherent biases of that origin. We must, therefore, point out the distinct economic risks of women involved in caring in a rural setting as opposed to the risks of women whose caring takes place in the urban middle-class environment that is the historical home of feminism.

CARING: CONTRACT VERSUS COVENANT

Caring has recently been identified as a central category of the moral self (Mayeroff, 1971; Noddings, 1984, 1991). Caring is the foundation of human existence from which all moral life springs. It is through caring that the voice of the mother is heard. The persistent attachment of many women, and in particular of rural women, to caring roles might be rooted in the "memory of caring" (Noddings, 1984, p. 107), the memory of the mother. With time, and as the male mothering role develops, it could be argued that the nature of this memory might change. The caring relationship defines the good life and is basic to self-image and happiness. If this is so, however, how do we account for the discrepancy between the aspirations of urban and rural women when it comes to caring roles and their demands? What is it about caring that elicits different responses in rural women and urban feminists?

Noddings (1984) described the ethic of caring as one of reciprocity. It is a reciprocal ethic, but one in which the cared-for does not promise to behave equitably. It is not a contractual ethic in which mistrust and mutual suspicion are assuaged by measurable accountability and pricing. An ethic of caring, on the contrary, suggests a covenant between the parties of the relationship and is firmly grounded in human trust. Within this ethic, there is a core in the human transaction that is radically resistant to quantification and pricing and yet is essential for survival, particularly in rural communities. It is also an ethic that can be easily exploited by the contractual capitalist paradigm.

The maintenance of caring requires habits that are extraneous to the ethic prevailing in urban, anomic capitalism. To achieve the status of the one-caring (Noddings, 1984) in a relationship, certain virtues must be developed. However, these virtues of kindness, patience, and humility have been mostly exiled from the marketplace, from the political arena, and from the concomitant vocabulary of success. Throughout history, many who practiced these qualities lived outside the mainstream and were members of utopian communities, many of which were rural (Martinez-Brawley, 1990). To the extent that capitalism and its corollaries, professionalism and technical success, have infiltrated caring as an area of human activity, the virtues that support caring have become superfluous or even troublesome. The people traditionally associated with the caring domain but not with professionalism also have become superfluous and anachronistic. Often they are massively replaced by a proletarianized workforce too frightened not to be docile and too young to be critical of a new order. The maternal ethos is often discarded in favor of a professional ethos of efficiency.

The intrinsic differences between the ethics of the free market and the ethics of caring are such that the human relations sustained by an ethos of caring cannot resist the predatory and expansionist tactics of the capitalist ethos. The contact points in which the ethic of caring becomes vulnerable to the efficient machinery of the marketplace have been identified as trust versus mistrust, contract versus covenant, accountability versus narrative, negotiation versus dialogue, collaboration versus competition, and rational efficiency versus nurturing. Women are specially affected by the coexistence of both models of ethics, but the impact these models have on rural and urban women is different because of the different degree to which both groups are tied to the capitalist and professional paradigms of human relations.

OWNERSHIP OF CARING

Marxist feminists have exposed the systematic appropriation and manipulation by those who control the means of production, or in Marxist terms, by capital, of a large amount of work, often caring work, done by women. The Marxist analysis has focused lately on the domestic sphere. Although not all that takes place in the domestic space and time is labor, caring, or women's labor, we can safely say that a great deal of what women do is caring and a great deal of it takes place in and around the home. Consequently, light that is shed on domestic labor inevitably sheds light onto women's caring work. On the basis of the results of previous debates on domestic labor, Glazer (1990) discussed the tenuous boundaries of concepts such as private and public, labor and leisure, work and home, and production and reproduction. The duality of those concepts, Glazer argued, masks the work transfer from paid workers to consumers, be they buyers, patients, or clients of state bureaucracies. The reorganization of work makes it possible for capital to insert unsalaried involuntary workers into the production process. These workers are, for the most part, women. "Women, rather than both sexes, bear most of the burden of the work transfer" (Glazer, 1990, p. 143). Self-service retailing, according to Glazer, illustrates the point. Without the benefit of new technology, but just by restructuring work, commercial capitalism has been able to eliminate paid clerk positions, pass the work to the consumer (for instance, locating products, getting information about them, and pushing them through the store), and pocket the savings. So, what in appearance is a private activity, belonging to the domestic realm and done during leisure time, is actually involuntary and unwaged labor, labor that is appropriated by capital. In economic terms, the boundaries between private and public in this case are ambiguous.

Glazer's example shows a historically specific mechanism through which the bourgeois mode of relations intrudes, transforms, and appropriates in insidious ways caring work. Shopping is work that many women do as caregivers, and even if it is instrumental, repetitious, tiresome, and time-consuming work, few women would experience buying as purely mechanical work, devoid of caring attributes. For instance, it takes some empathy and devotion to pick the weekly family groceries, to choose food that is within budget, appetizing to the sickly one, nutritious to the fast-growing teen, not too salty, not too fatty, tasty to all, varied from one day to the next, and so on. In this intimate, often unspoken conversation between the shopper and those she cares for, an intruder alienates the shopper from her caring. While she pushes and fills her cart with prepackaged items, the consumer is not just taking care of the family and being a steward of its resources but without knowing it, without consent, and without compensation, she is working for someone else's profit. On top of that, as Glazer noted, she also is working in lieu of a laborer (most likely another woman) who used to get a salary for what she now is doing for free.

The alienation of the *one-caring* (the one who cares) from her care goes even further. Glazer pointed out that self-service has transformed the act of buying. Shoppers are forced to perform many tasks. They must locate products, have knowledge of them, and so on. From the perspective of the one-caring, it is not enough to know that a cup of rice and a cup of beans provides lunch for x number of people in the family; she also needs to know what a 397-gram package of fortified rice costs per gram in relation to a 527-gram package of a competing brand. If one adds the tasks of being informed about sale prices, clipping coupons, keeping track of expiration dates, applying for refunds, and so forth, one realizes that it is not only just physical work that commercial capitalism has appropriated from the one-caring but also the very intimate attribute of caring and of mental engrossment. The shopper's mental space must be filled with absolutely useless knowledge and pointless calculations to be a good steward and keep true to her image as the one-caring. These useless efforts, which Illich (1981) called *shadow work,* colonize the caregiver's ethical self. The virtues and skills developed through a lifetime of caring provide little shield against this form of colonization.

The work transfer that has taken place in retailing also has taken place in other areas closely related to care. Health care, for instance, has been changed into a series of discrete commodities since the first quarter of the 20th century. Health care practices such as nursing sick and elderly people and caring for dying people that had been successfully performed by mothers, wives, daughters, and a diversity of community women were appropriated and controlled by the emerging power of professional medicine. The consequence for women caregivers was that their healing skills and knowledge became disabled by stigma and were soon forgotten. Once skills were lost, the women's work shifted from healing to managing access to services and following up on other people's orders, for instance, sitting in waiting rooms, holding on telephones, filling in forms—all examples of shadow work. Although medical practice is now in dire need of cost containment, there is great reluctance to give up profit. The medical field is now beginning to explore returning hands-on care to mothers, wives, and daughters. Glazer (1990) mentioned that in a major medical center, the labor of patients' family members is used to provide cooperative care, thus lowering costs without infringing on other lucrative sources of profit.

Professionalization of care and loss of skills by women have been the two faces of capital accumulation. As women forgot their power to heal and console, they became greater consumers of professional ministrations. However, this greater degree of consumption did not translate into timesaving for women. There was a shift in the content of tasks, and many women had to intensify their paid labor to buy these new commodities. The most profound effect for the caring relationship is in the shift in the content of caring. Women moved from dressing wounds to filling out forms and waiting in line; more important, they lost the power to do differently. Women are powerless to heal physical pain or emotional need. Somehow, the more urbanized a woman becomes, the more her confidence and emotional robustness appear to be eroded. New emotional needs are defined for her, new diagnostic labels are attached to her children, and new experts tell her what to do in her caring relationships.

In advanced capitalism, intimate dimensions of caring, including mental engrossment, are exploited. Because urban feminists are aware of this exploitation, it is not surprising that for many of them caring is not the actualization of the memory of the good life. Caring, therefore, is often perceived as an occupational hazard that must be shared with reluctant others, be they spouses, the state, or for-profit agents. There can be no doubt that women are burdened by the double duty of paid and domestic labor and that they do not get much help from their partners or support from their employers or the state. But we believe that a measure of the bitterness of many urban women about caring work is not against caring work itself, but against the expropriation of their caring and the worthlessness of what they must do and must learn to care. Under conditions of exploitation, "the joy [that] often accompanies a realization of our relatedness. . . [and which] represents a major reward for the one-caring," departs from us (Noddings, 1984, p. 132). During those conditions, the repeated rituals of ordinary life lose their joyous quality and become worthless sameness.

Noddings (1984) wrote that "oddly, many women look at domesticity as unrelieved sameness" (p. 126). She asked, "Are they simply lacking in imagination and appreciation, or is something else operating here?" (p. 126). Correctly, Noddings claimed caring as central to human life and joy as the basic effect of our relatedness and of our ordinary lives. She falls short in not seeing fully how the ethos of caring has been invaded by the ethos of capitalism, and how fragile caring is at the hands of capitalism. Although we may also fall short of definite solutions to this dilemma, we offer an alternative view that should help illuminate the practice of social workers.

CONCLUSION

Using rural women as our unit of analysis, we have shown the special vulnerability of caring work to economic exploitation and the vulnerability of those who do the caring. We have postulated that the ethics of caring and our contemporary commitment to a market economy are not compatible. If we accept the premise that ethics of caring are essential to the human condition and centrally important to social work, not only because social work is a caring profession but also because social workers want to support and enhance caring in its most complex sense, then the dilemma of reconciling what all women, but particularly rural women, do with the most prevalent feminist economic vision is the crux of the professional challenge.

Social workers believe that caring generates intrinsically worthwhile activities and want to guard against the dangers of exploitation of women for their caring capacities. What are the plausible solutions that have been postulated through the decades as answers to this dilemma? From a pragmatic perspective, what are the alternatives? In searching for practical solutions and policies that preserve and restore dignity to women's work, feminism has often conceived responses, proposals, or tactics based on the conceptual frameworks that have historically illuminated the feminist philosophy. Although this is perfectly logical, it is within the realm of feminist and social work scholarship to reveal the potential conflicts and contradictions inherent in that approach. It also is within the mandate of social work to devise alternatives that are both liberating and hospitable to the role of caring, which though not exclusively a woman's prerogative, is one in which women, particularly rural women, have traditionally excelled and often do not want to give up. Although we are not ready to propose concrete policies that address the question of rural women's caring work, we have suggested that the equal worth and social wage analytical frames offer richer alternatives that are perhaps more consistent with the aspirations and realities of rural women workers. We also have suggested that these frames advance feminist and social work values.

"In any human group," Kanter (1972) suggested, "there is a gap between what works and has functional or organizational value, and what is desirable or has personal or social value" (p. 235). Even in utopian communities, whenever attempts were made to narrow this gap, failures were more frequent than successes. Perhaps it is not feasible to reconcile the two ethics to which we have alluded within the context of contemporary capitalistic society, particularly in ways that can be replicated on a large scale and with costs that contemporary Americans are willing to pay.

Against this problematic context, the challenge of social work is to find solutions or at least to maintain a keen awareness of the powerful contradictory forces operating in women's lives, particularly in rural women's lives. If freedom means actualizing the desire to serve and care for others, then freedom might lead women to economic oppression and dependence. If, on the other hand, freedom means participation in the market economy, then actualizing their caring ethos might lead them to a different kind of exploitation, that of the appropriation of their work by capital.

The comparable worth and social wage perspectives are clearly neither panaceas nor even the best solutions for resolving these concerns. They do, however, represent less rigid ways of framing the issue of women's work. The free-market perspective might be myopic to the real issues confronted by women in relation to their work, particularly in rural areas. If we must frame the dilemma of rural women within current economic terms, then comparable worth and social wage proposals reveal postures that are more alert to the contradictions inherent in the free market and might generate more sensitive policy proposals.

REFERENCES

Bandura, A. (1977). Self-efficacy: Toward a unifying theory of behavioral change. *Psychological Review, 84,* 191–215.

Blum, L. (1991). *Between feminism and labor: The significance of the comparable worth movement.* Berkeley: University of California Press.

Collins, B. G. (1986). Defining feminist social work. *Social Work, 31,* 214–219.

Etzioni, A. (1992). Communitarian solutions/what communitarians think. *Council of State Governments, 65*(1), 9–11.

Evans, S. M., & Nelson, B. J. (1989). Comparable worth: The paradox of technocratic reform. *Feminist Studies, 15,* 171–190.

Glazer, N. (1990). Servants to capital: Unpaid domestic labor and paid work. In J. L. Collins & M. Gimenez (Eds.), *Work without wages: Domestic labor and self-employment within capitalism* (pp. 142–167). New York: State University of New York Press.

Hacker, S. L. (1990). Farming out the home: Women and agribusiness. In D. E. Smith & S. M. Turner (Eds.), *"Doing it the hard way": Investigations of gender and technology* (pp. 69–88). Boston: Unwin Hyman.

Illich, I. (1981). *Shadow work.* Boston: M. Boyars.

Kanter, R. M. (1972). *Commitment and community, communes and utopias in sociological perspective.* Cambridge, MA: Harvard University Press.

Kessler-Harris, A. (1988). The just price, the free market, and the value of women. *Feminist Studies, 14,* 235–249.

Lewenhak, S. (1988). *The revaluation of women's work.* London: Croom Helm.

Martinez-Brawley, E. E. (1990). *Perspectives on the small community: Humanistic views for practitioners.* Silver Spring, MD: NASW Press.

Martinez-Brawley, E. E., & Durbin, N. (1987). Women in the rural occupational structure. *Human Services in the Rural Environment, 10*(4), 29–39.

Mayeroff, M. (1971). *On caring.* New York: Harper & Row.

Noddings, N. (1984). *Caring: A feminine approach to ethics & moral education.* Berkeley: University of California Press.

Noddings, N. (1991). Stories in dialogue: Caring and interpersonal reasoning. In C. Whitherell & N. Noddings (Eds.), *Stories lives tell: Narrative and dialogue in education* (pp. 157–170). New York: Columbia University, Teachers College.

Rainwater, L. (1992). *The social wage in the income package of working parents.* Unpublished manuscript.

Rainwater, L., Rein, M., & Schwartz, J. (1986). *Income packaging in the welfare state: A comparative study.* Oxford, England: Oxford University Press.

Rhode, D. L. (1991). Gender equality and employment policy. In S. E. Rix (Ed.), *Women's Research and Education Institute for the American Woman: 1990–1991* (pp. 170–200). New York: W. W. Norton.

Sacks, C. (1983). *The invisible farmers, women in agricultural production.* Totowa, NJ: Rowan & Allanheld.

Shrage, L. (1988). Should there be a legally enforceable right to comparable worth? A reply to Paul Weiler's "No." *Frontiers, 10,* 45–48.

Stoper, E. (1991). Women's work, women's movement: Taking stock. *Political and Social Science, 551,* 151–162.

Trory, E. (1992). *The social wage: Its role under capitalism and the transition from socialism to communism.* Hove, England: Crabtree Press.

Weber, M. (1968). *Economy and society.* New York: Bedminster Press.

8

Women Actors for Women's Issues
A New Political Agenda

Elizabeth Segal and Stephanie Brzuzy

Women's issues are no longer new to the policy arena. In recent years significant progress has been made in getting women's issues to the forefront of political debate. During the 1970s there was tremendous controversy surrounding equal rights and reproductive choice for women. These issues continued to draw public debate through the 1980s and into the 1990s. During the past several congressional sessions, legislation for family leave, child care, reproductive rights, and other issues of concern to women were discussed and called to vote.

Since the mid-1970s successful efforts have been made in getting women's issues on the political agenda. However, such discussions have not led to the actual adoption of key legislation. In part, this is a reflection of the disproportionately low representation of women in policy-making positions. The absence of enacted legislation and the disproportionate representation of women in the political arena are salient to social work for two reasons: (1) The majority of social work clients and service providers are women, and (2) social work values are complementary to feminist values. This chapter presents a theoretical and practical approach, grounded in feminist values, to effect the creation, enactment, and implementation of legislation supportive of women's issues.

THE POLITICAL ROLE OF WOMEN
Women represent over half the population of this nation. In 1990 women accounted for 52.4 percent of the voting age population in

the United States (U.S. Bureau of the Census, 1991). Additionally, in recent years, a greater portion of women voted than men. In the 1988 election, 58.3 percent of women voted compared with 56.4 percent of men. Coupled with the greater number of women, this difference in voter turnout represented almost 7 million more votes cast by women than by men (U.S. Bureau of the Census, 1989). Despite this difference, the overwhelming majority of those in positions of political power and decision making are men. The disproportionately low representation of women involved in developing the governing legislation of this country suggests that women and issues of concern to women are not being adequately addressed.

Historically, key women have been involved in political debate and policy-making. Famous political and social policy activists such as Elizabeth Cady Stanton, Susan B. Anthony, Sojourner Truth, Margaret Sanger, and Jane Addams are remembered well. Modern political figures such as Bella Abzug, Barbara Jordan, Shirley Chisholm, Barbara Mikulski, Sandra Day O'Connor, Geraldine Ferraro, and Pat Schroeder are publicly recognized. However, the number of women politicians and activists is extremely small compared with the proportion of women in the overall population.

Statistics on elected national political figures demonstrate the underrepresentation of women (*Congressional Quarterly Almanac,* 1990; Stanley & Niemi, 1988). In 1971, 13 women served in the U.S. Congress, 12 in the House, and one in the Senate. This represented 2.4 percent of the 535 members. In 1991, 30 women, representing 5.6 percent of the congressional membership, served in Congress. The elections of 1992 brought a significant number of women into elected offices nationally and locally. In 1993 women comprised 9.9 percent of the membership of Congress, compared with 5.6 percent in 1991. From 1991 to 1993, there was an 11 percent increase in the number of women officeholders in state legislatures. However, women hold only 20 percent of all state legislative positions (Center for the American Woman & Politics, 1993). Although the increase in the number of women elected to Congress and at the state level is a major step forward in women holding major elected positions, it remains to be seen whether this is the beginning of a trend or a one-year anomaly. Most legislation is developed through the work of committees. In the 103rd Congress, not one major committee was chaired by a woman. At the average rate of increase in female representation over the past 20 years, it will take more than 60 years before women make up half the members of Congress.

The representation of women at the state level is better than at the national level but still falls far short of representing the number of women in the general population. In 1969, 4 percent of state legislators were women, compared with 16 percent in 1990 (Freeman & Lyons, 1990). The number of governorships held by women in 1990 was three, representing 6 percent of the states (*Congressional Quarterly Almanac*, 1990). Men continue to dominate at the state level, particularly in key positions. However, it is at the local level that women have made the most gains during the past 20 years. Because national officeholders usually "work their way up" through local politics before attempting to run for national office, the gains made at the local level may represent a foundation for increased representation of women at the national level.

Why Are Women Disproportionately Represented?

Over the years a number of reasons for the low participation of women in politics have emerged. Foremost is the power position of women. Women were not granted the vote until 1920. Not being allowed to participate in voting, the foundation of our political structure, severely limited women's participation. Until women could legally participate, it was virtually impossible for them to serve politically. The reasons for not getting the vote are steeped in social conditions and values that date back to the earliest history of this nation.

GENDER STRATIFICATION AND ECONOMICS

Gender stratification and economic inferiority have historically kept women out of decision-making and power positions. The way resources are distributed and who holds elite roles of power have traditionally been controlled by men. This control has led to inequality of power based on gender. The result is gender stratification in the structure of our institutions of power.

Gender stratification in the U.S. labor force significantly affects the economic stability of women in this country. In 1989, 45 percent of all labor force participants were women (U.S. Department of Labor, 1990). However, in 1989 the median income for year-round, full-time working women was only 68 percent of what men earned (U.S. Bureau of the Census, 1990). In addition, women continue to work in lower-paying, traditionally female jobs. For example, in 1989, 80 percent of administrative support workers and 68 percent of retail and personal sales workers were women. Women constituted only 40 percent of workers in executive, management, or administrative positions (U.S. Department of Labor, 1990). Women constituted 41 percent of state and local government employment in 1984 and averaged annual salaries that were 24 percent less than those of men in comparable positions (Stanley & Niemi, 1988).

These data demonstrate how resources and positions of power are disproportionately distributed among men and women. The structure of our society and the gender division of labor reinforce women's economic and emotional dependence on men, making poverty a women's issue (Sidel, 1986). Gender stratification is based on economic inequality that keeps women at a power disadvantage with men. Chafetz (1990) argued that the only way to change this system is to increase the number of women occupying elite power roles. The gender division of labor, male superiority in resource power, and consequently the male occupation of elite roles in society are the main factors that account for the maintenance and stability of gender inequity (Chafetz, 1990). Our political system, with male domination of elite roles and control of resources, is a clear example of gender stratification.

SOCIALIZATION AND DISCRIMINATION

A number of other factors contribute to the lack of proportionate representation and subsequently the minimal political participation of women. Renzetti and Curran (1992) cited five closely interrelated factors:

1. Women have been socialized not to be political.

2. Domestic demands have kept women at home.

3. These roles have created an image that women are not qualified or capable of understanding politics.

4. The pervasiveness of sexism and discrimination have kept women out of politics.

5. Networks of men and incumbency have closed access to women.

The involvement of women in the political process is subject to a number of factors. There is a sense that women are not socialized to think about or participate in politics. Clark and Clark (1986) examined this phenomenon and discovered that until the mid-1960s, women may have been limited in political activities because of childhood socialization but were able to overcome this socialization as they aged. By 1980 younger women voted more heavily than men. However, the measures of participation focused on voting, campaigning, and contact with elected officials, not on serving in political positions. Owen and Dennis (1988) revealed through interviews with children and adolescents that socialization still had an impact on politicization. Females demonstrated less interest and understanding of the political process than males. Owen and Dennis concluded that this stemmed from early childhood socialization toward politics.

ACCESS TO EXISTING POLITICAL STRUCTURE

Examination of campaign effectiveness suggests that male and female candidates have similar election results (Burrell, 1988). Women who run for office seem to perform equally as well as men in fundraising and getting the vote. However, women constitute less than 20 percent of candidates running for public office (Burrell, 1990). The opportunities to run for office are limited because of the strength of incumbency. Very few seats are available in each election so the inequality of representation is perpetuated. More than 95 percent of incumbents have been reelected to the House over the past 10 years (Katz, 1992). The strength of incumbency is waning, which could open the opportunity for more women to get elected. Even before the 1992 election, retirements, redistricting, and primary defeats already guaranteed greater turnover in the House than in the previous four elections (Katz, 1992).

Once elected to public office, women tend to be on the outside of the power structure. Until recently, women were often elected or appointed to Congress following the death of their husbands (Kendrigan, 1984). These women were perceived to be less knowledgeable and therefore simply filling in for the deceased spouse. When Dan Quayle vacated his Senate seat in 1988 to serve as vice president, there was significant talk of recruiting his wife to fill the role. Regardless of her qualifications, the emphasis was on her position as the vice president's wife, with incidental interest in her political skills.

Moving into the political system is aided through mentoring, networking, and prior experience (Hale & Kelly, 1989). Historically, much of this has been done for women through the family. Today, women interested in political involvement understand the need to work with mentors and pursue careers that lead to greater political involvement. However, until more women are in positions to serve as mentors and in careers leading to politics, they will have to depend on men to assist them in gaining access to the political process.

These studies suggest that women are equal to or greater than men in consumer participation, voting, and campaigning for a candidate but are less involved as key figures in the political process and in elected positions. Women are more likely to work behind the scenes than to make decisions and serve publicly (Evans, 1981; Stockard & Johnson, 1992). Women have traditionally worked as supporters and volunteers for men, and this behavior continues to be seen in the political realm. To a large extent, women must rely on men to assist in gaining entry into the system, which tends to perpetuate the gender stratification in the political arena.

FEMINIST THEORIES AND POLITICAL PARTICIPATION

Our political system does not stand alone. It functions in relation to other systems, including the economic, social, cultural, and religious arenas of our nation. The roles of women in the workplace, in the home, and in our social institutions affect their political position. Feminist theories relevant to political participation reflect an ecological approach. Such an approach stresses the interrelation of various systems as the foundation for the current political status of women.

Gender Equity

The women's movement has been influential in promoting a more egalitarian view of women and raising national consciousness. As a result, more women have achieved access to highly valued positions related to decision making and the development of policy. However, Chafetz (1990) stressed that for women to truly gain gender equity, they must occupy elite roles. Until women are equal partners in the elite power system, the gender division of labor and resources will maintain gender inequity.

Kendrigan (1984) differentiated between equality of opportunity and equality of results. For true gender equity to occur, emphasis must be placed on equality of results. Although equalizing opportunities opens the door to more women, it does not question the rules and expectations of the system. If the measure of success or access to a job relies on characteristics men have acquired, then giving women equal opportunity requires that they participate in ways common to men, which denies the uniqueness of women. Equality of results, on the other hand, stresses significant social changes that promote treating people as individuals.

Christy (1987) suggested that societal changes have created a growing acceptance of democratic participation by all. This shift has helped to open access to areas of political influence and resource acquisition previously off-limits to women. In addition, this increased involvement in the democratic system has led to greater government involvement in issues that previously were relegated to women and families (such as reproduction and economic security). Thus, although women's political involvement in the 1970s centered on a liberal agenda, growing gender equity in politics has also opened the way for women to promote a more conservative agenda. For example, women activists such as Phyllis Schlafly demonstrate that women are taking lead roles politically but are promoting positions that are contrary to a feminist agenda.

Consequently, in the political arena equality of results is not simply more women in positions of political power. Gender equity based on results is achieved when feminist issues are heard and when policy goals are attained. Having more women in Congress may not improve gender equity unless policy changes supportive of women's equality are realized.

Role Equity versus Role Change

Role equity involves the placement of women in positions equal to those of men, as opposed to role change, which involves structural alteration of the social system. On the basis of analyses of political issues relevant to women, Gelb and Palley (1982) discovered that role equity is easier to achieve than role change. Role change threatens current values and thus encourages powerful opposition. The fight over ratification of the Equal Rights Amendment was an example of the struggle between role equity and role change.

The Equal Rights Amendment enjoyed early widespread support because it was viewed as a technical correction of our civil liberties system. As time passed, opposition grew because of the perceived changes in the traditional roles of women in society that would result. Supporters argued for social analysis and legal support to reify sociocultural changes in women's roles, whereas opponents believed the Equal Rights Amendment represented social change and an assault on long-held social values (Mathews & De Hart, 1990).

Redefining and Reconceptualizing

Political power tends to be viewed as finite, and therefore participation is limited to the power elite who control access to rights, resources, and opportunities. However, feminist theory calls for reconceptualizing power as accessible to all, thus allowing people to take control of their lives (Van Den Bergh & Cooper, 1986). Redefining and reconceptualizing allows for different expressions of political activity (Jones, 1988), such as calling for decisions by consensus of the majority affected. Thus, policies related to women, particularly poor women, could be decided by those directly affected. The result would be a grassroots system for policy-making.

The Personal Is Political

A rallying cry of the early women's movement was that "the personal is political," meaning that one's personal life and actions represent a political position or reality (Van Den Bergh & Cooper, 1986). Research on those involved in the political arena reveals that the link between the personal and the political is stronger for women than for men. Carroll (1989) found that politically active men have been able to make personal choices without negatively affecting their political careers. For women, the public and the private are interrelated. Decisions related to a woman's political involvement are made with significant consideration of her personal life.

Integrating the feminist value of the personal is political into the political system could result in policies that enhance the interaction of public and private lives. Personal experience often brings greater interest, clarity, and advocacy efforts to the consideration of a political issue. The following example highlights the difference between women and men in deciding policy related to the personal.

During the 101st Congress in October 1989, the House and the Senate were involved in policy debate over the issue of federal funding for abortion in cases of rape or incest. The appropriation bill, House Resolution 2990 (1989), included funds to be authorized for the U.S. Department of Health and Human Services. Added to the bill was one sentence that stipulated that public funds could be used for medical abortions "for the victims of rape or incest, when such rape or incest has been reported promptly to a law enforcement agency or public health service." The bill passed both the House and the Senate with simple majorities but was subsequently vetoed by President Bush. The House reconsidered the bill through a vote on whether to override or sustain the president's veto.

The issue of federal funding for abortion addressed by this bill was of significant interest to women because abortion, rape, incest, and unwanted pregnancies are realities experienced by women. The question thus becomes, do women perceive this issue differently from men? According to an analysis of the voting patterns on this bill, women did vote differently from men, suggesting that the personal *is* political.

The 101st Congress debated this issue with 25 women members, representing 5.7 percent of the House membership. Of those women, 14 were Democrats and 11 were Republicans. Successful override of the president's veto required a two-thirds majority vote by Congress. Although the overall vote fell short with only 55 percent of Congress supporting the veto override, the distribution by

Table 8-1

Total Votes Cast on Override

Vote	Women		Men	
	%	n	%	n
Override	71	17	54	214
Sustain	29	7	46	184

NOTE: One woman and nine men did not vote; three seats were unfilled.

Table 8-2

Voting of Women by Party Affiliation

Vote	Democrat		Republican	
	%	n	%	n
Override	69	9	73	8
Sustain	31	4	27	3

NOTE: One Democratic woman did not vote.

gender resulted in 71 percent of the women favoring an override compared with 54 percent of the men (Table 8-1).

Consequently, women's identification with the issue demonstrated a break with party lines (Table 8-2). A total of 73 percent of the Republican women voted against the president.

Although this is only one issue, it demonstrates the gender stratification on a key women's issue. The question arises as to what the outcome of such a vote might be if women were proportionately represented in Congress. What if 51 percent of the membership were women? This example suggests that because women seem to vote differently based on values such as the personal is political and reconceptualizing power, policies might be very different than they are today.

A MODEL TO PROMOTE WOMEN AS POLITICAL ACTORS

Feminist theories provide a strong foundation to effect greater participation of women in the political process. The concepts of gender equity and equality of results stress social change based on examination of outcomes. The concept of the personal is political demands that all women consider the effect of social and political policies on their lives. Understanding the dynamics of role equity versus role change can help structure a women's political agenda to follow achievable goals.

A successful model for advancing women in the political structure includes a number of variables. Boneparth and Stoper (1988) outlined several elements of our political system that can promote or hinder successful policy-making. These include the decentralized nature of the political system and the strength of incrementalism in policy-making.

Our political system is decentralized and consequently is multi-layered and complex. This complexity means that change is difficult to achieve and when it does occur it can be circumvented on different levels. The abortion issue reflects the advantages and disadvantages of decentralization.

For example, abortion policies have been debated at several levels of government. Numerous state courts have upheld local laws that have tried to limit women's access and rights to abortion. These decisions have been used to force the U.S. Supreme Court to reconsider a woman's right to decide to have an abortion as outlined in the *Roe v. Wade* decision. These efforts have been partially successful in that access to abortion has been restricted, especially for poor women. However, the Supreme Court has failed to overturn *Roe v. Wade*. If the Supreme Court did overturn *Roe v. Wade*, the multilayered system could allow for passage of abortion rights legislation through the congressional process. In fact, the 1992 Democratic leadership of the House and Senate publicly announced that if *Roe v. Wade* was overturned by the Supreme Court, they would support legislation to legalize abortion.

The decentralized nature of our political system contributes to the incremental nature of policy-making. It is far easier to make adjustments to existing policies within the political system than to achieve wholesale change. This position requires patience, long-term goals, and sustained involvement in the political process.

ROLES FOR WOMEN IN POLITICS

It is important to clarify the different roles of women in the political system. Today, equity has been achieved in the area of voter participation, whereas tremendous disparity still exists for women occupying elected positions. Although voting is very important, those in elite positions of power control the political system and its resources and subsequently the policies that affect women's lives. The need exists to broaden women's historically relegated roles in the electoral process.

The model outlined in Table 8-3 presents different modes of political participation. Although the model is presented in a dichotomous format, that is not the case in application.

Table 8-3

Model for Women in Politics

Political Support	Direct Political Involvement
Campaign for candidates	Run for elected office
Vote	Conduct voter registration
Contact elected officials	Lobby
Contribute financially	Do fundraising
Volunteer	Work for elected officials and politicians as paid employee
Meet and organize locally	Serve in political parties
Understand the political process	Participate in the political process

To effect change in representation, public policy, and issues brought to debate, it is imperative that women involve themselves in both political support and direct political involvement. Traditionally, women have been found in political roles that tend to support the direct involvement of men. The political agenda for the 1990s and the 21st century calls for women to focus on ways to increase their own direct involvement. The example of female legislators' voting records on public funding for abortions (in the case of rape or incest) suggests that if women attain proportionate representation in elite positions, public policy might reflect a more feminist and women-centered position.

POLITICAL STRATEGIES

There are five important strategies to be implemented whether one is pursuing a support role, a direct involvement role, or both in the political process:

1. Stress technical change instead of structural overhaul (to limit opposition).

2. Focus on incremental change with identified long-term goals.

3. Aggressively pursue public positions in which incumbents are not running for reelection.

4. Understand the political process and know the key players.

5. Organize locally to establish a constituency and develop a power bloc.

IMPLICATIONS FOR SOCIAL WORK

A feminist agenda also promotes the values of social work. The *NASW Code of Ethics* (National Association of Social Workers, 1994) describes the responsibilities of social workers. The preamble states that "the code is based on the fundamental values of the social work profession that include the worth, dignity, and uniqueness of all persons as well as their rights and opportunities" (p. v). In addition, the code states that "the social worker should advocate changes in policy and legislation to improve social conditions and to promote social justice [and] encourage informed participation by the public in shaping social policies and institutions" (p. 10). Feminism also stresses the well-being of the individual as both a personal and a political issue.

Because social work strives to eliminate discrimination and inequality, gender equity and redefining power are also feminist values compatible with the profession's ethics. Proportionate representation of women in the political system would benefit social work because of the significant proportion of women who are both the clients and the providers of social work services. The feminist agenda outlined in the next section reflects issues social workers have struggled with since the earliest days of the profession.

A FEMINIST AGENDA FOR THE 21ST CENTURY

In testimony before the Senate (February 6, 1992), the Comptroller General presented some of the major issues facing the government (Bowsher, 1992): the federal budget; defense spending; crisis in the health care system; the financial condition of banks, savings institutions, and the insurance industry; interest on the deficit; social security trust fund surplus and the deficit; government fraud, waste, and abuse; and the infrastructure. These concerns are significant and relevant to the management of government affairs. However, with the exception of the need for improved access to health care, this list does not include issues identified as significant for a feminist political agenda. Feminist social policy concerns include guaranteeing freedom of choice in reproductive rights; securing equality of rights through an Equal Rights Amendment; ensuring economic parity regardless of gender by eliminating the feminization of poverty and guaranteeing equal pay as well as comparable worth; supporting family policy such as paternity and maternity leave, family leave, adequate and accessible child care, and enforcement of child support payments; and reducing sexual harassment and violence. In addition to these concerns, social work priorities that are congruent with feminist values include guaranteeing adequate and accessible health care; guaranteeing adequate and accessible housing; eliminating discrimination against any person or group; guaranteeing adequate income; and ensuring access to resources, services, and opportunities.

Unfortunately, issues identified as key to the well-being of women, which are also congruent with social work agendas, are not recognized as vitally important to the well-being of the nation. Although half of the population is female and the family is the primary institution in this country, national policy priorities ignore women's and family issues.

Political agendas are controlled by those in positions of power. Women must work toward proportionate representation to influence the agenda and the course of debate. In addition, women must be inclusive and support candidates who share feminist values and promote a feminist agenda. Until women achieve gender equity in the political system, they will be the recipients of a political system controlled by and for the political elite.

REFERENCES

Boneparth, E., & Stoper, E. (1988). Introduction: A framework for policy analysis. In E. Boneparth & E. Stoper (Eds.), *Women, power and policy* (2nd ed., pp. 1–19). New York: Pergamon Press.

Bowsher, C. A. (1992). *Government management: Major issues facing the Congress.* Washington, DC: General Accounting Office.

Burrell, B. C. (1988). The political opportunity of women candidates for the U.S. House of Representatives in 1984. *Women & Politics, 8*(1), 51–68.

Burrell, B. C. (1990). The presence of women candidates and the role of gender in campaigns for the state legislature in an urban setting: The case of Massachusetts. *Women & Politics, 10*(3), 85–102.

Carroll, S. J. (1989). The personal is political: The intersection of private lives and public roles among women and men in elective and appointive office. *Women & Politics, 9*(2), 51–67.

Center for the American Woman & Politics. (1993). *Fact sheet.* New Brunswick, NJ: Rutgers University, Eagleton Institute of Politics.

Chafetz, J. (1990). *Gender equity: An integrated theory of stability and change.* Newbury Park, CA: Sage Publications.

Christy, C. A. (1987). *Sex differences in political participation.* New York: Praeger.

Clark, C., & Clark, J. (1986). Models of gender and political participation in the United States. *Women & Politics, 6*(1), 5–25.

Congressional Quarterly Almanac. (1990). 1991 occupants of statehouses. *46,* p. 927. Washington, DC: Author.

Evans, J. (1981). USA. In J. Lovenduski & J. Hills (Eds.), *The politics of the second electorate* (pp. 31–51). London: Routledge & Kegan Paul.

Freeman, P. K., & Lyons, W. (1990). Legislators' perceptions of women in state legislatures. *Women & Politics, 10*(4), 121–131.

Gelb, J., & Palley, M. L. (1982). *Women and public policies.* Princeton, NJ: Princeton University Press.

Hale, M. M., & Kelly, R. M. (1989). (Eds.). *Gender, bureaucracy, and democracy.* Westport, CT: Greenwood Press.

H.R. 2990, Section 204, 101st Cong., 1st Sess., *Cong. Rec.,* Sept. 26, (1989).

Jones, K. B. (1988). Towards the revision of politics. In K. B. Jones & A. G. Jonasdottir (Eds.), *The political interests of gender* (pp. 11–32). Newbury Park, CA: Sage Publications.

Katz, J. L. (1992). For many incumbents, the House just isn't home anymore. *American Caucus, 1*(2), 4.

Kendrigan, M. L. (1984). *Political equality in a democratic society.* Westport, CT: Greenwood Press.

Mathews, D. G., & De Hart, J. S. (1990). *Sex, gender, and the politics of ERA.* New York: Oxford University Press.

National Association of Social Workers. (1994). *NASW code of ethics.* Washington, DC: Author.

Owen, D., & Dennis, J. (1988). Gender differences in the politicization of American children. *Women & Politics, 8*(2), 23–43.

Renzetti, C. M., & Curran, D. J. (1992). *Women, men, and society* (2nd ed.). Boston: Allyn & Bacon.

Roe v. Wade, 410 U.S. 113 (1973).

Sidel, R. (1986). *The plight of poor women in affluent America: Women and children last.* New York: Penguin Books.

Stanley, H. W., & Niemi, R. G. (1988). *Vital statistics on American politics*. Washington, DC: Congressional Quarterly.

Stockard, J., & Johnson, M. M. (1992). *Sex and gender in society* (2nd ed.). Englewood Cliffs, NJ: Prentice Hall.

U.S. Bureau of the Census. (1989). Voting and registration in the election of November 1988. In *Current population reports* (Series P-20, No. 440). Washington, DC: U.S. Government Printing Office.

U.S. Bureau of the Census. (1990). Money income and poverty status in the United States: 1989. In *Current population reports* (Series P-60, No. 168). Washington, DC: U.S. Government Printing Office.

U.S. Bureau of the Census. (1991). Voting and registration in the election of November 1990. In *Current population reports* (Series P-20, No. 453). Washington, DC: U.S. Government Printing Office.

U.S. Department of Labor. (1990). *20 facts on women workers*. Washington, DC: U.S. Government Printing Office.

Van Den Bergh, N., & Cooper, L. B. (1986). Introduction. In N. Van Den Bergh & L. B. Cooper (Eds.), *Feminist visions for social work* (pp. 1–28). Silver Spring, MD: National Association of Social Workers.

9

A Feminist Ethic
toward Peace

Dorothy Van Soest

P romoting peace and resisting nuclear war are consistent with both feminist values and officially articulated social work values. The basic premise of this chapter is that feminist values, particularly as they are explicated in a relational ethic of care (Imre, 1982; Noddings, 1984), provide the grounding for a social work position about the nuclear threat and militarism. A feminist ethic of care may even represent the core value that is most consistent with what social work is about.

Since the mid-1980s there have been some indications of an increased awareness and concern among social workers regarding militarization and its effects, the psychosocial consequences of the nuclear threat, and the professional responsibility to address those serious issues (Gil, 1989; Goldberg, 1984; Greenwald & Zeitlin, 1987; Iatridis, 1988; Korotkin, 1985; Rice & Mary, 1989; Schachter, 1986; Schaffner Goldberg & Rosen, 1992; Sewell & Kelly, 1988; Stenzel & Baeck, 1984; White, 1986; Williams, 1987; Zealley, 1987). For example, a recently published book on peace studies was written from a social work perspective (Keefe & Roberts, 1991). In addition, the National Association of Social Workers (NASW) Delegate Assemblies adopted peace as a social policy priority goal in 1982, 1986, and 1990. NASW also adopted an official policy statement on Peace and Social Welfare in 1987, its national board of directors has taken positions on military interventions in Central America and the Persian Gulf, and the association published a curriculum guide for incorporating peace and social justice issues into social work education in 1992. The International Federation of Social Workers adopted an International Policy on Peace and Disarmament in 1988. Although it might be concluded from such activities that there is an implicit understanding that violence, war, and the nuclear threat are antithetical to social work values and ethics, social workers, like the general population, are diverse in their ideological, personal, and professional orientations related to peace issues (Van Soest, Johnston, & Sullivan, 1987). Moreover, there is not even a consensus among social workers related to the values of the profession (Prigmore & Atherton, 1979). However, there have been serious attempts to identify the core values that give professional direction (Joseph, 1989; Levy, 1973).

During the late 1970s and the early 1980s, there was considerable feminist organizing around nuclear disarmament. Around the world women from all walks of life joined together in protests, peace camps, and other actions. Gioseffi's (1988) anthology illustrated the feminist view that the nuclear threat and militarism are far too important to be left to self-selected "experts"; that is, the opinions and feelings of women must be heard, and women must be included in any political and moral decisions that are made. Van Den Bergh and Cooper (1986) pointed out that because feminism is concerned with ending domination and resisting oppression, it is a worldview that can lend perspective to any issue.

It is clear that women's perspectives on peace are not always the same as men's. Since 1979 a number of initiatives have been introduced into the peace movement that could only have been introduced by women (Assiter, 1983). For example, the peace camp movement (which began at Greenham Common air base, a proposed cruise missile site) resulted in similar women's peace camps springing up around the world. The style and tactics of the whole operation were feminist in orientation, with an emphasis on relationships, a holistic approach to organizing and action, and nonhierarchical decision-making and consensual problem-solving processes. Another example of feminist organizing on this issue was the 1982 founding of Women Against Military Madness, a peace organization in Minnesota based on a women's model of process and empowerment.

The feminist movement's actions against the nuclear threat and violence of the last 15 years are based on a rich heritage of women's peacemaking. This tradition is symbolized by the story about women in the Iroquois Nation who, it has been purported, made the suggestion that one way to prevent war was to stop having sex with men if they persisted in bellicose behaviors. Social work activists at the beginning of the 20th century played pivotal roles in peace activities. Emily Greene Balch, who worked at the Dennison Settlement House in Boston, was cofounder of the Women's International League for Peace and Freedom. She was later fired from her position as an economics professor at Wellesley because of her peace activities. Jane Addams presided over the Women's Peace Conference at The Hague. She and Balch are the only two women from the United States ever to have won the Nobel Peace Prize for their contributions to peace. Lillian Wald was part of the first group of social workers to speak out against World War I; she wrote a Peace Manifesto and went to the Peace Conference at The Hague. Another notable woman, Jeannette Rankin (the first woman elected to Congress), voted against U.S. entry into war in 1917 and again in 1941 and led a women's anti–Vietnam War march on Washington in 1968 when she was 88 years old (Addams, 1906, 1922/1983; Bussey & Tims, 1965; Costin, 1982; Randall, 1964; Siegel, 1983; Sullivan, 1993).

The purpose of this chapter is to show that concerns for peace within the social work profession and the feminist movement can be seen as complementary by examining how both suggest a relational ethic of care, which can deter militarism and nuclear threat. Factual information and theoretical strategies are presented in the next section as an overview of the nuclear threat and militarism. This is followed by an articulation of feminist principles as espousing an ethic of care that can be used in analyzing the problem. This feminist ethic of care is contrasted with traditional philosophical ethics of principle, justice, and utility. In the final section, the implications of using a feminist ethical position to address the nuclear threat and disarmament are discussed for social work in general and clinical social workers in particular.

MILITARISM AND THE NUCLEAR THREAT

Militarism has taken over the world economy in a most deleterious way. World military statistics, compiled from a variety of official sources and updated annually (Sivard, 1991), indicate that nearly $900 billion was spent on weapons in 1990. U.S. military expenditures in 1991 were $303 billion, or $800 million per day; the Pentagon budget for 1992 was about $291 billion (Council of Economic Advisors, 1991). Sixty-six countries are in the business of selling arms. The United States and the former Soviet Union are the largest arms exporters. The biggest buyers of arms are Third World countries, with the Middle East being the most lucrative region.

Impact of Military Spending on Health and Welfare

Military spending tends to deter allocation of expenditures for social welfare needs such as health and education, which endangers the welfare of the country in the long run (Dumas, 1986; Iatridis, 1988; Korotkin, 1985; Russett, 1970). When Sivard (1991) compared the rankings of 142 countries, the 12 countries with the largest military expenditures in 1987 all made a poorer showing in socioeconomic standing than in military power. The United States ranked number one in military power but number 18 in infant mortality rate and number 22 in the mortality rate of children younger than five. Additional social indicators reveal that in the United States one child in five is poor, twice the child poverty rate in Canada, Sweden, and Germany; nearly one-fourth of poor families live in housing officially classified as inadequate; 5.5 million children younger than 12 suffer from hunger; and 32 million people live below the official poverty line. Sharp budget cuts in programs for the poor have been well documented (Children's Defense Fund, 1986); however, the middle class has also suffered from the combined effects of social disinvestments and military spending (Iatridis, 1988). Although increased military spending has lowered the standard of living for billions of people around the globe, by far the largest percentage of people living below the poverty line is found among female-headed households (Gioseffi, 1988). The current arms policy of the United States not only neglects the poor in the United States and the poor of other nations, but there is good reason to believe that it is destroying the U.S. economy (Barnet, 1981; Bluestone & Harrison, 1982; Galbraith, 1981; Mahony, 1982; Russett, 1970; Sivard, 1991).

Military Deaths

The toll of militarism on human lives illustrates war's realities. It is estimated that there are 26 million soldiers worldwide in regular armed forces and another 40 million in the military reserves. The United Nations estimates that 200,000 of these soldiers are children (Sivard, 1991). From 1500 to 1990, excluding the Persian Gulf War, there were an estimated 141,901,000 war-related deaths worldwide. Over one-half of the total killed were civilians; however, during the 1980s, 75 percent of all people killed in wars were civilians (Sivard, 1991). Since the end of World War II there have been 140 to 160 conflicts in which perhaps 10 million people have been killed (Edwards, 1986; Lefever & Hunt, 1982).

Nuclear Arms Proliferation

Although millions of people have suffered and died as a result of conventional wars, nuclear weapons have changed the nature and risks of war in a way that is unimaginable. In World War II the

United States used small nuclear weapons twice, causing catastrophic consequences for the people of Japan. Today's nuclear arsenals are lethal beyond imagination and the possibility that nuclear weapons could be used again is a reality the world faces. According to Sivard (1991), the United States and the former Soviet Union have an inventory of 52,000 nuclear weapons, a decrease of almost 10 percent from the former high of 56,400 as a result of arms control agreements and other factors. This represents an explosive force 1,600 times the firepower released in World War II, Korea, and Vietnam combined, during which 44 million peoplewere killed. A recent accord between the United States and Russia would reduce the number of U.S. and Russian strategic weapons by the year 2003 to the lowest level since 1969. However, a dangerous dilemma exists related to disposing of the plutonium from dismantled warheads. No safe, environmentally benign, or economically feasible method exists for disposing of the tons of this substance, the most lethal on earth. Worldwide attention is newly focused on the need to halt nuclear proliferation. At present there are six confirmed nuclear powers, and military analysts expect that 31 countries will be able to produce nuclear weapons by the year 2000, including India, Pakistan, Israel, South Africa, Argentina, Brazil, North Korea, Iran, Iraq, and Taiwan (Harris & Markusen, 1986; Sivard, 1991).

The nuclear threat brings an urgency to the way we view militarism because, as Albert Einstein predicted, "we drift toward unparalleled catastrophe" (White, 1986, p. xv). A large-scale nuclear war, according to a 1979 report by the U.S. Arms Control and Disarmament Agency, could cause 25 million to 100 million deaths within 30 days, with many more to follow. In addition, it is predicted that 65 percent to 90 percent of industry would be destroyed and 200 of the largest cities would be annihilated. Other studies suggested that a full-scale nuclear war could kill between 300 million and 1 billion people initially, with more to follow (Edwards, 1986). Studies by Sagan (1984) estimated that the firestorms generated by a large-scale nuclear attack would result in much of the earth being covered with sooty smoke for months, thus threatening the survival of the human species. Dyson (1984) predicted that the effects of a first nuclear war might not be severe enough to exterminate humankind; however, such a war would leave the human species incurably insane. The unparalleled suffering and hatred that would result might create a pattern of revenge and a succession of nuclear wars that would in the end make the planet uninhabitable. In his poignant and terrifying chapter, "The Fate of the Earth," Schell (1982) unequivocally contended that a nuclear war would mean extinction: "Two paths lie before us. One leads to death, the other to life. If we choose the first path—if we numbly refuse to acknowledge the nearness of extinction, all the while increasing our preparations to bring it about—then we in effect become the allies of death, and in everything we do our attachment to life will weaken" (p. 234).

PREVENTING NUCLEAR WAR AND PROMOTING PEACE

Given the range of scenarios about survivability, it is no surprise that there is widespread agreement that steps should be taken to prevent nuclear war. However, there is a wide divergence of opinions about how to do so and about the priority that should be given to militarism. Implicit in the five alternative strategies that follow are underlying values and ethical principles that may not be consciously held but are nevertheless very influential in shaping our judgments.

Nuclear Deterrence

Deterrence, combined with the concept of a limited nuclear war, is the official U.S. strategy. Because each superpower has the ability to incinerate the defenseless population of the other many times over, each nation refrains from attacking out of fear of retaliation. Each side knows that an attack on the other would be tantamount to suicide. Thus, the idea is that nuclear weapons are built never to be used and weapons aimed at people lessen the risk of war (Krauthammer, 1982). Deterrence proponents insist that although living in a world of deterrence is very uncomfortable, it has prevented the outbreak of nuclear war and has also placed a restraint on political behavior that has enabled people to feel reasonably secure (Edwards, 1986). Critics of the "balance of terror" or deterrent position maintain that deeply disturbing dangers to life and the environment make the existence of nuclear weapons barely credible. For example, one study revealed that there were 3,200 accidents involving nuclear navies in the 1980s. Dangers from nuclear testing include evidence of cancer rates 70 percent above the national average at the main Soviet test site near Semipalatinsk (Sivard, 1991). Recently, concerns have been expressed about the safety of the older Soviet-designed nuclear reactors in Eastern Europe.

Strategic Defense: A Self-Defense Strategy

If deterrence fails, there must be a defense against a nuclear attack once it has been initiated. The strategic defense strategy aims to move the arms race to defensive weaponry by making attack more difficult and costly and preventing attack by making its outcome uncertain. The idea of a protective shield against nuclear weapons and the Star Wars image presented by then-President Reagan appeal to the need for security. This approach does not imply, however, that offensive nuclear weapons would be eliminated. The weapons would be maintained in a manner similar to the present (Dyson, 1984). Proponents of the Strategic Defense Initiative (SDI) are hopeful that this new technology will ultimately ensure safety against nuclear weapons. This strategy appeals to the ethic that says self-defense is good and mass murder is evil. Opponents of SDI, however, have questioned whether it is technically feasible and maintain that it creates a dangerous illusion of safety that makes us more vulnerable. The concept does not diminish the chance that nuclear war might begin as a result of an accident or a miscalculation. It has even been asserted that SDI introduces a new danger that nuclear war might be triggered by some "overenthusiastic spaceman starting a shooting match in the sky" (Dyson, 1984, p. 256). Although charges of wasteful spending on worthless defense studies and criticisms of proposed programs that will not work have come from within the U.S. Department of Defense as well as from outside, SDI continues to have support in both Congress and the administration and to experience growth despite other cutbacks in defense spending.

Peace through Strength and a New World Order
An approach to security through military buildup is the position taken by the U.S. Department of Defense (1983). The first priority of this strategy has been the modernization of all components of the U.S. strategic nuclear forces and the readiness upgrade of U.S. conventional forces. Combined with the motivation to be secure from enemy attack is a defensive strategy called "coercive diplomacy" that involves threatening opponents with dire consequences if they don't abandon an aggressive action. With the collapse of the Soviet Union and political discussions about a cut in the defense budget, the threat-based arguments are surfacing in the form of identifying the new nature of the threat we must protect ourselves against. A Pentagon study prepared as the basis for budgetary planning through 1999 details seven hypothetical war scenarios ranging from regional hostilities to a global war. Some proponents of this strategy go beyond the fear-based defense argument and see the results of the Persian Gulf War as a gain in U.S. assets and opportunities to "shape the contours of a new international system" (George, 1992, p. 1), in other words, a new world order with the United States as essentially the only superpower.

Alternative Self-Defense Strategies

Opponents of the strategy of security through military buildup propose alternative means of defense. Nonnuclear resistance advocates (Dyson, 1984) propose complete unilateral nuclear disarmament combined with vigorous deployment of nonnuclear weapons and a willingness to use them. Nonviolent resistance, on the other hand, requires an active pacifism as put into practice by Gandhi in India. This strategy requires not shedding any person's blood except one's own, disobedience to unjust laws, and a refusal to collaborate with unjust authorities. Proponents of pacifism point to its long and honorable history and suggest that the abolition of nuclear weapons is a task of the same magnitude as the abolition of slavery (Dyson, 1984). Civilian-based defense is a national defense against internal usurpations and foreign invasions through prepared nonviolent noncooperation and defiance by the society's population and institutions (Sharp, 1985). Its aim is to become able to deny attackers their objectives, to become politically unruleable by would-be tyrants, and to subvert the attackers' troops and functionaries to unreliability and even mutiny. To be successful, this strategy would require full-scale attention on the same level that the military buildup has required in resources, training, and attitude preparation.

Swords into Plowshares Alternative: Economic Conversion

This position is essentially one that proposes the dismantling of a large portion of the world's war-making capabilities and transferring resources from military to civilian purposes through a planned process that would not cause social and economic dislocation. Economic conversion implies a reallocation of budgets to make funds available for nonviolent purposes. Research, production, and management practices in arms-producing factories would have to be adapted to civilian needs and criteria. Retraining of employees, refashioning of production equipment, and finding civilian uses for military bases and personnel would be required. Five economic conversion bills have been introduced in the House or Senate (Renner, 1990).

FEMINIST ETHICAL PRINCIPLES AS A VEHICLE FOR ANALYSIS

The alternative solutions and their underlying ethical principles reflect traditional individualistic ethics based on principles that are rational, logical, and quantifiable. Although the views focus on life-and-death issues of profound moral and personal concern to people, virtually no attention or credit is given to the affective and relational foundation of people's existence with each other. As Noddings

(1984) purported, "one who attempts to ignore or to climb above the human affect at the heart of ethicality may well be guilty of romantic rationalism. What is recommended in such a framework simply cannot be broadly applied in the actual world" (p. 3).

What is needed is an analysis of ethical principles about war and peace based on a feminist perspective rooted in receptivity, relatedness, and responsiveness (Noddings, 1984). What is proposed is an ethic of care that approaches conflicts relationally, based on reciprocity (Gilligan, 1982; Imre, 1982, 1989; Noddings, 1984, 1989; Rhodes, 1986). The perspective forms the criteria against which alternative strategies can be evaluated.

Feminist Perspective as a Relational Ethic of Care

When concerns about nuclear war and militarism are approached from a feminist view, a question that might be raised is: "If women were central to the argument, how would it be defined?" (Lerner, 1986, p. 228). The following quote (Soper, 1983) illustrates a feminist response to thinking about nuclear war that sounds strikingly different from the discussion thus far:

> It is when I think about children—my own and children in general—that I feel most despairing. [The despair] is more to do with a society that can allow such a total contradiction between the tender, patient, day-to-day care that parents and nurses and teachers bestow on children, and the callousness of nuclear decision-making .... Why, on the one hand, should I be able to see in nuclear weapons things that melt eyeballs, blast bodies to bloody fragments and burn the flesh to the bone of living people, while military strategists see in them only counters in a game? Why is it that while I flinch at every euphemism they produce, these experts continue to compute their equations of terror and to offer their dispassionate appraisals of "lethality factor" and "collateral damage"? Some part of the answer, I suspect, must lie in the fact that this largely masculine body of personnel has never had to attend to children, intimately, day after day, ministering to their simplest physical needs. These, of course, will be dismissed as emotive and feminine arguments . . . and that the point is how to prevent [nuclear war]. I will argue through the irrationality of deterrence and current nuclear policy with anyone who cares to take me on: I will do so in detail, coldly and even clinically. But in a final moment of feminine intuition, I might well want to add that much of the "rationality" of those who offer their "realistic" scenarios is utterly and completely out of touch with the reality of what nuclear weapons can do—and thus in turn with a significant part of the reason for not wanting to have them. (p. 178)

Noddings (1989) wrote about war from the perspective of one who has had responsibility for caring, maintaining, and nurturing. She maintained that an approach based on law and principle is the approach of the "detached one" and suggested that a feminist view, which is concerned with people, is an alternative that men can embrace as well as women. This feminist view is rooted in receptivity, relatedness, and responsiveness. It does not imply that logic should be discarded or that logic is alien to women. Noddings conceded that a relational approach may be more typical of women than men; however, the truth of that assumption must be empirically validated. A relational ethic concentrates on the moral health and vigor of relationships, not of individuals, and recognizes that moral judgments and decisions about how to act must take into account the relations in which moral agents live and find their identities. A relational ethic is rooted in and depends on natural caring, whereby we act on behalf of the other and the relationship is characterized by a reciprocal dependency. Maternal caregiving is an example of this basic structure of care and illustrates its source in biological life. The caring attitude expressed in our earliest memories of being nurtured is considered to be universally accessible.

Ruddick (1989) argued that the caring experience of women, above all the "preservative love" of women as mothers, is what can save us from a nuclear holocaust. She explored in detail the day-to-day caring of children by mothers and saw the peacemaking, flexibility, and patience it requires as a blueprint for the kind of work needed to promote peace. Others have also traced women's peculiar revolt against war to their experience as mothers (Addams, 1922/1983; Schreiner, 1911). Noddings (1989) saw ethical caring as a means to restore shaky relations to that preferred state of maternal caregiving. Although many women speak out strongly for peace (Gioseffi, 1988), this is not to argue that women are by nature or by socialization more pacific than men. The recent historical record is inconclusive, and feminists have posited conflicting theories on women's relation to war and peace. Women's historical linkage to pacifism (Florence, Marshall, & Ogden, 1915/1987) is counterbalanced by instances when women have espoused revolution with hope and war with enthusiasm (Ruddick, 1989). Women have fed, nursed, soothed, served, and attempted to relieve suffering while paradoxically they have also allowed themselves to support the infliction of suffering in their endorsement of wars and have sometimes expressed pride in the sacrifice of their sons. Noddings (1989) explained that women's acceptance of war does not seem to emerge from seeing striving as a virtue but rather from a desire to remain in positive relation with those who worship striving. "Women do not seem so much interested in overcoming opponents as they are in supporting their own combatants" (Noddings, 1989, p. 204).

Noddings (1989) developed the analysis further by defining moral evil as occurring when a person causes useless and intractable pain or fails to alleviate it when he or she is clearly in a position to do so. Cultural evil, which includes poverty, racism, war, and sexism, is another form of evil. War as a form of cultural evil is caused by a large moral evil—the neglect of relation. War can thus be defined as psychosis caused by an inability to see relationships. The neglect of relation causes separation and is instrumental in creating rivals and making enemies. It can be traced in part to the pervasive ideology of individualism that supports a competitive, adversarial way of life. Competition easily leads to enmity and the projection of evil onto others. Labeling people as enemies leads us to devalue their moral worth, and this devaluation allows us to treat them in ways that would be unthinkable if they were part of our moral community (Bok, 1979). U.S. foreign policy operates under the persistent belief that one is consummately safe only when secure from others (the enemy); an ethic of care insists that one is preeminently safe through the connectedness of relationships.

A relational ethic of care and feminist principles complement each other, providing a framework for deterring militarism and the threat of nuclear war. Feminist principles that are congruent with an ethic of care include focusing on relationships; valuing process between people as equally important as goal accomplishment; refusing to dichotomize phenomena or people into good or evil, allies or enemies; and emphasizing the value of personal relationships as creating a context for political, economic, and social structures and systems.

IMPLICATIONS FOR SOCIAL WORK

In examining the responsibility of social workers to be peacemakers, we are summoned to a deeper understanding of ourselves that transcends the usual us versus them mentality and does not polarize the situation into a simple good versus evil dichotomy. We are challenged professionally to define a core value or principle for social work that is deemed moral and just and that will provide the grounding for an ethical position about the nuclear threat and militarism. Because relationship and caring are integral to social work practice, they may represent the core value that is most consistent with what social work is about. Imre (1982) maintained that relationship, as a vital part of social work, has its roots in caring, which locates morality primarily in the ability to empathize (Noddings, 1984). Herein lies the key to the ethical position for the social work profession in relation to the nuclear threat, militarism, and war. By asserting that a truism in social work is that goodness is caring, we establish the primary foundation for both ethical behavior and practical actions for peace.

Indirect Practice Implications

Through a variety of strategies—lobbying, educating, organizing, forming coalitions, and policy advocacy—social workers can work to deter the nuclear threat and promote peace. Professional opposition to nuclear deterrence is endorsed on the grounds that it is a policy based on fear and separation, which destroy our ability to care for ourselves and others. The existence of nuclear and other weapons of mass destruction creates fear and separation and requires protection from "the other," or the enemy, rather than promoting connection and relation. For social workers who wish to adhere to a pacifist principle, such a position is consistent with an ethic of care when it is based on valuing and respecting people's connectedness rather than creating false dichotomies and artificial separations (Van Den Bergh & Cooper, 1986). When social workers support nonviolent approaches to self-defense, they open the possibility of relationship, whereas support of violence of any kind creates more separation. Economic conversion to a peacetime economy should be supported because it frees up resources to meet people's needs and restore the economy in a way that has the potential to create community among people.

Direct Practice Implications

The core conditions of the helping relationship that form a constellation of skills and attitudes for social work—genuineness or realness, caring or unconditional positive regard, and empathic understanding—are the same characteristics that are required of peacemakers. Practice issues related to the nuclear threat and militarism are thus not necessarily atypical or peculiar to social work practice, although they might not be comprehended readily or recognized as carrying the tremendous import they do in terms of threatening our ability to care. By grounding ethical dilemmas and practice decisions in an ethic of care and relation, social workers have a framework that makes it possible to examine practice issues from the perspective of what damages or supports caring and what heals relationships, rather than separating people from each other and perpetuating violence. As antidotes to violence and separation, the skills of active listening and communicating empathy provide social workers with the ability to contribute to peace through nonviolent conflict resolution.

Understanding one's professional role in responding specifically to the potential impact of the nuclear threat on individuals, families, and groups requires that social workers first face their own denial, psychic numbness, and sense of powerlessness about the issue. It also requires an understanding, from a psychosocial perspective, of how the nuclear threat affects mental and emotional health, the normal development of children, intergenerational relationships, and the family's ability to master various stages of the life cycle (Greenwald & Zeitlin, 1987). While being careful not to impose one's own concerns about the nuclear threat onto clients, it is important not to collude with clients' possible fears and helplessness that affect their ability to care, to feel effective in the world, and to engage in the change process.

CONCLUSION

Imre's (1982) basic presupposition that "goodness is caring" in social work grounds us as peacemakers. To act responsibly in the nuclear age, social workers must be informed of the situation, work toward healing relationships, and oppose any act that separates human beings from each other. This approach is consistent with feminist practice principles that value interrelationship, connectedness, empowerment rather than conflict and competition, and the development of community through a covenant of caring. Supporting these values as we move into the 21st century can do much to promote peace and deter nuclear proliferation.

REFERENCES

Addams, J. (1906). *Newer ideals of peace.* New York: Macmillan.

Addams, J. (1983). *Peace and bread in time of war.* Silver Spring, MD: National Association of Social Workers. (Original work published 1922)

Assiter, A. (1983). Womanpower and nuclear politics: Women and the peace movement. In D. Thompson (Ed.), *Over our dead bodies: Women against the bomb* (pp. 199–206). London: Virago Press.

Barnet, R. (1981). *Real security: Restoring American power in a dangerous decade.* New York: Atheneum.

Bluestone, B., & Harrison, B. (1982). *The deindustrialization of America.* New York: Basic Books.

Bok, S. (1979). *Lying: Moral choice in public and private life*. New York: Vintage Books.

Bussey, G., & Tims, M. (1965). *Women's International League for Peace and Freedom*. London: George Allen & Unwin.

Children's Defense Fund. (1986). *Children's Defense Fund budget: An analysis of the FY 1987 federal budget and children*. Washington, DC: Children's Defense Fund.

Costin, L. B. (1982). Feminism, pacifism, internationalism, and the 1915 International Congress of Women. *Women's Studies International Forum, 5*, 301–315.

Council of Economic Advisors. (1991). *Economic indicators: September 1991* (Report prepared for the Joint Economic Committee of the U.S. Congress). Washington, DC: U.S. Government Printing Office.

Dumas, L. J. (1986). The military albatross: How arms spending is destroying the economy. In J. Wallace (Ed.), *Waging peace: A handbook for the struggle to abolish nuclear weapons* (pp. 100–105). New York: Harper & Row.

Dyson, F. (1984). *Weapons and hope*. New York: Harper & Row.

Edwards, A.J.C. (1986). *Nuclear weapons, the balance of terror, the quest for peace*. Stonybrook: State University of New York Press.

Florence, M. S., Marshall, C., & Ogden, C. K. (1987). *Militarism versus feminism: Writings on women and war*. London: Virago Press. (Original work published 1915)

Galbraith, J. K. (1981, June/July). The economics of the arms race—and after. *Bulletin of Atomic Scientists*, pp. 13–16.

George, A. I. (1992). *Forceful persuasion: Coercive diplomacy as an alternative to war*. Washington, DC: U.S. Institute of Peace Press.

Gil, D. G. (1989, March). Work, violence, injustice and war. *Journal of Sociology and Social Welfare, 16*(1), 39–53.

Gilligan, C. (1982). *In a different voice: Psychological theory and women's development*. Cambridge, MA: Harvard University Press.

Gioseffi, D. (Ed.). (1988). *Women on war: Essential voices for the nuclear age*. New York: Touchstone.

Goldberg, G. S. (1984). Adding the arms race to the psychosocial equation. *Social Work, 29*, 481–483.

Greenwald, D., & Zeitlin, S. (1987). *No reason to talk about it: Families confront the nuclear taboo*. New York: W. W. Norton.

Harris, J. B., & Markusen, E. (Eds.). (1986). *Nuclear weapons and the threat of nuclear war*. New York: Harcourt Brace Jovanovich.

Iatridis, D. S. (1988). New social deficit: Neoconservatism's policy of social underdevelopment. *Social Work, 33,* 11–15.

Imre, R. W. (1982). *Knowing and caring*. Lanham, MD: University Press of America.

Imre, R. W. (1989). Moral theory for social work. *Social Thought, 15*(1), 18–27.

Joseph, M. V. (1989). Social work ethics: Historical and contemporary perspectives. *Social Thought, 15*(1), 3–4.

Keefe, T., & Roberts, R. E. (1991). *Realizing peace: An introduction to peace studies*. Ames: Iowa State University Press.

Korotkin, A. (1985). Impact of military spending on the nation's quality of life. *Social Work, 30,* 369–372.

Krauthammer, C. (1982). In defense of deterrence. In E. W. Lefever & E. S. Hunt (Eds.), *The apocalyptic premise: Nuclear arms debated* (pp. 69–81). Washington, DC: Ethics and Public Policy Center.

Lefever, E. W., & Hunt, E. S. (Eds.). (1982). *The apocalyptic premise: Nuclear arms debated*. Washington, DC: Ethics and Public Policy Center.

Lerner, G. (1986). *The creation of patriarchy*. New York: Oxford University Press.

Levy, C. S. (1973, Winter). The value base of social work. *Journal of Education for Social Work, 9*(1), 34–42.

Mahony, B. R. (1982). The case for nuclear pacifism. In E. W. Lefever & E. S. Hunt (Eds.), *The apocalyptic premise: Nuclear arms debated* (pp. 279–293). Washington, DC: Ethics and Public Policy Center.

Noddings, N. (1984). *Caring: A feminine approach to ethics and moral education*. Berkeley: University of California Press.

Noddings, N. (1989). *Women and evil*. Berkeley: University of California Press.

Prigmore, C. S., & Atherton, C. R. (1979). *Social welfare policy: Analysis and formulation*. Lexington, MA: D. C. Heath.

Randall, M. (1964). *Improper Bostonian: Emily Greene Balch*. New York: Twayne Publishers.

Renner, M. (1990, June). *Swords into plowshares: Converting to a peace economy* (Worldwatch Paper 96). Washington, DC: Worldwatch Institute.

Rhodes, M. L. (1986). *Ethical dilemmas in social work practice*. Boston: Routledge & Kegan Paul.

Rice, S., & Mary, N. L. (1989). Beyond war: A new perspective for social work. *Social Work, 34,* 175–178.

Ruddick, S. (1989). *Maternal thinking: Toward a politics of peace*. New York: Ballantine Books.

Russett, B. M. (1970). *What price vigilance? The burdens of national defense*. New Haven, CT: Yale University Press.

Sagan, C. (1984). Nuclear war and climatic catastrophe. *Foreign Affairs, 62,* 257–292.

Schachter, B. (1986). Growing up under the mushroom cloud. *Social Work, 31,* 187–192.

Schaffner Goldberg, G., & Rosen, S. (1992). Disengulfing the peace dividend. *Social Work, 37,* 87–93.

Schell, J. (1982). The fate of the earth. In E. W. Lefever & E. S. Hunt (Eds.), *The apocalyptic premise: Nuclear arms debated* (pp. 221–234). Washington, DC: Ethics and Public Policy Center.

Schreiner, O. (1911). *Women and labour*. London: Virago.

Sewell, S., & Kelly, A. (1988). *Professions in the nuclear age*. Brisbane, Australia: Boolarong Publications.

Sharp, G. (1985). *National security through civilian-based defense*. Omaha, NE: Association for Transarmament Studies.

Siegel, B. (1983). *Lillian Wald of Henry Street*. New York: Macmillan.

Sivard, R. L. (1991). *World military and social expenditures*. Washington, DC: World Priorities.

Soper, K. (1983). Contemplating a nuclear future: Nuclear war, politics and the individual. In D. Thompson (Ed.), *Over our dead bodies: Women against the bomb* (pp. 169–179). London: Virago Press.

Stenzel, A. K., & Baeck, A. (1983). Social work and human survival in the nuclear age: A call for action. *Social Work, 28,* 399–401.

Sullivan, M. (1993). Social work's legacy of peace. *Social Work, 38,* 513–520.

U.S. Department of Defense. (1983). *Soviet military power.* Washington, DC: Author.

Van Den Bergh, N., & Cooper, L. B. (Eds.). (1986). *Feminist visions for social work.* Silver Spring, MD: National Association of Social Workers.

Van Soest, D., Johnston, N., & Sullivan, M. (1987). Orientation to peace and justice in professional social work education in the United States. *Social Development Issues, 10*(3), 81–99.

White, R. K. (Ed.). (1986). *Psychology and the prevention of nuclear war.* New York: New York University Press.

Williams, L. F. (1987). Under the nuclear umbrella. *Social Work, 32,* 246–249.

Zealley, H. (1987). Professional voices. In H. Davis (Ed.), *Ethics and defense: Power and responsibility in the nuclear age* (pp. 226–240). New York: Basil Blackwell.

10

Global Feminist Zeitgeist Practice

Janice Wood Wetzel

Since the founding of the social work profession in the early 1900s, its members have espoused a person–environment model of practice, recognizing the importance of the impact of societal forces on emotional well-being, as well as the impact of personal attitudes and behaviors on the social environment. Throughout the 20th century, however, social critics have faulted professionals in the Western world for their heavy emphasis on the person, which too often resulted in blaming the victim. All too often, women have paid the price. Conversely, social work clinicians have faulted community organization and social development proponents for ignoring the psychological trauma of people in need of therapy. The debate has reached international proportions. Developing countries who have used Western literature and methods have found the concept of therapy inappropriate to meet the tremendous social needs of the people they serve, yet by ignoring emotional trauma they ignore reality. Since 1948, the World Health Organization has emphasized the need for a global perspective when addressing mental health concerns. Such a perspective emphasizes prevention of community mental health problems and decentralization of services (Mathews & Wagenfeld, 1992). Nevertheless, Western logic and values that emphasize cure and the problems within a patient, ignoring prevention and the impact of destructive attitudes toward women in their home and work environments, have dominated the world mental health scene. This is no less true in the United States.

Prevention and social intervention represent the most important challenge of the 21st century, whatever the country or culture (Viswanathan & Wetzel, 1993). Global Feminist Zeitgeist Practice, the model presented here, is designed to meet that challenge without sacrificing the significance of either societal influence or emotional well-being. It brings a new feminist vision of practice to the international social work community.

SOCIAL DEVELOPMENT AND WOMEN'S MENTAL HEALTH

Until a few years ago, efforts to enhance people and their societies throughout the world focused solely on social development, a term that was defined as political, legal, and economic advancement. After decades of efforts and billions of dollars, global research indicated that programs designed to enhance this definition of social development usually failed because the needs of women were largely ignored (Dixon, 1980). The enhancement of women's universally low self-esteem is essential to the realization of their advancement. Even when opportunities for advancement are available, they are not incorporated into women's lives when their emotional well-being is ignored. But global experience over the past few years has shown how resistant people are to concepts of prevention of mental illness and promotion of mental health. The incorporation of such concepts into social development was disregarded, even denigrated, by feminists. With few exceptions, it was generally held that such ideas were "frills of the Western world" that were inappropriate and irrelevant to those in the developing world who had more "substantive" problems.

The erroneous assumption was that women's economic, political, and legal social development would automatically circumscribe personal development. Global research and women's universal experience has awakened the world of women, but the initial resistance is understandable when one looks at women's history. Intrapsychic theories have been used for generations to label women who do not conform to male subjugation as mentally ill, translated as sick, crazy, or at the very least, misguided (Ballou & Gabalac, 1985; Broverman, Broverman, Clarkson, Rosenkrantz, & Vogel, 1970; Chesler, 1972). The stigma of mental illness is universal, thus keeping women in their place.

STIGMA AND WOMEN'S MENTAL HEALTH

Stigma regarding mental illness and therapy is a serious concern the world over. In some societies, persons labeled as mentally ill are ostracized, as are their families, even for generations after the branded person has died. In others, there are no words in the language for mental illness, so great are the stigma and attendant denial. Such realities are relevant to the United States as well, given its own inherent biases and the vast migration of people from other nations. The problem is compounded for women. Few people realize that more than 80 percent of the world's refugees are women and their children (*Nairobi Forward-Looking Strategies for the Advancement of Women*, 1985). Because of the extreme pressures and abuse these women and children have endured, their mental health problems are widespread. Yet, stigma blocks their use of services. Thus, a nonstigmatizing model of prevention and intervention is needed to integrate psychological and social elements for them. Such a model, based on prevention as well as intervention, is important to all women. Women are universally vulnerable, regardless of class and ethnicity, for they are subject to male domination and relegated to second-class status everywhere in the world.

WOMEN'S MENTAL HEALTH WORLDWIDE

Mental health has been defined by Women for Women, a group of scholarly feminist women in Bangladesh, as "more than the absence of disease. It implies a feeling of well-being and an ability to function in full capacity, physically, intellectually and emotionally" (Huq, Johan, & Begum, 1985, p. 48). The women of Bangladesh, like the women of the rest of the world, were found to be mentally ill at a 2:1 ratio compared with men and at a 3:1 ratio when it comes to depression, the world's leading mental health problem. They have a lower status in almost all aspects of society, including social, economic, educational, and political life. Comparing these findings with studies concerning the mental health of women throughout the world, Huq, Johan, and Begum concluded that depression was by far the largest category affecting all women. There are no socially acceptable outlets for their unhappiness, and the prognosis depends on how well they can "fight back the challenges of social conflict" (p. 65).

The mental health of women and their low social status are intricately intertwined. Hostile family, community, and work environments negatively affect women's emotional well-being. Any serious attempt to improve women's mental health condition must deal with the ways in which their mental health is affected negatively by social customs and cultural conditions. This includes the gamut of economic activity as well as unpaid work in the home, a combination that leaves women subject to chronic exhaustion. According to the United Nations, women do two-thirds of the world's work, yet two-thirds of the world's women live in poverty (Wetzel, 1993).

The women of the world often lack the knowledge and conviction that they are worthy human beings, that their inferior status as females is not natural and unchangeable. Women's perceptions that they have little importance and value are strongly reinforced by their political, educational, and cultural invisibility; limited rights and services; and society's often tacit acceptance of sexual exploitation and abuse. This is as true in North America, Europe, and the former Soviet Union as it is in the developing countries of Africa, Asia, Latin America, and Australia, differing only by degree from one society to another and based on a woman's personal situation and the culture in which she lives.

EVOLUTION OF GLOBAL FEMINIST ZEITGEIST PRACTICE
The concept of nonstigmatizing practice based on a Global Feminist Zeitgeist is the product of years of domestic and international study, both academic and experiential. There are three phases of the model's development.

Phase 1: Person–Environment Depression Research
The first phase of the model's evolution began with cross-cultural, gender-specific, person–environment research on depression in white women (Wetzel, 1978a, 1978b; Wetzel & Redmond, 1980). Dependence and independence characteristics, considered to be on a "developmental line" as conceptualized by Anna Freud (1963), subsequently were assessed in relation to Anglo, African American, and Mexican American women and men. The impact of family and work environments on mental health was also investigated. The results of the studies revealed that dependence or "secondary dependence" among independent people was so defined because they were not allowed to act in accord with their independence, which placed them at significant risk. So, too, did the presence of nonsupportive, controlling environments, whether at home or at work. Although men were found to be equally vulnerable when these conditions existed, they were much less likely to be socialized to dependence or to live and work in nonsupportive, controlling environments.

Phase 2: The Psychosocial Spectrum
In the second phase, more than a dozen major psychological, social, and existential theories espoused by both Eastern and Western traditions, plus research regarding depression and human development, were analyzed (Wetzel, 1991a, 1991b, 1992, 1993). Four significant qualities common to all perspectives emerged. The four themes had positive characteristics that reflect mental health and well-being and negative characteristics that reflect vulnerability to depression. Both the internal, psychological attributes of a person and his or her

external environmental situations can be either catalysts or barriers to well-being or dysfunction.

The four major themes are the qualities of connectedness, aloneness, action, and perception; these form what may be called the *psychosocial spectrum*. As an illustration of this, connectedness can reflect dependence at the negative end of the spectrum or relationality at the positive end. Aloneness can represent alienation or independence. Action can be destructive or constructive, and perception ranges from lack of self-worth to a sense of self-esteem. The matrix depicted in Table 10-1 is designed to clarify the concept.

Each theme is on a negative to positive continuum, thus shifting the focus from the previously conceptualized dependence–independence developmental line to four unfolding psychosocial continua, all of which have equal importance. The presence of negative psychological and social characteristics concerning people and the environments that affect their lives represents vulnerability, whereas the presence of positive attributes reflects the necessary components of personal development and preventive social conditions. This conceptual framework provides a matrix for understanding the impact of variable conditions on the lives of the world's women. Although both negative and positive internal and external realities encroach on everyone's lives, emotional well-being is not possible unless the positive aspects outweigh the negative aspects. Rather than applying stigmatizing models of mental health and illness, which label women destructively in most societies, nonstigmatizing, therapeutic experiences couched in an educational context should be fostered. Such programs would reduce psychological and environmental barriers to well-being while promoting preventive catalysts for the enhancement of mental health and personal development.

Although the work done with and on behalf of women should be therapeutic, there is no reason to label the work as treatment or therapy. Instead, one-on-one conversations and group programs that incorporate the psychosocial spectrum can be conceptualized as education for healthy living, rather than as mental health. Women and their families can be informed about causes for their problems or the symptoms they exhibit based on the psychosocial spectrum factors that are shared with them on an egalitarian basis.

Although everyone has aspects of both negative and positive dimensions of all four psychosocial attributes, depression occurs when the negatives outweigh the positives. Simply, practice should be designed to enhance the positive and decrease the negative internal and external psychosocial spectrum factors.

Table 10-1

The Psychosocial Spectrum

Psychosocial Dimensions	Negative Valence	Positive Valence
Connectedness	Dependent/living through others	Relational/healthy attachments
Aloneness	Alienated/lonely	Independent/unique
Action	Destructive/fragmented energy	Constructive/focused energy
Perception	Worthlessness/powerlessness	Self-esteem/hopefulness

Phase 3: The Global Feminist Zeitgeist

Finally, the Global Feminist Zeitgeist evolved via a global study of 150 successful women's programs in 14 nations (Wetzel, 1993). The study focused on grassroots, nongovernmental organization sectors; a few government-sponsored projects; and educational and service-oriented social work institutions. Selected programs met two criteria: First, the program had to address one or more of the issues put forth in the documented legacies of the United Nations Decade of Women, the *Nairobi Forward-Looking Strategies for the Advancement of Women* (1985) and the *Convention on the Elimination of All Forms of Discrimination Against Women* (1980). In short, a feminist human rights orientation was required. Second, the program had to incorporate most, and preferably all, aspects of human development and well-being reflected in the psychosocial spectrum.

GLOBAL FEMINIST ZEITGEIST PRACTICE

The international study of successful women's programs throughout the world indicated that they have much in common. A zeitgeist, "the spirit of the age," is in the air. A zeitgeist is a trend of thought and feeling that is applied in practice in similar ways. Even when women do not know there is a dynamic international women's movement, their successful programs around the globe share similar characteristics. Each component of the Global Feminist Zeitgeist is illustrated by focusing on a program that exemplifies the principle. Thus, a blueprint for universal practice is portrayed. Most of the programs could have been used to illustrate more than one component. But, of more significance, all four psychosocial spectrum dimensions are represented in all programs, hence, their effectiveness in promoting well-being and reducing dysfunction. The inclusion of all dimensions is an essential tenet to maintain while recognizing that ethnic groups and cultures will vary in the degree to which they are comfortable with each principle. Many cultures are more identified with connectedness, among them Latin American societies, whereas others, such as the white Anglo-Saxon population in the United States, view aloneness in the sense of independence as a virtue, although this is less true for females.

Although each program's emphasis may be different, all program activities are action-oriented in a positive sense, reducing negative activity and intrinsically changing self-perception and the perception about women from negative to positive. The women move from isolated, alienated aloneness to positive aloneness, affirming their uniqueness, while at the same time decreasing controlling connectedness and increasing supportive relationships. Empowerment leaves the realm of ideology as self-esteem becomes reality. Women's mental health is strengthened in the process, and they are never labeled as mentally ill or otherwise stigmatized. This is Global Feminist Zeitgeist Practice, the spirit of the age.

Principles in Action

Principle 1. *Raising consciousness regarding gender roles and the importance and worth of every female.* Recognizing domestic work as important work to be respected and counted on an equitable basis, women have adopted Freire's (1982) conscientization model even when they have never heard of him.

Filomena Tomaira Pacsi, an activist group of women in Lima, Peru, works with the wives of rural miners to reduce their feelings of isolation (negative aloneness), enhance their solidarity (positive connectedness), encourage social action, and increase their self-perception and sense of worth by recognizing how important their roles are to their husbands, children, and communities. The rural women, traditionally disparaged because they are women, are victims of their husbands' abuse and neglect. The urban women of *Filomena* joined with these rural women to raise their consciousness and change their lives. When the mines were being closed without notice, the rural women encouraged their husbands and families to make sacrifice marches hundreds of miles to the city. With the help of *Filomena,* the women of Lima began to realize how important they were to the mining struggle. The rural women took charge of the marches, feeding their families in community kitchens and providing education for their children along the way. The women also took responsibility for health care, surveying the needs of children and arranging for mobile health units staffed by paramedics who were organized by the Housewives Committee. *Filomena* adopted the slogan "Your tenderness will remain," to honor the concept of nurturance while expanding their roles to meet the needs of the larger community.

The presence of the urban women of *Filomena,* in the words of the rural women of the mines, brought them "tremendous joy, sweeping them off their feet." The solidarity and spirit of the two groups of women spread to the rural women's husbands, who stopped being violent toward their wives and showed them newfound respect. Respect for the rural women's roles was enhanced by bonding among the women and the recognition of their organizational expertise. It was the women who taught their husbands to advocate for better working conditions rather than to settle for their poor circumstances. The women opened their husbands' eyes to the responsibilities of companies and the rights of human beings in their employ (personal communication with Flora Rojas, Patricia Amat, Angelica Medrano, and Esther Hinostroza, *Filomena Tomaira Pacsi,* Lima, Peru, July 6, 1989).

Principle 2. *Forming interdisciplinary professional partnerships with poor women and training indigenous trainers to serve their own communities.* Professional women provide resources and supervision.

The Women in Development Consortium of Thailand is a joint project of Thailand's Chulalongkorn, Thammasat, and Khon Kaen universities, in cooperation with York University in Canada. Their joint Train the Trainers program in Bangkok is conducted by Friends of Women, an interdisciplinary group of professional women and a few men who are kindred spirits. These women and men are devoted to working in partnership with low-income female factory workers who are exploited. Using a nonhierarchical participative group approach, the professional facilitators train selected leaders from the factory, who in turn train the other female factory workers, hence, the Train the Trainers program title.

The five-day program begins with an orientation day designed to put the participants at ease, helping them counter their sense of alienation and loneliness (negative aloneness) by recognizing their shared roots and new relationship (positive connectedness). Most are rural women who have come to the city in search of work.

The second day focuses on occupational health issues, with particular attention to the women's bodies and their chronic exhaustion from devastating working conditions. On the third day, the discussion shifts to economic problems, using a micro approach. The women talk about their personal incomes and expenses, analyzing their situations in the context of their poor status.

The fourth day, conducted by feminist labor lawyers and educators, is concerned with law and politics. Labor protection laws, and the difference between de jure law (legislated) and de facto law (what is actually practiced), are discussed. The women also learn when and how to bargain collectively in the workplace and to lobby for political change at the national level.

Finally, on the fifth day the women receive a synthesis of all they have experienced. They chart the connections between personal and social problems and economic and political concerns. The necessity of working individually and collectively for social change becomes clear. In the process the women achieve a new sense of self-worth and possibility. The women become trainers themselves and their challenge is to bring the message to new trainees (personal communication with Malee Pruekpongsawalee, Women in Development Consortium, Bangkok, Thailand, January 18, 1989).

Principle 3. *Addressing the fundamental right of every woman to live without fear and domination, whether in the home or society, and to be educated and treated with respect.*

Academia Mexicana de Derechos Humanos, the Mexican Human Rights Academy in Mexico City, specifically addresses women's issues as human rights issues. A more sophisticated female grassroots citizenry and improved conditions have resulted from the academy's continuous dialogue with the public sector and the implementation of programs. A 66-hour Train the Trainers course was designed to teach social workers and nurses about existing legislation and the changes that must be made on behalf of women. A participative, consciousness-raising format focuses on women, their bodies, and human rights, with particular attention to confronting violence.

The program begins with a Gender Identity and Women's Bodies component in which the individual and collective experiences of both heterosexual and lesbian women are discussed. The participants address the questions, "Who are we as women? What is the status quo—our roles and our education? What are we taught to believe about ourselves and our bodies?"

The second phase of the program focuses on women's bodies and violence. Discussion centers on consideration of the character, forms, conditions, and processes of violence, particularly violence having to do with women's bodies. The women ask each other, "What violence have you experienced in your lifetime? What aspects of your life have been free of violence? What is the relationship between violence and your body?"

A component on sexuality and violence differentiates sex from sexuality and gender and addresses sexuality and violence in pregnancy, contraception, and the right to choose whether or not to bear a child. Next, a family and violence component focuses on the character of the traditional family in terms of hierarchy, power, and roles and covers forms of violence within the family such as beatings and other maltreatment, injuries, rape, forced obedience, dependency, and prohibitions. A discussion of civil and family codes is followed by attention to different forms of family unions, the treatment of women and the recognition of children in their lives, and the causes and types of divorce.

In a final component, seminar participants discuss alternatives to victimization and how to confront violence. Solutions and practical applications include avoiding the paralysis of victimization, organizing women's collectives, and establishing informal legal offices (personal communication with Mariclaire Acosta, *Academia Mexicana de Derechos Humanos*, Mexico City, Mexico, June 23, 1989).

Empowered to demand respect and repel violence, these women no longer experience aloneness in a negative sense. They are connected in a positive way, involved in social action on behalf of themselves and their sisters, and their perceptions have changed markedly.

Principle 4. *Sharing home maintenance and child care with men on an equal basis; restructuring the family and society from a human rights perspective.*

This mandate was considered radical when the women of nonaligned countries included it in a resolution at the first Decade of Women Conference in Mexico City in 1975. Today the mandate is a mainstream demand of women throughout the world who recognize its necessity if justice and equity are ever to prevail. Although there are many examples of individual change and general progress in changing societal attitudes, there is not yet a program that reflects success in this regard, despite the fact that hundreds of programs advocate for such structural change. Even so, advocacy efforts of such groups increase connectedness and decrease negative aloneness among women. They also increase positive action and decrease negative perceptions of homemakers and their work. In the process, women's self-esteem is enhanced and the future holds promise.

The Norwegian Housewives Association of Oslo is perhaps the largest and most active political pressure group of this kind, making its views known at local, national, and international political levels. It has programs serving 2,000 study groups to encourage, among other goals, greater awareness of the need for shared responsibility and economic equality. By including unpaid work in the home and community (regardless of who is doing it) in the gross national product statistical reports worldwide, the association contends that recognition for such labor would be ensured (personal communication with Ingunn Birkeland, Norwegian Housewives Association, United Nations, New York, January 16, 1988).

Principle 5. *Teaching fundamental rights regarding health needs, both emotional and physical, including the individual and mutual need for nurturance, freedom from exhaustion, and participation in decision making, within and outside the home.*

Save the Children–USA in Dhaka, Bangladesh, finally realized after almost 10 years of working in rural areas of the country that the lives of children would not improve unless their mothers' lives also improved. As is typical, despite the overwhelming responsibilities and considerable skills of the women of Bangladesh, the women felt they were useless, unworthy, helpless, dependent members of society. Save the Children created a three-pronged two-week program called An Expanded World of Women to counter the misperceptions of women and to help fulfill their unrecognized human need for nurturance and support (positive connectedness). In the process, the perceptions of women by others and by women themselves are forever changed, passed on to their husbands and children and to other women and their families in an ever-expanding community. No longer isolated and alone, but recognizing the need for healthy personal development (positive aloneness), the women learn to join hands with other women in terms of mutual nurturance and economic support (positive connectedness).

The concepts were pretested by the women themselves when an artist came into the community with group facilitators and sketched pictures of the work the women were doing. The artist encouraged the women to correct the drawings until they met with the women's approval. The final products were silk-screened on the first of three cloth flip charts designed to be used in the training sessions. The use of pictures was necessary because the women were illiterate. (Women throughout the world are illiterate at a ratio of 3:2 compared with men, so the method would be useful elsewhere as well. Even among literate women the use of pictures as a communication medium may be preferable. I saw such a descriptive poster at a Women and Work program in the Netherlands.)

The first flip chart, filled with images of the women at work, makes a dynamic impression on them. Never have the women recognized the extent of their labor, nor the importance of it. Time is spent talking about the women's multiple roles. The second flip chart, introduced after a few days, uses pictures of seeds and their flowering growth as analogues to the needs of women. As rural women, they understand agricultural necessities such as sunlight, water, weeding plants, and treating the plants with care. But because of their socialization, the women have been unaware that they, too, require nurturing, rest, and nutritious food. Women throughout the world are taught to nurture others, but no one is taught to nurture them. To provide time for themselves is considered selfish, contributing to women's universal vulnerability to depression (Wetzel, 1991a).

A depiction of different types of trees helps the women understand the concept of embracing unity in diversity. Although women may differ in any number of ways, they share universal needs and concerns and they deserve equal respect. They learn that regard for individual and cultural differences and the importance of everyone's unique gifts does not obviate the common needs and rights of all women.

The third flip chart expands the world of women to recognize that "changing the world begins with us." They review how women are perceived, what hampers their growth, the isolation and restrictions of society, and the poverty, hunger, ill health, compulsory childbearing, and lack of opportunity and security they experience. For the first time in their lives, the women recognize their right to a fair share of the money their efforts have reaped for their husbands. The collective, through role play and support, helps the women communicate with their families as they make changes. By forming savings groups, the women learn to finance the development of income-generating projects though individual efforts, collective savings, and credit unions that they establish themselves. The women reach out in ever-widening circles to include new participants into their fold (personal communication with Jobunnesse Lily, Save the Children–USA, Dhaka, Bangladesh, January 26, 1989).

Principle 6. *Teaching women that both personal development and action, as well as collective social development and action, are essential if their lives are to change for the better.*

All of the successful programs emphasize the two-fold efforts that must be made by women. Personal development is essential but not sufficient. The same is true of economic, legal, and political development. Nor can social development and social action be achieved in isolation; it is a collaborative enterprise.

Stree Mukti Sanghatana, an activist street theater group in Bombay, India, devoted to raising consciousness on behalf of the advancement of women's rights, provides an unusual example. The group creates awareness concerning women's exploitation and abuse (changing perceptions) through the medium of the performing arts. By making a point of involving boys and men as well as girls and women, the group mobilizes members of the audience to become active in its organization. Everyone can play a part behind the scenes or on the stage. In the process, the people develop as individuals, reaching out to the community to create new attitudes and actions. Written materials, posters, and slide shows supplement the group's performances. The imagination of the people is captured by grounding their ideology in tangible programs. Examples of the group's theatrical productions are *No Dowry, Please; We Will Smash the Prison;* and *A Girl is Born,* all of which address traumatic examples of female subordination (personal communication with Sharde Sathe, *Stree Mukti Sanghatana,* Bombay, India, January 31, 1989).

Principle 7. *Teaching women about their existing rights, such as how to execute legal and political critical analyses and how to develop legislation and policies.* This process always begins with personal experience, then generalizes it to national and international policies so that the connection becomes real.

The Association for the Advancement of Feminism in Wan Chai, Hong Kong, works closely with women, teaching them how to analyze social policies and facilitating their awareness (perception) of the connections between personal issues and discriminating legislation and other social policies. The group always begins with the personal experiences of the women (negative aloneness) before making the connection between those experiences and the larger political and legal arena. Though often illiterate, the women become adept at policy analysis, having examined such issues as family life education, women's care of developmentally disabled and elderly individuals, women and social security, battered wives, child care services, labor, and law and housing policies in relation to women. They follow up with social action, designing policies to improve the situation of women, and advocating for change (personal communication with Cheung Choi Wan, Association for the Advancement of Feminism, Wan Chai, Hong Kong, January 11, 1989).

Principle 8. *Engaging in participative social action research, culminating in new policies and laws, as well as participative psychosocial programs for social change.*

The Center for Latin American Social Work (CELATS) in Miraflores, Peru, has completely changed the direction of Latin

American social workers in recent years by focusing on the social problems that confront the people of its country. The ultimate purpose of this new focus is to help the people take control of their lives so they can begin to solve their problems. Because women are most likely to be among the poorest and most marginal of the population, many projects are devoted to them. CELATS members begin with participative social action research that links theoretical issues and practical intervention. CELATS researchers analyze the characteristics of the poorest sectors of society and of the social policies that affect them. Case studies are often used in which women not only are invited to the presentation of the findings, but the women themselves develop proposals based on the findings. Once the data concerning the collection of practical experiences are analyzed, the findings are interpreted by the women and presented to social work practitioners who adapt them for purposes of problem prevention and intervention.

The findings are also reinforced by the training department of CELATS, again adapted to the various fields of action. The communications department follows up with publications and instructional materials that are distributed to the membership of 3,000 social workers in 21 countries. This four-pronged structure is marked from beginning to end by the fundamental purpose that drives the organization: service to deepen and enrich professional action in the neediest sectors of the continent, with professional training required to fulfill that purpose. The objective is clear from the selection of research themes to the practical experiences of individual women (countering negative aloneness and changing their perceptions of themselves as empowered people). The women's collective efforts (connectedness) are supported and encouraged, as is the content of training and social action programs in which they participate as full partners (personal communication with Marcela Chueca, Monica Escobar, Esperanza Reyes, Margareta Rosa, and Norma Rottier, CELATS, Miraflores, Peru, July 4, 1989).

Principle 9. Developing credit unions and coupling personal development with social and economic development of women, never ignoring either end of the spectrum; recognizing women's right to be paid equitably for their work.

The Grameen Bank was founded in 1976 by Muhammed Yunus (1982), an economics professor teaching in rural Bangladesh who was appalled at the condition of women. The bank is probably the most well-known credit union for low-income people in the world. Women, the majority of those who participate in the program, are taught to organize as a collective, using their group as collateral to guarantee each loan made to individual women. The guarantee is seldom needed. The concepts of stressing the value of connectedness, or countering negative fiscal aloneness, of fostering positive entrepreneurial independence (positive aloneness), and of changing poor women's perceptions of themselves and others' perceptions of them are thus taken to the nth degree.

The Grameen Bank does more than operate as a public bank. Women grantees are provided services, extending to a Train the Trainers program, that enhance their mental and physical health and consequently their productivity. Services are based on the principle that poor women should have equal opportunities, but they must be provided the psychological as well as the financial means of becoming productive citizens. Banking becomes a way of achieving human rights and dignity without losing sight of the goal that the poor should receive what would be theirs already if justice prevailed. In the bargain, the subservient condition of future generations of females will be forever transformed (personal communication with Jannat Quanine, Grameen Bank, Dhaka, Bangladesh, 1989).

FEMINIST WAYS OF BEING

Global Feminist Zeitgeist Practice is ideologically and operationally consistent with feminist "ways of being," the theme of this book. Interconnectedness and concern for collective welfare are illustrative of positive connectedness; naming one's reality could easily define positive aspects of aloneness and perception; and valuing a process orientation and encouraging empowerment certainly characterize positive action, encourage positive connectedness, and reduce negative aloneness. Singly and in combination, these efforts result in women's positive perception of themselves. The outcome is not only mental health in the 21st century, but a future that holds promise for the women of the world and for the myriad lives that they touch.

The feminist concept of "personal is political" is also exemplary. In almost all successful programs, women are asked to reflect on the relationship between their personal experience and the wider social, economic, and political conditions of women in their countries. Empowerment results from linking the personal and the political, which is achieved through positive action, positive self-perception, and positive connectedness.

Finally, the feminist theme of eliminating dichotomies is accomplished in four ways through the Global Feminist Zeitgeist model:

(1) through a positive perception of women's traditional roles and contributions to society, as well as their work outside the home; (2) through the establishment of partnerships between professional and low-income women, otherwise estranged and unable to achieve what they can collectively; (3) through bridging the artificial division between personal and social development (or clinical practice and social policy practice) by respecting both the internal and the external worlds of women, the psychological and the social duality; and (4) through embracing the concept of unity in diversity, whereby the tensions between the false dichotomy of gender and race dissolve. When we observe the discrimination common to all people of color throughout the world (regardless of race, ethnicity, or culture), concern about the universal ugliness of racism forges bonds with women and men around the globe. Accordingly, when we recognize the common subservient conditions of women throughout the world (regardless of race, ethnicity, or culture), the international bonds of sisterhood are mobilized and women join together with a growing cadre of supportive brothers.

Women's concerns *are* the concerns of the world. Their well-being is directly linked to the well-being of families, communities, and nations. To practice effectively in the 21st century, therefore, social workers must view women as a priority. Women are not only our nation's and the world's majority, but their concerns are central to the success of social development in the United States and around the globe. Indeed, international research revealed more than a decade ago that ignoring women and their contributions to societies leads to failure in social development (Dixon, 1980). Although this fact continues to be reliable, women continue to be disregarded and marginalized as a special issue population. If economic, political, or social conditions ranging from health care to education are to improve, the advancement of women from a human rights perspective must be embraced as a concept, indeed as a mission. To do so is to advance not only women, but men and children alike—in short, the people of the world. Global Feminist Zeitgeist Practice provides a realistic means to this visionary end. As all social workers know, the process is the product.

REFERENCES

Ballou, M., & Gabalac, N. W. (1985). *A feminist position on mental health.* Springfield, IL: Charles C Thomas.

Broverman, I. K., Broverman, D. M., Clarkson, F. E., Rosenkrantz, P. S., & Vogel, S. (1970). Sex role stereotypes and clinical judgments of mental health. *Journal of Consulting and Clinical Psychology, 34,* 1–7.

Chesler, P. (1972). *Women and madness.* Garden City, NY: Doubleday.

Convention on the Elimination of All Forms of Discrimination Against Women. (1980). New York: United Nations.

Dixon, R. (1980). *Assessing the impact of development projects on women* (Program Evaluation Paper No. 8, PN-AAH-725). Washington, DC: Agency for International Development.

Freire, P. (1982). *Pedagogy of the oppressed.* New York: Continuum Publishing. (Original work published 1970)

Freud, A. (1963). The concept of developmental lines. In *The psychoanalytic study of the child* (Vol. 18, pp. 245–266). New York: International Universities Press.

Huq, J., Johan, R., & Begum, H. A. (1985). *Women and health.* Dhaka, Bangladesh: Brac Printers.

Mathews, G., & Wagenfeld, M. O. (1992). A cross-cultural perspective on selected mental health systems [Special Issue on Mental Health Services]. *Journal of Sociology and Social Welfare, 28*(2), 155–163.

Nairobi Forward-Looking Strategies for the Advancement of Women. (1985). New York: United Nations.

Viswanathan, N., & Wetzel, J. W. (1993). Concepts and trends in mental health: A global overview. In P. Mane & K. Y. Gandevia (Eds.), *Mental health in India: Issues and concerns* (pp. 43–69). Bombay, India: Tata Press.

Wetzel, J. W. (1978a). Depression and dependence upon unsustaining environments. *Clinical Social Work Journal, 6*(2), 75–89.

Wetzel, J. W. (1978b). The work environment and depression: Implications for intervention. In J. W. Hanks (Ed.), *Toward human dignity: Social work in practice* (pp. 236–245). Washington, DC: National Association of Social Workers.

Wetzel, J. W. (1991a). *Clinical handbook of depression.* New York: Gardner Press.

Wetzel, J. W. (1991b). Universal mental health classification systems: Reclaiming women's experience. *Affilia, 6*(3), 8–31.

Wetzel, J. W. (1992). Profiles on women: A global perspective. *Social Work in Health Care, 163,* 13–27.

Wetzel, J. W. (1993). *The world of women: In pursuit of human rights.* New York: New York University Press.

Wetzel, J. W., & Redmond, R. C. (1980). A person–environment study of depression. *Social Service Review, 54,* 363–375.

Yunus, M. (1982). *Grameen Bank project in Bangladesh: A poverty focused rural development programme.* Dhaka, Bangladesh: Imperial Press.

Special Populations

11

Women of Color and Culturally Competent Feminist Social Work Practice

Zulema E. Suarez, Edith A. Lewis, and June Clark

Much of what we do as individual, family, group, and community practitioners is driven by values or beliefs, although our society promotes rationality. Our work and lives are often governed by subjective truths we regard as desirable, worthy, or right (Lewis, 1988). Current exercises in futuring, the study and envisioning of the future, which includes "focusing on the array of alternatives open to decision-makers" for the purpose, among others, of inducing social change (Toffler, 1972, p. 4), also hold fast to some subjective set of values that is not always made explicit. Yet, these values and their ordering may not be shared by all people (Attneave, 1982) and seldom do we think of the implications of our futuring efforts for those with varying class, ethnic, racial, and gender lenses. To create more hopeful and useful images of feminist practice with women of color, we must name and alter value orientations, philosophies of treatment, and professional habits that may have little use for them.

This chapter addresses the issue of culturally competent feminist practice as we approach the 21st century (Lewis & Kissman, 1989). We begin by exploring current work in futuring and its use for women of color. The need for alternative visions of futuring, which includes an acknowledgment of the historical, social, and political realities of women of color, is then addressed. Finally, a model for culturally competent feminist practice and its implications for 21st century social work are presented.

Although most of the recommendations made in this chapter directly address the experiences of African American and Latina women, many will be useful for other populations as well. As Latina and African American women, the authors have chosen to highlight these umbrella groups not to be exclusionary but to give voice to our collective experiences as social work practitioners and scholars. The voices of other women of color must also be heard. Moreover, the authors believe the recommendations made in this chapter to be consistent with sound social work practice with all peoples in the 21st century.

FUTURING AND WOMEN OF COLOR

Looking toward the future requires shifting our attention from our day-to-day concerns and committing ourselves to conjecturing about an unknown. Futurists, people who systematically think about the long-term implications of a broad range of social issues, do just that. Unfortunately, the daily struggles of women of color in this society deny them the same luxury.

Women of color, however, must become actively involved in futuring, which includes characterizing society, generating coherent images of the future, and recommending how society can move toward these images (M. L. Bundy, 1976). Inclusion in these activities is critical for the improvement of the status of women of color in the 21st century. Thinking about the future, according to McHale (1969), is an idealistic and value-bound enterprise. Hence, human values and choices drive the direction of innovation and help determine the future through action and policy (Coates & Jarrett, 1989). Because futurists are virtually all white male professionals and intellectuals who, for the most part, continue to shape the world in their own image, the blueprint for tomorrow reflects a masculine worldview.

Although some people have rationalized the overwhelmingly Caucasian, male aspect of the futures movement in the United States as "not having yet drawn the attention of minorities" (Coates & Jarrett, 1989, p. 9), others see it as overtly racist, sexist, and elitist (R. V. Bundy, 1976). By excluding women and people of color from futuring, one group is able to maintain ownership of today while simultaneously claiming tomorrow. This, of course, creates a Catch-22 situation in which women of color cannot have power if they do not actively participate in forging the future but cannot forge the future because they do not have power. If we are to have a more inclusive and humane society, women and men of color must be included in the design of future paradigms.

Some futurists (Brown, 1976; Coates & Jarrett, 1989) argue that we urgently need a new social ethic that is humanistic, collectivist, universal, flexible, and not culturally biased. Indeed, feminist scholars argue that the individual problems of women are embedded within the inequalities of extant patriarchal systems (Bricker-Jenkins & Hooyman, 1983). Yet, the "innovative ethic" proposed by these futurists is not new. Instead, it reflects values traditionally espoused by people of color, feminists, and social work (Collins, 1986; Giele, 1978; Lewis & Kissman, 1989).

EXISTING PARADIGMS AND THEIR EFFECT ON WOMEN OF COLOR

A patriarchal society embodies what has been called a masculine ethos: "a philosophical ordering of the world, such that the building blocks of social reality are assumed to be dichotomous, polarized categories arranged in hierarchical order—superior to inferior, superordinate to subordinate" (Collins, 1986, pp. 215–216). Mackinnon (1987) argued that under this social hierarchy, men are dominant and women are subordinate. This hierarchy, along with the penchant for rationality and empiricism, leads to reductionism, fragmentation, and estrangement. Under the current social system, social policies and programs are developed according to this masculine framework. Hence, not only does this society fail to nurture women of color but neither do the social welfare programs and policies that profess to alleviate their social problems.

Within a masculine framework, problems are narrowly defined in order to be studied and understood by the linear Western mind. One aspect of the framework, the tendency to dichotomize, is palpable in this society's views on health and in the delivery of health services. Whereas feminist and non-Western views of health and mental health are holistic and do not "make the rigid separation of physical health and social psychological well-being that characterizes Western thinking" (Green, 1982, p. 29), in the masculine framework health is seen as a dichotomy, as physical versus mental. This is not only disaffirming of the worldview of women of color, but it results in the fragmentation of health and mental health services. Instead of battling with one overwhelming and alienating bureaucracy, women of color must suffer through two. Moreover, under the current reductionistic framework, health is viewed through a disease model that isolates the part from the whole or the context. Hence, a woman of color's depression is treated with medication and psychotherapy but the poverty she lives in goes untouched (Gutierrez, 1992).

Individualism, "the very core of American culture" (Bellah, Madsen, Sullivan, Swidler, & Tipton, 1985, p. 27), was highly adaptive during the frontier days when vast geographic distances and rudimentary transportation forced families to be self-sufficient. That value is inadequate, however, in an interdependent world. By placing the responsibility of social well-being on each citizen and not on the collective, individualism promotes the well-being of patriarchal society while victimizing women and men of color. This value may lead to the erroneous conclusion that personal lifestyle choices are the greatest threat to health, ignoring the myriad environmental and social problems confronting society today. For example, Coates and Jarrett (1989) suggested that the greatest opportunity for improved health "lies in nutrition, exercise, altered lifestyles, and using the automobile analogy—preventive maintenance. Unfortunately, rural, impoverished, small town people and new ethnics tend to be inattentive to these health promoting factors" (p. 295). Individualism victimizes women, deemphasizes public health, and promotes one-to-one interventions that are not cost-effective. It may also lead to simplistic national health and mental health campaigns such as expecting adolescents of color to "just say no" to drugs and sex to prevent substance abuse, teenage pregnancy, and acquired immune deficiency syndrome.

Another basic cultural tenet noxious to women of color is that of having dominion over nature. The need to subjugate the environment to meet our needs has deleterious consequences. Not only is this tenet "partly responsible for the worsening environmental crisis" (Brown, 1976, p. 91) but it affects social spending. Under the current system a disproportionate amount of our social resources is invested in technology to control nature, such as genetic engineering and reproductive technology, and focused on the excessive postponement of the lives of a few while disregarding the overall welfare of others.

MODEL FOR CULTURALLY COMPETENT FEMINIST SOCIAL WORK PRACTICE WITH WOMEN OF COLOR

Much has been written about the tenets of culturally competent feminist practice in social work (Comas-Diaz, 1988; Gutierrez & Lewis, 1990; Lara, 1992; Lewis & Kissman, 1989), which combines elements of ethnic-sensitive and feminist conceptual frameworks. This section briefly highlights some of the critical elements of culturally competent feminist practice and their implications for women of color and for those working with these diverse populations.

Understanding Contexts

Understanding the social, political, and historical contexts of women in a society has long been recognized as important to feminist analysis.

The first tenet of the culturally competent practice model also emphasizes this knowledge and its potential differences for women whose ultimate gender lens is also potentially related to their economic status, class background construction, ethnicity, and race. All of these factors must be taken into account in the analysis of the woman of color in her social context. Much of the culturally competent practice literature addresses ways in which this can be accomplished (Boyd-Franklin, 1990; Devore & Schlesinger, 1987; Lum, 1992; Solomon, 1976).

Because of the importance of context for all women in this society and the heightened oppression of women of color, culturally competent feminist practice must go beyond analysis when working with individual women to involve the women and their constituents in social action. The feminist notion of the personal is political proposes that, because our conditions and consciousness are shaped by political forces, we are so intertwined with our environment that there are no private solutions for our troubles (Bricker-Jenkins & Hooyman, 1983). Therefore, individual and societal change become aspects of the process of political change (Gould, 1987). Through consciousness-raising, women are helped "to grasp the collective reality of women's condition and learn how to use their personal experience as a starting point for social change" (Gould, 1987, p. 8).

Recognizing Strengths

Recognizing the strengths of women of color is a second tenet of culturally competent feminist social work practice. This usually incorporates a thorough analysis of a woman's support system, abilities, and resources. It also requires viewing women of color as actors with the potential for meeting their individual, family, and community needs, rather than as victims. This is accomplished by becoming familiar with the historical strengths of women of color in their communities of origin. Much literature is available on the roles of mutual support and aid in communities of color that, in many cases, led to the development of national social welfare programs (Macht & Quam, 1986).

Taking an Empowerment Perspective

Culturally competent feminist social work practice includes the need for taking a generalist, empowerment perspective in assessment and intervention (Gutierrez, 1992; Gutierrez & Lewis, 1990). In this instance, empowerment is viewed in its complexity as a goal, change process, and method. Consonant with the principles stated above, the target of intervention is not restricted to the individual but includes the different systems that form her context. This requires an ongoing analysis of the interaction between individual change and its consequences at the familial, community, and societal levels. Illustrations of empowerment in practice are given later in this chapter.

Undergoing Self-Assessment

In working with women of color, the culturally competent social worker must recognize how she personally has benefited from the racism, sexism, and classism that dominate the lives of the women she has worked with. Despite any recognition the social worker has about how individual "isms" have affected her life, the deeply embedded roots of the others are often less easy to admit and change. She must therefore be willing to undergo a self-assessment to understand the dynamics of how her own racism or classism can impede the consumer's progress. Without this recognition the social worker can be of little assistance to consumers who are often struggling with issues of race, ethnicity, class, economic well-being, and their own constructions of gender. This is one reason why instead of serving as a speaker for women of color, the culturally competent social worker must facilitate opportunities whereby women of color can speak their own truths.

Acknowledging Limits and Fears

The culturally competent feminist social worker acknowledges her own limitations and fears when doing this work. Because feminist perspectives are relatively new to social work, despite the strong presence of women in the profession, feminist social work practice has not been consistent in espousing the concepts of cultural competence (Lewis & Kissman, 1989). One implication of this emerging paradigm for culturally competent feminist practitioners is that it will be discredited by practitioners unfamiliar with this paradigm shift. Culturally competent feminist practitioners must be able to articulate a firm response that, without the inclusion of feminist and diverse ethnic voices, social work practice merely perpetuates an exclusionary framework. To do this, however, the culturally competent feminist practitioner must confront and deal with her fears about professional criticism and her feelings of powerlessness. How can the practitioner help women of color to advocate for themselves if she is unable to model that behavior for them?

Recognizing Dichotomous Thinking

The culturally competent feminist social worker recognizes the entrenchment of dichotomous thinking and monoculturalism in this society and in her thinking and reflects on how these affect her work with women of color. Understanding how dichotomous thinking has pitted white women and women of color against each other is crucial. The choices made by service consumers must be evaluated through a lens that appreciates "shades of gray" rather than simple dichotomies. Similarly, culturally competent feminist social workers must recognize that time orientations vary across cultures and that the Western perspective is futuristic rather than present-oriented (McGoldrick, Pearce, & Giordano, 1992). This continual focus on the future implies a sense that it can be controlled by the individual, an assumption that takes on a deitylike posture.

Women of color must be included in futuring exercises if they are to contribute to the forging of future visions of society. However, asking women of color to conjecture about the future while ignoring their present-time orientation is victimizing and unaffirming of their worldview. For some women of color, a present-time orientation suggests an awareness of the importance of the process as well as the end goal. Thus, futuring exercises should also address and honor the present reality. In other words, the articulation of a better tomorrow should also be accompanied by attention to "their basic needs and objective conditions" (Bricker-Jenkins & Hooyman, 1983, p. 19) as well as to immediate strategies for improving today. Thus, the focus would be not only on future outcome but also on current processes.

Focusing on Processes

Culturally competent feminist practice requires a focus on processes as well as outcomes (Gutierrez & Lewis, 1990). It necessitates careful attention to the use of words and space in practice. Do the words practitioners use in their assessment and intervention have the same meanings for service consumers? Are the instruments and interventions used normed for or tested with the populations in question? Culturally competent feminist practice requires transformation on the part of both practitioners and consumers. This transformation connotes a sharing of power within working relationships.

The next two sections focus on applying the culturally competent feminist social work practice model to specific practice settings. The following two cases are composites of actual practice experiences and indicate the ways in which elements of the model are useful.

MODEL APPLICATION ONE: CORAZON

Corazon is a 32-year-old woman who identifies herself as a Mexican national. She has been married since age 14 to Juan and has three teenage daughters. Corazon and Juan worked in migrant camps across the country for several years but were able to get permanent status three years ago and have since been working in a factory in a large midwestern city.

Corazon came to the attention of the community mental health center because of a domestic violence incident involving Juan. The area police and domestic violence shelter team responding to the 911 call for assistance removed Juan from the home under the area's mandatory arrest policy and informed Corazon of her options under the law. A bilingual, bicultural translator was part of the team and was able to ascertain that this incident was one of many involving physical and sexual abuse. Corazon declined the option to move to a shelter, preferring to remain in her community, but did agree to seek assistance through the community mental health center.

Corazon was assigned to see a social worker for her first visit rather than the regular intake worker because it was felt that she would not return if expected to wade through the regular bureaucracy of the agency. The social worker was of Cuban descent and made that known to Corazon during their initial meeting. The worker was aware that it was important to determine how Corazon viewed the importance of her own as well as the worker's ethnicity. Although both women might be thought of as Latinas, the worker was aware of the potential cultural differences because the cultural influences for Cubans are primarily African and European, whereas those for Mexicans are Indian and European.

On the basis of the client's definition of why she wanted assistance, the social worker also had to clarify early in the intervention Corazon's willingness to engage in the working relationship. Because Corazon was minimally educated in Mexican schools and could neither read nor write English, it would have been very easy for a formally educated social worker to decide that Corazon would need extensive help to determine her own goals. Instead, the practitioner used a strategic goal-setting program, the Network Utilization Project (Lewis & Ford, 1990), to help determine Corazon's strengths and resources. No standardized assessment instruments were used because there were none normed for women like Corazon. The worker made the assumption that there was nothing a normed instrument could provide that was unavailable through a proper multicultural therapeutic alliance.

The interaction between the worker and Corazon ultimately required many instances of back-translation in which the worker listened to Corazon and then made certain that the words and phrases used had consistent meaning to them both. The worker was aware that language is often based on one's ethnic group of origin; hence, her own use of Spanish might differ from the client's understanding. Thus, the practitioner demonstrated her bicultural as well as bilingual abilities using the bilingual protocol established by the agency (Lara, 1992).

One of the strengths identified for Corazon was that she had the ability to be simultaneously analytic and process-oriented. Other strengths included her ability to continue to raise her children and work while faced with spousal abuse. The social worker contracted with Corazon for a combined intervention of insight-oriented therapy to help her understand and tease out "what was and was not due to herself rather than to forces in society" (Gould, 1987, p. 12) and case management services linking her to resources within the formal social service network. It should be stressed that the choice of the intervention was not based on the practitioner's theory of choice but on Corazon's problem-solving style. Social workers require flexibility in their use of interventions so that they may identify those most appropriate for working with particular individuals in their social and political contexts.

The goals Corazon chose included returning to school to increase her English literacy, learning to drive to have more mobility, and finding additional income sources for her family. She began by taking literacy classes. The social worker asked Corazon to keep a journal of her feelings about the therapy and its impact on her life. At first, a group of symbols and colors were created so that Corazon could express her thoughts and feelings without the use of extensive English. As her literacy increased, however, her reflections were modified to include the new words and phrases she had learned to read and write.

Midway through the therapeutic relationship, Corazon decided to leave her husband. She and the girls moved out of their home and Corazon applied for public assistance. As a result, Juan stalked both Corazon and the social worker, and Corazon's neighbors chastised her for leaving her husband. In this predominantly Catholic Latino community, there was little support for women in abusive situations, in part because of the value of familialism, the belief that the family must stay together at all costs. Corazon and the social worker began an effort to help Corazon build a new community to offset her loss of support. This effort included working with classmates in her literacy program and participating in the women's groups offered in the local Catholic church. They also discussed her spirituality and reframed the community consensus that she was a bad person for leaving her husband. The church group offered Corazon support in her construction of a loving God who would support her self-actualization.

The social worker constantly had to be aware of her own values as they affected the relationship between herself and Corazon. For example, spirituality did not have the same importance for the practitioner, but she was able to appreciate its importance for Corazon. The strategy of using public assistance was also somewhat problematic for the social worker, whose family of origin had viewed the receipt of public funding as an admission of weakness. Receipt of public assistance in Corazon's case was a strength because it allowed her to meet individual goals. Without receiving Aid to Families with Dependent Children, Corazon would not have been able to attend school. The additional education resulted in her ability to find more lucrative employment. Armed with an increased consciousness of herself and of the societal institutions that had sustained her oppression, Corazon became an advocate for Latinas through her volunteer work at the local domestic violence shelter and eventually helped to organize a self-help group for physically abused women. At work, she was very active in her union, advocating for the rights of Latina factory workers.

When Corazon eventually began a romantic relationship with another man, the social worker needed to reexamine her own values regarding the timing of this emerging relationship. It was imperative to the worker that her own family and community views of life did not interfere with the ability to work effectively with Corazon. Because there were no other Latina professionals within the agency for case consultation, the social worker sought help from other Latinas in the city. The worker also engaged in self-reflection, pursuant to this case, with other social workers she supervised in the agency who had worked with diverse populations. In this way, she became both student and teacher.

Corazon's case highlights many aspects of culturally competent feminist social work practice. The helping relationship was built on the existing strengths of the service consumer, while considering the social and political context of her community, with the goal of assisting her to live fully within her life setting. This case also illustrates the social worker's need for establishing a balance between reflection and action in her work. Although it is optimal that this work be done within the agency context, it can be accomplished by empowering workers to seek out learning opportunities within professional communities and organizations of color.

MODEL APPLICATION TWO: IMANI
Imani is a 40-year-old African American social worker who, in conjunction with her 45-year-old Irish American colleague, Tisch,

cofacilitates a group of 10 women who are working on individual and community goals. Imani and Tisch have worked together in an agency for several years but have not attempted to cofacilitate a group before. As coworkers, they have tried to talk with each other to confront their own experiences with classism, racism, and sexism. Their conversations revealed much about their sociobiological development and the ways in which they viewed themselves as women and as feminist practitioners. Through their conversations Imani and Tisch established how their distinct constructions of gender complement and diverge from each other (Childers & Hooks, 1990). They modeled this style of paying specific attention to ethnicity, race, gender, class, and sexual orientation in the group.

Special attention was paid to group composition. The women who had been contacted about their interest in participating in a group came from various ethnic backgrounds and different sexual orientations. Of the 10 women, three were African American, two identified themselves as black, two considered themselves American, and three were both religiously and culturally Jewish. In the pregroup interviews with each potential participant, Imani and Tisch focused on the differences and similarities in the proposed group and ascertained the willingness of each participant to work through individual variations to find commonalities, mutual aid, and support. In the initial group meetings, the cofacilitators focused on questions that helped build group cohesiveness: What were the different constructions of gender within the group (using the process undertaken earlier by the group facilitators), what values had shaped their lives, and what values had they adopted as adults? An ethnographic charting exercise (Lewis & Ford, 1990) was completed in the second group session to identify the resources of individual group members outside the group, including family, friends, partners, spiritual networks, and other formal or informal supports. The resources and skills of group members were also discussed and charted as a way to build community. The differential use of language was uncovered by group members' participation in a free-association exercise on language to draw attention to the potential for difference in verbal interaction. The term "bad," for example, was found to have several different meanings related to familial background and ethnic group membership. Communication styles that might be more prominent for some group members were also discussed via an exercise on conflict management styles. The cofacilitators deemed it important to recognize the potential for conflict and backlash and drew attention to it directly when it arose. This initial work within the group helped participants construct a basis for interpersonal interaction and develop multicultural ground rules to guide further discussion and work.

While looking at the subject of difference, Imani and Tisch engaged the group in exercises to raise consciousness about how issues of racism, sexism, classism, and ethnicity united them in their experiences. Group members were able to share experiences related to the effect of "isms" on their lives. Reflecting collectively on the commonalities of prejudice and its consequences, group members were assisted in developing intimacy with each other, which was similar to the process experienced by the cofacilitators in their earlier discussions with each other.

Group members continued to develop strategies for meeting their individual and community goals in the course of the meetings. These strategies were shared in the group, and sometimes other participants offered helpful problem-solving strategies from their own experiences. This empowered both the person looking for a solution and the one offering the suggestion.

During the course of the group, one member revealed a problem with her lesbian partner. The African American group members began to withdraw from the full group, thus subgrouping with each other, exchanging snickers and glances and limiting their interaction with the lesbian member. At the same time, they expressed ambivalence about their ability to continue in the group. Imani and Tisch had anticipated this potential conflict and immediately moved the group discussion to the development of messages around homosexuality and feminism. Imani took the lead in addressing the issue of homophobia in African American communities and the need for the development of a safe space for all group members. The withdrawn group members were asked to examine the strengths of the relationships within the group and any learning that had taken place for them. They were able to express their caring for the lesbian group member, revisiting their commonality in oppression without developing a hierarchy in the group pursuant to who is more oppressed. Both workers recognized the need for Imani's leadership in this discussion as well as the benefit of her modeling alternative behaviors based on acquiring new knowledge about individuals' differences. The expertise of the lesbian member and of another African American group member were also used to present composite pictures of the components of homophobia and its consequences for lesbians and gay men within the inner city.

In time, group members chose to learn group facilitation skills and then paired off in multiethnic teams to serve as cofacilitators for other women's groups sponsored by the agency and other local agencies. Having the awareness that the needs of women are not uniform because they are affected by class, ethnicity, and sexual orientation (Gould, 1987), these groups eventually formed inter-community coalitions that advocated for some of the different priorities confronting the women of color, lesbians, and white women who participated in the groups.

This case illustrates the importance of constant attention to differences and similarities on a conscious level in the design and implementation of groups. Many exercises can help culturally competent feminist practitioners working with heterogenous groups to build effective group cohesion. These exercises, combined with the reflective action of group workers, can enhance the probability of successful heterogenous groups and coalitions.

SUMMARY

This chapter has considered culturally competent feminist practice with women of color as one way of shaping a futuristic framework in social work practice. This style of practice relies on flexibility rather than dichotomous thinking and on the practitioner's ability to live with multifocal lenses. It encourages the use of different truths in practice to provide more accurate depictions of the lives of women of color. Generalist practice is considered to be one way of uncovering these truths and implementing them in the development of sound interventions.

The culturally competent feminist practice model demonstrates that learning takes place when one views people who are living marginally as having strengths and as being able to add much to the development of future perspectives. This chapter offers two recommendations: (1) the conscious inclusion of women of color in leadership roles within agencies and other societal institutions and (2) the direct exploration of differences and similarities within therapeutic interaction so that commonalities can be identified and established for future work.

The authors believe that this framework is a sound model for social work practice with individuals and groups in general, not just with women of color, other women, or men of color. The feminist adage that the personal is political and social work's emphasis on the person within the environment both dictate the need to change the societal institutions that contribute to the oppression of women of color. This imperative stands today as it will stand tomorrow. Futurist culturally competent feminist practice reaffirms the need for personal change as a starting point for structural change. Today, as in the 21st century, social workers must help women of color extend their strengths and their voices beyond the boundaries of their communities to the societal arena because visions of the future are being sketched without their input. Efforts must also be made to recognize the women of color who are futurists so that others can hear the values and visions that they have always articulated. Thus, the strengths of women of color and their roles as actors are affirmed. Continued use of traditional individualistic practice models when working with women of color may engender their dependency on the very institutions that attempt to disempower them.

Yet, given the profession's discomfort with alternative conceptual frameworks (Pinkney, 1993), the authors recognize that some might view this model as constituting "political correctness" and therefore be suspicious of its generalizability (Schoem, Frankel, Zuniga, & Lewis, 1993). We can spend our energy and limited human resources confronting the backlash that will accompany use of these recommendations in practice, as other practitioners have braved allegations of the inappropriateness of cognitive–behavioral practice and feminist practice in general, or we can stop arguing and attend to the need of preparing ourselves and our constituents for the challenges of the 21st century.

REFERENCES

Attneave, C. (1982). American Indians and Alaska native families: Emigrants in their own homeland. In M. McGoldrick, J. Pearce, & J. Giordano (Eds.), *Ethnicity and family therapy* (pp. 55–83). New York: Guilford Press.

Bellah, R., Madsen, R., Sullivan, W. M., Swidler, A., & Tipton, S. M. (1985). *Habits of the heart: Middle America observed.* London: Hutchinson.

Boyd-Franklin, N. (1990). *Black families in therapy: A multi-system approach.* New York: Guilford Press.

Bricker-Jenkins, M., & Hooyman, N. R. (1983). A feminist world view: Ideological themes from the feminist movement. In M. Bricker-Jenkins & N. R. Hooyman (Eds.), *Not for women only: Social work practice for a feminist future* (pp. 7–22). Silver Spring, MD: National Association of Social Workers.

Brown, L. R. (1976). Issues of human welfare. In R. V. Bundy (Ed.), *Images of the future* (pp. 81–95). Buffalo, NY: Prometheus Books.

Bundy, M. L. (1976). A nonmale image of the future. In R. V. Bundy (Ed.), *Images of the future* (pp. 152–158). Buffalo, NY: Prometheus Books.

Bundy, R. V. (1976). Up the downward path: The futures movement and the social imagination. In R. V. Bundy (Ed.), *Images of the future* (pp. 66–72). Buffalo, NY: Prometheus Books.

Childers, M., & Hooks, B. (1990). A conversation about race and class. In M. Hirsch & E. Fox Keller (Eds.), *Conflicts in feminism* (pp. 60–81). New York: Routledge.

Coates, J. F., & Jarrett, J. (1989). *What futurists believe.* Mt. Airy, MD: Lomond Publications.

Collins, B. G. (1986). Defining feminist social work. *Social Work, 31,* 214–220.

Comas-Diaz, L. (1988). Cross-cultural mental health treatment. In L. Comas-Diaz & E. S. Griffith (Eds.), *Clinical guidelines in cross-cultural mental health* (pp. 337–361). New York: John Wiley & Sons.

Devore, W., & Schlesinger, E. (1987). *Ethnic-sensitive social work practice.* St. Louis: C. V. Mosby.

Giele, J. Z. (1978). *Women and the future: Changing sex roles in modern America.* New York: Random House.

Gould, K. (1987). Feminist principles and minority concerns: Contributions, problems and solutions. *Affilia, 2,* 6–19.

Green, J. (1982). *Cultural awareness in the human services.* Englewood Cliffs, NJ: Prentice Hall.

Gutierrez, L. (1992, October). *Macro practice for the 21st century: An empowerment perspective.* Paper presented at the First Annual Conference on Social Work and Social Science, Ann Arbor, MI.

Gutierrez, L., & Lewis, E. (1990). A feminist perspective on organizing with women of color. In J. Erlich & F. Rivera (Eds.), *Organizing with people of color: Changing and emerging communities* (pp. 113–132). Chicago: Aldine de Gruyter.

Lara, G. (1992). Effective communication: A non-deficit approach. *Discharge Planning Update, 12*(3), 3–4.

Lewis, E. (1988). Role strengths and strains of African-American mothers: Social support as a prevention strategy. *Journal of Primary Prevention, 9*(1), 77–91.

Lewis, E., & Ford, B. (1990). The network utilization project: Incorporating traditional strengths of African-American families into group work practice. *Social Work with Groups, 8*(3), 7–22.

Lewis, E., & Kissman, K. (1989). Factors in ethnic-sensitive feminist social work practice. *Arete, 14*(2), 23–31.

Lum, D. (1992). *Social work practice and people of color: A process-stage approach* (2nd ed.). Monterey, CA: Brooks/Cole.

Macht, M., & Quam, J. (1986). *Social work: An introduction.* Columbus, OH: Charles E. Merrill.

Mackinnon, C. A. (1987). *Feminism unmodified: Discourses on life and law.* Cambridge, MA: Harvard University Press.

McGoldrick, M., Pearce, J., & Giordano, J. (Eds.). (1992). *Ethnicity and family therapy.* New York: Guilford Press.

McHale, J. (1969). *The future of the future.* New York: George Braziller.

Pinkney, A. (1993). *Black Americans* (4th ed.). Englewood Cliffs, NJ: Prentice Hall.

Schoem, D., Frankel, L., Zuniga, X., & Lewis, E. (1993). *Multicultural teaching in the university.* New York: Praeger.

Solomon, B. (1976). *Black empowerment: Social work in oppressed communities.* New York: Columbia University Press.

Toffler, A. (Ed.). (1972). *The futurists.* New York: Random House.

12

From Tenement Class to Dangerous Class to Underclass
Blaming Women for Social Problems

Mimi Abramovitz

The Bible says the poor will always be with us but does not say why. Since biblical times, observers have tried to determine both the causes of social problems and their enduring persistence. The resulting mainstream theories fall into two key groups: (1) the liberal or institutional analysis, which links social problems such as poverty to imperfect labor markets and other systemic malfunctions, and (2) the conservative or behavioral analysis, which attributes social problems to defective character and individual dysfunctions.

Behavioral theories explaining the causes of social problems have always exerted a deep influence on social work practice and social welfare policy. But they have not served women very well. From the "lumpen proletariat" to the "tenement class" to the "dangerous class" to the "underclass," experts have linked poverty and other social problems to a failed work ethic among men and to a failed family ethic among women. The theories not only blame women for social problems but argue that the persistence of social problems reflects the transmission of unproductive values and behaviors from one generation to the next. Given the gender division of labor, these analyses, especially the theory of intergenerational transmission of social problems, implicitly blame mothers for society's problems. From social Darwinism to eugenics to psychoanalysis to the culture of poverty, intergenerational explanations of social problems have reflected a deep-seated distrust of the capacity of poor women to raise their children properly. From the morally defective family to the schizophrenogenic mother to the welfare queen, 20th century behavioral theories have been deeply misogynist.

Behavioral theories typically gain strength when developments in the political economy threaten the status quo. These theories become popular in hard times when economic crises indict the market economy for its inability to provide enough jobs or income for the average person and in disruptive times such as when rapid changes in women's roles appear to undermine patriarchal family arrangements. The resurgence of behavioral theories at these times can assume a political role. By explaining the crises in individual rather than systemic terms, they help to protect the system from itself.

The following historical review of behavioral theories focuses on the currently popular and influential idea that families transmit social problems from one generation to the next. The review was undertaken as a critical response to what I perceive as a feminization of the theory of the underclass, a negative view of poor women as lazy, immoral, and responsible for the transmission of a "tangle of pathologies" across generations.

An examination of earlier social problem theories uncovered a similar pattern of blaming mothers for poverty, for the antisocial behavior of children and adults, and for a host of other social problems. These theories merit a careful critique because of their long history and current popularity and because their pejorative views of poor women have historically fueled opposition to social welfare programs. The underclass theory of poverty rationalized the devastating social welfare cutbacks of the 1980s and punitive welfare "reforms" of the 1990s. The latter, known as workfare, wedfare, learnfare, and healthfare, promote the use of government dollars to control the work, marriage, and childbearing behavior of poor women. President Clinton's welfare reform plan, announced in June 1994, promised to "end welfare as we know it" by putting a two-year limit on the receipt of Aid to Families with Dependent Children (AFDC) and mandating hospital-based paternity establishment, among many other harsh measures. The clues suggest that when it comes to poor women, the behavioral theories of poverty still prevail.

THEORIES OF THE INTERGENERATIONAL TRANSMISSION OF POVERTY

Long before welfare dependency became a household word, women were blamed for transmitting undesirable values and behavior across generations. The harsh critique of poor women as breeders of the tenement class, the dangerous class, and most recently, the underclass has persistently linked poverty, deviance, and other social problems to the home. The means of transmission have changed over time from moral contagion to genetic transmission to psychological internalization to cultural dissemination.

Moral Contagion

One of the earliest behavioral theories explained social problems as the product of moral deficiencies transmitted in the home from one generation to the next. This thinking gained ground in the early 1800s as the industrial revolution made many people dependent on an uncertain market economy. The economic transformation dislodged many people from the land and left others jobless during economic depressions; fueled the development of cities and large-scale immigration from Europe; and forced marginalized workers and impoverished people to move from town to town in search of work, to beg and steal, and to live in overcrowded slums.

The new theory of social problems sought to explain poverty, joblessness, and the degradation of individuals that accompanied the industrial revolution. It labeled workers and people who lived in slums as lazy, ignorant, drunkards, gamblers, spendthrifts, sinners, and foreigners and saw them as a "tenement class" whose character and behavior created their own plight. The prevailing social theory held that the tenement class was devoid of moral feeling and a sense of shame and that the chief evils of poverty were more "moral in their origin and character," than economic (Boyer, 1978, p. 90). Therefore, "the principal cause of poverty and crime is the want of an early mental and moral culture" (New York Association for Improving the Condition of the Poor, 1860, p. 31). Slum life was seen then as "a commingled mass of venomous filth and seething sin" (Bremner, 1964, p. 6); poor children were cursed "not by poverty principally, but by the ungoverned appetite, bad habits, and vices of their parents" (Brace 1872/1973, p. 165); and social evils were "attributed to something wrong at home" (Boyer, 1978, p. 39). Such families were characterized by a lack of self-control, discipline, thrift, sobriety, sexual restraint, and self-sacrifice (Scott & Wishy, 1982), and commentators held that they were "more deteriorated by the defects of their habitations, corrupting associations, and surrounding nuisances. . . than by the greatest pecuniary want to which they are subjected" (Stansell, 1986, p. 202).

The moral contagion theory blamed poverty and the condition of the tenement class on the home life of the victims instead of on the dynamics of capitalist development. Blaming social problems on an improper home gained added credibility from the redefinition of the home and gender roles that accompanied the industrial revolution's separation of household and market production. The transformation of the market economy privatized the family, sent men to work in the factories, and made women the moral guardians of the home and community. The emerging ideology defined the increasingly privatized middle-class home as a refuge that protected the family from the corrupt and dangerous commercial world outside and defined the home as the woman's place. Previously the father's domain, the task of raising children to be moral and productive citizens who would fit into the economic order became women's work (Mathaie, 1982; Ryan, 1975; Scott & Wishy, 1982).

In this ideological context, the normal patterns of poor and working-class life appeared deviant. From the vantage of the middle class, poor families and neighborhoods were the breeding grounds of degeneracy, the "parent of constant disorder and the nursery of increasing vices" (Stansell, 1986, p. 202). The teeming street life, the ramshackle tenements without bathtubs or private toilets, the crowded neighborhoods, and the widespread presence of children outdoors became "evidence" of parental neglect, family disintegration, and a pervasive social pathology rather than an expected outcome of life in overcrowded apartments and communities (Ryan, 1975; Stansell, 1986). The Society for the Prevention of Cruelty to Children defined as cruel those parents who sent their children to work, gave them excessive responsibility for the home, or left children unattended (Gordon, 1988). Reform manuals of the 1850s frequently depicted working-class mothers, especially if employed or single, as a subhuman species: bestially drunk; abusive; indifferent as well as unwomanly; and neglectful, if not dangerous, to future generations (Stansell, 1986). The moral contagion theory effectively condemned mothers for the inferior quality of life industrialization offered to the poor.

The popular cure for social problems corresponded to the prevailing definition of the problem. Instead of combating the problem, social policies sought to prevent the "moral contagion" by removing children from the home, resocializing their mothers, and seeking support from their fathers (Stansell, 1986). After visiting a poor woman and her two children, a Children's Aid Society worker reported, "though for her pure young children too much could hardly be done, in such a woman there is little confidence to be put. . . it is probably some cursed vice has thus reduced her and that, if her children not be separated from her, she will drag them down too"

(Stansell, 1986, p. 193). During the last quarter of the 19th century, the child-saving movement, led by Charles Loring Brace, moved young boys to rural foster homes theoretically under the care of better families. They sent poor young girls to industrial schools and lodging homes to learn the skills of industry and domesticity. To be sure that mothers ceased passing defective morals on to their children, they were enrolled in classes on virtuous motherhood (Stansell, 1990). By condemning the homes of poor people in the early 1800s and again in the 1870s, social theories sanctioned institutionalizing poor people by replacing public aid with the more punitive poorhouse and workhouse. Later, this relief was cut, and the orphanage, asylum, prison, and other institutions became the primary response to the poor.

During most of this period, African Americans were enslaved, treated as property, and forced to work the land and to breed future slaves. If the middle class saw the homes of the white poor as the moral pests of society that should be broken up, white society granted African Americans no family rights at all. The law of the land denied African American females any rights of womanhood, outlawed their marriages, and tore their families apart (Davis, 1983; Glenn, 1985). The denial of liberty and humanity to African Americans was justified during and after slavery by doctrines of racial inferiority that defined black individuals as lazy, immoral, and criminal and by widespread views that black people had no sense of family life and needed to "be made faithful to the marriage bond and taught [their] sense of ancestry" (Fitzhugh, cited in Gutman, 1983, p. 463).

Genetic Transmission

Between the Civil War and World War I, social Darwinism and the eugenics movement legitimized the idea that undesirable values and behaviors were transmitted across generations. Both theories attributed the social problems that accompanied the period's rapid industrialization, urbanization, and immigration to laws of natural selection and inheritance. Social Darwinism transformed Darwin's theory of biological evolution based on natural selection and survival of the fittest into a theory of social selection in which the struggle of economic survival differentiated the fit and the unfit. In this competitive environment those with courage, enterprise, good training, intelligence, and perseverance naturally rose to the top, whereas those with physical, moral, or mental weaknesses fell to the bottom. The highly racist eugenics movement equated the fit with people who were rich, native born, and white and the unfit with people who were poor, foreign born, and nonwhite and believed that the traits of both were inherited. Some members even wanted to prevent reproduction by the unfit (J. H. Ehrenreich, 1985; Hofstadter, 1955; Katz, 1986).

These theories shaped social policy. A well-known report on the poorhouse stated that "the vices and weaknesses [of the poor] are very frequently, if not universally, the result of tendencies which are to a greater or lesser degree hereditary in character" and that many poorhouse inmates had "inherited their distaste of work and their fondness for drink from their pauper parents" (Katz, 1986, pp. 86–87). Studies of foreign-born families such as the Jukes and the Kallikaks concluded that feeblemindedness was inherited and was largely responsible for paupers, criminals, prostitutes, and drunkards and that family types and whole racial groups spawned endless generations of "defectives" (Gordon, 1988; Katz, 1986; Trattner, 1989). Charity reformers believed that only "by snapping the bonds between pauper parents and their children" could the transmission of dependence from one generation to the next be prevented (Katz, 1986, p. 106). Others believed that the urban slums stimulated (or some thought, were predicated on) a biological incapacity to resist deviant behavior (Solinger, 1992).

The belief in the intergenerational transmission of deviant behavior through bad genes reflected deep nativist fears that the influx of immigrants threatened the purity and integrity of the racial stock of the native born. Nativists believed that the disappearance of native-born Americans in a flood of foreign-born immigrants was lowering the standard of American intelligence, slowing down the economy, and undermining the nation. Nativists believed that if the situation was left unchecked, the human race would be overrun by a wave of undesirables (Hofstadter, 1955). By supporting white domination as naturally ordained, social Darwinism and eugenics also fueled the virulent racism that assured the legalization of segregation after the Civil War (Allen, 1975).

The hereditarian theories of the period clearly implicated women as genetic transmitters of deviant behavior. As the biological and social reproducers of the next generation, women were blamed for social problems and expected to protect the future of the race. Fears of race suicide were linked to the falling birthrate among native-born, college-educated women and the increasing number of wage-earning women. Theodore Roosevelt accused native-born white women who refused to have large families of being "criminals against the race" (Ladd-Taylor, 1987, p. 2). To protect the racial stock, policymakers glorified motherhood (Mother's Day was first observed in 1908) but condemned individual mothers who did not measure up to the ideal (Ladd-Taylor, 1987).

The leading reformer, Josephine Shaw Lowell, regarded "degraded women" as "the visible links in the direful chain of hereditary pauperism and disease" and questioned the right of the "diseased and viscous" to reproduce their kind and bring into the world beings whose existence must be one long misery to themselves and others. "We do not hesitate to cut off, where it is possible, the evil of insanity by incarcerating for life the incurably insane: Why should we not also prevent the transmission of moral insanity as fatal as that of the mind" (Lowell, 1879, p. 192). She concluded that the unrestrained liberty of "vagrant and degraded" women was a dangerous cause of increased crime, pauperism, and insanity and recommended long-term incarceration for all women younger than 30 arrested for misdemeanors or on the birth of a second illegitimate child (Lowell, 1879). The public viewed black women as prostitutes and their families as dysfunctional (Gilkes, 1983). A highly praised 1910 study of black people insisted that "in [their] home life the Negro is filthy, careless and indecent. . . as destitute of morals as many of the lower animals. . . [and with] little knowledge of the sanctity of the home or marital relations (Odum, 1910, p. 38).

In 1870, poorhouse superintendents heard that the "surest way of correcting the great evil of hereditary pauperism now growing rapidly in our state was to separate children from their parents" (Katz, 1986, p. 107). To a New York State reformer, keeping pauper families together contradicted sound public policy. Another leader warned that society neglects its duty "when it allows a child to remain with a parent that persistently teaches it beggary and crime" (Abramovitz, 1992, p. 153). Given the gender division of labor, mothers were the parent in mind. The eugenics movement called for and won institutional segregation of the feebleminded, immigration quotas, marriage restrictions, compulsory sterilization, and family break-up to prevent the hereditary transmission of mental and moral characteristics (Katz, 1986; Lubove, 1965). By the end of World War I, immigrants and poor people filled state institutions, and by 1917 25 states had a sterilization law. Family break-up became the cornerstone of public policy.

The eugenics movement finally lost ground to new scientific findings, its inherent racism, and its use by Hitler in the 1930s. But the deep distrust of poor women's ability to socialize their children properly persisted as the idea of the intergenerational transmission of deviant values and behaviors by women reappeared in new forms.

Psychological Internalization

Twentieth-century theorists transformed theories of the intergenerational transmission of undesirable values and behavior from a biological to a psychological event and extended the antiwoman analysis to the middle class. Having rejected moral and genetic contagion as the conveyor of social problems from one generation to the next, the new theories emphasized psychological transmission through the mother–child tie (B. Ehrenreich & English, 1979).

Dubbed "scientific motherhood," the new child-rearing ideas meshed with economic trends and the Progressive Era's drive for rationality, efficiency, and order in all spheres of life. With profits and productivity increasingly dependent on mass production techniques, especially the routinization of the work process based on scientific management, workers had to accept new levels of discipline and efficiency. Mounting labor unrest also placed a premium on conformity. Scientific homemaking and scientific mothering paralleled these trends. Both doctrines expected mothers to produce children whose personalities would fit into the changing economic order (B. Ehrenreich & English, 1979; Mintz & Kellog, 1988).

Scientific mothering replaced reliance on traditional maternal care with the advice of child-rearing experts inspired by the new field of psychology. In the late 1890s, mothers learned that children would grow into responsible adults through good maternal examples and mother-love. By the turn of the 20th century, the idea of the child as a passive receptor to be molded by proper role models was supplanted by the idea of children as active and malleable creatures whose personalities could be shaped by systematic child-rearing methods. This idea devalued mother-love as too sentimental and spontaneous. Mother-love came to be seen as a dangerous instrument that spoiled children and encouraged them to be dependent, undisciplined, and nonconforming. Instead, scientific mothering called for strict feeding and sleeping schedules, early toilet training, minimal maternal affection, and other stern practices needed to instill the habits of regularity demanded by the rapidly industrializing economy (Ladd-Taylor, 1987; Mintz & Kellog, 1988; Scott & Wishy, 1982). Scientific footing for this idea was provided by behaviorism, which purported that children, like machines, could be programmed to fit any culture (B. Ehrenreich & English, 1979).

Guided by the assumption that faulty child rearing led to larger social problems such as poverty, delinquency, and class antagonism, proponents hoped scientific mothering would instill future workers with obedience, punctuality, and good citizenship long before they could get out of line (Mintz & Kellog, 1988). The director of the Boston Psychopathic Hospital stated that all the workers in a 1920 strike "had something wrong with them from a nervous or mental standpoint" (J. H. Ehrenreich, 1985, p. 67). Such thinking allowed the mental health field to pay little attention to the social realities of living and working in a highly industrialized and fiercely competitive society (Woodruff, 1964).

Although scientific mothering blamed all mothers for family and social problems, poor and working-class women were especially suspect and vulnerable to failing the test of scientific motherhood. Watson argued that "no one should have a child until she could afford to give the child a room of its own" (B. Ehrenreich & English, 1979, p. 205). Others felt that poor and working-class women should not have children at all. Taking the middle ground, the Laura Spelman Rockefeller Foundation funded programs to train teachers and home economists to be parent educators who would teach poor and working-class mothers proper child rearing. By the 1920s, a nationwide parent education network existed in schools, social welfare agencies, religious organizations, and government programs (B. Ehrenreich & English, 1979).

Scientific mothering and behaviorism coexisted with a growing body of theory that stressed the child's emotional development rather than discipline and control. The mental hygiene field, for example, held that the family's prime duty was to furnish a nurturing environment that met children's needs. It maintained that the quality of emotional ties in the home determined the difference between the normal and the abnormal personality. Normal adjustment was defined as being able to accept frustration, deprivation, external authority, and one's station in life. Echoing this thinking, a Rockefeller Foundation official stated that "the personality development of a child who had received proper parenting would display the characteristic submissiveness to authority and acceptance of the limitations of income and possessions. . . largely because the underlying feeling tone toward life, derived from breast feeding and mothering, will prevent any strong resentment and foster an attitude of cheerful acceptance" (J. H. Ehrenreich, 1985, p. 69). The mental hygiene movement popularized the concept of normality and devised standardized tests to measure it, sending parents to search for infantile, neurotic, or other signs of abnormal behavior in their children (J. H. Ehrenreich, 1985; Mathaie, 1982).

The move away from discipline and self-control toward more responsive parenting was influenced as well by the work of Freud and others who argued against undue repression of children's needs, which could result in life-long psychological damage. New theories urged flexible rather than rigid child-rearing practices on the grounds that responsiveness rather than control produced well-adjusted children. By the early 1930s Gesell had written about stages of child development and recommended that the child's demands dictate the timing of feeding, weaning, and toilet training. Gesell believed that the ideal mother relied on understanding, patience, and indirectness to allow children self-determination and that she followed the child's lead, never bucking the phase (B. Ehrenreich & English, 1979; Ladd-Taylor, 1987; Mintz & Kellog, 1988; Ryan, 1975).

Psychoanalysis intensified the focus on women by suggesting that mothering was biologically grounded in women's maternal instinct, which made them natural mothers. According to psychoanalytic theory, the ideal mother achieved self-fulfillment in meeting her children's needs rather than her own. She desired no companionship other than her own child. To want anything else abnormally violated the terms of women's psychosexual maturity. With the mother no longer needing to discipline children, her job was to meet children's needs for play, stimulation, and nurturance; to encourage children's impulses; and to offer more and more full-time unconditional love (B. Ehrenreich & English, 1979). Social workers said that poverty and the need for relief stemmed from deeply rooted childhood dependency wishes and that rising crime, idiocy, poverty, and suicide were the result of inadequate parenting.

The move toward greater permissiveness and away from carefully conditioned patterns of behavior coincided with the post–World War I rise of mass-produced goods and services and the intensification of the consumer culture. If Americans had to follow the industrial clock before World War I, after the war the distribution of a growing supply of mass-produced goods demanded that Americans drop their spartan habits of frugality for greater indulgence and self-gratification. Previously suppressed impulses were now encouraged as healthy for personality development and the wider economy (B. Ehrenreich & English, 1979).

But the shift toward permissiveness did not take mothers off the hook. Instead, the mother's personality rather than her child-rearing methods risked producing a psychologically scarred child prone to deviant behavior as an adult. Suspicion about mothers grew during and after World War II as only a wholly domestic nonworking mother could hope to achieve the required ideal state. Mother-blaming reached new heights during World War II, fueled by changing times and women's changing roles. With poverty pushed to the back burner and men away at the war front, public attention focused on new problems, including the massive entry of married women into the labor force. The effort to blame wartime hardships and postwar social problems on mothers reflected the major changes in family life initiated by the war and was an effort to reverse these changes.

Experts translated public fears about the changing roles of women into questions about the ability of women to raise children.

When more than 2 million men were rejected for service for psychological reasons, the military blamed mothers. The armed services' psychiatric consultant accused "America's traditional sweet, doting, self-sacrificing mom" of having "failed in the elementary mother function of weaning offspring emotionally as well as physically" (Mintz & Kellog, 1988, p. 164). Wylie's (1942) best-selling *A Generation of Vipers* claimed that overpowering women and megaloid mom worship, called "momism," led to psychological and emotional immaturity in children (Mintz & Kellog, 1988). The theme of overbearing mother and absent father was continued into the late 1950s by social observers who critiqued fathers as nighttime residents and weekend guests. But the focus on absent men quickly translated into a description of the middle-class suburban family as problematically child-centered and female-dominated (Mintz & Kellog, 1988). B. Ehrenreich and English (1979) speculated that the fear of mothers reflected a growing sense among men that ongoing changes had somehow deprived them of power.

The postwar growth of female employment as well as rising rates of divorce, nonmarital births, illegal abortions, juvenile delinquency, and homosexuality fueled fears about the decline of the patriarchal family. By the end of World War II the romantic picture of the loving mother had given way to two negative images: (1) the rejecting mother who scarred her children and society by working outside the home or having interests of her own and (2) the overprotective mother who was alone with her children all day and became overinvolved and overpowering.

In the late 1940s Lundberg and Farnham's (1947) book *The Modern Women: The Lost Sex* purported that "the spawning ground of most neurosis in Western Civilization is the home. The basis for it is laid in childhood. . . . And as we have pointed out, the principal agent laying the groundwork for it is the mother" (p. 303). This widely read book claimed that only half of America's mothers were "healthy, fully maternal mothers" who "merely loved their children" (Mathaie, 1982, p. 268). The other half were unhealthy; they were rejecting, overprotective, or dominating.

Bowlby's theory of maternal deprivation also captured public attention after the war and reinforced the psychoanalytic reprimand of women. Bowlby's research on World War II orphans living in hospitals for a long time with minimal attention accurately depicted the children's seriously withdrawn state. But Bowlby overextended his conclusions about the dangers of maternal deprivation to the home. Although it was not supported by his research, Bowlby claimed that the symptoms of maternal deprivation could occur whenever the mother was not present in the home full-time. In an updated version of the intergenerational theory of social problems, he claimed that "deprived children, whether in their own homes or out of them, are a source of social infection as real and serious as the carriers of diphtheria and typhoid" (B. Ehrenreich & English, 1979, p. 231). Bowlby called for a public health campaign to detect cases of deprivation on a mass scale, equating the effort with earlier campaigns to rid communities of disease.

Hoping to control these seemingly dangerous trends, postwar observers advised working mothers to quit their jobs and return to their natural state of motherhood. Experts argued that normal child development depended on having a mother at home. Dr. Spock and many social workers stressed the mother–child bond. Other professionals also argued that to satisfy their children's needs for love, attention, and care, women should stay home. Backed by Bowlby's studies of maternal deprivation, the Freudian theory of female sexuality, and sociologist Parson's one breadwinner–one homemaker model of the nuclear family, mental health professionals, like many others, told mothers that their employment impaired their children's ability to form intense emotional relationships. Guilt-inducing pundits accused those who did not or could not conform to these patterns of child deprivation and unnatural female instincts (Mintz & Kellog, 1988). Working mothers also were blamed for a vast array of problems ranging from bed-wetting to juvenile delinquency to schizophrenia. Single mothers were seen as fallen women raising illegitimate children in unstable families or broken homes, especially if they were African American (Solinger, 1992). Lesbians were simply seen as sick.

Although working women were heavily rebuked, full-time homemakers did not escape reproach. Experts admonished women to be full-time mothers but then told them that this devotion damaged their children. Women were condemned as overprotective and neurotically overinvolved with their children and were told they were responsible for any dependency, delinquency, or dissent manifested by their offspring (Brienes, 1992). In psychoanalytic terms, such overprotective mothers were aggressive and expressed unconscious hostilities and destructive urges and often exerted undue power and influence over their children (B. Ehrenreich & English, 1979). According to Brienes (1992) the fear that mothers would incapacitate their children was really a fear that they would emasculate their sons, thereby creating dependent and weak men and spoiling their sons' (and the nation's) chances of success.

The mother's personality continued to be the focus of blame throughout the 1950s. With more white middle-class mothers restlessly confined to the home, experts increasingly linked childhood psychological disorders to the mother's mental health. Mental health specialists in all disciplines traced childhood psychological problems to the unmet developmental needs of mothers and suggested that mothers subconsciously displaced their own frustrations and needs for independence and achievement onto their children. Maladjusted, sociopathic, or otherwise deviant behavior of children now reflected unresolved mental conflicts, unsatisfied inner needs, and other outcomes of poor mothering (Lubove, 1965). Well-known psychiatrists such as Erikson and Lidz linked these patterns of maternal care to schizophrenia, homosexuality, and an inability to assume adult commitments (Mintz & Kellog, 1988). Between the 1940s and the early 1960s

> it was suddenly discovered that the mother could be blamed for everything. In every case history of the troubled child; alcoholic, suicidal, schizophrenic, psychopathic, neurotic adult; impotent, homosexual male; frigid, promiscuous female; ulcerous, asthmatic and otherwise disturbed American could be found a mother. A frustrated, repressed, disturbed, martyred, never satisfied, unhappy woman. A rejecting, overprotecting, dominating mother. (Mintz & Kellog, 1988, p. 189)

Whereas postwar mother-blaming accused white women of momism, African American women suffered degrading racist stereotypes. Black women were Sapphires, the overbearing wife of Kingfish on the "Amos 'n Andy" show, or the castrating matriarchs who ruled the female-headed household, overpowered their men, emasculated their sons, and transmitted low social and moral standards to family members (Collins, 1990; Gilkes, 1983; Solinger, 1992). White unwed mothers were regarded as neurotic and curable and were urged to give their babies up for adoption. But black unwed mothers were tarred with centuries-old racist myths of black women as the hypersexual Jezebel or as the warm and simple black Mammy who possessed a natural affection for children. Among other things, these stereotypes were used to justify the lack of maternity homes and adoption services for African Americans and the use of black women as domestic servants (B. Ehrenreich & English, 1979; Solinger, 1992).

After World War II, as more unmarried African American mothers became eligible for AFDC, many states passed surveillance laws that allowed special investigating units to ferret out unwed mothers and disqualify them for aid (Bell, 1965). Most white experts believed that the African American personality was negatively and immutably shaped by biology and slavery, leaving African American mothers prone to "unrestrained sexuality" and "unsuitable homes" and generally inferior, both morally and psychologically, to white mothers (Solinger, 1992).

The argument that pathological behavior is transmitted from parent to child through the mother's impaired psychological development and the inadequate socialization of children continues to this day. Perhaps it was a coincidence that in the 1970s, at the height of the women's movement, natural childbirth, breast-feeding, and the theory of maternal–child bonding came into vogue. Despite little evidence that bonding made any difference, one pediatric expert declared that infants who do not bond properly can become terrorists (Noble, 1993). A *New York Times Magazine* article titled "Mothers: Tired of Taking the Rap," (Smith, 1990) concluded that "mothers have been made the cause of everything from colic to mass murder" (p. 32). Mother–child relationships cannot be discounted as an important factor in shaping children's adult personality. But singling out mothers and ignoring the role of fathers and of wider social conditions leads to a highly distorted view of social problems and sanctions punitive social work practices and social policies.

Cultural Dissemination

The psychological analysis of social problems was directed largely to the white middle class. But blaming women's psyche for social problems also trickled down to the white and black working classes as well as to the poor. Reviews of child protection records indicate that the previously neglectful parent became the neurotic or pathological mother (Gordon, 1988). With the "rediscovery of poverty" in the 1960s, the behavioral theory of poverty and belief in its intergenerational transmission reappeared. This time, however, the source of contagion was a defective culture rather than defective morals, genes, and psyche. Based on anthropological studies of Mexican and Puerto Rican barrios, Lewis (1961, 1966) posited the existence of a culture of poverty that tends to perpetuate itself from generation to generation by preventing children from using the few opportunities that come their way. He argued that the culture of poverty was a by-product of capitalism and a means by which the poor adapted to their marginalized position in a class-stratified society.

Neoconservatives such as Banfield and Moynihan picked up the culture of poverty theory but stressed the victim-blaming rather than the structural features of Lewis's analysis. Moynihan's (1965) report, *The Negro Family,* openly blamed poverty and other social problems faced by the African American community on its large number of female-headed families, even though until very recently the overwhelming majority of black families had two parents. Moynihan argued that women living alone deprived their children of a male role model and a proper authority figure. The women trapped their families in a tangle of pathology and a cycle of poverty. Moynihan stated that the structure of the black family, rather than poverty and racism, caused crime, drug addiction, school failure, male unemployment, and the need for welfare. To some it was no accident that a victim-blaming analysis resurfaced just when the increasingly militant civil rights movement drew more public attention to racial injustice (Gresham, 1989).

The culture of poverty theory lay dormant during the turbulent 1960s after the storm unleashed by Moynihan's report. But it reappeared in the currently popular theory of the underclass (Wilson, 1985). The underclass theory initially focused on poor men as unmotivated workers, irresponsible fathers, and inadequate providers and portrayed them as street hustlers, drug addicts, and criminals. But the already racialized theory, which increasingly depicted women as incubators of deviant values and "breeders" of underclass behaviors, has been feminized.

FEMINIZATION AND RACIALIZATION OF THE UNDERCLASS

Social scientists describe the underclass today as a socially isolated segment of poor people, living in disorganized neighborhoods characterized by high rates of crime, hustling, drug abuse, dropping out of school, joblessness, teenage pregnancy, female-headed households, out-of-wedlock births, and welfare use (Mincy, Sawhill, & Wolf, 1990; Ricketts & Sawhill, 1988). You do not have to listen too hard to hear the message that crime, drug use, and dropping out of school are among the "tangle of pathologies" transmitted from one generation to another by women of color heading families or that mother-only households keep their families mired in poverty and dependent on the state from one generation to the next.

Implications for Social Policy

Underclass theorists have no trouble placing welfare mothers in the same class as drug users, criminals, and other antisocial groups. The negative stereotypes of poor women contained in the theory of the underclass have become firmly embedded in the current social dogma and fuel support for increasingly punitive social policies for poor women. During the 1980s, the major initiatives directed toward poor families, especially those headed by women, were social program cutbacks that forced thousands of women off AFDC, eroded benefits by nearly a third, and made it more difficult for women to get housing, food stamps, Medicaid, and social services.

Another major initiative has been the use of government dollars to regulate the lives of women. The new "personal responsibility" legislation known as workfare, wedfare, learnfare, and healthfare seeks to dictate the work, marital, and childbearing decisions of women on welfare rather than simply to provide income support. These programs assume that the culture of poverty is transmitted from deviant mother to deviant child and imply that poor women cannot manage without government directives and do not deserve aid unless they act correctly.

Workfare, the first of the new reforms, became the centerpiece of the 1988 Family Support Act, which transformed AFDC from an income support program, to help single mothers stay home with their children, into a mandatory work program. As is the case with Clinton's proposed two-year cap on welfare benefits, workfare advocates see welfare mothers as irresponsible parents and poor role models who will not work unless forced to by the government.

The second reform to use government dollars to change women's behavior is wedfare, which seeks to control women's marital and childbearing decisions. The image of welfare mothers as lazy and unmotivated is seconded only by the popular perception that women on welfare have large families, have children for money, and keep their families trapped on welfare for many generations. Based on this myth, several states now want to deny benefits to children conceived or born while the mother was on welfare. Other states have considered, but have rejected, rewarding the use of the Norplant contraceptive or making it a condition of aid. Is forced sterilization far behind?

The use of government dollars to condition the mother's behavior also is present in learnfare, which reduces AFDC benefits for any child who fails to meet specified school attendance requirements. Similarly, healthfare docks a family's check if prescribed health schedules for children are not followed. Both programs imply that poor women on welfare do not know how to care for their children.

The most negative response to the idea of women as irresponsible breeders is the increasing criminalization of women's reproductive behavior. In the name of "fetal protection," states are prosecuting women whose infants test positive for drugs, alcohol, or the human immunodeficiency virus as child abusers or drug pushers (Chavkin, 1990). Instead of receiving needed services the women face long jail terms and the loss of parental rights (Bader, 1990; Lewin, 1989, 1990). These charges do not always stand, but the number of prosecutions has shot up from less than one every five years to 60 in less than a year. Virtually all prosecutions involved poor women, mostly women of color. The former drug and education czar, William Bennett, suggested that children be removed from drug-plagued homes and neighborhoods and placed in orphanages. An Ohio legislator recently proposed mandatory sterilization of women who give birth to a second addicted baby. Some states are already fingerprinting welfare mothers.

WHAT THE FUTURE HOLDS

Clearly conservative theories of poverty that blame social and economic problems on women rather than the profit-oriented decisions of business and the state have captured and continue to shape the social policy agenda. But how much have we been seduced or co-opted by them? How far have terms such as underclass, welfare dependency, culture of poverty, reverse discrimination, and welfare reform crept into our personal and professional language? Do we realize that images about women, race, and poverty buried in these words violate the interests of those whom they profess to describe and that, as race code words, they have been used to justify attacks on the welfare state?

By using this language, we become hostage to conservative definitions of people, poverty, and society and let them shape our consciousness and our behavior. To claim the future for women and feminism, we must first resist the massive dose of antiwomen and racist ideology and then seek progressive social change. We must expose the misogynist practice of blaming social problems on women to protect the failed decisions of business and the state, eliminate social policies that enforce stereotypic roles for women by rewarding those who comply with prescribed wife and mother roles and punishing those who cannot or choose not to do so, and subject all social policies, new and old, to a gender test to ensure they promote equal rights and responsibility for all in the home, workplace, political system, and society.

This is no small order. These tasks require that we identify, reclaim, and reinstate the profession's long-standing liberal and radical heritages and make them compatible with feminist analysis and action. We must challenge and restructure the linchpin of patriarchy, namely, the gender division of labor, which structures inequality between the sexes into the family, the workplace, the welfare state, and the entire social order, leaving women holding the short end of the stick.

To accomplish this enormous task, to make social policy, if not all societal institutions, responsive to women and supportive of their needs, we must join forces with those women who refuse to take the blame, punishment, or coercion. This includes welfare mothers who have begun to organize and protest across the nation. These political actions are critical. The historical record shows that the "powers that be" rarely act, and social policy rarely changes, unless pressured from below.

REFERENCES

Abramovitz, M. (1992). *Regulating the lives of women: Social welfare policy from colonial times to the present.* Boston: South End Press.

Allen, R. (1975). *Reluctant reformers: Racism and social reform movements in the United States.* New York: Anchor Books.

Bader, E. (1990, March/April). Pregnant drug users face jail. *New Directions for Women,* pp. 1, 8.

Bell, W. (1965). *Aid to dependent children.* New York: Columbia University Press.

Boyer, P. (1978). *Urban masses and moral order in America, 1820–1920.* Cambridge, MA: Harvard University Press.

Brace, C. L. (1973). *The dangerous classes of New York.* Washington, DC: National Association Social Workers. (Original work published 1872)

Bremner, R. H. (1964). *From the depths: The discovery of poverty in the United States.* New York: New York University Press.

Brienes, W. (1992). *Young, white and miserable: Growing up female in the 1950s.* Boston: Beacon Press.

Chavkin, W. (1990). Drug addiction and pregnancy: Policy crossroads. *American Journal of Public Health, 80,* 483–487.

Collins, P. H. (1990). *Black feminist thought: Knowledge, consciousness, and the politics of empowerment.* London: HarperCollins.

Davis, A. (1983). *Women, race and class.* New York: Vintage.

Ehrenreich, B., & English, D. (1979). *For her own good: 100 years of the experts' advice to women.* New York: Anchor Books.

Ehrenreich, J. H. (1985). *The altruistic imagination: A history of social work and social policy in the United States.* Ithaca, NY: Cornell University Press.

Family Support Act of 1988, P. L. 100-485, 102 Stat. 2343.

Gilkes, C. T. (1983). From slavery to social welfare: Racism and the control of black women. In A. Swerdloow & H. Lessinger (Eds.), *Class, race and sex: The dynamics of control.* Boston: G. K. Hall.

Glenn, E. N. (1985). Racial ethnic women's labor: The intersection of race, gender and class oppression. *Review of Radical Political Economics, 17*(3), 86–108.

Gordon, L. (1988). *Heroes of their own lives: The politics and history of family violence.* New York: Penguin Books.

Gresham, J. H. (1989, July 24). The politics of family in America. *Nation,* pp. 116–122.

Gutman, H. C. (1983). Persistent myths about the Afro-American Family. In M. Gordon (Ed.), *The American family in social–historical perspective* (pp. 459–481). New York: St. Martin's Press.

Hofstadter, R. (1955). *Social Darwinism in American thought.* Boston: Beacon Press.

Katz, M. B. (1986). *In the shadow of the poorhouse: A social history of welfare in America.* New York: Basic Books.

Ladd-Taylor, M. (1987). *Mother-work, ideology, public policy and the mother's movement.* Unpublished doctoral dissertation, Yale University, New Haven, CT.

Lewin, T. (1989, January 9). When courts take chage of the unborn. *New York Times,* pp. 1, 11.

Lewin, T. (1990, February 5). Drug use in pregnancy: New issue for the courts. *New York Times,* p. 14.

Lewis, O. (1961). *The children of Sanchez.* New York: Random House.

Lewis, O. (1966, October). The culture of poverty. *Scientific American, 215,* 19–25.

Lowell, J. S. (1879, June) One means of preventing pauperism. In *Proceedings of the sixth annual conference of charities* (pp. 189–200). Boston.

Lubove, R. (1965). *The professional altruist: The emergence of social work as a career, 1880–1930.* Cambridge, MA: Harvard University Press.

Lundberg, F., & Farnham, M. (1947). *The modern women: The lost sex.* New York: Harper & Brothers.

Mathaie, J. A. (1982). *An economic history of women in America: Women's work, the sexual division of labor and the development of capitalism.* New York: Schoken Books.

Mincy, R., Sawhill, I. V., & Wolf, D. A. (1990). The underclass: Definition and measurement. *Science, 248,* 450–453.

Mintz, S., & Kellog, S. (1988). *Domestic revolutions: A social history of American family life.* New York: Free Press.

Moynihan, D. P. (1965). *The Negro family: The case for national action.* Washington, DC: U.S. Government Printing Office.

New York Association for Improving the Condition of the Poor. (1860). *Seventeenth annual report.* New York: Author.

Noble, B. P. (1993, February 21). Infant bonding and guilty mothers. *New York Times,* p. 25.

Odum, H. (1910). *Social and mental traits of the Negro: Research into the basic conditions of the Negro race in southern towns.* New York.

Ricketts, E. R., & Sawhill, I. V. (1988). Defining and measuring the underclass. *Journal of Policy Analysis and Management, 7*(2), 316–325.

Ryan, M. (1975). *Womanhood in America: From colonial times to the present.* New York: New Viewpoints.

Scott, D. M., & Wishy, B. (1982). *America's families: A documentary history.* New York: Harper & Row.

Smith, J. M. (1990, June 10). Mothers: Tired of taking the rap. *New York Times Magazine,* pp. 2–33, 38.

Solinger, R. (1992). *Wake up little Susie: Single pregnancy and race relations before Roe v. Wade.* New York: Routledge.

Stansell, C. (1986). *City of women: Sex and class in New York, 1789–1860.* Urbana, IL: University of Illinois Press.

Stansell, C. (1990). Women, children and the uses of the stress: Class and gender conflict in New York City, 1850–1860. In E. C. DuBois & V. L. Ruiz (Eds.), *Unequal sisters: A multicultural reader in U.S. women's history* (pp. 92–108). New York: Routledge.

Trattner, W. I. (1989). *From poor law to welfare state: A history of social welfare in America.* New York: Free Press.

Wilson, W. J. (1985). Cycles of deprivation and the underclass debate. *Social Service Review, 56*(4), 541–559.

Woodruff, K. (1964). *From charity to social work in England and the United States.* London: Routledge & Kegan Paul.

Wylie, P. (1942). *A generation of vipers.* New York: Farrar & Rinehart.

A version of this chapter was presented at Stony Brook School of Social Work, State University of New York at Stony Brook, on October 20, 1994.

13

Homeless Women and Feminist Social Work Practice

Alice K. Johnson and Rosalie N. Richards

W hen a woman is categorized as "a homeless woman" she has lost an ingredient integral to her identity. She is now known in terms of being without, as being less than. She is without the identity a home affords.

To understand what it means to be homeless, an image of what home, with all of its ramifications, means to our sense of self must be created. Virginia Woolf wrote in *A Room of One's Own* that "a woman must have money and a room of her own if she is to write fiction" (Woolf, 1929, p. 4). Just as having children is a way a woman in this society can establish her sense of self-expression, so having a home is a basic way of establishing her creative identity. Home is a secure place (Rainwater, 1966), a sacred place (Eliade, 1959), the epitome of a meaningful relationship between a woman and her environment.

Women living in neighborhoods described as depressed, as war zones, and as violence- and poverty-plagued may not aspire to express their creativeness through writing and may not require a room that only they need ever enter. However, they do want, and they do creatively express themselves in, a place they call home.

To be homeless is to suffer a stigmatized loss of identity, as is having a child taken away by protective services. Both catastrophic events mean a loss of part of one's creative expression, of one's identity. Homeless women are less.

Home is further connected with security and power. Dovey (1985) explained that

> home is a center of security, of possessed territory, a place of freedom
> where our own order can become manifest, secure from the impositions

of others. This aspect of home as a place of autonomy is also fundamentally linked to home as identity; it gives a connection to the future. . . a certain freedom of interaction between present and future, between our experiences and dreams. Knowing that we have the power to remain in a place and change it permits us to act upon and build our dreams. (p. 43)

Homeless women are torn out of this image of creative space and power. Instead they find themselves in an often-changing environment over which they have little control. They find themselves trying to cope with stressful demands in shelters created with no one in particular in mind. They must negotiate complex and impersonal welfare and support services systems without having a space to return to that speaks of self that was created out of one's thoughts and feelings. Worse than that, to be homeless means to have little control over chaos: papers get lost; appointments are missed; long lines are expected; and, for the mothers, little children never quit needing attention and testing limits in the midst of this chaos. For homeless women, space, security, order, and self-expression are lost in impersonal surroundings, stressful changes, and bureaucratic lines.

The image of being silenced parallels the homeless woman's loss of creative space. In describing the multitude of obstacles women must overcome in developing the power of their minds, Belenky, Clinchy, Goldberger, and Tarule (1986) developed the image of the silent woman who lives "cut off from others in a world full of rumor and innuendo. Words arise out of wrath, and they provoke wrath" (p. 25). Noise may come from the homeless woman and may surround her, but she is truly the silent woman, for the symbolic room of her own is not afforded her. Without this room she cannot express herself because she has no protected space that makes it possible for her to hear her own soul, her personal thoughts.

As these lines suggest, homelessness has a distinct meaning for women. This chapter begins by examining the extent of the contemporary problem of homelessness for women. Single women and women with children emerge as distinct subpopulations with different service needs, and these will be discussed next. A feminist analysis of homelessness follows. This includes a challenge to the myopic approach of feminist thought that has opted to develop feminist struggle with a class instead of a gender agenda. Finally, we discuss how feminist values in practice can assist homeless women to recover their homes.

EXTENT OF THE PROBLEM FOR WOMEN

Homelessness emerged as a contemporary social problem on the streets of U.S. cities in the early 1980s (Stern, 1984). At the local level, lawsuits charged city governments to respond to the shelter needs of homeless people (Chackes, 1988; Johnson, Kreuger, & Stretch, 1989) and new service systems developed (Johnson & Banerjee, 1992). At the federal level, policy entrepreneurs successfully tacked homelessness legislation onto other bills. As a result, despite federal retrenchment in other areas, legislation to aid homeless shelters became law (Arnold, 1989).

Early estimates of the extent of the homeless problem ranged from 250,000 people (U.S. Department of Housing and Urban Development, 1984) to more than 3 million people (Hombs & Snyder, 1982). As advocates (Hopper, 1984) and government agencies (U.S. General Accounting Office, 1988) challenged the validity of these estimates, methodological and measurement techniques for assessing homeless people received increased attention (Johnson, 1989b; Tauber, 1991), and the 1990 census marked the first time the U.S. government attempted to enumerate people living both in shelters and on the street. Currently, however, the federal government officially uses the Urban Institute's national estimate of 567,000 to 600,000 homeless individuals (Kondratas, 1991). Families with children make up approximately 10 percent of the homeless population (Burt & Cohen, 1989a).

One indication of the growing problem of homelessness for women is the rapid increase in the demand for homeless shelters. From 1984 to 1988 the number of single homeless women in shelters rose 180 percent and the number of homeless families in shelters more than quadrupled, reaching more than 60,000 (U.S. Department of Housing and Urban Development, 1989). In 1986 the demand for family shelter had increased by 80 percent in 25 surveyed cities, making female-headed families the fastest growing subgroup in the homeless population (Reyes & Waxman, 1987). The National Academy of Sciences estimated that 100,000 children under the age of 18, not including those who have been forced to leave their parents' homes, are homeless on any given night (Institute of Medicine, 1988).

Homeless single women and homeless mothers and children are two different groups of homeless persons. A review of the literature on single women and on mothers with children will be presented below in preparation for viewing homelessness from a feminist perspective.

Single Women

Homeless women were first recognized as alcoholics on skid row (Garrett & Bahr, 1973) and later as middle-aged and elderly, often mentally ill, women living on the streets in New York City (Baxter

& Hopper, 1984; Rousseau, 1981). Gender-based differences between homeless women and homeless men have been noted by numerous authors (Benda, 1990; Hagen, 1987; D. Roth, Toomey, & First, 1987). Crystal's (1984) early research in New York shelters suggested that women do not fit the criteria of disaffiliation commonly associated with homelessness among men (Bahr, 1973). Homeless women are more often found to have been previously married and are more likely to continue contact with their children. In a random sample of 298 men and 230 women from Baltimore missions, shelters, and jails, more than one-half of the women, compared with about one-fourth of the men, remained in continuous contact with their families (Breakey et al., 1989). Also in Baltimore, Russell's (1991) ethnographic research with single homeless women showed the same tendency toward affiliation: "Not only did many of them have regular contact with a female relative or friend, but also they tried to maintain contact with their children. Affiliation and concern for their children was their principle [sic] interest" (p. 106).

Except for personality disorders, which have equal rates, homeless women show a higher prevalence of mental illness than homeless men (Breakey et al., 1989). In St. Louis, homeless women are less likely than homeless men to have drinking problems or alcohol treatment histories and are more likely to have been sexually abused. Homeless women also express a greater need for social support and use a wider support network than homeless men (Calsyn & Morse, 1990). As a result, women are more likely to be situationally homeless (Bachrach, 1987). African Americans are disproportionately represented among homeless women (First, Roth, & Arewa, 1988).

Not only are homeless women distinct from homeless men, but they make up a heterogeneous group with diverse service needs (Hagen, 1990; Stoner, 1984). On the basis of whether or not the homeless woman is accompanied by dependent children, two distinct groups emerge. Women not accompanied by dependent children are generally older white women. These women have been homeless longer and are more likely to have been hospitalized for psychiatric problems, have had recent contact with a mental health professional, drink, and have a drinking problem (Johnson & Kreuger, 1989). Single homeless women, sometimes referred to as "shopping bag ladies," live anonymously, make little use of social services, and are socially isolated (Schein, 1979).

National comparisons of single women, single men, and women accompanied by children indicate that single women and single men are more likely to have histories of mental hospitalization and to have attempted suicide. Single women have double the rate of chemical dependency treatment of women accompanied by children but half the treatment rate of single men. Criminal involvement is much less likely for women than men, with a slightly higher rate for single women with children (Burt & Cohen, 1989b).

Women with Children

Compared with single women and single men, homeless women with children are the youngest, have the least education, and are the most likely to be nonwhite. They also have been homeless for the shortest time, are least likely to have held a steady job, and are most likely to rely on welfare for income. Nevertheless, the actual amount of welfare income they receive per person is less than what single men and women receive from their cash sources (Burt & Cohen, 1989b). Homeless mothers are, however, well informed about and use community services (Hagen & Ivanoff, 1988). They have greater access to financial assistance, health care, counseling services, and sufficient quantities of daily food (Anderson, Boe, & Smith, 1988). According to Burt and Cohen (1989b), "in many ways, homeless women with children differ from homeless men. Women bring gender responsibilities with them into the homeless situation" (p. 509).

Research on homeless families began with interviews of 80 families in 14 Boston shelters (Bassuk, Rubin, & Lauriat, 1986). Homeless mothers are young, single women of color with a high school education or less, a poor job history, and have an average of two children, of which at least one is a preschooler. They have typically supported themselves through Aid to Families with Dependent Children (AFDC) since the birth of their first child. This profile is remarkably consistent in studies of sheltered families across geographically diverse regions of the country, including Detroit (Mills & Ota, 1989); King County, Washington (Miller & Linn, 1988); Los Angeles (McChesney, 1986); New York City (Phillips, DeChillo, Kronenfeld, & Middleton-Jeter, 1988); Philadelphia (L. Roth & Fox, 1990); northern California (Stanford Center for the Study of Families, Children and Youth, 1991); and St. Louis (Johnson, 1989a).

Comparative research has tried to assess how the situation of homeless families differs from that of poor housed families. Los Angeles includes a large number of two-parent homeless families. Homeless mothers disclose more spouse and child abuse and more substance abuse and mental health problems (Wood, Valdez, Hayashi, & Shen, 1990). Though not residing in shelters specifically designed for battered women, homeless mothers show high rates of domestic violence and long histories of abuse (Bassuk & Rosenberg, 1988; Redmond & Brackmann, 1990; Shinn, Knickman, & Weitzman, 1991).

Lack of affordable housing is indicated as the primary cause of homelessness, with interpersonal conflict playing a role, particularly in female-headed families. In the context of the St. Louis low-income housing market, two scenarios emerge. In the first case, families who have never managed an independent household are doubled up with friends or family members. Doubling up leads to family friction and the dependent family becomes homeless. In the second scenario, housing conditions precipitate homelessness for families housed in their own place of tenure. Whenever possible, these families also stay with other households until this resource is no longer available. Ultimately, inadequate welfare benefits, the lack of affordable housing, and family friction lead to homelessness (Johnson, 1989a).

In New York City, homeless mothers use up their social support networks before turning to public shelter (Shinn et al., 1991) and follow one of three paths to homelessness. The first group of primary tenants is usually welfare families who take a quick path to homelessness. Difficult housing conditions, including substandard housing and eviction, disrupt previously stable tenancy. A second group of primary tenants takes a slower path in which their housing situations grow more and more marginal over time. Doubling up, combined with personal problems, leads to entering a shelter. A third group of families who have never been primary tenants moves rapidly into shelters when their doubled-up situation ends (Weitzman, Knickman, & Shinn, 1990). In a Los Angeles study, a recent loss of AFDC payments accounted for 43 percent of the homeless cases, and 20 percent of the housed families had been homeless in the previous five years (Wood et al., 1990).

Homeless Children

Homelessness is a serious risk to the well-being and development of children (Molnar, Rath, & Klein, 1990; Rafferty & Shinn, 1991). Nearly one-half (47 percent) of 156 homeless children in Boston shelters demonstrated at least one developmental lag (Bassuk & Rubin, 1987) and a higher incidence of developmental delay compared with poor housed children (Bassuk & Rosenberg, 1988). In addition to significant emotional and behavioral problems, children in New York welfare hotels had cognitive functioning far below average (Fox, Barrnett, Davies, & Bird, 1990). In St. Louis, children 5 months to 18 years old exhibited cognitive delays in the mentally retarded or borderline range at three times the expected rate. Low verbal skills indicated neither a normal nor a retarded pattern but one more comparable to those reported in abused and neglected children (Whitman, Accardo, Boyert, & Kendagor, 1990).

A random sample of 83 homeless preschool children in Philadelphia shelters indicated differential effects of ability, achievement, and adjustment. Compared with a matched control group of inner-city children, preschool homeless children exhibited slower development and more emotional and behavioral problems than their housed peers, whereas homeless children 6 to 12 years old were not significantly different (Rescorla, Parker, & Stolley, 1991). Nonetheless, homelessness necessitates school transfers, leads to erratic attendance, and negatively affects school performance in reading and math for school-age children. In New York City, 15 percent of those students interviewed were repeating their prior grade and more than 12 percent of all homeless students were two or more years older than the usual age for their grade (Rafferty, 1991).

Health also is negatively affected by homelessness. According to L. Roth and Fox (1990), children living in shelters are more likely to be in fair or poor health than children coping only with poverty. Alperstein, Rappaport, and Flanagan (1988) reported higher blood lead levels, higher rates of child abuse and neglect, and more hospitalizations for homeless preschool children compared with low-income preschool children in New York City. Homeless children also suffer difficult birth outcomes, especially low birth weight and high rates of infant mortality (Chavkin, Kristal, Seabron, & Guigli, 1987); delayed immunizations (Miller & Linn, 1988); higher levels of nutritional disorders and acute and chronic illnesses, including ear infections and anemia (Wright, 1991); and limited access to preventive and primary health care (Hu, Covell, Morgan, & Arcia, 1989). Using national data from the Johnson-Pew Health Care for the Homeless Program, Wright (1991) concluded: "The evidently disproportionate rate of illness observed among homeless children, in short, is not just a simple consequence of their impoverished circumstances. Homelessness is an independent and quite consequential risk factor in its own right" (p. 88).

VIEWING HOMELESSNESS THROUGH A FEMINIST PERSPECTIVE

Across the lifespan, women are at risk of becoming homeless. In addition, as suggested in the literature, the untoward effects of homelessness on women are severe. Yet, with the exception of two ethnographic studies of single homeless women (Harris, 1991; Russell, 1991), almost no work has been done to elucidate a feminist perspective on homelessness. Women are so underrepresented in the literature on homeless people that "gender status is sometimes subsumed under the nongender-specific, depersonalized status of *the homeless* (Milburn & D'Ercole, 1991, p. 1161). Noting that homeless women are victimized by patriarchal society and obstructed by unequal opportunity structures, Benda and Dattalo (1990) suggested that "a feminist perspective, which points to invidious socialization practices, abusive affiliations, limited opportunity, deviance and dysfunction, has particular utility for explaining why women are homeless" (p. 74).

The multiple causal factors commonly associated with homelessness for women include the feminization of poverty, the shortage of affordable housing, unemployment, teenage pregnancy, domestic violence, and family disruption (Sullivan & Damrosch, 1987). From a feminist perspective, these can be summarized under two oppressive and victimizing themes, the feminization of poverty and abuse.

The Feminization of Poverty

The feminization of poverty is a fact of life for homeless women. Homeless women and children are affected by changes both in the labor market and in public policies designed for dependent populations (Battle, 1990). Some women may be discouraged workers who never recovered from the recessions of 1979 and 1982 and their high unemployment rates (Hopper & Hamburg, 1986). Others may be women with personal disabilities such as drug abuse or mental illness who turn to general assistance (GA) in states and counties where it is available, Supplemental Security Income (SSI), and food stamps. Recent cutbacks, however, have added to the level of their poverty. For example, approximately 160,000, or 12 percent, of chronically mentally ill SSI recipients were dropped from the rolls during the Reagan administration. Approximately 65 percent of these cases have been reinstated, but tighter eligibility requirements prohibit new applicants from obtaining benefits (Burt & Pittman, 1985).

Macroeconomic issues also negatively affect poor families (McChesney, 1991). During recent recessions, more families have become poor because of the rise in unemployment, inadequate unemployment and disability insurance, employment in a secondary labor market of unstable jobs with no benefits, deindustrialization and the move to a global economy, and radical discrimination. Single mothers are even more negatively affected by discrimination in pink-collar occupations where women are paid less than men and by the failure of many fathers to pay child support. Single mothers without labor market skills and male support are forced to turn to welfare for economic support and medical care, but this income is so meager that these mothers and children live below the poverty line. McChesney (1991) observed the following:

In summary, single mothers are poor because they are women, which means that they experience significant sex discrimination in the labor market, because they are not economically connected to men, because they have sole responsibility for both the support and the care of their children, and because the safety net benefits (AFDC) are inadequate. (p. 160)

Housing Assistance

Unlike other safety net programs that serve poor households, housing assistance is not an entitlement. Rather, the number of eligible households that receive benefits is determined by the amount of money Congress appropriates for housing programs (Leonard, Dolbeare, & Lazere, 1989). As a result, only one-third of eligible low-income households receive federally assisted housing (Reyes & Waxman, 1987). Although little is actually known about how means-tested welfare payments such as AFDC and SSI interact with housing assistance programs, the housing affordability costs of poor people who receive both types of benefits are about 33 percent lower than the average housing costs of persons receiving welfare benefits alone (Newman & Schnare, 1989). With decreasing opportunities for low-income home ownership (Johnson & Sherraden, 1992), the rise in the number of poor households, poor renter households, and poor households that have grown poorer (Apgar, 1989) has increased the demand for assisted rental housing since 1978. For example, the average wait for subsidized housing is nearly two years (Reyes & Waxman, 1987). In some cities, such as New York and Los Angeles, the wait is considerably longer and large families who require three or more bedrooms must wait even longer.

The shortage of affordable housing is considerably worsened by the decrease in federal rental subsidies. Adjusted for inflation, federally subsidized housing outlays were cut more than 80 percent between 1978 and 1988. The short supply of low-cost housing is hindered further by a 19 percent decline in the number of low-income rental units since 1970 (Leonard et al., 1989). This shortage of affordable rental housing is attributed to various factors, including the demolition of single room occupancy (SRO) hotels (Kasinitz, 1984); gentrification (Adams, 1986); government eminent domain actions and urban redevelopment (Johnson, 1992b); condominium conversion and displacement (Wright & Lam, 1987); and fire, arson, abandonment, and inadequate construction levels (Hartman, 1986). In addition, the rapid inflation from 1974 through the mid-1980s and the decline in the average income of renter households exacerbated the problems of affordability and housing adequacy for low-income renters (Apgar, 1989). Birch (1985) discussed housing problems in terms of gender.

As a group, female householders constitute more than 40 percent of the nation's housing problem. Being a female householder means that a woman has one in three chances of being cost burdened and a one in eight chance of living in an inadequate dwelling. . . . If she is a single parent, she has more than a 50 percent chance of having a housing problem. . . . Today a female householder has less than a 50 percent chance of achieving homeowner status; a single parent has a 40 percent chance. (p. 44)

In linking poverty and the shortage of affordable housing for women, it is evident that homelessness results when there are too many poor households and not enough low-cost housing. According to McChesney (1991) women

are too poor. . . to be able to pay the market rate for housing—in the context of a shortage of affordable housing. . . because they are unable to work (sick, disabled, or without child care), because they are unable to find work (involuntarily unemployed, discouraged workers), or because they are unable to find work that pays more than a poverty wage (working poor). (p. 164)

Abuse

From a feminist perspective, the interpersonal causes of homelessness can be widely defined as abuse, including self-abuse, spouse abuse, child abuse and neglect, and the abuse of living in unsafe neighborhoods. Single homeless women most often are described in terms of self-abuse. There is tentative support for the hypothesis that mentally ill and substance-abusing single women, similar to single men with these problems, drift downward toward homelessness. This slow deterioration at the margin of society stems from personal backgrounds that include some types of mental illness, attempted suicide, substance abuse (including prescription drugs), and a history of victimization in abusive relationships (Benda, 1990; Brown & Ziefert, 1990; D'Ercole & Struening, 1990). The route to homelessness for single women suggests a close link between personal oppression and homelessness, but the various combinations of abuse and the sequence of oppressive events is unknown.

In the case of homeless families, McChesney's (1992) interviews with 80 homeless families in Los Angeles shelters identified four different groups' paths to homelessness: (1) unemployed couples, (2) mothers leaving relationships, (3) mothers receiving AFDC, and (4) mothers who had been homeless as teenagers. Only in the case of unemployed couples was there no direct evidence of abuse contributing to homelessness. Mothers leaving relationships had lived in a stable housing arrangement with a man who supported the family. Most were leaving their relationship, however, because of abuse. These homeless battered women who had not worked outside the home for several years were now without income and without access to child care. Mothers in the third group had always relied almost completely on AFDC income as the main source of support for themselves and their children. The current primary relationships in their lives were with unemployed male companions who had never supported the family. In some cases, drug problems were superimposed on their situation of homelessness. Either the women or their boyfriends were using crack cocaine. The final group of mothers who had been homeless as teenagers had histories of severe abuse in their families of origin. Multiple foster care placements were terminated by running away, often because of sexual abuse. As homeless teenagers, they had learned to survive through subsistence prostitution until the birth of their first child, which made them eligible for AFDC.

Interviews with formerly homeless women in New Haven, Connecticut, indicate that the removal of children from their care because of child abuse and neglect resulting from drug addiction precipitates homelessness for some mothers. For addicted mothers, the removal of children means the end of AFDC as an income support, but some mothers are able to obtain drug treatment while on general assistance. Other mothers who are not involved in substance abuse become homeless in their effort to leave unsafe neighborhoods where gang violence, crime, and drug dealing threaten the welfare of their children (Johnson, 1992a).

FEMINIST VALUES AND SOCIAL WORK PRACTICE WITH HOMELESS WOMEN

To be a homeless woman is not easy. It involves shouldering the burden of a stigmatized identity. It includes frequent moves, unstable personal relationships, the lack of work or work skills, victimization through violence and abuse, stress, loneliness, and depression. Being a homeless woman includes having chaotic living conditions and little control over outer circumstances. The task of putting order into life decisions is thus made gargantuan.

Without social support, homeless women are truly alone. Having no social support means no help with transportation to the various appointments required by state and local agencies or to emergency rooms, which are the private physician equivalent for welfare clients. A lack of social support means no day care for children and no respite for mothers. It means a lack of food and a stable living environment and estrangement from families. It means being in and coming from a vulnerable family that has become dysfunctional.

Whatever previous problems homeless women may have had with prioritizing, making and following lists, creating filing systems, and keeping up with appointments are exaggerated by the state of living communally in a homeless shelter. Religious persons living in a convent (with silence and no children) attest to the fact that living communally is difficult, even when a person has chosen this lifestyle because of her spirituality. To be thrust into a strange place called a shelter and to be immediately faced with negotiating interactions with people who are similarly stressed, depressed, and angry does not help a woman collect her thoughts and prioritize her life. From this experience of confusion and turmoil, she must interface with complicated welfare, medical, and support agencies on her own behalf and, if she is a mother, on behalf of her children. She is required to do this without having space of her own and without transportation. She often acts out, abuses substances, and misses appointments.

The issues of homeless women, then, are issues of identity, power, and security—all symbolized by and literally contained in a home of one's own. What can be done to reinstate a support system for older, psychiatrically disabled, single women living in poverty at the margin of society? What can be done to empower the young mother of color to enable her to acquire a home and to find and claim her own identity, power, and inner security?

Feminist values focus on relationships, connectedness, concern with family, and concern with the welfare of others. Four feminist themes (Bricker-Jenkins & Hooyman, 1986; Van Den Bergh & Cooper, 1986) provide a beginning direction for social work practice with homeless women: (1) the personal is political, (2) renaming, (3) valuing process as equal to outcome, and (4) reconceptualizing power.

The Personal Is Political

It is important for homeless women to see how their personal situation relates to political realities. Given their extremely difficult situation, homeless women must understand that system inequities are at the root of much personal misfortune. We must create a macro view that informs homeless women of inequalities in the housing market, the feminization of poverty, and their victimization in abusive relationships. It must be personally and publicly acknowledged, as McChesney (1990) clearly stated, that the only real solution to homelessness is either an increase in the supply of affordable housing or a reduction in poverty for women and children.

The chronic stress and depression common among homeless woman could be dealt with by referral to a local mental health agency and evaluation for psychotropic medication, if appropriate. However, social histories may reveal that extant depression is situational rather than caused by a chemical imbalance (Goodman, Saxe, & Harvey, 1991). Wetzel (1991) emphasized this common misdiagnosis and the resulting mistreatment of depression in poor women of color. Lack of control over an unstable environment (Rosenberg, Solarz, & Bailey, 1991), lack of self-expression, and lack of perceived power all feed into learned helplessness and a lowered sense of self-esteem. The homeless woman experiences all of these things.

Consequently, the failure to deal with the cause of a homeless woman's depression is a failure to heal the illness. A homeless woman can be empowered by focusing treatment on her understanding of the etiology of stress and depression as affected by the societal inequities of oppression and victimization. Focusing on lack of social supports, inadequate income, lack of child care, abusive relationships, and lack of adequate education and training can actually create a series of goals to pursue. Support in strengthening intrafamilial relationships is critical (Ziefert & Brown, 1991). Having occasional respite care and achieving goals that create power, control, a positive identity, and a home would be a better healing force for the homeless mother than medication for stress and depression.

Renaming

Silences (Olsen, 1978) documented the history of women writers and pointed out the relative silence of women as literary voices. Gilligan (1982) identified the importance of voice in woman's development and identified a different voice when women talk about personal moral crises and decisions. Belenky et al. (1986) reported from their interviews with women that women graphically referred to voice or silence in terms of their affirmed or negated identity. Terms such as "speaking out" or "being silenced" relate to a woman's sense of self-esteem and power.

In feminist thought, renaming eliminates self-negation. For the homeless woman to rename her situation, she must reflect on her story. How did she get here? Where is she going? What is important to her? Reflecting on her story and her experiences leading to homelessness can function as a method of individual empowerment and problem solving. Recounting her history can help her to define a sense of self, rather than submitting to stereotypes of who she is based on her homeless condition. Renaming recognizes one's strengths and coping abilities. It also builds bonds of mutual support and friendship.

Valuing Process as Equal to Outcome

Valuing process as equal to outcome includes accepting "progress before perfection." In other words, significant changes cannot be expected to come immediately. For the homeless woman, the extensive problem solving necessary to gain stability and power can start during the actual crisis period of homelessness. What can a woman learn about herself while in a shelter? What are her strengths? If the situation she left behind is worse, then is she moving forward? How will she get there? What is the first step in this next direction? The process by which homeless women solve their problems and the skills and strengths that they muster by addressing the homeless dilemma are actually as important as exiting homelessness.

Reconceptualizing Power

Homeless women can be empowered through understanding that their difficult situation is not just a personal problem but that female homelessness relates to gender, class, and racial oppression. Whereas it may be easier for a homeless client to implicate skin color as related to her victimization, many women can be in denial about the salience of gender as an explanatory variable of their oppressed reality.

Homeless women can feel less victimized by acquiring an understanding that extant social policies related to income security, housing, and health care can actually predispose one to homelessness. For instance, welfare mothers can be systematically barred from legally marrying their children's fathers. A woman could choose to marry her male partner; however, she would lose her entitlement benefits. Her partner may be no more competitive in the job market than she, so a choice to marry could lead to more chaos than her present circumstances involve.

USING FEMINIST VALUES IN PRACTICE

Feminist practice can empower homeless women through several avenues. First, homelessness can be reframed as an indicator of systematic inequities. These systemic injustices should be addressed at the bureaucratic level. For instance, there must be a major revamping of the welfare system so that it does not penalize women who desire to marry. In the meantime, opportunities for training, work, and child care must be created that provide an economic incentive to be in a job situation. Legislation should be passed that provides for housing assistance to meet the current demand.

Second, feminist practitioners can create an atmosphere within the shelter system that is a reflection of what a home can symbolize, including curtains, pictures on walls, and interactions between people based on seeing each other as a family. Consideration can be given to how private space can be carved out within shelters and what touches of comfort and beauty can be added.

Third, knowing that stressed mothers are most likely to act aggressively toward their acting-out children and that depressed mothers are more likely to communicate less with their children and be less sensitive to their infants' actions (Hammen, 1991), feminist practitioners can develop respite programs for mothers. These services would provide children with opportunities to play, tell stories, act out dramas, and grow in literacy skills and self-esteem. At the bureaucratic level, a case must be made for preschoolers in homeless households similar to the one made for migrant youths in the 1960s when amendments to the Elementary and Secondary School Act created the Bureau of Migrant Education. By amending existing social legislation, the structure and financing for a special program similar to Head Start can be built into the homeless shelter system. Such a program would include nutritious food; a nurturing and personalized environment; and developmentally appropriate literacy, self-esteem, and school readiness activities.

Finally, feminist practice within homeless shelters should include helping women and children understand and strengthen the innate abilities they have used to survive and cope with their homeless situation. Work must focus on encouraging the further development of homeless women and their children. In this way, a program not only supports personal strengths, it also helps clients internalize the sense of identity a home can symbolize and foster.

Shelter providers also need a forum for sharing methods and feminist processes that work to foster these empowering elements. Some examples follow.

One small organization, New Haven Home Recovery in New Haven, Connecticut, has addressed these issues and can be viewed as a beginning model in developing a feminist practice. The elements found to enhance feminist goals include having peer counselors, in this case women of color who have themselves experienced and overcome great difficulties, including homelessness. These counselors relate to residents more like extended family members than clients and they possess the empathy that encompasses the art of social work practice (Germain & Gitterman, 1980). They are remarkably successful both in providing case management—the task most often found lacking in shelter services—and in finding permanent housing for the stable families and further shelter services for the more vulnerable families—the task commonly cited as the most difficult for shelter workers (Hagen & Hutchison, 1988).

The staff at New Haven Home Recovery creates connectedness through informal visits on the front porch and barbecues in the backyard. Personal stories are shared by clients and staff over cups of coffee or during rides to appointments. Interviews with former clients reveal that the homeless women take with them a sense of empowerment as they leave the shelter and claim the strengths and skills they have used in overcoming homelessness. Former clients name the connectedness they feel with staff role models and with some of their homeless peers as what has strengthened them during and after their homeless experience (Johnson, 1992a).

To address the cognitive and emotional difficulties homeless children confront, New Haven Home Recovery also offers a four-day preschool program for children of residents (Richards, 1993). To build self-esteem this program focuses on the importance of each child. Coat and jacket hooks are marked with each child's name. The leaders and the children name and greet each other in song. Nutritious food is provided. Reading events, part of the literacy aspect of the program, include a time for each child to make up a story, which the leader writes down and the group dramatizes. Each story is illustrated by the child and is hung on the wall. Another aspect of the program, school readiness, develops simple but essential skills for entering school. These include the ability to focus on a project for minutes at a time, to raise one's hand to enter a group discussion, and to hear and follow directions. To help them prepare for their children's educational process, mothers participate in the process and are affirmed by the leaders as well.

Our Sister's Place in Hartford, Connecticut, seeks to politically empower women during their shelter stays. The shelter is in a house, with curtains and doilies on armchairs, which creates a home-like atmosphere. A cadre of former clients forms the base for a women's group at the shelter. Women are encouraged to see their own homelessness as an expression of oppression through sexism and of the barriers imposed by rigid and limiting welfare policies. Lobbying at the state capitol for welfare reform and housing benefits is a concrete expression of women's growing awareness (Lee & Beaumont, 1992). Lee's (1986, 1990, 1991) empowerment-based practice model for working with homeless women is exemplary. Though not derived solely from feminist thought, her group work approach closely aligns with feminist principles. Other empowerment-oriented approaches are recommended for working with homeless families

(Johnson & Castengera, 1994) and single, mentally ill homeless women (Berman-Rossi & Cohen, 1988; Breton, 1988; Martin & Nayowith, 1991).

All of these exercises are beneficial in and of themselves, but taken as a whole, they give homeless women a model or a sense of what can be a part of their meaning of home. These policy and program suggestions are inherently feminist and synchronistic with core social work values. They focus on well-being and supportive relationships, they encourage empowerment, and they seek to preclude gender oppression and discrimination. Currently, however, there is no comprehensive articulation of a feminist practice approach for working with homeless women. This chapter's discussion begins, therefore, a formalized and much-needed discussion concerning the development of shelter-based feminist practice for homeless women. At a minimum, a viable model for homeless women must combine aspects of the meaning of home, interpersonal connectedness, and empowerment.

CONCLUSION

The problems women are faced with, such as the stigmatized loss of identity brought about by being homeless and other issues resulting from sexism and female-pejorative discrimination, will not disappear in the 21st century. The suggestions discussed here for dealing with homelessness from a feminist perspective are not operative only for homeless women. These approaches are informative for effective social work practice with all clients struggling with problems affected by gender, class, and racial injustice as well as with the particularly stigmatized group of women branded homeless.

But that which we are only beginning to articulate here—a feminist practice model with basic tenets of shared struggles, of mutuality, of identity through community, and of a vision of oneself and of others as worthy of deepest respect—needs further clarity in theory and in practice. Homeless women need assistance in their struggle to give voice to the "I am" hidden within every person whose identity has been co-opted into the silence and invisibility caused by gender, class, and racial injustice. We must continue to develop models based on empowerment group work such as Lee's (1991). A model of feminist shelter practice that combines peer counseling with the supervised casework methodology that Hagen and Hutchison (1988) find so often lacking must be developed. And the relationship between the peer counselor and the supervisor must be based on feminist empowerment practice as well.

In *Blood, Bread, and Poetry* Adrienne Rich (1986) described her struggle to understand the particular forms oppression took to cause her particular silences—the hiatuses in her own identity. She addressed the need for the feminist movement to see past the delusion that it has been universally applicable without having acknowledged its own racial, class, and ethnic perspectives. To dispel this delusion, each woman who is attending to the task of growing in consciousness must also face her fears of differences in other women. Homeless women share in each woman's oppression but their "otherness" provides a cloak that can mask the dreadful forces that cause the silence and the lies in each woman's struggle for beingness. One step in formulating the feminist practice model is to give voice to the homeless women themselves; to hear their own articulations and struggles of chaos and bitterness, of identity and strength. A further step is to give voice to the children of these women, to hear and encourage their distinct stories as they express their own "I am." Feminist practitioners must not make the mistake of the oppressor who assumes to speak for the oppressed. Ultimately the goal of social work practice with homeless women and children is to help them discover the symbolic room of their own, the place from which an articulation of their own identities can be creatively expressed.

REFERENCES

Adams, C. T. (1986). Homelessness in the post industrial city: Views from London and Philadelphia. *Urban Affairs Quarterly, 21,* 527–549.

Alperstein, G., Rappaport, C., & Flanagan, J. M. (1988). Health problems of homeless children in New York City. *American Journal of Public Health, 78,* 1232–1233.

Anderson, S. C., Boe, T., & Smith, S. (1988). Homeless women. *Affilia, 3*(1), 62–70.

Apgar, W. C., Jr. (1989). Recent trends in housing quality and affordability: A reassessment. In S. Rosenberry & C. Hartman (Eds.), *Housing issues of the 1990s* (pp. 37–62). New York: Praeger.

Arnold, C. A. (1989). Beyond self-interest: Policy entrepreneurs and aid to the homeless. *Policy Studies Journal, 18*(1), 47–66.

Bachrach, L. L. (1987). Homeless women: A context for health planning. *Milbank Quarterly, 65,* 371–396.

Bahr, H. M. (1973). *Skid row: An introduction to disaffiliation.* New York: Oxford University Press.

Bassuk, E. L., & Rosenberg, L. (1988). Why does family homelessness occur? A case-control study. *American Journal of Public Health, 78,* 783–788.

Bassuk, E. L., & Rubin, L. (1987). Homeless children: A neglected population. *American Journal of Orthopsychiatry, 5*(2), 1–9.

Bassuk, E. L., Rubin, L., & Lauriat, A. S. (1986). Characteristics of sheltered homeless families. *American Journal of Public Health, 76,* 1097–1101.

Battle, S. (1990). Homeless women and children: The question of poverty. In N. A. Boxill (Ed.), *Homeless children: The watchers and the waiters* (pp. 111–127). New York: Haworth Press.

Baxter, E., & Hopper, K. (1984). *Private lives/public spaces: Homeless adults on the streets of New York City.* New York: Community Service Society.

Belenky, M. F., Clinchy, B. M., Goldberger, N. R., & Tarule, J. M. (1986). *Women's ways of knowing: The development of self, voice, and mind.* New York: Basic Books.

Benda, B. B. (1990). Crime, drug abuse and mental illness: A comparison of homeless men and women. *Journal of Social Service Research, 13*(3), 39–60.

Benda, B. B., & Dattalo, P. (1990). Homeless women and men: Their problems and use of services. *Affilia, 5*(3), 50–82.

Berman-Rossi, T., & Cohen, M. B. (1988). Group development and shared decision making: Working with the homeless mentally ill. *Social Work with Groups, 11*(4), 63–74.

Birch, E. L. (Ed.). (1985). *The unsheltered woman: Women and housing in the 1980s.* New Brunswick, NJ: Rutgers University, Center for Urban Policy Research.

Breakey, W. R., Fischer, P. J., Kramer, M., Nestadt, G., Romanoski, A. J., Ross, A., Royall, R. M., & Stine, O. C. (1989). Health and mental health problems of homeless men and women in Baltimore. *Journal of the American Medical Association, 262,* 1352–1357.

Breton, M. (1988). The need for mutual-aid groups in a drop-in for homeless women: The sistering case. *Social Work with Groups, 11*(4), 47–59.

Bricker-Jenkins, M., & Hooyman, N. R. (Eds.). (1986). *Not for women only: Social work practice for a feminist future.* Silver Spring, MD: National Association of Social Workers.

Brown, K. S., & Ziefert, M. (1990). A feminist approach to working with homeless women. *Affilia, 5*(1), 6–20.

Burt, M. R., & Cohen, B. E. (1989a). *America's homeless: Numbers, characteristics, and the programs that serve them.* Washington, DC: Urban Institute.

Burt, M. R., & Cohen, B. E. (1989b). Differences among homeless single women, women with children, and single men. *Social Problems, 36,* 508–524.

Burt, M., & Pittman, K. J. (1985). *Testing the social safety net.* Washington, DC: Urban Institute.

Calsyn, R. J., & Morse, G. (1990). Homeless men and women: Commonalities and service gender gap. *American Journal of Community Psychology, 18,* 597–608.

Chackes, K. M. (1988). Sheltering the homeless: Judicial enforcement of government's duties to the poor. *Journal of Urban and Contemporary Law, 31,* 155–199.

Chavkin, W., Kristal, A., Seabron, C., & Guigli, P. E. (1987). The reproductive experience of women living in hotels for the homeless in New York City. *New York State Journal of Medicine, 87,* 10–13.

Crystal, S. (1984). Homeless men and homeless women: The gender gap. *Urban and Social Change Review, 17*(2), 2–6.

D'Ercole, A., & Struening, E. (1990). Victimization among homeless women: Implications for service delivery. *Journal of Community Psychology, 18,* 141–152.

Dovey, K. (1985). Home and homelessness. In I. Altman & C. M. Werner (Eds.), *Home environments* (pp. 33–64). New York: Plenum Press.

Eliade, M. (1959). *The sacred and the profane.* New York: Harcourt, Brace & World.

First, R. J., Roth, D., & Arewa, B. D. (1988). Homelessness: Understanding the problem for minorities. *Social Work, 33,* 120–124.

Fox, S. J., Barrnett, R. J., Davies, M., & Bird, H. R. (1990). Psychopathology and developmental delay in homeless children: A pilot study. *Journal of the American Academy of Child and Adolescent Psychiatry, 29*(5), 732–735.

Garrett, G. R., & Bahr, H. M. (1973). Women on skid row. *Quarterly Journal of Studies on Alcohol, 34,* 1228–1243.

Germain, C. B., & Gitterman, A. (1980). *The life model of social work practice.* New York: Columbia University Press.

Gilligan, C. (1982). *In a different voice: Psychological theory and women's development.* Cambridge, MA: Harvard University Press.

Goodman, L., Saxe, L., & Harvey, M. (1991). Homelessness as psychological trauma: Broadening perspectives. *American Psychologist, 46,* 1219–1226.

Hagen, J. L. (1987). Gender and homelessness. *Social Work, 32,* 312–316.

Hagen, J. L. (1990). Designing services for homeless women. *Journal of Health & Social Policy, 1*(3), 1–16.

Hagen, J. L., & Hutchison, E. (1988). Who's serving the homeless? *Social Casework, 69,* 491–497.

Hagen, J. L., & Ivanoff, A. M. (1988). Homeless women: A high-risk population. *Affilia, 3*(1), 19–33.

Hammen, C. (1991). Parenting. In E. L. Bassuk & D. A. Cohen (Eds.), *Homeless families with children: Research perspectives* (pp. 30–36). Rockville, MD: U.S. Department of Health and Human Services.

Harris, M. (1991). *Sisters of the shadow.* Norman: University of Oklahoma Press.

Hartman, C. (1986). The housing part of the homelessness problem. In E. L. Bassuk (Ed.), *The mental health needs of homeless persons* (pp. 71–85). San Francisco: Jossey-Bass.

Hombs, M. E., & Snyder, M. (1982). *Homelessness in America: A forced march to nowhere.* Washington, DC: Community for Creative Non-Violence.

Hopper, K. (1984). Whose lives are these anyway? A comment on the recently issued report on the homeless and emergency shelters by the Department of Housing and Urban Development. *Urban and Social Change Review, 17*(2), 12–13.

Hopper, K., & Hamburg, J. (1986). The making of America's homeless: From skid row to new poor, 1945–1984. In R. G. Bratt, C. Hartman, & A. Meyerson (Eds.), *Critical perspectives on housing* (pp. 12–40). Philadelphia: Temple University Press.

Hu, D. J., Covell, R. M., Morgan, J., & Arcia, J. (1989). Health care needs for children of the recently homeless. *Journal of Community Health, 14*(1), 2–8.

Institute of Medicine. (1988). *Homelessness, health and human needs*. Washington, DC: National Academy Press.

Johnson, A. K. (1989a). Female-headed homeless families: A comparative profile. *Affilia, 4*(4), 23–39.

Johnson, A. K. (1989b). Measurement and methodology: Problems and issues in research on homelessness. *Social Work Research & Abstracts, 25*(4), 12–26.

Johnson, A. K. (1992a). *Interviews with formerly homeless families*. Unpublished manuscript, New Haven Home Recovery, New Haven, CT.

Johnson, A. K. (1992b). Urban redevelopment law and the loss of affordable housing: A reassessment. *Journal of Law and Social Work, 3*(1), 29–43.

Johnson, A. K., & Banerjee, M. (1992). Purchase of service contracts for the homeless: The development of a city-wide network. *Journal of Applied Social Sciences, 16*, 129–141.

Johnson, A. K., & Castengera, A. R. (1994). Integrated program persons. *Journal of Community Practice: Organizing, Planning, Development, and Change, 1*(3), 29–47.

Johnson, A. K., & Kreuger, L. W. (1989). Toward a better understanding of homeless women. *Social Work, 34*, 537–540.

Johnson, A. K., Kreuger, L. W., & Stretch, J. J. (1989). A court-ordered consent decree for the homeless: Process, conflicts and control. *Journal of Sociology and Social Welfare, 16*(3), 29–42.

Johnson, A. K., & Sherraden, M. (1992). Asset-based welfare policy: Homeownership for the poor. *Journal of Sociology and Social Welfare, 19*(3), 61–78.

Kasinitz, P. (1984). Gentrification and homelessness: The single room occupant and the inner city revival. *Urban and Social Change Review, 17*(1), 9–14.

Kondratas, A. (1991). Ending homelessness: Policy challenges. *American Psychologist, 46*, 1232–1238.

Lee, J.A.B. (1986). No place to go: Homeless women. In A. Gitterman & L. Schulman (Eds.), *Mutual aid groups and the life cycle* (pp. 245–263). Itasca, IL: F. E. Peacock.

Lee, J.A.B. (1990). When I was well, I was a sister: Social work with homeless women. *Jewish Social Work Forum, 26*, 22–30.

Lee, J.A.B. (1991). Empowerment through mutual aid groups: A practice grounded conceptual framework. *Groupwork, 4*(1), 5–21.

Lee, J.A.B., & Beaumont, J. (1992, May). Empowering the homeless woman. In *Building bridges: Integrating homeless families into the service network*. Symposium conducted at a conference for service providers for homeless families, New Haven, CT.

Leonard, P. A., Dolbeare, C. N. & Lazere, E. B. (1989). *A place to call home: The crisis in housing for the poor*. Washington, DC: Center for Budget and Policy Priorities and Low Income Housing Information Service.

Martin, M. S., & Nayowith, S. A. (1991). Group work with homeless mentally ill: In shelters, drop-in centers and SRO hotels. In M. Weil, K. Chau, & D. Southerland (Eds.), *Theory and practice in social group work: Creative connections* (pp. 137–152). New York: Haworth Press.

McChesney, K. Y. (1986). Families: The new homeless. *Family Professional, 1,* 13–14.

McChesney, K. Y. (1990). Family homelessness: A systemic problem. *Journal of Social Issues, 46*(4), 191–205.

McChesney, K. Y. (1991). Macroeconomic issues in poverty: Implications for child and youth homelessness. In J. J. Kryer-Coe, L. M. Salamon, & J. M. Molnar (Eds.), *Homeless children and youth: A new American dilemma* (pp. 143–173). New Brunswick, NJ: Transaction.

McChesney, K. Y. (1992). Homeless families: Four patterns of poverty. In M. J. Robertson & M. Greenblatt (Eds.), *Homelessness: A national perspective* (pp. 245–256). New York: Plenum Press.

Milburn, N., & D'Ercole, A. (1991). Homeless women: Moving toward a comprehensive model. *American Psychologist, 46,* 1159–1169.

Miller, D. S., & Linn, E. H. B. (1988). Children in sheltered homeless families: Reported health status and use of health services. *Pediatrics, 81,* 668–673.

Mills, C., & Ota, H. (1989). Homeless women with minor children in the Detroit metropolitan area. *Social Work, 34,* 485–489.

Molnar, J. M., Rath, W. R., & Klein, T. P. (1990). Constantly compromised: The impact of homelessness on children. *Journal of Social Issues, 46*(4), 109–124.

Newman, S. J., & Schnare, A. B. (1989). Reassessing shelter assistance: The interrelationship between welfare and housing programs. In S. Rosenberry & C. Hartman (Eds.), *Housing issues of the 1990s* (pp. 121–153). New York: Praeger.

Olsen, T. (1978). *Silences.* New York: Delacorte Press/Seymour Lawrence.

Phillips, M. H., DeChillo, N., Kronenfeld, D., & Middleton-Jeter, V. (1988). Homeless families: Services make a difference. *Social Casework, 69,* 48–53.

Rafferty, Y. (1991). Developmental and educational consequences of homelessness on children and youth. In J. J. Kryer-Coe, L. M. Salamon, & J. M. Molnar (Eds.), *Homeless children and youth: A new American dilemma* (pp. 105–139). New Brunswick, NJ: Transaction Publishers.

Rafferty, Y., & Shinn, M. (1991). The impact of homelessness on children. *American Psychologist, 46,* 1170–1177.

Rainwater, L. (1966). Fear and the house as haven in the lower class. *Journal of the American Institute of Planners, 32,* 23–31.

Redmond, S. P., & Brackmann, J. (1990). Homeless children and their caretakers. In J. A. Momeni (Ed.), *Homelessness in the United States: Data and issues* (Vol. 2, pp. 123–132). New York: Greenwood Press.

Rescorla, L., Parker, R., & Stolley, P. (1991). Ability, achievement, and adjustment in homeless children. *American Journal of Orthopsychiatry, 61*(2), 210–220.

Reyes, L., & Waxman L. (1987). *The continuing growth of hunger, homelessness and poverty in America's cities: 1987.* Washington, DC: U.S. Conference of Mayors.

Rich, A. (1986). *Blood, bread, and poverty: Selected prose, 1979–1985.* New York: W. W. Norton.

Richards, R. (1993). *This is my story: A homeless children's program for developing self-esteem, literacy and school readiness.* Unpublished manuscript, New Haven Home Recovery, New Haven, CT.

Rosenberg, A. A., Solarz, A. L., & Bailey, W. A. (1991). Psychology and homelessness: A public policy and advocacy agenda. *American Psychologist, 46,* 1239–1244.

Roth, D., Toomey, B. G., & First, R. J. (1987). Homeless women: Characteristics and needs. *Affilia, 2*(4), 6–19.

Roth, L., & Fox, E. R. (1990). Children of homeless families: Health status and access to health care. *Journal of Community Health, 15*(4), 275–284.

Rousseau, A. M. (1981). *Shopping bag ladies: Homeless women speak about their lives.* New York: Pilgrim Press.

Russell, B. G. (1991). *Silent sisters: A study of homeless women.* New York: Hemisphere Publishing.

Schein, L. (1979). A hard-to-reach population: Shopping bag women. *Journal of Gerontological Social Work, 2*(1), 29–41.

Shinn, M., Knickman, J., & Weitzman, B. C. (1991). Social relationships and vulnerability to becoming homeless among poor families. *American Psychologist, 46,* 1180–1187.

Stanford Center for the Study of Families, Children and Youth. (1991). *The Stanford studies of homeless families, children, and youth.* Stanford, CA: Stanford University.

Stern, M. J. (1984). The emergence of homelessness as a public problem. *Social Service Review, 58,* 291–301.

Stoner, M. R. (1984). The plight of homeless women. *Social Service Review, 57,* 565–581.

Sullivan, P. A., & Damrosch, S. P. (1987). Homeless women and children. In R. D. Bingham, R. E. Green, & S. B. White (Eds.), *The homeless in contemporary society* (pp. 82–98). Newbury Park, CA: Sage Publications.

Tauber, C. M. (Ed.). (1991). *Enumerating homeless persons: Methods and data needs.* Washington, DC: U.S. Department of Commerce.

U.S. Department of Housing and Urban Development. (1984). *A report to the secretary on the homeless and emergency shelters.* Washington, DC: Author.

U.S. Department of Housing and Urban Development. (1989). *A report on the 1988 National Survey of Shelters for the Homeless.* Washington, DC: Author.

U.S. General Accounting Office. (1988). *Homeless mentally ill: Problems and options in estimating numbers and trends.* Washington, DC: Author.

Van Den Bergh, N., & Cooper, L. B. (Eds.). (1986). *Feminist visions for social work.* Silver Spring, MD: National Association of Social Workers.

Weitzman, B. C., Knickman, J. R., & Shinn, M. (1990). Pathways to homelessness among New York City families. *Journal of Social Issues, 46(4)*, 125–140.

Wetzel, J. W. (1991). *Clinical handbook of depression.* New York: Gardner Press.

Whitman, B. Y., Accardo, P., Boyert, M., & Kendagor, R. (1990). Homelessness and cognitive performance in children: A possible link. *Social Work, 35,* 516–519.

Wood, D., Valdez, B., Hayashi, T., & Shen, A. (1990). Homeless and housed families in Los Angeles: A study comparing demographic, economic, and family function characteristics. *American Journal of Public Health, 80,* 1049–1052.

Woolf, V. (1929). *A room of one's own.* New York: Gardner Press.

Wright, J. D. (1991). Poverty, homelessness, health, nutrition, and children. In J. J. Kryer-Coe, L. M. Salamon, & J. M. Molnar (Eds.), *Homeless children and youth: A new American dilemma* (pp. 71–103). New Brunswick, NJ: Transaction.

Wright, J., & Lam, J. (1987). Homelessness and the low income housing supply. *Social Policy, 17(4)*, 182–191.

Ziefert, M., & Brown, K. S. (1991). Skill building for effective intervention with homeless families. *Families in Society, 72(4)*, 212–219.

14

Substance Abuse and the Feminist Perspective

Ann A. Abbott

As the 21st century approaches, a major concern among service providers and policymakers is the increase in the number of individuals identified as being "under the influence," that is, either using or abusing alcohol and other drugs or suffering from the ramifications of a significant family member's substance abuse. On the basis of this broad definition, alcoholism could easily account for 20 percent to 40 percent of all human services clients (Gary & Gary, 1985–1986; Googins, 1984). If other drugs are included, this estimate could swell considerably. Of special concern is the growing awareness of the different dimensions of the problem among women.

This chapter focuses on developing an understanding the addiction problem for this at-risk population and providing guidelines for effective treatment and intervention. The primary emphasis here is based on a feminist perspective grounded in recognition of the vital role played by societal inequalities, especially as related to power or lack of power, and accompanying variations in self-esteem and vulnerability to substance use and abuse.

Our society is dominated by a philosophy determined primarily by white males. Historically, the dynamics and treatment surrounding substance abuse and dependence have been developed along a similar dimension. Before 1970, only a handful of articles on women and substance abuse had been published (Clemmons, 1985). Most literature lumped all substance abusers into one category, that of white males (Ettorre, 1986, 1989; Mandel, Schulman, & Monteiro, 1979). Although a congressional mandate for increased attention to alcoholism among women brought a limited increase in relevant research in the 1970s, it wasn't until the 1980s, when the rise of a feminist perspective occurred, that a major increase in attention was directed toward understanding female substance use and abuse and the accompanying treatment (Corrigan, 1980, 1985; Corrigan & Anderson, 1982; Fillmore, 1984, 1987; Harrison & Belille, 1987; Hser, Anglin, & Booth, 1987; Nichols, 1985; Robbins & Clayton, 1989). Initially, because of the magnitude of the task, this new research viewed women as a homogeneous group. However, the above-mentioned studies began to examine the influence of diversity based on such factors as socioeconomic status, employment history, age, and racial and ethnic background. Because of the nature of the problem, attention to it remains limited, and additional examination is needed (Blume, 1992).

EXTENT OF THE SUBSTANCE ABUSE PROBLEM

Because of secrecy and the illegal aspects of substance abuse, determining the number of substance abusers is difficult. Gathering information on women is more difficult because of their frequent isolation in the role of homemaker and the tendency of society to deny or overlook the problem as incompatible with the feminine role. At times, the shame and fragile or limited self-esteem of women have contributed to the cover-up (Forth-Finegan, 1991).

Approximate numbers can be garnered from two perspectives: (1) research based on national surveys and (2) treatment statistics. Research based on national surveys is suspect because most findings are limited by the accuracy of self-reports. The validity of treatment statistics depends on the availability of appropriate treatment, a matter of special concern for women. For many women, participation in treatment programs also depends on availability of child care, reducing the threat of losing their children while they pursue out-of-home treatment, adequate insurance coverage, and employer support and approval of the time demands of treatment.

In examining alcohol use in general, the National Institute on Drug Abuse (NIDA) (1989) found that 60 percent of the males and 46.7 percent of the females studied reported using alcohol during the previous month. Earlier findings by the U.S. Department of Health and Human Services (DHHS) (1983) indicated that 60 percent of adult women drink alcohol. Of course, use does not guarantee abuse; however, it is a prerequisite. Among users, the reported ratios of male to female alcohol abusers range from 1:1 to 7:1 (Babcock & Connor, 1981; Gary & Gary, 1985–1986; Googins, 1984; McCrady, 1982; Robins et al., 1984).

In a special report to Congress, the National Institute on Alcoholism and Alcohol Abuse (NIAAA) (1985) indicated that approximately 6 million women (6 percent of adult females) abused alcohol or were dependent on alcohol (Clark & Midanik, 1982). About 14 percent of adult males fell into a similar category, thus suggesting an approximate 2:1 ratio of males to females. NIAAA's annual report five years later (1990) supported a similar ratio. However, some minor changes in patterns of use were noted along with more detailed data on women. A slight decrease in per capita alcohol consumption was reported, supported by a minor decrease in indicators of alcohol abuse, such as mortality from liver cirrhosis. Research by Hilton and Clark (1987) that covered the 17-year period from 1967 to 1984 found few significant changes in consumption patterns. Hilton and Clark found that the drinking patterns of women had not changed over the 17-year period, whereas a significant increase occurred in the proportion of men reporting no alcohol use.

Although alcohol use is more prevalent among males than females, the reverse holds true for psychotropic drugs, which females are twice as likely to use as males (Cafferata & Kasper, 1983; Corrigan, 1985). Compared with men, women report more frequent use of prescribed drugs (Robbins & Clayton, 1989) and use of over-the-counter medications (Verbrugge, 1982). Prather and Minkow (1991) reported that women receive almost two-thirds of prescriptions for such drugs. For problems involving other drugs such as marijuana, cocaine, or heroin, one of four reported users is female (Van Den Bergh, 1991b). Almost half of the callers to the national cocaine hotline are women, women spend two times as much money per week on cocaine as men, and heroin addiction is growing faster among women than men (Peluso & Peluso, 1988; Van Den Bergh, 1991b).

Whereas information on drinking patterns of females in general is limited, data on drinking patterns of African American women are even more limited (Gary & Gary, 1985–1986) as are data on females from other racial and ethnic groups (Levin, 1987). National data suggest that, although a smaller percentage of African Americans drink, a larger percentage is classified as having a drinking problem (Gary & Gary, 1985–1986). Collectively, African American and Hispanic individuals constitute a smaller percentage of drug and alcohol users than do white individuals; however, the problem is very serious in many African American and Hispanic communities. For example, African American men who drink are more likely than their white counterparts to use other drugs; African Americans who abuse substances have much higher rates of serious health problems; African American communities cannot easily avoid the indirect effects of drug activity such as crime; and, similar to the position of women, strong cultural barriers to successful treatment may exist (NIDA, 1989). In an early study, Cahalan and Cisin (1968) determined that 38 percent of African American women, compared with 11 percent of white women, could be classified as heavy drinkers. Later studies confirmed these findings (Kane, 1981; K. D. Miller, Lescault, Heller, & Bernstein, 1980).

Not surprisingly, research based on substance abuse treatment statistics illustrates that men outnumber women. What is surprising is that the disparity between males and females is reflected in a 5:1 (Beckman & Amaro, 1984) or 4:1 (Harrison & Belille, 1987) treatment ratio given the 2:1 prevalence rates previously quoted. Within the 12-step approach of Alcoholics Anonymous, a ratio of males to females of approximately 3:1 was noted (National Council on Alcoholism, 1990). In 1978 less than 3 percent of the 578 NIAAA-funded treatment programs were designed specifically for women (Babcock & Connor, 1981; Van Den Bergh, 1991b). In examining research studies from 1972 to 1980, Vannicelli (1984) found that slightly more than 2 percent of treatment outcome studies focused solely on women; 44 percent of the remainder included a small number of female subjects. These findings tend to minimize the problem among women and most likely are a direct reflection of the biases in operation and the accompanying difficulties women experience in procuring treatment. These findings also suggest that substance abuse among women is a disguised yet serious risk that warrants attention. I contend that similar risks exist in relation to other minority populations and that treatment initiatives have begun to address the problem only marginally. (In this chapter, the term minority is used to define power base in relation to society as a whole and is not used to suggest a specific racial or ethnic population.)

SETTING THE STAGE FOR AT-RISK
CONDITIONS THAT LEAD TO ADDICTION

Typically, substance abuse has been identified as a male issue, and treatment has been developed accordingly. This is not surprising in a world guided by a patriarchal hierarchy and vision. Although this hierarchy is being challenged, the system has traditionally been defined by men, with women being cast into a subservient, less-important position (Friedan, 1963; J. B. Miller, 1983; Millett, 1970). For the most part, power or control has been in the hands of white males, with all others being relegated to the ranks of the disempowered (M. Lerner, 1991). Being cast into this realm leads to a belief that nothing can or will change, which frequently results in hopelessness, helplessness, low self-esteem, depression, and, ultimately, despair and the inability to act on one's behalf (Connor & Babcock, 1980). With this mind-set in place, the disempowered become their own jail keepers (M. Lerner, 1991). Thus, the effects of sexism and racism can be seen (Connor & Babcock, 1980; Greene, 1992). With this overarching perspective in place, the sense of being controlled, rather than being in control, makes the struggle of those seeking equality a futile battle.

These social conditions set the stage for addictions to develop (Schaef, 1987; Van Den Bergh, 1991a, 1991b). Because of the sense of worthlessness generated in women and other minorities in a patriarchal society, the tone is set to pursue something that will make them feel complete and in control. In addition, because value is determined by an outside force, the solution frequently is sought in an external source, in this case a mind-altering substance. It is in this context that women seek to deal with their frustration and powerlessness. By using alcohol and other drugs, women seek a paradoxical solution. They initially feel power over the decision to use a substance and seize the opportunity to control their intake of that substance to help them escape their social plight. In the process, as dependence on and tolerance of the substance develop, women are once again controlled by an external force, becoming powerless against it. An additional attraction is that the use of alcohol and other drugs represents equal access to an area that was frequently forbidden or unavailable to women (Morrissey, 1986). In their quest for equality, female substance abusers relinquish what little power they have attained.

SPECIAL PROBLEMS AND NEEDS OF
ALCOHOLIC AND DRUG-DEPENDENT WOMEN
Powerlessness

With these conditions in place, the special needs of the female drug and alcohol abuser can be identified. Given the predominant cultural mind-set, the role of powerlessness among women and other disenfranchised groups is evident. With their disempowered position can come self-deprecatory feelings, lowered self-esteem, alienation, and depression (Connor & Babcock, 1980; Corrigan, 1991; H. G. Lerner, 1988; Mandel et al., 1979; Van Den Bergh, 1991b).

Depression

Whether such depression is biologically based or culturally induced remains open to debate. Some believe the effects of alcohol and drug abuse mask the breadth of the depression problem; others purport that the diagnosis of depression masks the prevalence of substance abuse (Corrigan, 1991; Merikangas, Weissman, Prusoff, Pauls, & Leckman, 1985; Yalisove, 1992). Alcohol acts as a depressant. Although it is difficult to determine the cause-and-effect relationship, a consensus exists about the interactive link between depression and the development of addictive behavior (Van Den Bergh, 1991b). Depression is frequently given as one of the primary reasons women initially begin to use alcohol or drugs. A woman's knowledge that she is abusing alcohol and other drugs can lead to lowered self-esteem and increased depression. Thus, the two are frequently entwined in the spiral of substance abuse and addiction.

Relationship Orientation
Women typically advance a value scheme that differs from that of the predominant male culture. For example, women give increased importance to human relationships versus the acquisition of external goods. Simply stated, women place more value on relationships than men do (Gilligan, 1982). Not surprisingly, women cite problematic interpersonal relationships as contributing to their substance use and abuse more frequently than men do (Gomberg & Lisansky, 1984; Hser et al., 1987; Rosenbaum, 1981).

Victimization
Statistics show that women are victimized far more often than men; this fact can be construed as additional evidence of the male–female power differential. Research indicates that a history of victimization among substance-abusing women is more the norm than the exception (Bass & Davis, 1988; Miller, Downs, & Gondoli, 1989; Miller, Downs, Gondoli, & Keil, 1987; Peluso & Peluso, 1988; Van Den Bergh, 1991b; Wallace, 1992; Wilsnack, 1984; Winfield, George, Swartz, & Blazer, 1990).

Sex-Role Stereotyping
Sex-role stereotyping and gender socialization, to a large extent determined by males, have had definite bearing on the recognition of substance abuse among women and the involvement of women in treatment, to say nothing of the actual substance abuse scenario (Blume, 1992; Forth-Finegan, 1991). Historically, the favored view of women has been as soft, frilly, passive, young, innocent, helpless, pure, fragile beings who do not use or abuse substances to an extent that alters behavior beyond the desired definition and certainly not to an extent sufficient to require treatment (Youcha, 1978). As a result of this double standard for males and females, the problem of

substance abuse among women is frequently glossed over or disguised by anyone who buys into the traditional stereotypes. This biased vision is promoted not only by family members but frequently by program planners, policy developers, and service providers.

Physiological Risks

Not only are women at risk psychologically and socially, they are also at risk biologically. Because women's ratio of body fat to water differs from that of males, alcohol enters their system at a less diluted rate, resulting in a higher blood alcohol level for a similar amount of alcohol and a more potent impact (Blume, 1992; Corrigan, 1985; Van Den Bergh, 1991b). Corrigan (1980) also noted the more rapid progression of alcoholism in females, a process commonly referred to as telescoping (Lisansky, 1957). This process not only applies to the progression from abstinence to problem drinking, but, on a positive note, also refers to the time between the presence of problem drinking and seeking treatment, which is generally shorter for women than for men. Research revealed a later onset of problem drinking among women than men; however, with the influence of the telescoping effect, the age at which women enter treatment begins to approximate that of males (Corrigan, 1980). Despite their shorter time span as problem drinkers, reported death rates are 50 to 100 times higher among alcoholic women than alchoholic men. This higher death rate may be caused in part by the reduced ability of the female body to metabolize alcohol and to its decreased protective barrier for the stomach (Van Den Bergh, 1991b).

Fetal Alcohol Syndrome

Additional needs of women surface when examining their role in reproduction and parenting. Not only does alcohol affect the mother, it also can have a profound, irreversible effect on her fetus (Youcha, 1978). Reported prevalence rates for fetal alcohol syndrome range from 1 to 3 per 1,000 live births (DHHS, 1983). In addition, substance abuse can limit the ability of women to provide a caring, nurturing environment for the growth and development of children. Although the permanent impact of other drug abuse on fetal development has not been fully documented, the presence of neonatal addiction is evident as is the inability of the drug-abusing mother to fulfill her mothering role. Another indication of the far-reaching impact of substance abuse is the increased need for grandparents to assume parental responsibility for their grandchildren when their daughters are unable to parent because of substance abuse.

Other Special Treatment Considerations

Women have special needs that must be considered in setting up the most effective treatment plan. These frequently include the need for child care facilities; treatment for dual addiction; long-term living facilities such as halfway houses; special women's groups in which women can feel safe discussing sexual experiences, fears, anger, and frustrations; programs that address the unique needs of lesbians; a choice of male or female counselors; and insurance coverage and medical leave time sufficient to cover necessary treatment (Pape, 1993; Walker, Eric, Pivnick, & Drucker, 1991; Youcha, 1978). In addition, women need programs that are ethnically and culturally sensitive (Greene, 1992; Leland, 1984). Although the importance of these needs was specified years ago, programs incorporating these needs are still being developed. Youcha (1978) noted that 50 percent of women returned to drinking within six weeks of inpatient treatment and remarked that "the impression over the years has been that women are harder to engage in treatment, leave more quickly, and are more difficult to manage. It may be that treatment has yet to be designed which captures the needs of women and thus allows them to be more successful" (p. 202). Youcha also noted that women treated with a recognition of their needs got better faster and may have slightly higher success rates than their male counterparts. More recently, McIntyre (1993) reinforced this notion that sensitivity to issues of gender is paramount in successful treatment initiatives.

FEMINIST TREATMENT OF SUBSTANCE ABUSE DIFFICULTIES

The primary approach to substance abuse treatment has been based on the biopsychosocial model. The feminist approach expands on the more traditional underpinnings of this model and its overall vision (Van Den Bergh & Cooper, 1986). The three major components of the model (the biological, the psychological, and the social) are not viewed as mutually exclusive but rather as strongly entwined. The feminist model reinforces this systemic interactional perspective, which recognizes the genetic or biological and the intrapsychic and, most important, provides greater explication of the combined social and cultural contexts as determinants of human behavior. By doing so, the model challenges the beliefs that historically have assigned increased value to particular physical, cultural, and behavioral variations (H. E. Lerner, 1982). For example, certain values are applied differently to males and females, to ethnic group members, and to disenfranchised individuals. Our white, male-dominated society places greater value on male attributes such as being competitive, independent, and rational and less value on traditionally female attributes such as being cooperative, dependent, and emotional (Sturdivant, 1980). The feminist approach challenges these gender and cultural disparities.

Because of their alternative culture, women and other minorities have been oppressed and devalued by the dominant value system. The feminist philosophy seeks to offset or challenge the impact of the dominant value scheme's sex-role stereotyping, racism, sexism, homophobia, and the power, economic, and political differentials the dominant culture assigns to various positions (Laidlow, Malmo, & Associates, 1990; Nichols, 1985). Feminism is based on empowerment and the elimination of power differentials, valuing family and personal life equally to public life, encouraging the renaming of one's reality, valuing differences, eliminating artificial separations or dichotomies (in particular, those that create and maintain disempowered conditions), and encouraging affiliations and connections with others and the community. The feminist perspective is founded on advocacy for women and other minorities rather than on a vendetta against male domination (Sturdivant, 1980). The feminist approach moves from focusing primarily on the patient's unique individual history to identifying contributions in the larger cultural context. This perspective challenges the more traditional structures (economic, social, and political) that historically have dictated and explained behavior. Basically, feminism is concerned with ending domination and oppression as defined by existing social structures and beliefs (Van Den Bergh & Cooper, 1986; Worell & Remer, 1992). Feminism forces examination of problems within the societal context of inequality and power and suggests alternatives that enhance equality, respectful recognition of diversity, and empowerment (Bepko, 1991).

Treatment based on these feminist principles advances the following five goals: (1) challenging the axiom that biology may be destiny, especially as defined by gender and race, and reframing it to include the importance of the disease model; (2) eliminating dichotomized thinking or false dichotomies; (3) promoting programs that are sensitive to diverse population needs; (4) encouraging empowerment for all; and (5) supporting policies that enhance treatment accessibility.

Reframing the Role of Biology as Destiny
The reframed biological piece focuses on the disease model, which is grounded on the idea of genetic predisposition to addiction and physiological dependence on substances. These beliefs are not being

challenged; rather it is the beliefs based on sex-role stereotyping, sexism, and racism, which some argue may predispose one to alcohol and drug abuse, that are being challenged. On the one hand, in the realm of addiction, biology based solely on gender and racial genotypes does not determine destiny. On the other hand, biological determinism in the form of physiological or metabolic difference is critical. In other words, the alcoholic individual, whether male or female, black or white, metabolizes alcohol less rapidly and efficiently than does the nonalcoholic individual, similar to the way that sugar is metabolized by the diabetic individual compared with the nondiabetic individual. The feminist approach shifts the attention to physiological difference as opposed to societally assigned constitutional difference or weakness. It challenges the idea that alcoholism is equivalent to an inherent constitutional weakness and recognizes the importance of difference in relation to biological processes such as metabolization.

Altering Dichotomized Thinking

Preconceived ideas about what is good or bad set the tone for intrapsychic value. Typically, self-esteem is strongly influenced by the value the predominant culture assigns to role, gender, status, and race. Strength and the accompanying sense of power, or the ability to control one's destiny, also are frequently based on external reality. On the larger social level, if the worldview diminishes the power of a particular group, then helplessness, hopelessness, and depression make up the bulk of that group's psychic beliefs and strongly influence its ability to act on its own behalf. In addition, the dominant culture determines who gets treatment, as well as when, where, how, and why they get treatment. Such rigid categorical thinking leaves little if any room for diversity and individual differences and sets the tone for addictions to develop (Van Den Bergh, 1991a, 1991b; Van Den Bergh & Cooper, 1986).

Historically, dichotomous thinking has been the rule (Van Den Bergh, 1991a): good versus bad, in-group versus out-group, male versus female. Anyone who does not fit the desired prototype is cast into a lesser position. Women bear the burden of this either–or thinking. To feel complete or empowered or to overcome feelings of inadequacy, women frequently resort to substance abuse. With this in mind and with the introduction of the feminist perspective of holistic versus dichotomous thinking (for example, the incorporation of androgyny versus male or female), women and men can learn to be more accepting of self and others. In addition, they can learn that recovery is a continuous process, not an either–or position. This perspective is especially important in relation to treatment that specifically delineates between right and wrong ways to be clean and sober. The feminist perspective encourages flexibility and diversity in relation to avenues of recovery, with abstinence being the bottom line.

Promoting Diversity

As service providers and practitioners, we must bring issues of sex-role stereotyping, sexism, and racism out into the open and confront them directly. This action allows practitioners to serve as role models for empowerment and change. Respect for the individual value of each person and for the richness of diversity must be cultivated. We must highlight awareness of the oppressive nature of sexism and racism and how this discrimination may play out in the area of substance abuse.

We must develop programs that take the needs of special populations to heart. We must design programs that are ethnically and culturally sensitive, and make certain they take gender-based needs into account, including the special needs of gay men and lesbians. Program components should speak to the special problems of women, such as dual addictions and child care needs, and should guarantee client access to a diverse counseling staff that reflects client interests and needs.

Treatment initiatives based on the feminist model are firmly grounded on respect for diversity and individual needs. A demographically diverse staff allows participants a wide choice of treatment providers and role models. Treatment plans, including length of treatment, are developed based on a range of individual client needs rather than forcing clients into preconceived treatment models. Support services, such as child care and a range of medical support and living services, are made available. In some cases, services such as providing food, clothing, and shelter are essential. In other cases, advocacy and intervention with an employer, landlord, or social welfare agency may be paramount. Although economic security may be of greater importance to some clients, emotional security may play a greater role in the recovery of others. The underlying key to feminist treatment is flexibility in relation to the diversity of individual needs. Feminist philosophy recognizes that great diversity exists among and between groups. Although women are not the same as men, they are definitely not a homogeneous group. Both facts must be woven into the fabric of substance abuse treatment.

Encouraging Empowerment

The feminist approach recognizes the role that disempowerment plays in addictions and the role that empowerment plays in successful treatment. This approach provides a responsive format, not only for women but for all types of clients. It is an approach that speaks to the importance of the power differential as it pertains to the behavior of all groups, whether they are ethnic groups, women, or disenfranchised males.

Psychologically, disempowered people are blamed for their lack of ability or power just as substance abusers are blamed for their addiction. The disease model has done much to move us from blaming the victim toward empowering the abuser to seek treatment. Incorporation of the feminist model, with its increased awareness of the sources and manifestations of the overall power differential and its accompanying shame and lowered self-esteem, will activate this empowerment and reduce personal blame for failure. Empowerment from a feminist perspective also entails reconceptualizing power as an internal source of personal control rather than as control or power over others. It gives the individual much greater say over her or his destiny and in turn recognizes and heightens the value of the self. From this perspective, recovery from substance abuse is defined as the process of "rediscovering oneself and reclarifying one's meaning and purpose in living" (Van Den Bergh, 1991a, p. 33).

On the basis of feminist principles, self-esteem should not be determined externally but rather should flow from internal empowerment. Women and other disempowered groups can be taught and encouraged to have increased control over their own destinies. Individual women may not be able to single-handedly change the social, political, and economic forces that govern society. However, in substance abuse treatment, each person can make the decision to strive for abstinence and sobriety. Each person can admit powerlessness over a substance and by doing so, such as in a 12-step program, can become empowered (Clemmons, 1991). Admitting powerlessness may seem paradoxical to becoming empowered. However, by accepting powerlessness over alcohol, individuals can free their psychic energy from maintaining the addiction and use it to promote growth, development, and sobriety. We must establish treatment programs that encourage and provide opportunities for women and members of other disenfranchised groups to take control of their lives. In a similar vein, women and men alike can be enlightened about the effect the current worldview can have on human behavior and how self-esteem can influence the ability of an individual to perform and push for change (Young-Eisendrath & Wiedemann, 1987). In turn, these women and men can challenge the status quo and change their personal views as well as those of the larger society.

Supporting Policies

In addition to modifying programs, we must advocate for adequate universal insurance coverage, medical leave time, and sufficient resources for research and program development. We should support and endorse programs based on the feminist model and should encourage the education of service providers and policymakers about the importance of feminist-based practice in facilitating and sustaining a reduction in substance use and abuse.

SUMMARY

Historically, opportunities for women to find appropriate treatment for substance abuse have been limited. The lack of opportunities has been compounded because the primary referral route for many women in need of treatment has been the male physician, who has not been adequately prepared to diagnose substance-abusing women or to select or design appropriate treatment. Often it was easier to treat these women with antidepressants through more acceptable mental health channels. Such an alternative allowed the health care provider to avoid confrontation surrounding the shameful problem of female addiction. In the process of this alternative prescribing, the tone was set for cross-addictions to develop in an addicted population (Sandmaier, 1980).

As knowledge of substance abuse has grown, I hope that we have moved beyond these limitations. Although evidence of sex-role stereotyping and male dominance continues to exist, focused attention and solid research are beginning to shed important light on both the dynamics and treatment of female substance abuse. This progress is expected to continue.

The reframing of the biopsychosocial framework in light of feminist ideology opens doors for growth, change, hope, individuality, and respect, all ingredients necessary for successful substance abuse treatment (Kravetz & Jones, 1988). As practitioners we must carry this feminist reframing a bit further. We must ask ourselves the following questions:

- Are we purveyors of the more traditional male-dominated mind-set?

- Do we cast substance abusers, minorities, and disenfranchised people into powerless positions?

- Do we reinforce their already impoverished estimates of self-worth and power?

- Do we advance program guidelines that perpetuate powerlessness?

- Do we blame the victims, leaving society immune from responsibility?

- Do we, as practitioners, buy into the hazards of disempowerment with its accompanying immobilization and loss of hope for change?

The feminist perspective "is not so much a collection of specific techniques as it is an attitude. . . [that] attempts to free men and women from the constraints and handicaps that traditional gender-role stereotypes have on their well-being" (Mitchell, 1992, p. 6). It also attempts to free individuals from the ravages of racism and other prejudicial thinking.

Our job has just begun. Those populations currently vulnerable to addictions are likely to be similarly at risk in the 21st century because of the increasingly complex nature of societal demands for resources, especially in light of retrenchment economics. The current burgeoning of 12-step and other self-help and mutual-aid groups suggests the need for people to feel both empowered and included. Hence, in a paradoxical way, the increase in addictions, especially viewed from a feminist perspective, brings to light the importance of a solution near and dear to the underlying philosophy and commitment of social work to building a greater sense of community and enhancing the collective welfare. A feminist perspective that builds on social work principles of empowerment, equality, inclusion, and respect for diversity advances accessibility to treatment and ultimately to effective addiction reduction.

Once our self-assessment and commitment to change have begun, our changing beliefs will be transferred to our fellow workers, program protocols, and clients. This empowerment should serve us well as we move on to the challenges ahead, especially with substance abuse. Although the perspective advanced here is labeled feminist, its techniques do not apply solely to women but can be applied to all who are disenfranchised or disempowered. The result should be a more responsive and more effective substance abuse treatment effort in the future.

REFERENCES

Babcock, M., & Connor, B. (1981). Sexism and treatment of the female alcoholic: A review. *Social Work, 26,* 233–238.

Bass, E., & Davis, L. (1988). *The courage to heal: A guide for women survivors of child sexual abuse.* New York: Harper & Row.

Beckman, L., & Amaro, H. (1984). Patterns of women's use of alcohol treatment agencies. In S. Wilsnack & L. Beckman (Eds.), *Alcohol problems in women* (pp. 319–348). New York: Guilford Press.

Bepko, C. (Ed.). (1991). *Feminism and addiction.* New York: Haworth Press. (Also published as *Journal of Feminist Family Therapy, 3*[3/4])

Blume, S. B. (1992). Alcohol and other drug problems in women. In J. H. Lowinson, P. Ruiz, & R. B. Millman (Eds.) and J. G. Langrod (Assoc. Ed.), *Substance abuse* (2nd ed., pp. 794–807). Baltimore, MD: Williams & Wilkins.

Cafferata, G. L., & Kasper, J. A. (1983). *National health care expenditure study, data preview 14; psychotropic drugs: Use, expenditures, and sources of payment* (DHHS Publication No. PHS 83–3335). Washington, DC: U.S. Department of Health and Human Services, National Center for Health Services Research.

Cahalan, D., & Cisin, I. (1968). American drinking practices: Summary of findings from a national probability sample. *Quarterly Journal of Studies on Alcohol, 29,* 130–151.

Clark, W. B., & Midanik, L. (1982). Alcohol use and alcohol problems among U.S. adults: Results of the 1979 national survey. In *Alcoholism consumption and related problems.* (DHHS Publication No. ADM 82–1190, pp. 3–52). Washington, DC: U.S. Government Printing Office.

Clemmons, P. (1985). Reflections of social thought in research on women and alcoholism. *Journal of Drug Issues, 15*(1), 73–80.

Clemmons, P. (1991). Feminists, spirituality, and the twelve steps of Alcoholics Anonymous. *Women and Therapy, 11*(2), 97–109.

Connor, B., & Babcock, M. L. (1980). The impact of feminist psychotherapy on the treatment of women alcoholics. *Focus on Women: Journal of Addictions and Health, 1*(2), 77–92.

Corrigan, E. M. (1980). *Alcoholic women in treatment.* New York: Oxford University Press.

Corrigan, E. M. (1985). Gender differences in alcohol and other drug use. *Addictive Behaviors, 10,* 313–317.

Corrigan, E. M. (1991). Psychosocial factors in women's alcoholism. In N. Van Den Bergh (Ed.), *Feminist perspectives on addictions* (pp. 61–71). New York: Springer.

Corrigan, E. M., & Anderson, S. C. (1982). Black alcoholic women in treatment. *Focus on Women: Journal of Addictions and Health, 3,* 49–58.

Ettorre, B. (1986). Women and drunken sociology: Developing a feminist analysis. *Women's Studies International Forum, 9,* 515–520.

Ettorre, B. (1989). Women and substance use/abuse: Towards a feminist perspective or how to make dust fly. *Women's Studies International Forum, 12*(6), 593–602.

Fillmore, K. M. (1984). When angels fall: Women's drinking as cultural preoccupation and as reality. In S. Wilsnack & L. Beckman (Eds.), *Alcohol problems in women* (pp. 7–36). New York: Guilford Press.

Fillmore, K. M. (1987). Women's drinking across the adult life course as compared to men's. *British Journal of Addictions, 82,* 801–811.

Forth-Finegan, J. L. (1991). Sugar and spice and everything nice: Gender socialization and women's addiction—A literature review. In C. Bepko (Ed.), *Feminism and addiction* (pp. 19–48). New York: Haworth Press.

Friedan, B. (1963). *The feminine mystique.* New York: Dell.

Gary, L. E., & Gary, R. B. (1985–1986). Treatment needs of black alcoholic women. *Alcoholism Treatment Quarterly, 2*(3), 97–114.

Gilligan, C. (1982). *In a different voice.* Cambridge, MA: Harvard University Press.

Gomberg, E.S.L., & Lisansky, J. M. (1984). Antecedents of alcohol problems in women. In S. Wilsnack & L. Beckman (Eds.), *Alcohol problems in women* (pp. 233–259). New York: Guilford Press.

Googins, B. (1984). Avoidance of the alcoholic client. *Social Work, 29,* 161–166.

Greene, B. (1992). Still here: A perspective on psychotherapy with African American women. In J. C. Chrisler & D. Howard (Eds.), *New directions in feminist psychology* (pp. 13–27). New York: Springer.

Harrison, P. A., & Belille, C. A. (1987). Women in treatment: Beyond the stereotype. *Journal of Studies on Alcohol, 48*(6), 574–578.

Hilton, M. E., & Clark, W. B. (1987). Changes in American drinking patterns and problems, 1967-84. *Journal of Studies on Alcohol, 48*(6), 515–522.

Hser, Y., Anglin, M. D., & Booth, M. W. (1987). Sex differences in addict careers: 3. Addiction. *American Journal of Drug and Alcohol Abuse, 13*(3), 231–251.

Kane, G. P. (1981). *Inner-city alcoholism: An ecological analysis and cross-cultural study.* New York: Human Services Press.

Kravetz, D., & Jones, L. E. (1988). Women reaching women: A project on alcohol and other drug abuse. *Administration in Social Work, 12*(2), 45–58.

Laidlow, T. A., Malmo, C., & Associates. (1990). *Healing voices: Feminist approaches to therapy with women.* San Francisco: Jossey-Bass.

Leland, J. (1984). Alcohol use and abuse in ethnic minority women. In S. Wilsnack & L. Beckman (Eds.), *Alcohol problems in women* (pp. 66–96). New York: Guilford Press.

Lerner, H. E. (1982). Special issues for women in psychotherapy. In M. T. Notman & C. C. Nadelson (Eds.), *The woman patient: Volume 3. Aggression, adaptations, and psychotherapy* (pp. 273–386). New York: Plenum Press.

Lerner, H. G. (1988). *Women in therapy.* Northvale, NJ: Jason Aronson.

Lerner, M. (1991). *Surplus powerlessness.* Atlantic Highlands, NJ: Humanities Press International. (Original work published 1986)

Levin, J. D. (1987). *Treatment of alcoholism and other addictions.* Northvale, NJ: Jason Aronson.

Lisansky, E. S. (1957). Alcoholism in women: Social and psychological concomitants. *Quarterly Journal of Studies on Alcohol, 18,* 588–623.

Mandel, L., Schulman, J., & Monteiro, R. (1979). A feminist approach for the treatment of drug-abusing women in a coed therapeutic community. *International Journal of Addictions, 14*(5), 589–597.

McCrady, B. S. (1982). Women and alcohol abuse. In M. T. Notman & C. C. Nadelson (Eds.), *The woman patient: Volume 3. Aggression, adaptations, and psychotherapy* (pp. 217–244). New York: Plenum Press.

McIntyre, J. R. (1993). Family treatment of substance abuse. In S.L.A. Straussner (Ed.), *Clinical work with substance abusing clients* (pp. 171–195). New York: Guilford Press.

Merikangas, K. R., Weissman, M. M., Prusoff, B. A., Pauls, D. L., & Leckman, J. K. (1985). Depressives with secondary alcoholism: Psychiatric disorders in offspring. *Journal of Studies on Alcohol, 46,* 199–204.

Miller, B. A., Downs, W. R., & Gondoli, D. M. (1989). Spousal violence among alcoholic women as compared to a random household sample of women. *Journal of Studies on Alcohol, 50,* 533–540.

Miller, B. A., Downs, W. R., Gondoli, D. M., & Keil, A. (1987). The role of childhood sexual abuse in the development of alcoholism in women. *Violence and Victims, 2,* 157–172.

Miller, J. B. (1983). The necessity of conflict. *Women and Therapy, 2*(2/3), 3–10.

Miller, K. D., Lescault, B. A., Heller, B. S., & Bernstein, B. (1980). Differences in demographic characteristics, drinking, history and response to treatment in black and white women seen at an alcohol detoxification center. *Focus on Women: Journal of Addictions and Health, 1,* 136–144.

Millett, K. (1970). *Sexual politics.* New York: Doubleday.

Mitchell, W. E. (1992). Psychotherapy for bulimia from a feminist perspective. In J. C. Chrisler & D. Howard (Eds.), *New directions in feminist psychology* (pp. 3–12). New York: Springer.

Morrissey, E. R. (1986). Contradictions inhering in liberal feminist ideology: Promotion and control of women's drinking. *Contemporary Drug Problems, 13*(1), 65–88.

National Council on Alcoholism. (1990). *NCADD factsheet: Alcoholism, other drug addictions and related problems among women.* New York: Author.

National Institute on Alcoholism and Alcohol Abuse. (1985). *Alcohol and health: Second special report to the U.S. Congress.* Washington, DC: U.S. Government Printing Office.

National Institute on Alcoholism and Alcohol Abuse. (1990). *Alcohol and health: Seventh special report to the U.S. Congress.* Washington, DC: U.S. Government Printing Office.

National Institute on Drug Abuse. (1989). *National household survey on drug abuse: Population estimates, 1988* (DHHS Publication No. ADM 89-1638). Washington, DC: U.S. Department of Health and Human Services, Public Health Service.

Nichols, M. (1985). Theoretical concerns in the clinical treatment of substance abusing women: A feminist analysis. *Alcoholism Treatment Quarterly, 2*(1), 79–90.

Pape, P. A. (1993). Issues in assessment and intervention with alcohol- and drug-abusing women. In S.L.A. Straussner (Ed.), *Clinical work with substance abusing clients* (pp. 251–269). New York: Guilford Press.

Peluso, E., & Peluso, L. (1988). *Women and drugs: Getting hooked, getting clean.* Minneapolis: Compucare.

Prather, J. E., & Minkow, N. V. (1991). Prescription for despair: Women and psychotropic drugs. In N. Van Den Bergh (Ed.), *Feminist perspectives on addictions* (pp. 87–99). New York: Springer.

Robbins, C., & Clayton, R. R. (1989). Gender-related differences in psychoactive drug use among older adults. *Journal of Drug Issues, 19*(2), 207–219.

Robins, L. N., Helzer, J. E., Weissman, M. M., Orvaschel, H., Gruenberg, E., Burke, J. D., & Regier, D. A. (1984). Lifetime prevalence of specific psychiatric disorders in three sites. *Archives of General Psychiatry, 41,* 949–967.

Rosenbaum, M. (1981). Sex roles among deviants: The woman addict. *International Journal of Addictions, 16,* 859–877.

Sandmaier, M. (1980). *The invisible alcoholics.* New York: McGraw-Hill.

Schaef, A. (1987). *When society becomes an addict.* San Francisco: Harper & Row.

Sturdivant, S. (1980). *Therapy with women: A feminist philosophy of treatment.* New York: Springer.

U.S. Department of Health and Human Services. (1983). *Fifth special report to the U.S. Congress on alcohol and health.* Washington, DC: U.S. Government Printing Office.

Van Den Bergh, N. (1991a). A feminist perspective on addictions. *Addiction and Recovery, 11*(4), 30–33.

Van Den Bergh, N. (1991b). Having bitten the apple: A feminist perspective on addictions. In N. Van Den Bergh (Ed.), *Feminist perspectives on addictions* (pp. 3–30). New York: Springer.

Van Den Bergh, N., & Cooper, L. B. (1986). Introduction. In N. Van Den Bergh & L. B. Cooper (Eds.), *Feminist visions for social work* (pp. 1–28). Silver Spring, MD: National Association of Social Workers.

Vannicelli, M. (1984). Treatment outcome of alcoholic women: The state of the art in relation to sex bias and expectancy effects. In S. Wilsnack & L. Beckman (Eds.), *Alcohol problems in women* (pp. 369–412). New York: Guilford Press.

Verbrugge, L. (1982). Sex differences in legal drug use. *Journal of Social Issues, 38*(2), 59–76.

Walker, G., Eric, K., Pivnick, A., & Drucker, E. (1991). A descriptive outline of a program for cocaine-using mothers and their babies. In C. Bepko (Ed.), *Feminism and addiction* (pp. 7–17). New York: Haworth Press.

Wallace, B. C. (1992). The therapeutic community as a treatment modality and the role of the professional consultant: Spotlight on Damon House. In B. C. Wallace (Ed.), *The chemically dependent: Phases of treatment and recovery* (pp. 39–57). New York: Brunner/Mazel.

Wilsnack, S. (1984). Drinking, sexuality and sexual dysfunction in women. In S. Wilsnack & L. Beckman (Eds.), *Alcohol problems in women* (pp. 189–227). New York: Guilford Press.

Winfield, I., George, L. K., Swartz, M., & Blazer, D. G. (1990). Sexual assault and psychiatric disorders among a community sample of women. *American Journal of Psychiatry, 147,* 335–341.

Worell, J., & Remer, P. (1992). *Feminist perspectives in therapy: An empowerment model for women.* New York: John Wiley & Sons.

Yalisove, D. L. (1992). Survey of contemporary psychoanalytically oriented clinicians: A synthesis. In B. C. Wallace (Ed.), *The chemically dependent: Phases of treatment and recovery* (pp. 61–81). New York: Brunner/Mazel.

Youcha, G. (1978). *A dangerous pleasure.* New York: Hawthorn Books.

Young-Eisendrath, P., & Wiedemann, F. L. (1987). *Female authority: Empowering women through psychotherapy.* New York: Guilford Press.

15

Feminist Social Work Practice with Lesbian and Gay Clients

Eileen F. Levy

esbian–feminist theorist and poet Adrienne Rich (1979) wrote "Black and white feminists have in common a commitment . . . to a profound transformation of world society and of human relationships; and that we agree that such a transformation requires minimally that every woman be self-identifying and self-defining, with the right to determine how, when, and for whom she will exercise her sexuality and her reproductive powers" (p. 279). Rich's words are meaningful for feminist social workers who work with lesbian, gay, and bisexual clients, and embrace the ideas of transformation, self-identification, and self-definition in their work.

The commitment of feminist social workers to transformation informs their practice. To provide relevant services that empower lesbians and gay men to achieve competence and strength, each social worker must know and understand the life experiences of their clients. Lesbians and gay men make up one of the most diverse communities in the United States and face unique challenges in a heterosexist, homophobic environment. Prejudice and oppression in the social environment represent the most critical sources of stress to gay men and lesbians. Social workers need to be knowledgeable and aware of the needs and issues of lesbian and gay clients to help create change, transformation, and empowerment.

This chapter discusses feminist social work practice with lesbian, gay, and bisexual clients, and identifies some of their significant needs. It also addresses relevant practice approaches that promote individual and collective empowerment, such as the ecological perspective (Germain, 1979) and the strengths perspective (Saleebey, 1992).

DEMOGRAPHICS AND BACKGROUND
Beginning with studies by Alfred Kinsey in the late 1940s and early 1950s, it has been both widely accepted and disputed that 10 percent of the population could be considered gay or lesbian. On the basis of interviews of more than 12,000 men and 8,000 women, Kinsey reported that gay and lesbian people existed in every geographic region of the country, in every occupation, social class, and age group, and concluded that if there were no social restraints such as homophobia or heterosexism, homosexual activity would appear in a much larger portion of the population. Because of the difficulty in collecting accurate data about lesbian and gay people, there are probably similar proportions of lesbians and gay men throughout all social classes and ethnic and racial communities (Blumenfeld & Raymond, 1993). The current diversity of the gay and lesbian community is a validation of Kinsey's assumption that gay men and lesbians exist in every subgroup of society: a part of every group and apart from every group (Pierce, 1991).

CIVIL RIGHTS ISSUES
Although the "percentage" debate continues today, lesbian and gay people are experiencing the most significant changes in their social status since the Stonewall riots of 1969, which marked the beginning of the contemporary lesbian and gay liberation movement. On June 27, 1969, after a police raid on the Stonewall Inn in New York City, which was common at many gay bars in New York, people rallied and fought the police, demanding social recognition and an end to harassment of gay men and lesbians (Blumenfeld & Raymond, 1993). The Stonewall riots began the contemporary struggle for equal rights for gay men and lesbians in this country. Many gay liberation organizations were founded to fight heterosexism and homophobia and to promote visibility and respect for gay and lesbian people.

LESBIANISM IN THE WOMEN'S MOVEMENT
In the early 1970s, the contemporary women's liberation movement began to challenge sex role norms, economic discrimination, violence against women, and reproductive rights. Many of the leaders in this movement were lesbians. Because of the pervasiveness of

homophobia, the issue of lesbianism became a source of conflict and tension within the women's movement. Heterosexual women perceived the presence of lesbians in the movement as a threat to the legitimacy of the issues. Lesbian caucuses were formed in many women's liberation organizations, and lesbians developed separate organizations that specifically addressed their concerns.

Bisexual people and profeminist men also began to organize in the late 1970s. These groups began to raise the consciousness of society about sexuality and played a role in the emergence of a new definition of homosexuality, from that of a sickness or perversion, to an alternative lifestyle (Blumenfeld & Raymond, 1993):

> By the mid-1970s, homosexuals constituted a bona fide and legitimate minority group sharing many commonalities with other disenfranchised groups, but unlike these other groups who for some time had a sense of their past and a feeling of community, the gay and lesbian minority was for the first time creating its own true feeling of identity and shared sense of community. (p. 309)

CURRENT LESBIAN AND GAY ACTIVISM

The election of Bill Clinton as president in 1992 has put gay and lesbian visibility on the political agenda. From the debates about gay men and lesbians in the military to the appointment of Roberta Achtenberg, an open lesbian, as assistant secretary at Housing and Urban Development (HUD), lesbians and gay men are finding themselves "out there" in ways unimaginable to the many gay men and lesbians who spent years hiding in closets and living dual lives. The "post-Stonewall generation" of lesbians and gay men, for many who may see being closeted as unthinkable, their activist, sometimes radical politics, often challenge the "established" gay and lesbian community whose members are actively seeking visibility and legal recognition. The 1993 March for Gay/Lesbian/Bisexual Rights drew approximately 1 million people to Washington, DC, and the sense of empowerment, entitlement, and pride felt by members of the community is one indication that equal rights for lesbians and gay men are high on the community's national political agenda.

Even though gay and lesbian issues have had much recent positive media coverage and have been part of a national debate, lesbians and gay men continue to experience oppression and discrimination. The outright homophobia and hatred that occurred during the Senate confirmation hearings of HUD Secretary Roberta Achtenberg in April 1993 demonstrates that lesbians and gay men continue to be feared, hated, rejected, and challenged because of their sexual orientation. There is no state in which gay and lesbian marriages are considered legal. Few cities and states offer domestic partner benefits to gay and lesbian families. Gay and lesbian adoption and foster parenting continues to be under scrutiny, if allowed at all, and gay and lesbian people in the military are being asked to make a vow of silence, secrecy, and celibacy under President Clinton's "don't ask, don't tell, don't pursue" policy of July 1993. Gay men and lesbians struggle with human immunodeficiency virus (HIV) and acquired immune deficiency syndrome (AIDS), cancer, and other life-threatening illnesses, and many do not receive adequate, sensitive health care (Robertson, 1992). Much work needs to be done.

CONTEXT OF HETEROSEXISM AND HOMOPHOBIA

Social workers working with lesbian or gay clients need to understand what it means to be a gay man or lesbian in a heterosexist and homophobic society. Although the social context appears to be rapidly transforming, gay men and lesbians occupy a marginal status. According to Blumenfeld and Raymond (1993), "heterosexism is discrimination by neglect, omission, and/or distortion . . . homophobia is discrimination by intent and design" (p. 245). Heterosexism means that heterosexuality is the only legitimate and compulsory form of sexuality; no other acceptable choice exists. Furthermore,

> Because this norm is so pervasive, heterosexism is difficult to detect . . . when parents automatically expect that their children will marry a person of the other sex . . . and will rear children within this union . . . when teachers presume all of their students are straight and teach only about the contributions of heterosexuals—these are examples of heterosexism. (Blumenfeld & Raymond, 1993, p. 244)

A climate for homophobia is created by the assumption that the world is and must be heterosexual. Heterosexism and homophobia together enforce compulsory heterosexuality. To ensure its predominance, heterosexism is backed by societal institutions that serve as systematic enforcers of homophobia. Heterosexism compels lesbian and gay people to confront and struggle with their invisibility and makes it difficult to develop a positive sexual identity. Accurate representations of lesbians and gay men are rarely provided by the media and other institutions. Instead, homosexuality is represented as perverse, a crime against nature, and an unnatural act. Heterosexual love, sex, and romance are idealized by the dominant culture and serve as a form of social control by reinforcing heterosexuality as the preferred, superior, and acceptable sexuality. Those who are heterosexual have access to heterosexual privilege, which are the benefits for men and women who are heterosexual. These benefits may include legitimacy of oneself as a person through attachment to an opposite sex partner, social and familial acceptance, economic security, and legal and physical protection. Heterosexism occurs within the framework of institutionalized homophobia, the social and cultural fear of homosexuality.

CHALLENGES FACING GAY MEN AND LESBIANS CREATE A NEED FOR SOCIAL WORK SERVICES

The discussion presented above of both the historical and current status of lesbians and gay men in the United States indicates that there is a tremendous need for social work services to help empower this vast disenfranchised community. Proactive social workers are needed to work with lesbians and gay men and direct their efforts to both personal support and environmental change.

Some of the most difficult challenges that lesbians and gay men face and that may influence them to seek social work services include coming out; lesbian and gay parenting issues; the impact of HIV and AIDS on gay men and lesbians and their families and communities; and issues of domestic violence in the lesbian and gay community.

Coming Out: Issues of Self-Acceptance

Feminist practice principles, such as valuing, renaming, encouraging process, eliminating splitting or dichotomizing, and taking actions to self-empower, are useful in working with clients who are coming out and constructing their lesbian and gay identities. Social workers may play a significant role in helping lesbians and gay men make decisions about coming out. According to Grace (1985), coming out is identifying and respecting one's homosexuality and disclosing this positive identity. For most lesbians and gay men, coming out is complex; social workers need to be aware of both the risks and the advantages associated with disclosure of one's gay or lesbian identity.

During the coming-out process, many gay men and lesbians seek help from social workers, who need to be sensitive to the complexities that encompass these life choices. Coming out and subsequent identity formation is a process, not an isolated, finite event. The feminist belief in the value of process as equal to product may help social workers validate the coming-out experience for clients.

Because of the different life tasks required of gay men and lesbians in each of the different "stages" of coming out, social workers may serve a variety of functions, such as support, advocacy, education, intervention, prevention, and mediation.

Several researchers have developed models of coming out that explain the process of developing gay and lesbian identities in a heterosexist, homophobic environment (Cass, 1979; Coleman, 1985; Lewis, 1984). Cass's (1979) model contains six interconnected stages: (1) identity confusion (the "who am I?" stage); (2) identity comparison (the rationalization or bargaining stage); (3) identity tolerance (reaching out to other lesbians and gay men and feeling less belonging with heterosexuals); (4) identity acceptance (developing close ties with other lesbians and gay men and accepting rather than tolerating a gay or lesbian identity); (5) identity pride (marked by increased disclosure of one's sexual orientation and a feeling of community with other gay men and lesbians); and (6) identity synthesis (where anger at heterosexual institutions lessens, the gay or lesbian individual sees heterosexuals as possible allies, the individual sense of pride increases, and the identity becomes integrated as part of the personality structure of the individual). Coleman's (1985) model uses five stages and focuses more on relational attachments: (1) pre–coming out (not yet conscious of having feelings of attraction for same-sex individuals but a pervasive feeling of being different from others); (2) coming out (where one acknowledges having homosexual feelings, may discuss these with close friends, and may make some contact with others who identify as gay men or lesbians); (3) exploration (trying on a new sexual identity and interacting more frequently with other gay men and lesbians); (4) first relationship (desire to create a more stable relationship and combine emotional and physical attraction); and (5) integration (the final stage when the public and private identities are unified and continue for the remainder of the person's life). Most gay men and lesbians maintain well-developed coping strategies in this final stage to manage life in a homophobic environment. Although Lewis's (1984) model deals specifically with lesbian identity, it can be generalized to gay men as well. Her five-stage model includes (1) dealing with being different, (2) experiencing dissonance and inner turmoil, (3) building relationships and dealing with family, (4) forming a stable lesbian identity, and (5) integrating that identity into a healthy self-concept.

These models depict general patterns of coming out that may occur in gay men and lesbians and do not suggest that there is a "correct" way to move through the process. The process is not linear, and people may go through some phases simultaneously or more than once. Gay men and lesbians continually assess the risks and benefits and make decisions regarding disclosure throughout their lives. According to Lee (1992), environmental response is a critical factor in the coming-out process. If the gay man or lesbian feels acceptance, validation, and warmth from those who know of his or her sexual orientation, he or she will move through the process with less stress than someone whose environment is unwelcoming and hostile. Grace (1992) explored the harmful effects of homophobia on the pace and quality of the coming-out process. He concluded that, if throughout one's coming out the person is focused on survival and defense, rather than intimacy and growth, and if the person's perception of the world is that of a threatening and dangerous place, he or she is likely to disguise his or her true identity, become alienated, and develop a shame-based perception of oneself as a gay or lesbian person. "Repeated experiences of homophobia-inspired shame may add to a person's sense that private self is defective, worthless, bad, unlovable, that it is to be hidden at all costs rather than exposed" (Grace, 1992, p. 40).

Gender, race, and ethnicity also affect the coming-out process. Gender issues, such as roles and socialization, account for some significant differences in the coming-out process for men and women. Men come out and have more homosexual experiences earlier than women (Gagnon, 1977). Women are socialized to form intimate, long-term, monogamous relationships through which many derive their identities, while identity of men is largely derived through what one does in the world. These differences affect the stress experienced by men and women and need to be recognized by social workers when helping clients understand and navigate the coming-out process. Clients of color and those strongly identified with ethnic communities often face difficulties in coming out and being open about their sexual identity. Disclosing one's sexual orientation may present conflicts for gay men and lesbians of color who fear rejection and alienation from their communities. Social workers need to be sensitive to and knowledgeable of the client's cultural background to better help the client make informed choices about coming out.

Many gay men and lesbians are encouraged to be open about their identity, largely because doing so may have a positive impact on self-esteem (Levy, 1989). Yet clients also need information regarding possible risks involved in making these decisions (for example, lesbians who are involved in custody disputes with former spouses). Information about sexual orientation is often used prejudicially in making custody determinations in the court system (Rivera, 1987) and in denying equal access and opportunities to gay men and lesbians in such areas as employment and housing. Clients need to assess the possible consequences when they disclose their gay or lesbian status. Social workers can help these clients validate their experience and assist them in making informed choices. They can help clients develop strategies and support them in coming out to families, children, friends, work associates, and other people important to the client (Levy, 1992).

Coming out requires a shift in self-concept, and clients may need help with identity development. Because identity change involves grieving the loss of the "old self," social workers can help their clients create more accurate self-definitions. Internalized homophobia may surface for gay men and lesbians during the identity development process; workers need to know about internalized homophobia and know effective interventive strategies. Interventions that challenge negative self-perceptions and help clients feel good about their gay or lesbian identity are important in helping them combat internalized homophobia. These strategies help empower gay and lesbian clients to develop skills and strategies to influence their environment.

The feminist model of practice includes validating clients and helping them value their life experience. This requires that the social worker not merely tolerate but accept their lesbian and gay clients. If clients receive validation from social workers, who truly value gay and lesbian people equally with heterosexuals, it can make a tremendous difference in the perception lesbians or gay men have of themselves.

Acceptance of Gay and Lesbian Families

Lesbian and gay families exist in every social group in society, yet they are largely invisible. Currently, an estimated 6 to 14 million children have a lesbian or gay parent. Lesbians and gay men create families in a context of societal homophobia, ignorance, insensitivity, stereotyped thinking, outright prejudice, hostility, violence, and institutionalized discrimination; their status is continually questioned by mainstream society.

Conceptual work focused on family structural frameworks, "normal family processes," or "family life cycle models" have largely been based on a heterosexual family model. Traditional definitions of family are restrictive and institutionalize the heterosexual nuclear family as the domain where procreation, socialization of future generations, and nurturance of its members occurs. The family is where basic human needs are met (for example, companionship, intimacy, economic security, and procreation).

The existence of alternative family structures indicates that the traditionally defined norm does not meet the needs of a diverse society. Families who deviate from the nuclear family structure often encounter negative social pressures as a result of their marginal status. Lesbian and gay families challenge assumptions about traditional family structures. These families are viable structures that carry out culturally defined needs. Because parenthood is sanctioned only within the institution of heterosexuality, the position of the lesbian and gay parent in society is confusing. On the one hand, society says it is good to be a parent; on the other, it is bad to be a gay man or lesbian.

The idea that lesbians and gay men are capable of both creating and maintaining environments where children can thrive and mature into healthy, self-sufficient adults is revolutionary in a society that fears difference. Currently in the United States, an estimated 3 million lesbians are mothers, and between 1 and 3 million gay men are natural fathers (Bozett, 1987). Most lesbian mothers and gay fathers have had their children through heterosexual relationships, primarily marriages, before coming out as gay or lesbian. Today, with the "lesbian baby boom," many lesbians are choosing to have children through insemination with a known or unknown donor, through sexual intercourse with men, or through adoption. Gay men are choosing to adopt on their own or forming families with women for the purposes of raising children and creating a family together. Current literature on lesbian and gay male families (Bozett, 1987; Burke, 1993; Crawford, 1987; Gunter, 1992; Levy, 1989, 1992; Martin, 1993; McCandlish, 1987; Weston, 1991) reinforces the marginal social status of lesbian and gay families. These families are a direct challenge to the patriarchal family assumption. Thus, the family often lives in a hostile social environment, resulting in additional stress. The lesbian mother and gay father, because they are parents, continually interact with heterosexist societal institutions. These institutions and social services are designed to serve heterosexual families and, if not blatantly opposed to homosexuality families are certainly oblivious to the special needs of these families (Levy, 1992). In addition, the lesbian and gay community, a source of support for many, often fails to support lesbian mothers and gay fathers because of community ambivalence toward children. In addition to the daily stressors of a heterosexist environment, there are unique stressor events in the lesbian or gay family life cycle. These include deciding to parent a child, coming out to the children, child custody issues, a child beginning or changing schools, and dealing with a family of origin.

It is important that social workers understand the social context of lesbian and gay parents and appreciate their particular strengths and resources. These parents need to feel supported and validated by their peers and by professionals. It may be particularly helpful and esteem-building to involve lesbian and gay parents in a support-ive group experience with others who are dealing with similar life issues (Levy, 1992). Many lesbian and gay families feel isolated, and workers knowledgeable about community resources can connect clients with support groups or develop support groups where none exist. They also can encourage clients to create informal links with other gay and lesbian parents; these social networks are helpful resources. In addition, social workers can provide supportive services to children of lesbian and gay families as part of a feminist, family-centered approach to social work intervention.

People with HIV and AIDS
The increasing number of lesbians and gay men with HIV and AIDS shows a growing need for feminist social workers to provide meaningful services to this community. Social work practitioners have played an instrumental role in creating and organizing support programs for people with AIDS and HIV and in identifying the needs of people with AIDS and the needs of people who love them. Social workers have established links and networks between social service and health care agencies by the creation of new agencies. The empowerment of the community has helped fuel major volunteer efforts, such as support groups, community education, school-based programs, home care, recreational services, legal services, and fundraising (Shattls & Shernoff, 1992). It was the lack of institutions or social services that initially caused these volunteer organizations to be created where no services existed. The needs of this population are tremendous, and social work practitioners who understand the issues and challenges to this increasing population within the gay and lesbian community are required. Gay men in particular are dealing with the realities associated with premature death and need help to empower themselves to cope with end-of-life issues. Many of these men never came out to their parents and now face death; their families need assistance to cope with the many life tasks that confront them as they move through the grief process.

In a study by Siegel and Krauss (1991) of men living with HIV infection, the researchers interviewed 55 HIV-positive gay men regarding their decision making. Three categories of decision making emerged from these interviews: (1) dealing with possibility of shortened life span, (2) dealing with reactions to stigmatizing illness, and (3) developing strategies for maintaining physical and emotional health. Gay men, particularly in cities with a high incidence of AIDS-related deaths, grieve the loss of their lovers, friends, and community. They may feel guilt that they have survived.

Many people with AIDS experience loss of employment and income because of the homophobic policies of many workplaces and experience loss of health benefits during a time of need. People with AIDS suffer much stigmatization and marginalization, even within the gay community, because their presence is a reminder of mortality. People with AIDS experience a slow and painful death, and many people suffer from dementia and AIDS-related blindness as a final assault. Health care practitioners need to be educated about the needs and issues of these clients.

Social workers can assist clients with self-acceptance and spiritual acceptance of the reality confronting them. Empowerment practices with clients who are HIV-positive can include supporting them to make changes in their priorities, such as building support networks. Social workers can be involved in designing interventions so people with AIDS and their communities can be aware of the daily challenges these people face.

Domestic Violence
Feminist social workers also need to be aware of the prevalence of domestic violence in the lesbian and gay communities, in some cases another outcome of internalized homophobia. Domestic violence largely has been invisible within the gay and lesbian communities because of the unwillingness of the communities to recognize these crimes. Although the invisibility is challenged as the silence is broken, societal homophobia prevents lesbian and gay victims of domestic violence from receiving support and intervention. The victims of domestic violence do not receive help or protection from their batterers, and the batterers are not usually held accountable for their abusive behavior. Shelters for battered women usually are not hospitable to lesbian clients. Most services for batterers are designed for men, which precludes lesbian batterers from receiving necessary intervention (Leeder, 1988; Lobel, 1986). Identification of victims and batterers can be difficult in lesbian and gay relationships. The more aggressive partner is usually assumed to be the batterer, although relationship dynamics might indicate otherwise.

The dynamics of control, intimidation, and violence that characterize all battering relationships are present in lesbian and gay abusive relationships, but it may be necessary to redefine the victim–abuser dichotomy for this population (Hart, 1986). The feminist concept of renaming can be applied to the situation of battered lesbians and gay men, who have been categorized within a heterosexist framework of relationship dynamics. Lesbians, for example, may tend to physically fight back against their batterers more frequently then heterosexual women (Porat, 1986); consequently, the distinction between batterer and abused may be blurred, and the batterer may claim to have been abused by the victim. Social workers need to be aware of the relationship dynamics in lesbian and gay couples and accurately assess underlying power dynamics in abusive relationships. They can empower clients by accepting their stories as truth. Social workers need to listen to lesbian and gay clients who come for help.

Helping professionals can play an important role by assisting victims in freeing themselves from the abuse and not reinforcing an abusive relationship (Renzetti, 1992). If the battering is not named or is denied or it is implied that the victim caused the abuse, the victim will likely experience self-blame and isolation. If the worker names the violence as battering and challenges the use of violence in the relationship, the victim may feel empowered and continue to seek help, possibly leaving the abusive relationship (Renzetti, 1992). For lesbians in particular, it is critical that the myth of lesbian domestic violence as less destructive, dangerous, and terrifying than abuse experienced in heterosexual relationships be challenged. Workers need to believe and support battered lesbians and gay men and confront batterers to take responsibility for their behavior.

IMPLICATIONS FOR FEMINIST SOCIAL WORK PRACTICE

Two practice approaches, the ecological perspective (Germain, 1979) and the strengths perspective (Saleebey, 1992), are compatible with a feminist model of social work practice.

Ecological Perspective

The ecological perspective focuses partly on the "goodness of fit" between people and their environments. It emphasizes the dual concern of social work for the adaptive potential of people and the nutritive qualities of their environments (Germain, 1979). The ecological perspective is concerned with the growth, development, and potential of people and the properties in the environment that support or fail to support one's potential. Social work practice, from this perspective, is directed toward improving the transactions between people and environments (Germain, 1979). This perspective is consistent with a feminist vision. It examines the relationship between the person and environment and regards the "transactions" that occur within these dimensions as the problem focus; it is closely aligned with the feminist principle that the "personal is political" and demonstrates a connectedness between individuals and the social structure.

Strengths Perspective

The strengths perspective (Saleebey, 1992) is based on five assumptions that are consistent with a feminist world view: (1) respecting client strengths, (2) recognizing and fostering client strengths, (3) collaboration between social worker and client, (4) avoiding the victim mind-set, and (5) noticing the resources within an environment. The model places importance on the concept of empowerment, helping people discover their own personal, familial, and community power. Empowerment requires that people have the right and responsibility to participate in actions that define their world (Saleebey, 1992) and resonates with the feminist practice principle of reconceptualizing power, aiding clients to develop skills that would influence their personal lives as well as their environment. The strengths perspective "seeks to develop abilities and capacities in clients . . . it assumes that clients already have a number of competencies and resources that may be used to improve their situation" (Saleebey, 1992, p. 15). It allows social workers to reframe their perspective from the negative to the positive; rather than focus on "what's wrong" with their clients, it allows social workers to focus on strengths and "what's right" about their clients. The strengths perspective challenges the notion of "normal human development" that has hurt lesbians and gay men who do not "fit" within these normative models and leads us to "develop a more fluid and expansive sense of how human beings grow and change" (Weick, 1992, p. 22). According to Weick, three essential assumptions ground the strengths perspective: (1) every person has an inherent power, and this power may be stimulated through the process of empowerment; (2) power is a form of knowledge that can guide personal and social transformation; and (3) when people's positive capacities are supported, they are more likely to act on their strengths (belief in inherent capacity for growth and well-being). The strengths perspective brings us to another level of truth regarding practice: "that each person already carries the seeds for his or her own transformation" (Weick, 1992, p. 25). These perspectives provide social workers with a useful paradigm to guide their work with lesbian and gay clients and further reinforce feminist practice principles of renaming, valuing process, and empowerment.

IMPLICATIONS FOR THE FUTURE
Policy Implications

Social workers can play leadership roles and help organize within professional and community organizations to work for progressive social change. They can actively promote and work for policy changes on such issues as gay and lesbian civil rights, domestic partnership legislation, and the military ban on homosexuality. Gay and lesbian civil rights have been challenged in several states, including Oregon and Colorado; referenda against these rights have gained momentum across the country as the antigay tactics of right-wing religious and conservative groups take hold. Although the social environment has become safer for lesbians and gay men, the backlash against the community has become stronger. Domestic partnership legislation is being passed in many states; businesses and institutions are extending health care and other benefits to partners of gay and lesbian employees. These benefits validate the reality of lesbian and gay families and are an important step in achieving equal rights and protection under the law. Social workers can advocate for domestic partner benefits and legislation in their agencies and communities. They can work to ensure that homophobic military policy and procedures are challenged so lesbians and gay men who want to openly serve their country may do so.

Program Implications

In addition to policy changes, there is a need for increasing social services for gay men and lesbians, especially programs for youths, senior citizens, and protection from workplace harassment. Homosexual youths are an especially vulnerable, high-risk group; they lack positive gay and lesbian role models and usually have limited or no support systems. Studies of gay, lesbian, and bisexual youths show that many engage in intentional self-destructive behavior and repeatedly attempt suicide (Remafedi, Farrow, & Deisher, 1993). Many of these suicide attempts are related to internal or interpersonal conflict about sexual identity. Social programs, particularly in schools, that address the needs of these youths could significantly affect the stress associated with coming out during adolescence. Social workers can play an important part in establishing such programs in their communities by educating agency staff about the needs of gay and lesbian youths, writing grants to obtain funding for innovative programs, and organizing collaboratives of gay and lesbian service providers.

As the population grows, there will be an increasing need to provide services and advocacy for gay and lesbian senior citizens. Of concern to this population are issues of bereavement, physical disability, and stigmatization (Kimmel, 1993). Older lesbians and gay men frequently confront the loss of lovers and friends; these losses often go unnoticed because many seniors are not comfortable being open about their homosexuality because of lack of societal acceptance during much of their lives. Many lesbian and gay seniors need to be hospitalized or placed in nursing homes, where staff do not understand or respect their relationships with lovers or friends (Kimmel, 1993). Gay and lesbian seniors also encounter ageism within the gay community, which may negatively affect their self-esteem and identity. Social workers can help provide seniors with the services and programs they need, such as bereavement support groups, counseling, health care advocacy, or referrals to sensitive community programs.

Lesbians and gay men frequently encounter discrimination in the workplace because of their sexual orientation. Social workers can help organize training programs or workshops to educate staff about homophobia and heterosexism. They can provide sensitive vocational counseling to lesbian and gay employees around issues of visibility in the workplace, sexual harassment, or discrimination because of sexual orientation.

Feminist social work practitioners need to take an active, transformative role as we enter the 21st century; there is much work to be done. Social workers need to be educated about the myriad issues that affect the lives of gay men and lesbians and be committed to incorporating feminist approaches in their practice that validate their clients' experiences, advocate for their social and civil rights, and help create change, transformation, and empowerment.

REFERENCES

Blumenfeld, W. J., & Raymond, D. (1993). *Looking at gay and lesbian life*. Boston: Beacon Press.

Bozett, F. W., Ed. (1987). *Gay and lesbian parents*. New York: Praeger.

Burke, P. (1993). *Family values: Two moms and their son*. New York: Random House.

Cass, V. (1979). Homosexual identity formation: A theoretical model. *Journal of Homosexuality, 4,* 219–235.

Coleman, E. (1985). Developmental stages of the coming out process. In J. C. Gonsiorek (Ed.), *A guide to psychotherapy with gay and lesbian clients* (pp. 31–43). New York: Harrington Park Press.

Crawford, S. (1987). Lesbian families: Psychosocial stress and the family-building process. In Boston Lesbian Psychologies Collective (Eds.), *Lesbian psychologies: Explorations and challenges* (pp. 195–214). Chicago: University of Illinois Press.

Gagnon, J. H. (1977). *Human sexualities.* Glenview, IL: Scott, Foresman.

Germain, C. B. (Ed.). (1979). *Social work practice: People and environments: An ecological perspective.* New York: Columbia University Press.

Grace, J. (1985). Coming out in social work. In H. Hidalgo, T. L. Peterson, & N. J. Woodman (Eds.), *Lesbian and gay issues: A resource manual for social workers.* Silver Spring, MD: National Association of Social Workers.

Grace, J. (1992). Affirming gay and lesbian adulthood. In N. J. Woodman (Ed.), *Lesbian and gay lifestyles* (pp. 33–48). New York: Irvington.

Gunter, P. (1992). Social work with non-traditional families. In N. J. Woodman (Ed.), *Lesbian and gay lifestyles* (pp. 87–110). New York: Irvington.

Hart, B. (1986). Lesbian battering: An examination. In K. Lobel (Ed.), *Naming the violence* (pp. 95–97). Seattle: Seal Press.

Kimmel, D. C. (1993). Adult development and aging: A gay perspective. In L. D. Garnets & D. C. Kimmel (Eds.), *Psychological perspectives on lesbian and gay male experiences* (pp. 517–534). New York: Columbia University Press.

Lee, J.A.B. (1992). Teaching content related to lesbian and gay identity formation. In N. J. Woodman (Ed.), *Lesbian and gay lifestyles* (pp. 1–22). New York: Irvington.

Leeder, E. (1988). Enmeshed in pain: Counseling the lesbian battering couple. *Women and Therapy, 7*(1), 81-99.

Levy, E. F. (1989). *Lesbian motherhood: Identity and social support. Affilia, 4*(4), 40–53.

Levy, E. F. (1992). Strengthening the coping resources of lesbian families. *Families in Society, 73*(1), 23–31.

Lewis, L. (1984). The coming-out process for lesbians: Integrating a stable identity. *Social Work, 29,* 464–469.

Lobel, K. (Ed.). (1986). *Naming the violence.* Seattle: Seal Press.

Martin, A. (1993). *The lesbian and gay parenting handbook.* New York: Harper Perennial.

McCandlish, B. M. (1987). Against all odds: Lesbian mother family dynamics. In F. W. Bozett (Ed.), *Gay and lesbian parents* (pp. 23–28). New York: Praeger.

Pierce, D. (1991, May). *Building bridges: Notes on developing a framework for social work practice with lesbian and gay people.* Invitational paper presented at Building Bridges, Gay and Lesbian Social Work Conference, University of Maryland at Baltimore.

Porat, N. (1986). Support groups for battered lesbians. In K. Lobel (Ed.), *Naming the violence* (pp. 80–87). Seattle: Seal Press.

Remafedi, G., Farrow, J. A., & Deisher, R. W. (1993). Risk factors for attempted suicide in gay and bisexual youth. In L. D. Garnets & D. C. Kimmel (Eds.), *Psychological perspectives on lesbian and gay male experiences* (pp. 486–499). New York: Columbia University Press.

Renzetti, C. M. (1992). *Violent betrayal: Partner abuse in lesbian relationships.* Newbury Park, CA: Sage Publications.

Rich, A. (1979). Disloyal to civilization: Feminism, racism, gynephobia. In A. Rich, *On lies, secrets, and silence: Selected prose 1966–1978* (pp. 275–310). New York: W. W. Norton.

Rivera, R. R. (1987). Legal issues in gay and lesbian parenting. In F. W. Bozett (Ed.), *Gay and lesbian parents* (pp. 199–230). New York: Praeger.

Robertson, M. M. (1992). Lesbians and an invisible minority in the health services arena. *Health Care for Women International, 13,* 155–163.

Saleebey, D. (Ed.). (1992). *The strengths perspective in social work practice.* New York: Longman.

Shattls, W. D., & Shernoff, M. (1992). Field placements in AIDS service provider agencies. In N. Woodman (Ed.), *Lesbian and gay lifestyles* (pp. 277–292). New York: Irvington.

Siegel, K., & Krauss, B. J. (1991). Living with HIV infection: Adaptive tasks of seropositive gay men. *Journal of Health and Social Behavior, 32*(1), 17–32.

Weick, A. (1992). Building a strengths perspective for social work. In D. Saleebey (Ed.), *The strengths perspective in social work practice* (pp. 18–26). New York: Longman.

Weston, K. (1991). *Families we choose.* New York: Columbia University Press.

The author thanks D. Jeanette Nichols, RN, for support and editorial assistance throughout the writing of this chapter.

16

Women and AIDS
Feminist Principles in Practice

Jane Miller and Mary Ann Kuszelewicz

The serious and immense task involved in developing a coherent and useful analysis of policy, research, and practice issues relevant to the acquired immune deficiency syndrome (AIDS) epidemic among women is a significant challenge confronting social workers (Amaro, 1990). The task also exposes the complexities involved in attempting to discuss the ramifications that this disease has introduced into women's lives. This chapter focuses on feminist principles and how they can be applied on both the micro and the macro level when working with women in the human immunodeficiency virus (HIV) spectrum. Before expanding on these feminist principles, it is critical to discuss the history, demographics, extent, and degree of the HIV and AIDS phenomena.

A BRIEF HISTORY OF THE AIDS EPIDEMIC
Origins and Prevalence of the Problem
The first cases of AIDS were published in 1981, although the exact date of the disease's origin is not known. The Centers for Disease Control (CDC) traced the first cases to 1978 (Grmek, 1990). In And the Band Played On, Shilts (1987) implied that AIDS was introduced into the United States in 1976 during the bicentennial celebration. This, of course, cannot be substantiated. AIDS has a very high mortality rate, which some researchers believe is 100 percent. AIDS has no cure although some drugs, such as azidothymidine (AZT), seem to help prolong the lives of people who are able to tolerate the possible severe side effects.

The World Health Organization has begun to define AIDS as the final phase in what they call HIV disease. Individuals become infected with HIV and several months to a year later develop antibodies to the virus, at which point they are considered seropositive. They may live many years with no symptoms, but they can infect other people through risky behavior. As the infected individual develops antibodies, he or she may or may not experience time-limited symptoms similar to the flu. As the HIV disease progresses, symptoms may include night sweats, persistently swollen lymph glands, and the return of flulike symptoms. This state was once referred to as AIDS-related complex (ARC). The time interval from this stage to full-blown AIDS is variable and can be related to general health status, access to medical care, nutrition, and abstinence from drug and alcohol use. AIDS is a constellation of opportunistic infections that the HIV-infected individual is susceptible to because of a severely compromised immune system.

AIDS was first identified as a gay male disease and was called gay-related immune deficiency (GRID). It was then expanded to include the four Hs: homosexuals (males), Haitians, hemophiliacs (mostly men), and heroin users (mostly men). A culture of silence early in the AIDS epidemic led to misinformation and stereotyping. The information published by journalists and physicians linked AIDS to the sexual behavior of male homosexuals. The debate began to focus on gay male bathhouses as the vector of the illness (Bayer, 1989).

The culture of silence continued as hemophiliacs contracted the illness. Although CDC spokespeople advocated for the disease to be seen as transmitted through blood, as is hepatitis B, blood banks were reluctant to make this acknowledgment. Thus, the focus remained on AIDS as a disease of gay men (Shilts, 1987). Funding for research on HIV and AIDS remained sparse in the early years of the epidemic. It did not become a public health issue until the announcement that Rock Hudson, a Hollywood actor, was symptomatic (Brandt, 1988; Shilts, 1987). Even in 1991, the major media focus on AIDS concerned Earvin "Magic" Johnson, an African American all-star basketball player who was diagnosed as HIV-positive, rather than the millions of anonymous individuals affected by this disease.

Although AIDS continues to affect gay men, it is now more commonly a disease of minorities, injecting drug users, and women. The more the disease is stigmatized as a "gay male disease," the more unthinkable it becomes to conclude that women may be at risk (Murphy, 1988). The phrase "risk groups" perpetuates the myth that individuals not within designated risk groups are immune to contracting the virus. In essence, that omission has stigmatized many people, including injecting drug users, workers in the sex industries, and gay men, and has obscured the real risk factors, which are behavioral. Being a gay man or an injecting drug user does not automatically put one at risk for exposure to the virus; rather, practicing unsafe behavior puts one at risk (Santee, 1988).

Women and AIDS

Sexism, racism, classism, and heterosexism all contribute to the lack of public awareness about women with HIV and AIDS and the fact that women constitute at least 10 percent of the HIV and AIDS cases in the United States (Padian, 1991). HIV-positive women remain invisible.

As of October 1993, 328,392 Americans had been diagnosed with AIDS (Centers for Disease Control and Prevention, 1993). The disease has been affecting women in increasing numbers. Since the late 1980s AIDS has been the leading cause of death among women ages 25 to 29 in some areas of the country, particularly in the northeastern United States (Patton & Kelly, 1987). There were at least 42,019 females diagnosed with AIDS in 1993 (Centers for Disease Control and Prevention, 1993), and the majority of them were women from racial and ethnic groups who were more likely to be facing the issues of poverty and disenfranchisement. There are problems in assessing not only the number of women with HIV and AIDS but also the ways in which the women are affected. Many of the illnesses that affect women with HIV or AIDS, specifically pelvic inflammatory disease and gynecological cancers, are not included in the 1984 CDC definition of the AIDS diagnosis (Maggenti, 1989). National statistics are not available for the total number of HIV-positive women and only an estimated number is available for the women diagnosed with AIDS. Therefore, when reading information pertaining to HIV and AIDS, one frequently discovers the contradictions, variations, and conflicts with the statistics and materials provided, which enhance the level of frustration as one attempts to uncover the realities of this epidemic.

Women are frequently omitted from media coverage and AIDS brochures and are eclipsed in medical research. If and when women are included, public health officials frequently hold prostitutes responsible for AIDS. This is an unsubstantiated and sexist claim (Murphy, 1988). At the level of media coverage, women must be seen as being at risk and not as vectors for the illness. Even children, who constitute approximately 1 percent of the U.S. AIDS cases, continue to gain more attention and research than infected women, even though almost all of the pediatric AIDS cases are acquired during pregnancy (Murphy, 1988). Research money is more plentiful today than at the beginning of this epidemic, yet research and written material pertaining to women with HIV and AIDS remain minimal.

Lesbians are a group of women even less frequently addressed on the topic of HIV and AIDS in the academic press, the media, or even within the alternative presses. This group's level of risk for HIV remains a controversial subject. For the first decade of this epidemic, lesbians were considered the lowest-risk group (Kaspar, 1989), although the number of lesbians with HIV and AIDS is increasing (Denenberg, 1991). Some of the behaviors that place lesbians at risk are injecting drug use, heterosexual sex with infected men, sexual contact with bisexual women, blood-to-blood contact, partnering with injecting drug users, and alternative fertilization (Kaspar, 1989). Risk of woman-to-woman transmission remains unclear, although two case examples have appeared in the medical literature (Marmor, Weiss, & Lyden, 1986; Monzon & Capellan, 1987).

Epidemiology and Natural History of HIV and AIDS in Women
Most women with AIDS are young; approximately one-third are between the ages of 20 and 29 at the age of diagnosis. Given the long latency period of HIV disease before becoming full-blown AIDS, many of these women possibly were infected as teenagers. Eighty-five percent of the women with AIDS are considered to be of reproductive age (15 to 44 years of age), and many of them find out they are HIV-positive at the time of pregnancy or delivery (Carovano, 1991; Ellerbrock & Rogers, 1990). Seventy-five percent of the women with AIDS reside in eight states along the Atlantic coast, the District of Columbia, and Puerto Rico (Ellerbrock & Rogers, 1990).

Injecting drug use is involved in approximately 71 percent of the female AIDS cases, with 52 percent of the women injecting drugs themselves and 19 percent being the sexual partner of an injecting drug user (Ellerbrock & Rogers, 1990). Nearly one-half of the women with AIDS are African American and about 20 percent are Hispanic (Campbell, 1990). Unfortunately, many women do not perceive themselves as at risk for HIV (Carovano, 1991). Consequently, unprotected heterosexual intercourse continues to be a significant risk factor. Unprotected heterosexual intercourse is the second largest transmission category for women and has increased annually for the past seven years (Campbell, 1990). Women remain in a position of less power in decision making regarding sex. They are at high risk for infection as long as their only means of protection is to advocate for male condom use. Unfortunately, many males are reluctant to take responsibility for pregnancy prevention (Carovano, 1991;

Macks, 1988), and it is unlikely that they will take responsibility for preventing HIV transmission.

One cannot assume that HIV infection will take the identical course in women as it has in men. Differences have already been identified in the course of the illness between homosexual men and injecting drug users; one could expect similar differences in the presentation of the disease within women. To date, there are few cohort studies of the progression of the disease in either drug users or women (Brettle & Leen, 1991). Prospective studies of symptomatic HIV-infected women and the progression of the disease during pregnancy are not available (Ellerbrock & Rogers, 1990). In studies that looked at the effect of pregnancy on asymptomatic HIV-infected women, Brettle and Leen (1991) discovered that pregnancy seemed to accelerate progression of HIV disease, but later studies have not replicated this finding. Hence, the effect of pregnancy on HIV disease is equivocal.

The clinical problems for HIV-infected women include a higher risk for development of urinary tract infections and other lower genital tract infections (such as genital warts) than has been observed in males infected with HIV. Kaposi's sarcoma, a common cancer associated with HIV and AIDS, is rarely seen in women. However, when present, it seems to attack women's immune systems, severely shortening their life span. A cancer that does affect women with HIV or AIDS disproportionately is neoplasia of the genital tract, including cervical dysplasia. Women have a lower incidence of pneumocystis carinii pneumonia (PCP) but frequently have yeast infections of the esophagus and HIV-related wasting syndrome. No studies of the effects of HIV and AIDS on the sex hormone levels of women have been implemented. Women are more likely to be anemic than men. AZT treatment, of which anemia is a side effect, may be more difficult for women to tolerate (Brettle & Leen, 1991). One of the gynecologic conditions seen in women with HIV or AIDS is a recurrent or persistent candidiasis that is more difficult to treat. Once a woman is infected with the human papilloma virus (HPV), spontaneous regression of genital warts is not often seen. The cervical disease caused by HPV is the most serious gynecological disease faced by women with HIV or AIDS and can be fatal (Marte & Allen, 1991, 1992).

Women have a significantly poorer survival rate then men. This may be related to many factors, including a relationship between drug use and gender. More important is women's lack of access to medical knowledge and care, leading them to seek medical care later in the course of the illness when little can be done to extend their lives significantly (Brettle & Leen, 1991). Another issue is the lack of access women have had to the clinical trials of experimental drugs. Consequently, little is known about the effects of drug therapy on women with HIV or AIDS (Campbell, 1990). What little research does exist focuses on women as vectors of the illness through the sex industries or pregnancy (Kaspar, 1989).

After political pressure was applied by those who attended the Women and AIDS Conference held in December 1990 in Washington, DC, clinical trials were cautiously provided for women. For the first time the federal government funded a large study, referred to as the 076 project. Continuing the focus on women as vectors, the study sought to determine whether HIV transmission between mother and neonate could be prevented through treatment with AZT. This clinical trial was funded with a background of no previous studies on the effects of AZT on women, no prospective studies of disease progression in symptomatic HIV-positive pregnant women, and many other unexplored areas affecting women. As one author stated, "Efforts to prevent AIDS among women have been the result not of concern for women but rather a concern that is primarily about protecting the health of men and children" (Carovano, 1991, p. 131); the same can be said about the priorities for research. Yet studies consistently show that the transmission rate from males to their female partners is 20 percent. Results from studies on transmission from women to men are much less consistent, ranging from zero to half the rate of male-to-female transmission (Padian, 1991).

Disenfranchisement of Women in the AIDS Epidemic
AIDS is a reflection of the existing problems and preexisting weaknesses present in our system. One needs to question why women are not considered important enough to warrant HIV and AIDS education programs and research. HIV and AIDS expose the already prevalent disenfranchisement existing among the sexes, classes, and races (Mitchell, 1988). One needs to remain insightful to understand that maintaining basic fundamental needs such as housing and food is a priority for many women with the disease. HIV and AIDS clearly demonstrate a paradigm for all of the critical issues that have historically beleaguered women. Social workers and all members of society must remain aware and informed of the barriers that face women with HIV or AIDS and women in general (Khalili, 1987):

> *Deeply ingrained societal racism and sexism; inadequate quality of and lack of access to health care, including outpatient, hospice and respite care, as well as more traditional modes of care; absence of decent affordable housing, particularly for female-headed households, the*

impoverished, and the working poor; insufficient child care facilities and support services for raising children; and unequal educational opportunities and illiteracy. (p. 46)

Although we have attempted to dispel some of the myths and misrepresentations present in society, it is important to examine how social workers can provide services to HIV-positive women using a feminist approach both at the micro and the macro level. We begin by defining feminist practice principles and then describe how we envision their incorporation into social work practice.

FEMINIST PRACTICE PRINCIPLES

Feminist theory and values are not static but are always evolving and changing, a process in development that is advanced through dialogue (Van Den Bergh & Cooper, 1986). A multitude of feminist theories cannot be reduced to a single definition in this chapter. Instead, rather than explore various feminist theories that are politically based (liberal, socialist, or radical) we examine a number of feminist concepts that are based on a theoretical framework that can be applied and integrated into practice.

The principles described below are all interrelated and underlie the core of practice implemented by feminist practitioners. The principles are an end to patriarchy, empowerment, the personal is political, unity and diversity, validation of the nonrational, valuing process, and consciousness-raising (Bricker-Jenkins & Hooyman, 1986). These themes are the foundation of feminist practices, and how they are implemented is critical. Specifically, the practitioner values the client, acknowledges the client's potential, and sees the client as a competent, worthy, capable human being, not as pathological. The therapist varies the techniques used depending on where the client is and with awareness of the client's diagnosis, using the diagnosis as an analytical tool in the best interest of the client. These principles can be demonstrated by a clinician through nonverbal feedback, body language, role modeling, and a multitude of other techniques. Feminist therapists will not set their own agendas but will work hand-in-hand with their clients, discussing approaches and interventions and setting goals together.

Feminist therapists have an obligation to use their power to effect change by consciously and actively sharing power and making an effort to equalize power (Brown, 1985). "An equalitarian relationship between therapist and client then becomes one in which equality is viewed as equal worth rather than equal power" (Rosewater & Walker, 1985, p. xxii). Feminist therapists implement their power inequity and privilege on their clients' behalf, achieving the least desperate balance of power overall (Douglas, 1985). The clinician is a catalyst for the client's growth, providing a supportive environment where the client is met on his or her own terms. Clients are empowered to discard restrictive behaviors and ideas and are provided with new information, skills, and resources with which to consider their alternatives (Valentich, 1986).

Because the feminist principles are intertwined, feminist therapists will integrate approaches when working with HIV-positive and AIDS clients while constantly discovering new ways of constructively developing these ideologies within their practice. For example, a therapist might empower an HIV-positive client to work toward ending patriarchy after her or his consciousness has been raised. The brief examples presented are provided to illustrate specific pragmatic approaches based on the feminist principles that clinicians can use when working with HIV-positive and AIDS clients. The principles of valuing process and consciousness-raising are not specifically discussed because they are present within the context of the other themes. We show how these ideologies overlap, intersect, and are basic underlying tenets to feminist philosophies.

An End to Patriarchy

The feminist therapist provides the skills and knowledge to solve problems and meet the needs of clients with HIV or AIDS, demystifying the patriarchal system by collaborating with clients to give them access to the rights and privileges they have been denied. A clinician will provide skills and knowledge to expand each woman's vision of her rights and capabilities at the same time advocating to end all institutionalized systems of oppression that affect women with HIV or AIDS. Each woman's values must be validated, respected, and honored, while providing her with opportunities to question and discover alternative ways of gaining access to child care, health care, financial support, and legal advice, so that she no longer must rely on the patriarchal system to fulfill her needs. Feminist social workers must recognize that all aspects of our lives, public and private, are deeply marked by patriarchy and must be reframed, reassessed, and revised in the therapeutic relationship.

Medical, physical, and mental health care have been more accessible to men affected by HIV and AIDS, especially upper-middle-class men. On the other hand, women with HIV or AIDS have frequently been disregarded on the basis of deeply ingrained sexism, classism, racism, and other unfounded assumptions and stigmas. Social workers must collaborate with their clients to obtain the necessary information to fight for the medical, financial, housing, and child care programs that HIV-infected women deserve. Additionally, social workers must stay abreast of and share pertinent information on the complex medical, psychological, and social services systems that exist or do not exist for women in the HIV spectrum and their care providers.

Clinicians discover that when they respect clients by valuing their experiences in dealing with their HIV or AIDS status, they will learn from their clients. Social workers also can gain insights and support from other professionals in the field. Feminist therapists must connect with other professionals not only to learn from each other, share information, and support each other but also to confront one another in examining their own biases.

Some women with HIV or AIDS seen in clinical practices have not received quality medical care from physicians who have had previous experience treating this population. These physicians lack necessary information pertaining to the different course that HIV and AIDS has taken in women. Additionally, these doctors have not been knowledgeable about treatment options and their impact on women.

Many clients have discovered that AZT seems to affect their menstrual cycles, and they have not been able to find medical information on possible underlying reasons and their potential association with the use of AZT. Many women have demanded that physicians and researchers explore these areas. They also have networked with each other to find mutual support as they face these experiences.

The clinician's role would be to raise the consciousness of and empower these women to voice their angers and frustrations by encouraging them to share their feelings and build support systems. In doing so, they can work toward diminishing the obstacles they are faced with, thereby no longer feeling marginalized and invisible. By voicing their demands these women may avoid feeling exploited and dominated by the patriarchal system.

Empowerment

Smith and Douglas (1990) found that

> empowerment forms the core definition of feminist therapy, together with the continual analysis of the societal inequities that dictate unequal access to resources (power) for oppressed groups. Empowerment is the process by which clients are encouraged to make their own decisions, honor their own feelings and choose their own actions. (p. 43)

Feminist therapists can help clients get in touch with the power they already have, but are not aware of, by using various consciousness-raising techniques. Clinicians must encourage women with HIV or AIDS to discover their interpersonal power and strengths by validating their experiences and enabling them to rename certain aspects of their behaviors. Feminist therapy focuses on empowering women to realize their potential, support their values, and achieve their goals while learning about themselves throughout the process (Smith & Siegle, 1985).

The therapist is faced with a healthy struggle between advocacy and enabling, with the goal of empowering clients by monitoring and evaluating the influence and effect the clinician has on clients. Empowering women with HIV or AIDS, whether on a personal or an interpersonal level, is at the core of all feminist principles. For example, one's consciousness cannot be raised unless one feels empowered and one cannot feel empowered if one's consciousness has not been raised. Hence, feminist principles are interwoven in the feminist therapist's approach to working with clients.

A woman's feelings of powerlessness can be decreased if a clinician remains nonjudgmental and supportive, validates her perceptions, and encourages her to make her own decisions. Redefining power, reducing guilt, affirming the client's reality, identifying the costs and benefits, and providing necessary information can empower the client to make informed decisions.

The Personal Is Political

As feminist therapists, a key belief is that as we change ourselves we change the world. The belief that the personal is political deeply affects and influences our work and our lives, in essence working to eradicate the pervasive racism, classism, sexism, and heterosexism we face. The following is an example of how the personal became the political in a client's life.

The client with AIDS was working full-time, had not missed any work, and had not told her employer of her diagnosis. The client entered the hospital over a weekend and the employer then discovered the client's HIV status. The employer immediately fired the client after five years of service, even though she was still capable of performing her job and no health reasons justified the termination. Her termination was a blatant act of discrimination. In addition, the health insurance coverage provided by her employer had an AIDS clause that provided coverage far below the provisions for other catastrophic illnesses—another example of discrimination.

Although eight months had passed, the events were still emotionally tumultuous for the client. It also was the beginning of a transformation from an apolitical to a politically active role wherein the client became a militant activist. The therapist worked with the client, empowering her to express her anger through role playing and to use it as a catalyst to fight for positive changes. The client constructively used her personal experiences to fight for an end to discrimination against people living with AIDS or HIV. She learned strategic tactics and methods of organizing by unifying forces to protest the discrimination that affected her life and the lives of many individuals with this virus. The feminist therapist provided the necessary information and support as well as assistance as an educator, liaison, referral source, coalition builder, and role model. The therapist took an active role in all phases of this process by advocating, empowering, and encouraging the client toward political action while honoring the client's own desires and decisions.

Unity and Diversity

Working with women with HIV or AIDS who come from diverse backgrounds and experiences and trying to discover ways to bring them together is an exciting, and at times arduous, endeavor. It brings to the surface the challenges one faces when confronting differences and the possibilities of creating solidarity between women in the HIV spectrum. Women are frequently isolated and even when they share a common behavior, their backgrounds may be so diverse that it causes difficulties when they connect with one another (Kaspar, 1989).

One of the authors saw a number of HIV-positive lesbian clients in her practice who were isolated because the support groups available were primarily composed of gay men or heterosexual women dealing with issues revolving around the men in their lives. According to Leonard (1990), "Lesbians have been absent from most discussions of HIV infection. The most common attitude seems to be that AIDS is not a lesbian problem" (p. 113). Lesbians have been ignored by the media and the medical and academic presses, a situation that has promoted ignorance of the possible risks they have for contracting HIV.

The lesbian HIV-positive clients felt stigmatized because they were not "supposed" to be at risk, and the perception of stigma only added to their feelings of isolation. Although these women were a diverse and small group, it seemed worthwhile to attempt to unify them. Because so few HIV-positive lesbians have come out with their HIV status or have been tested, the therapist's role was as a referral source and networker, while assisting them in acknowledging their differences and preserving and honoring their uniqueness.

Validation of the Nonrational

As a feminist practitioner, one can explore nontraditional techniques that are not widely used in counseling with HIV-positive clients who are interested in or open to examining them (Valentich, 1986). These techniques include relaxation, meditation, and visualization. The practitioner also provides resources to discover additional avenues of holistic or alternative healing methods, such as massotherapists, acupuncturists, art or dance therapists, herbalists, polarity specialists, and healing weekends as well as HIV-specific relaxation and visualization tapes and recommendations of available books about healing. Feminist practitioners must instill the value of the therapeutic process, not just the therapeutic product, by encouraging the client to take appropriate risks and discover the multitude of healing methods available. Many clients with HIV or AIDS are already involved in alternative healing methods, so the therapist's role is to encourage, support, and assist clients in finding whatever paths they choose to bring about spiritual, emotional, and physical growth and healing in their lives.

MACRO-LEVEL ISSUES

Macro-level issues that would concern a social worker focusing on HIV and women include research, policy, and organizational issues. A few areas of research that still must be explored include symptomatology specific to women, the effects of contraceptive use on risk of HIV transmission, the effect of AZT on menstrual cycles, menstrual disorders seen in HIV-infected women, and the gynecology protocols for clinical trials. To date, the largest female-specific research effort funded by the government is the 076 project. This research continues to focus on women merely as vectors who are not deserving of research themselves. "Women deserve more and better health care, but in the nation's inner cities, the 076 protocol may be the only choice available" for minority women and women without health care benefits who seek access to AZT (Byron, 1991, p. 95). Social workers must intervene in the health care system to influence it to provide equal access to women for treatment, drug rehabilitation, and psychological services. Women with HIV need appropriate child care, housing, and respite care for their children—all areas to be targeted at the policy level. The Ryan White Comprehensive AIDS Resources Emergency Act (a legislative action named after a young man who died of AIDS) authorized resources for AIDS-related services; social workers must organize, lobby, and demand implementation of female-specific legislation and access to the Ryan White money for women's services.

At the public health and educational levels, interventions for preventing the spread of the illness to women have remained ineffective. Educational materials that worked well with gay men are not relevant to women. Pamphlets, videos, and health education must be culturally and socially applicable; women must be able to identify with materials and hear their voices. With women's lowered sense of power in sexual relationships, education that focuses on women taking responsibility for condom use is an inadequate and insensitive response to this epidemic.

Women's lower economic status in this society places them at greater risk for substance abuse and participation as sex workers. Social workers can work at the societal level to eliminate the multiple causes of unequal access to employment and the wage gap women face. The successful community organizing that gay men orchestrated in the early days of the AIDS epidemic can be an example for social workers interested in intervening at the macro level for the needs of HIV-positive women, their children, and their caregivers. How different the AIDS response would have been if instead of first affecting gay men, who were organized and politically conscious, it had hit drug users or minority women (Bayer, 1989).

As social workers, we must confront institutionalized prejudice and discrimination. By providing inadequate health care benefits, emotional and financial support, and job protection, organizations are not caring for their most vulnerable members. Jobs that provide benefits are systematically unavailable to disenfranchised women because of sexism, racism, and classism. This negatively affects a woman's life whether she is HIV-positive and in need of services or is caring for a loved one who has HIV or AIDS. Organizational interventions are needed and appropriate. Kaspar (1989) discussed the role of sexual politics:

> As is true of other areas, sexual politics plays an important role in the social response to both women with AIDS and women who are at risk for developing it. Such issues as the formulation of policy, drug testing, and the provision of services are all influenced by the fact that women have little political and personal power. (pp. 7–8)

The women's movement of the 1970s taught women that the personal is the political. This very personal illness must be treated as a political problem, and social workers can help empower their female clients with HIV or AIDS to take political action. The political agenda of this country has made this an illness that disproportionately affects the politically and socially disenfranchised and leaves them with limited, if any, resources and support services.

Women who have HIV or AIDS, as well as caregivers of those with HIV (who disproportionately are women), do not benefit from rhetoric; they need a kinder and gentler society.

This chapter captures and illustrates the bleak realities that women living with HIV and AIDS face. We are now beginning to confront and expose the challenges this epidemic poses for women. As we move into the 21st century, the conditions that place women at risk for HIV infection will remain salient and most likely will expand. Women's second-class political and economic status and the sexist, pejorative assumptions about women as "sexual objects" have hindered significant initiatives to undertake research on women and HIV disease progression and on effective treatments for women with HIV.

One might argue that AIDS, in general, has been a subject marginalized because of the stigma associated with the groups first affected by this disease, specifically gay men and lesbians, minority group members, sex industry workers, and injecting drug users. The paradox of heightened awareness of HIV risks may be that as it begins to affect white, middle-class, heterosexual persons, greater interest and resources will be invested in finding solutions to this public health problem.

Through using such feminist principles as empowerment, valuing diversity, eliminating discriminating and dichotomizing practices, and community building, it is hoped that the solutions to the HIV crisis will be applicable and available to all persons infected regardless of race, gender, sexual orientation, or class. Feminist principles resonate with the core of social work values; hence, social work practice within the field of HIV and AIDS must be derived from a feminist model.

We hope this discussion provokes social workers to examine the impact of policies and practices related to HIV infection and AIDS on women's health and reminds social workers that we have a responsibility to take a leadership role in the policies, program planning, and educational materials that affect all women. By implementing the feminist principles explored in this chapter, we have an opportunity to take a more powerful role in effecting positive changes in the lives of women with HIV and AIDS and in the population at large.

REFERENCES

Amaro, H. (1990). Women's reproductive rights in the age of AIDS: New threats to informed consent. In M. Gerber Fried (Ed.), *From abortion to reproductive freedom: Transforming a movement* (pp. 245–254). Boston: South End Press.

Bayer, R. (1989). *Private acts, social consequences: AIDS and the politics of public health.* New York: Free Press.

Brandt, A. M. (1988). AIDS: From social history to social policy. In E. Fee & D. M. Fox (Eds.), *AIDS: The burdens of history.* Berkeley: University of California Press.

Brettle, R. P., & Leen, C.L.S. (1991). The natural history of HIV and AIDS in women. *AIDS, 5,* 1283–1292.

Bricker-Jenkins, M., & Hooyman, N. (Eds.). (1986). *Not for women only: Social work practice for a feminist future.* Silver Spring, MD: National Association of Social Workers.

Brown, L. (1985). Ethics and business practices in feminist therapy. In L. B. Rosewater & L.E.A. Walker (Eds.), *Handbook of feminist therapy: Women's issues in psychotherapy* (pp. 297–304). New York: Springer.

Byron, P. (1991). Feds to study women with HIV. *Ms., 2*(1), p. 95.

Campbell, C. A. (1990). Women and AIDS. *Social Science and Medicine, 30*(4), 407–415.

Carovano, K. (1991). More than mothers and whores: Redefining the AIDS prevention needs of women. *International Journal of Health Services, 21*(1), 131–142.

Centers for Disease Control and Prevention. (1993). *HIV/AIDS surveillance report.* Atlanta: Author.

Denenberg, R. (1991, July/August). A decade of denial: Lesbians and HIV. *On Our Backs,* pp. 22–21, 38–41.

Douglas, M. A. (1985). Role of power in feminist therapy: A reformulation. In L. B. Rosewater & L.E.A. Walker (Eds.), *Handbook of feminist therapy: Women's issues and psychotherapy* (pp. 241–249). New York: Springer.

Ellerbrock, T. V., & Rogers, M. F. (1990). Epidemiology of human immunodeficiency virus infection in women in the United States. *Obstetrics and Gynecology Clinics of North America, 17*(3), 523–544.

Grmek, M. D. (1990). *History of AIDS.* Princeton, NJ: Princeton University Press.

Kaspar, B. (1989). Women and AIDS: A psycho-social perspective. *Affilia, 4*(4), 7–22.

Khalili, A. (1987). Summary of testimony. In *AIDS: Its impact on women, children and families* (pp. 44–46). New York: New York State Division for Women.

Leonard, Z. (1990). Lesbians and the AIDS crisis. In ACT UP–New York Women & AIDS Book Group Staff & New York Women's Handbook Group Staff (Eds.), *Women, AIDS & activism* (pp. 113–118). Boston: South End Press.

Macks, J. (1988). Women and AIDS: Countertransference issues. *Social Casework, 69*(6), 340–347.

Maggenti, M. (Ed.). (1989). *The Act Up Women's Caucus: Women and AIDS handbook.* New York: AIDS Coalition to Unleash Power.

Marmor, M., Weiss, L. R., & Lyden, M. (1986). Possible female-to-female transmission of the human immunodeficiency virus. *Annals of Internal Medicine, 105,* 969.

Marte, C., & Allen, M. (1991). HIV-related gynecologic conditions: Overlooked complications. *Focus: A Guide to AIDS Research and Counseling, 7*(1), 1–4.

Marte, C., & Allen, M. (1992). *Gynecology protocol for HIV-infected women.* Unpublished manuscript, Beth Israel Hospital, Methadone Program, New York.

Mitchell, J. (1988). What about the mothers of the HIV infected babies? *National AIDS Network Multi-Cultural Notes on AIDS Education and Service, 10*(1), 1–2.

Monzon, O. T., & Capellan, J.M.B. (1987). Female-to-female transmission of HIV. *Lancet, 2*(40), 44–45.

Murphy, J. S. (1988). Women with AIDS: Sexual ethics in an epidemic. In I. B. Corless & M. Pittman-Lindeman (Eds.), *AIDS: Principles, practices and politics* (pp. 65–77). New York: Hemisphere.

Padian, N. (1991). Epidemiology of AIDS and heterosexually transmitted HIV in women. *Clinical Notes: AIDS File, 5*(3), 1–8.

Patton, C., & Kelly, J. (1987). *Making it: A woman's guide to sex in the age of AIDS.* New York: Firebrand Books.

Rosewater, L. B., & Walker, L.E.A. (Eds.). (1985). *Handbook of feminist therapy: Women's issues in psychotherapy.* New York: Springer.

Ryan White Comprehensive AIDS Resources Emergency Act of 1990, P.L. 101-381, 104 Stat. 576.

Santee, B. (1988). *Women and AIDS: The silent epidemic*. New York: Women and AIDS Resource Network.

Shilts, R. (1987). *And the band played on*. New York: St. Martin's Press.

Smith, A. J., & Douglas, M. A. (1990). Empowerment as ethical imperative. In H. Lerman & N. Porter (Eds.), *Feminist ethics in psychotherapy* (pp. 43–50). New York: Springer.

Smith, A. J., & Siegle, R. F. (1985). Feminist therapy: Redefining power for the powerless. In L. B. Rosewater & L.E.A. Walker (Eds.), *Handbook of feminist therapy: Women's issues in psychotherapy* (pp. 13–21). New York: Springer.

Valentich, M. (1986). Feminism and social work practice. In F. Turner (Ed.), *Social work treatment: Interlocking theoretical approaches* (3rd ed., pp. 564–589). New York: Free Press.

Van Den Bergh, N., & Cooper, L. B. (1986). Introduction. In N. Van Den Bergh & L. B. Cooper (Eds.), *Feminist visions for social work* (pp. 1–28). Silver Spring, MD: National Association of Social Workers.

Violence against Women

Barrie Levy

Violence against women is "not random violence; the risk factor is being female" (Heise, 1989, p. 3). As Lenore Walker (1992) said in a recent speech, "Susan Brownmiller called rapists the shock troops that keep women in their place. . . and, Ann Jones added, batterers are the home guard. It could happen to every one of us: violence is an equal opportunity affair." Women live in fear based entirely on gender. Discrimination and violence have restricted the aspirations and freedom of women because they must maintain a socially prescribed status quo or risk victimization at work, at home, in the streets, indeed, in all public spheres. Women are subject to domination and control by men and they struggle to control their own bodies. Sexual violence reflects the misogyny of this social order. Even when not inflicted by governments, violence against women is condoned or sanctioned by legal systems and government policy (Bunch, 1991).

The feminist movement of the 1970s and 1980s continued the analyses of sexism of previous feminist movements and confronted the manifestations of sexism in society and in the lives of women. To uncover the erroneous representations of women by a society that makes women invisible, the movement encouraged women to speak out about their experiences. Women and girls recognized that violence is a shockingly common occurrence in their lives. In speaking out about formerly unspeakable experiences with violence, feminists discovered what researchers later validated: Large numbers of women in the United States experience rape, incest, sexual abuse, date violence, wife abuse, marital rape, and sexual harassment. A rape is committed every six minutes (Federal Bureau of Investigation, 1988), and a woman is beaten every 15 seconds. Each day at least four women are killed by their batterers (U.S. Department of Justice, Bureau of Justice Statistics, 1986). Researchers have found that 42 percent to 88 percent of working women experience some form of sexual harassment in the workplace (Kaplan, 1991).

Violence against women is increasing in the United States. From the number of reported rapes in 1990, it is evident that the rape rate has increased four times faster than the overall crime rate in the last 10 years, and unreported rapes may be increasing even faster (U.S. Senate Committee on the Judiciary, 1992). By the 21st century, it is possible that federal legislation in the United States and United Nations policy will have defined violence against women as a hate crime. A global view of the civil rights of women has been stimulated by the increasing multiculturalism of the United States, the involvement of the United States in the affairs of nations all over the world, and a global women's movement in which localized efforts to improve the status of women are being supported by women in other countries.

Sexual violence targets women because they are women. In a society that devalues and restricts women, violence functions as a reinforcer of the status quo that limits women's power and maintains their dependence on men. Violence against women of color is dehumanizing racism and demoralizes and weakens communities of color.

PRACTICE ISSUES FOR THE 21ST CENTURY
Previous Social Work Response

Feminist social workers in the 1970s and 1980s participated in the development of strategies to deal with violence against women. Social workers joined activists in community organizing to change public attitudes and to improve community responsiveness to women survivors of violence. The feminist social workers developed protocols for sensitive treatment of victims by police officers and health, social services, and mental health agencies. Social workers joined psychologists and health care professionals to identify patterns of response to sexual victimization, such as posttraumatic stress disorder, rape trauma syndrome, and battered woman syndrome, and to implement models for supportive and empowering interventions with survivors. Social workers supported the growth of self-help movements for survivors. In addition, social workers developed models for prevention education and for psychoeducational interventions with men who are violent toward women to resocialize them regarding gender-role expectations and attitudes that sanction violence against women and girls.

As the end of the 20th century approaches, we are challenged by new and unresolved issues in dealing with violence against women and we are challenged by a backlash against feminism. This chapter addresses the implications of these issues for social work practice.

Cross-Cultural Perspectives on Violence against Women

The United States is increasingly multicultural, and responses to violence against women take place in a cultural context. Social workers have an important role to play in developing culturally sensitive approaches to intervention both with survivors and with perpetrators of violence against women.

Although there are many aspects of different cultures that are antithetical to violence against women (for example, the emphasis in Asian cultures on harmony and good relations at home), the possibility of violence increases with certain characteristics of a culture (Levinson, 1989; Ogawa, 1990). Levinson's (1989) cross-cultural study of 90 small and peasant societies found that the relationship between wife beating and inequality was not clear except in areas of economic and family domain. Where female work groups were absent, where men controlled distribution of the fruits of family labor, where women could not acquire independent wealth, where men owned the dwelling, and where men had the real power in the household, victimization was more likely. Levinson noted that "men control the wealth, have the final say in household decision-making, and are able to prevent their wives from escaping from marriage through divorce" (p. 73).

Sanday (1981) identified "rape-prone" societies in her cross-cultural study of 156 societies from a representative sample of the world's well-known and well-described societies. She found positive correlations with rape to be intensity of interpersonal violence, the presence of an ideology that encourages men to be tough and aggressive, frequent or endemic warfare, low female power and authority, and greater sexual separation. This configuration evolves in societies faced with depleting food resources, migration, or other factors that contribute to a dependence on destructive capacities rather than fertility.

She concluded that "rape is part of a broader struggle for control in the face of difficult circumstances. Where men are in harmony with their environment, rape is usually absent. . . . Men who are conditioned to respect the female virtues of growth and the sacredness of life do not violate women" (Sanday, 1981, p. 25).

Social change and environmental stresses seem to have an impact on levels of sexual violence toward women. Because norms regarding women's status and sexuality are highly resistant to change, women are still seen as acceptable targets of violence in the midst of rapid social change in gender-role expectations (White & Sorenson,

1992). Pressures on immigrant families, such as imbalances in traditional roles required for survival, test former customs and practices for two or three generations. "It may in fact be the collision of social and cultural values which has more to do with funneling frustrations and anger toward the incidence of domestic violence than deficits of traditional mores" (Ogawa, 1990, p. 69). Domestic violence may be culturally related in that it becomes attached to elements of the culture as a symptom of stresses and maladaptations (and is not restricted to the poor) (Ogawa, 1990).

Prejudices and stereotypes of ethnic minority cultures become "false cultures" as the dominant majority culture redefines characteristics of the minority culture to justify excess and abuse and to destroy the culture itself (Ogawa, 1990). For example, a teacher told me that her school does not bother to intervene in cases of family violence because abuse is "part of the Latino culture." Campbell (1992) observed the following:

> *Cultural evidence does not indicate whether this individual act [of wife beating] arose out of patriarchal, behavioral, ethnological or psychological imperatives, but it does indicate difference in the society's response to the beating. . . . Sexual jealousy and failure to adhere to prescribed female role behavior are close to universal issues whether they stem from parental certainty concerns or patriarchy. However, community acceptance of these reasons (or excuses) for violence against wives varies. (p. 23)*

Moreover, cultural differences in perceptions of violence influence the effects of sexual victimization on the victim. The victim's reactions and the way she seeks help may vary significantly. In addition, experiences with violence are complicated by racism and discrimination.

Differences in history and cultural values as well as stereotypes about who meets the social criteria to be a "real" victim affect responses to victimization. Although the posttraumatic stress disorder responses to rape are similar for all women, ethnic group members may perceive rape differently than others. According to research by Wyatt (1992), African American women tend to perceive rape as a likely rather than an unlikely occurrence in their lives based on hearing the myth that they are likely to be victims of sexual violence. African American women are less likely to report rape than Anglo American women because they do not perceive their experiences as "real rape." Their credibility is never established as firmly as for white women; racial discrimination pervades the identification of cases that can be successfully prosecuted (Wyatt, 1992).

Torres's (1987) study of Hispanic American and Anglo American women residing in shelters for battered women found no significant differences in severity and frequency of abuse but did find differences in perceptions of abuse. The Hispanic women did not consider verbal abuse and failure to provide adequate food and shelter as abuse and showed more tolerance for acts considered to be "emotional." Hispanic women reported that they stayed in the relationship because of their children and threats to family members. Anglo women stayed because of love for their abuser and a lack of alternatives to living with their abuser.

Perceptions of violence also are affected by ways in which women are viewed in various cultures. For example, although self-blame is typical of battered women of every culture, self-blame and shame are "especially potent force[s] with Asian/Pacific women because of cultural beliefs that dysfunction [battering or rape] results from immoral behavior" (Crites, 1991, p. 10), and because their status as women gives them little cause to believe that they have a right to be treated with respect and dignity by men.

The threat of violence affects virtually all women, and to defend herself from this devastating awareness, a woman may think herself safe by stereotyping certain "other" women as likely victims. Wife beating and sexual violence are psychologically, physically, and spiritually damaging to all victims. There are important variations in the ways in which the damage is experienced based on differences in culture and history. To the extent that any culture tolerates violence against women, either historically or based on current cultural stresses, cultural norms must be challenged as well as understood.

DEPATHOLOGIZING VICTIMIZATION

Researchers and mental health professionals have recognized the relevance of the traumas of sexual assault, incest, battering, and sexual harassment to symptoms of mental illness (Asher, 1988; Kilpatrick, Veronen, & Best, 1984; Koss & Harvey, 1991; Saunders, Villeponteaux, Lipovsky, Kilpatrick, & Veronen, 1992; Walker, 1984). Before the late 1970s, assessment and intervention often overlooked the patterns of response to these traumatic experiences. Either women did not speak of these experiences or practitioners failed to consider them relevant (Abarbanel, 1976; Davis 1987; Schuyler, 1976).

Awareness of the nature of women's experiences with violence, and of how common they are, spawned the growth of self-help, mutual support, and crisis-oriented programs to help women confront the violence in their lives.

However, feminists and mental health practitioners have disagreed on

the issue of whether it is useful to view socially created problems arising from power differentials as abnormal, with feminists saying no and mental health practitioners answering yes. . . . Rather than label battering as pathology or a family systems failure, [feminists] have challenged mental health practitioners to assume that violence against women, like that directed toward children, is behavior approved of and sanctioned in many parts of the culture. Extreme cases in which women are mutilated by psychotic men are only one end of a continuum of violent behavior, the more moderate forms of which are viewed as normal. (Schechter, 1982, p. 215)

This disagreement continues and has been further exacerbated during the 1990s by an increasing tendency to pathologize women, which has been influenced by the backlash against feminism and by co-optation of "women's problems" by the medical system. Medical models treat female victims as helpless, dependent, and sick and extend the experience of powerlessness inherent in the victimization itself. Social work participation in medical treatment models for women who are victims of sexual, family, and relationship violence has increased in the 1990s because more social workers are employed by medical systems, and medical systems now diagnose and treat women who have experienced violence.

Although it has been recognized that the traumatic impact of violence against women causes symptoms of mental illness, it is likely that these symptoms are misdiagnosed as character disorders. Gender-biased diagnostic systems used by social workers, such as the *Diagnostic and Statistical Manual of Mental Disorders, Third Edition– Revised* (DSM-III-R) (American Psychiatric Association, 1987), categorize as character disorders (such as dependent personality disorder, borderline personality disorder, or the new self-defeating personality disorder) sets of symptoms that are typical reactions to battering or sexual abuse. These diagnoses can have damaging effects on women, who are blamed for their victimization (in treatment and in court), treated as sick and incurable rather than as coping with traumatic situations, and punished for fulfilling feminine roles prized by their families and their cultures.

Masochistic Personality Disorder

By the 1970s, "the notion of an innate feminine masochism seemed a quaint relic" of the Victorian era (Faludi, 1991, p. 356). In 1991

Wetzel said that masochistic personality disorder was "a concept that has been discredited for some years as a pejorative, discriminatory term that had been applied mainly to women and other subordinate groups" (p. 16). In 1985, in what can only be explained as an outgrowth of anger over women's autonomy and feminism, masochistic personality disorder was introduced as a "new" disorder to be included in the DSM-III-R (Symonds, 1986). The criteria consisted of characteristics of "ideal femininity" and behaviors that also are typical of posttraumatic stress responses to wife beating. Studies of battered women have consistently found no evidence of childhood-developed personality disorders (Rosewater, 1985). Despite evidence that this diagnostic category is invalid, it was kept in the appendix to the DSM-III-R, its name was changed to self-defeating personality disorder, and it was given a code number (not usually done with controversial categories). This diagnosis has been removed from the 1994 edition of the manual (American Psychiatric Association, 1994).

Similar criticisms have been directed at the use of the diagnosis of borderline personality disorder. Recent research indicates that many of the symptoms that are criteria for a diagnosis of borderline personality disorder represent strategies any person would use to survive a situation in which he or she was being terrorized and victimized (Graham & Rawlings, 1991; Rosewater, 1985). The hostage syndrome or the Stockholm syndrome refers to the phenomenon of bonding to one's captor, batterer, or rapist as a survival strategy. Graham and Rawlings (1987) identified four outcomes of prolonged Stockholm syndrome: (1) splitting, (2) intense push–pull dynamics in relationships to others, (3) displaced anger, and (4) lack of sense of self. They later noted the similarity to borderline personality disorder and indicated that posttraumatic reactions to terrorization experienced from battering (or sexual assault) can appear to be borderline personality disorder.

Another major concern about character disorder diagnosis and treatment for women stems from the fact that violence against women is so widespread. Large numbers of women have been victims of domestic violence, acquaintance rape, sexual assault, childhood sexual molestation, or sexual harassment (S. J. Kaplan, 1991; Kilpatrick, Saunders, Veronen, Best, & Von, 1987; Koss, Gidycz, & Wisniewski, 1987). These women are not masochistic and do not have personality disorders. If violence against women is a mainstream experience affecting a majority of women, then 21st-century social work strategies to deal with it must address this violence as a normative cultural phenomenon rather than as idiosyncratic pathology.

Another version of the psychiatric self-defeating personality disorder is the "codependency movement," which engages women in the process of examining what they do to make men treat them badly. Both clinicians and the recovery movement tend to treat women for lifelong, incurable diseases (Tavris, 1992). Popular psychology books and recovery groups have adopted the useful concept of the enabler (Greenleaf, 1981; Paolino & McCrady, 1977) and misapply it to suggest that women are to be blamed for their victimization by men, which absolves males of responsibility for their behavior. Evidence of a backlash against feminism lies in attacks on women for being too independent or, conversely, for loving "too much" (Faludi, 1991; Schechter, 1982; Tavris, 1992; Walters, 1990; Wetzel, 1991). There is no similar focus on the problem of "men who treat women badly" nor are there diagnoses related to character disorders for male independence or lack of empathy, particularly toward women (M. Kaplan, 1983).

Other aspects of gender-based maltreatment of women by mental health systems are of concern as well. Women who are "heavy users" of inpatient psychiatric units are often medicated for symptoms without discovery of their histories of physical and sexual abuse (Rose, Peabody, & Stratigeas, 1991). A recent trend toward developing specialized hospital units to treat "disorders" such as reactions to sexual abuse may change this practice. However, this trend may be influenced by the potential of hospitals to receive insurance reimbursement for these new disorders. Although some women can benefit from the environment of a hospital program when symptoms make it impossible to function, there is an alarming trend to label women as sick and incurable and to promote medical treatments that isolate them, keeping them from dealing with the social context of their experiences. Whereas the focus and growth of medical treatment for victims have increased, treatment systems for individual perpetrators of violence against women have been absent.

Intervention with Perpetrators

Treatment for batterers and rapists has been controversial, and feminist social workers in the 21st century may influence future directions in this area. There is no real consensus regarding what causes violent behavior. However, feminist research indicates that power differentials, the need to control women, anger toward women, and patterns of violence learned during childhood, accompanied by social sanctions and a perception of women as "natural" victims, are important contributing factors (Burt, 1980; Groth, 1979; Malamuth, 1986; Pence & Paymar, 1990; Straus, 1977).

A priority for feminists in addressing violence against women has been to change attitudes toward violence against women. These efforts have been essential to overcoming the invisibility and tolerance of violence against women and to confronting social attitudes that blame women for their victimization. Although it is essential to continue these efforts, it is also essential to increase attention on the male perpetrators. Media coverage, educational efforts, and various intervention systems have already begun to refocus on the problem of the rapist, the batterer, and the molester, as opposed to seeing the victim as the problem. Victims empowered to see themselves as survivors must direct attention beyond survival to the real problem: Our social system produces large numbers of rapists, batterers, and molesters.

Rapists and batterers may psychologically test without pathology, but they clearly have a problem with aggressiveness toward women. In other words, they tend to fall within a range of behavior that is considered normal for men. Society must redefine what normal masculinity is so that violent behavior toward women is seen as pathological and unacceptable. This change does not require categorization of violent behavior as a medically diagnosable pattern or disease but as behavior for which the perpetrator is held responsible. For example, young men in high school are generally ignored when they are seen pushing or hitting their girlfriends and are often surprised when accused of date rape. Their concepts of normal masculinity are shaken when confronted with the criminality of their behavior (Levy, 1991).

Massive education, resocialization, and social support are needed for the redefinition of masculinity to preclude violence, particularly as it is directed against women. Mental health practitioners must rigorously recognize and intervene when early signs of violent behavior manifest. Collaboration between criminal justice and mental health systems should be established to effectively provide treatment for perpetrators.

Lesbian Batterers

Feminists have been challenged by the recent recognition that women as well as men can be violent and that domestic violence takes place in same-sex relationships at about the same rate as in heterosexual relationships (Brand & Kidd, 1986). Although the overwhelming majority of sex crimes are committed by heterosexual males, the incidence of interpersonal violence committed by females cannot be ignored. A new challenge for the 21st century is to expand the understanding of the complex factors contributing to interpersonal violence so that violence and abuse committed by women are not ignored and people who are victimized in these situations are not denied a supportive response by feminists or community services. The need to address these complex factors is made more challenging by the backlash against feminism, which depicts battering in gay male and lesbian relationships as proof that feminists have been unfair in seeing gender-role socialization and power differences between men and women as causes of violence against women.

The imposition of power and control is a major motivating factor for lesbian as well as heterosexual male batterers (Carlson, 1992; Hart, 1986). This need for control may be caused by a combination of factors, especially by a need to compensate for actual or perceived lack of power (Carlson, 1992) or by overdependency (Renzetti, 1992). Issues of power and control as they arise in relationships are influenced by social norms that promulgate relationship models based on dominance and submission. Although associated with masculinity and femininity, these norms are associated with social relationships regardless of gender or ethnicity within patriarchal, capitalistic, and socially stressed societies (Carlson, 1992; Walker, 1992).

IMPLICATIONS FOR SOCIAL WORK PRACTICE
Social work intervention in the 21st century must be guided by a definition of rape and battering as hate crimes against women, rather than seeing them exclusively as acts by "a sick person." To be consistent with feminist principles, intervention must be implemented in a sociohistorical context that takes into account the interplay between sexism and racism and the universality as well as the diversity of women's experiences with violence. Specific strategies to address issues of ethnic diversity, depathologizing victimization, and intervention with perpetrators are recommended.

Cultural Diversity
On the basis of cultural variations in women's perceptions of violence against them, it is recommended that social workers in any setting use these culturally sensitive practices:

- acquire cultural, social, and ethnic information and history
- use cultural strengths for client empowerment
- challenge aspects of client's culture that might interfere with safety, rights, equality, or self-esteem
- do not assume that a client's behavior or feelings are the same as those expected by cultural stereotypes

- approach violence as an outcome of social disorder

- help clients understand the social context in which violence against women takes place

- design programs using input and leadership from the cultural group members themselves. (Boyd, 1990; Fulani, 1987; Ho, 1990; Ogawa, 1990)

As Campbell (1992) indicated by virtue of her cultural analysis, "societal structures and anticipatory community mechanisms can overcome individual propensities to violence" (p. 23).

DEPATHOLOGIZING WOMEN'S VICTIMIZATION

To continue to counter the trend toward pathologizing women who are victims of violence, it is recommended that social workers in the 21st century use empowerment and social change models for intervention that depathologize survivors' symptoms of distress and advocate for removal of gender bias in diagnosis. The recognition that violence against women may be a mainstream experience must be accounted for within intervention models. Consciousness-raising groups for men and for women should be revived and expanded to appreciate culturally diverse experiences of being male or female (Kamen, 1991). Mental health intervention must include classic feminist consciousness-raising. Social therapy, a group therapy approach that strengthens a sense of community by addressing cultural, historical, social, and emotional dimensions of a client's experiences, also is recommended (Fulani, 1987). Models for mental health intervention that do not pathologize women's experiences include psychosocial, nonstigmatizing assessment; non-gender-biased, cross-culturally relevant therapy; self-help and mutual support groups; and feminist therapy (NiCarthy, Merriam, & Coffman, 1984; Rosewater & Walker, 1985; Walker, 1992; Wetzel, 1991).

Diagnosis and treatment for delayed or acute posttraumatic stress disorder to deal with symptoms of trauma is recommended rather than erroneously labeling character disorders. Symptoms should be recognized as coping strategies or reactions to loss. Treatment should be experientially focused and empowering, encourage restoration of mastery following experiences that deprive one of a sense of power and security, and support strengths used in coping with untenable situations.

Intervention with Perpetrators

A comprehensive system of policies and practices that reflect social change regarding tolerance for violence against women is needed to effectively intervene with perpetrators. Laws must be enforced so that there are clear consequences to acts of violence against women. Social workers in health, mental health, protective services, and criminal justice settings can work closely with police officers and the courts to hold rapists, batterers, sexual harassers, and molesters equally accountable for their behavior. There is no justice for white women or for women of color if there is a double standard of justice in which men of color are held more accountable than white men. Mandatory arrest policies can often make a difference if perpetrators are jailed, particularly if there is concurrent social work or mental health intervention (Adams, 1988; personal communication with A. LaViolette, therapist, Alternatives to Violence, Long Beach, California, April 8, 1992; Sherman & Berk, 1984).

Programs in the 21st century can build on current program models for teaching children and adolescents skills for healthy relationships such as communication, problem solving, managing anger, assertiveness, mutual respect, flexibility and nonstereotyping of gender roles, empathy, stress management, conflict resolution, acceptance of the variations of human sexuality, and responsible and respectful sexuality (Levy, 1984, 1991). School policies can reflect consistent and absolute intolerance for verbal abuse or physical violence, including support of prohibitions against violence within families or intimate relationships. Schools can become examples of nonviolent social environments by creating clear policies regarding the consequences of verbally or physically violent behavior as well as supporting alternatives for resolving conflict. Innovative program models have been created but not widely developed or disseminated (McKenna, 1985; Powell, 1991; Sousa, 1991).

Feminists who believe that rapists and batterers can control and change their behavior have developed psychoeducational group counseling models to change these men's relationships with women. Most programs emphasize the following nine points: (1) the perpetrator's responsibility for and ability to control violent behavior; (2) awareness of the seriousness, danger, and consequences of violent behavior; (3) awareness of one's motivation (and sense of entitlement) to dominate and control women as socially sanctioned, and sometimes as an outgrowth of feelings of powerlessness displaced onto women; (4) anger management techniques; (5) empathy with women; (6) relationship skills, such as communication, assertiveness, and problem solving; (7) stress-reduction skills; (8) development of social support; and (9) dealing with substance abuse. Psychoeducational groups can be effective with men who have recognized their tendency to be violent and are motivated to change. These groups encourage participants to question their perspectives, beliefs, and values as well as to use behavioral techniques for managing feelings and behavior (Adams, 1988; personal communication with A. LaViolette, therapist, Alternatives to Violence, Long Beach, California, April 8, 1992; Pence & Paymar, 1990; Sonkin, Martin, & Walker, 1985).

Similar program models have been developed for lesbian and gay male batterers (Island & Letellier, 1991; Minnesota Coalition for Battered Women, 1990). Additional outreach efforts and program components are needed with lesbians and gay men to overcome the invisibility and discrimination they experience. It is recommended that social workers provide services to lesbians and gay men that are affirming and accessible to them.

A feminist approach to group work with perpetrators of violence against women must carefully prevent participants from interpreting social support by the group as justification for violence. Empathy and understanding is important; however, the use of violence is never justified or condoned. Programs must include the perspective of victims and survivors to prevent the objectification of women (Adams, 1988; Shepard, 1991). Effective group models include formerly battered or raped women who lead groups or speak at group meetings. Perpetrators are not reliable sources of information regarding their own behavior, so it is important to include the women in their lives for feedback. Coordination among group leaders, individual clinicians, and the criminal justice system is essential. Although such program models have already been developed and implemented in the United States, it is recommended that feminist social workers expand these to reach more people; generate other models to fill the gaps in effective intervention with perpetrators; address the need for comprehensive, coordinated, widespread programs that prioritize the elimination of violence against women; and advocate for a feminist theoretical base for further program development.

CONCLUSION

Feminist social work practice that aims to eliminate violence against women must address the problem as a violation of human rights. Social power dynamics between oppressor and oppressed, which are associated with sexism, racism, classism, and heterosexism, create a context that supports victimization. Consequently, it is crucial that there be ongoing advocacy for acceptance of diversity and elimination of discrimination against women. Community programs that support nonviolence and egalitarian relationships must be undertaken with serious social sanctions against violence against women.

Perpetrators must be held responsible for violating those sanctions, and women must be helped to see that they have a right to be treated with respect and dignity by men.

Violence against women is a complex social problem, and social work perspectives are influenced by a backlash against feminism and by subtle new forms of victim blame, such as the codependency movement and trends toward pathologizing the victim. Sexual violence is not always perpetrated by men against women, which indicates that the sexist social context cannot be isolated from other aspects of social power dynamics to explain the prevalence of violence against women.

Social workers in clinical and community practice can help prevent violence against women by

- encouraging partnership rather than dominance and subordination in relationships
- redefining masculinity and femininity
- recognizing power dynamics and violence against women as a socially sanctioned abuse of power
- recognizing victims' strengths rather than pathologizing their responses to violence
- valuing the diversity of women's experiences
- seeking solutions through community and social change as well as through individual change.

By making these principles a priority, the social work profession can contribute to a nonviolent 21st century.

REFERENCES

Abarbanel, G. (1976). Helping victims of rape. *Social Work, 21,* 478–482.

Adams, D. (1988). Treatment models of men who batter: A profeminist analysis. In K. Yllo & M. Bograd (Eds.), *Feminist perspectives on wife abuse* (pp. 176–199). Newbury Park, CA: Sage Publications.

American Psychiatric Association. (1987). *Diagnostic and statistical manual of mental disorders* (3rd ed., rev.). Washington, DC: Author.

American Psychiatric Association. (1994). *Diagnostic and statistical manual of mental disorders* (4th ed.). Washington, DC: Author.

Asher, S. (1988). The effects of childhood sexual abuse: A review of the issues and evidence. In L. Walker (Ed.), *Handbook on sexual abuse of children* (pp. 3–18). New York: Springer.

Boyd, J. (1990). Ethnic and cultural diversity: Keys to power. *Women and Therapy, 9*(1/2), 151–167.

Brand, P., & Kidd, A. (1986). Frequency of physical aggression in heterosexual and female homosexual dyads. *Psychological Reports, 59,* 1307–1313.

Bunch, C. (1991). Recognizing women's rights as human rights. *Response, 13*(4), 13–16.

Burt, M. (1980). Cultural myths and supports for rape. *Journal of Personality and Social Psychology, 15,* 217–230.

Campbell, J. (1992). Prevention of wife battering: Insights from cultural analysis. *Response, 14*(3), 18–24.

Carlson, B. (1992). Questioning the party line on family violence. *Affilia, 7*(2), 94–110.

Crites, L. (1991). Cross-cultural counseling in wife beating cases. *Response, 13*(4), 8–12.

Davis, L. (1987). Battered women: The transformation of a social problem. *Social Work, 32,* 306–311.

Faludi, S. (1991). *Backlash: The undeclared war against American women.* New York: Crown.

Federal Bureau of Investigation. (1988). *Uniform crime reports.* Washington, DC: U.S. Government Printing Office.

Fulani, L. (1987). Poor women of color do great therapy. *Women and Therapy, 6*(4), 111–120.

Graham, D., & Rawlings, E. (1987) Psychological mechanisms, psychodynamics, and indicators. In D. Graham (Ed.), *Loving to survive: Men and women as hostages.* Unpublished manuscript.

Graham, D., & Rawlings, E. (1991). Bonding with abusive dating partners: Dynamics of Stockholm syndrome. In B. Levy (Ed.), *Dating violence: Young women in danger* (pp. 119–135). Seattle: Seal Press.

Greenleaf, J. (1981, April). *Co-alcoholic, para-alcoholic: Who's who and what's the difference?* Paper presented at the National Council on Alcoholism Annual Alcoholism Forum, New Orleans.

Groth, N. (1979). *Men who rape: The psychology of the offender.* New York: Plenum Press.

Hart, B. (1986). Lesbian battering: An examination. In K. Lobel (Ed.), *Naming the violence: Speaking out about lesbian battering* (pp. 173–189). Seattle: Seal Press.

Heise, L. (1989). International dimensions of violence against women. *Response, 12*(1), 3–11.

Ho, C. (1990). Analysis of domestic violence in Asian American communities. *Women and Therapy, 9*(1/2), 129–150.

Island, D., & Letellier, P. (1991). *Men who beat the men who love them.* New York: Haworth Press.

Kamen, P. (1991). *Feminist fatale.* New York: Donald Fine.

Kaplan, M. (1983, July). A woman's view of DSM-III. *American Psychologist, 38,* 786–792.

Kaplan, S. J. (1991). Consequences of sexual harassment in the workplace. *Affilia, 6*(3), 50–65.

Kilpatrick, D., Saunders, B., Veronen, L., Best, C., & Von, J. (1987). Criminal victimization: Lifetime prevalence, reporting to police and psychological impact. *Crime and Delinquency, 33,* 479–489.

Kilpatrick, D., Veronen, L., & Best, C. (1984). Factors predicting psychological distress among rape victims. In C. R. Figley (Ed.), *Trauma and its wake: The study and treatment of post-traumatic stress disorder* (pp. 113–141). New York: Brunner/Mazel.

Koss, M., Gidycz, C., & Wisniewski, N. (1987). The scope of rape: Incidence and prevalence of sexual aggression and victimization in a national sample of higher education students. *Journal of Consulting and Clinical Psychology, 55,* 162–170.

Koss, M., & Harvey, M. (1991). *The rape victim: Clinical and community interventions.* Newbury Park, CA; Sage Publications.

Levinson, D. (1989). *Family violence in cross-cultural perspectives.* Newbury Park, CA: Sage Publications.

Levy, B. (1984). *Skills for violence-free relationships.* (Available from the Southern California Coalition for Battered Women, P.O. Box 5036, Santa Monica, CA 90405)

Levy, B. (1991). *Dating violence: Young women in danger.* Seattle, WA: Seal Press.

Malamuth, N. (1986). Predictors of naturalistic sexual aggression. *Journal of Personality and Social Psychology, 50,* 953–962.

McKenna, G. (1985). *Acceptance speech*. Los Angeles Commission on Assaults Against Women Humanitarian Awards.

Minnesota Coalition for Battered Women. (1990). *Confronting lesbian battering: A manual for the battered women's movement*. (Available from Minnesota Coalition for Battered Women, 570 Asbury Street, No. 210, St. Paul, MN 55104)

NiCarthy, G., Merriam, K., & Coffman, S. (1984). *Talking it out: A guide to groups for abused women*. Seattle: Seal Press.

Ogawa, B. (1990). *The color of justice*. Sacramento, CA: Office of Criminal Justice Planning.

Paolino, T. J., Jr., & McCrady, B. S. (1977). *The alcoholic marriage: Alternative perspectives*. New York: Grune & Stratton.

Pence, E., & Paymar, M. (1990). *Power and control: Tactics of men who batter*. (Available from Minnesota Program Development, 206 West 4th Street, Duluth, MN 55806)

Powell, C. (1991). Dealing with dating violence in schools. In B. Levy (Ed.), *Dating violence* (pp. 279–283). Seattle: Seal Press.

Renzetti, C. (1992). *Violent betrayal: Partner abuse in lesbian relationships*. Newbury Park, CA: Sage Publications.

Rose, S., Peabody, C., & Stratigeas, B. (1991). Responding to hidden abuse: A role for social work in reforming mental health systems. *Social Work, 36*, 408–413.

Rosewater, L. (1985). Schizophrenic, borderline, or battered? In L. Rosewater & L. Walker (Eds.), *Handbook of feminist therapy* (pp. 215–225). New York: Springer.

Rosewater, L., & Walker, L. (1985). *Handbook of feminist therapy*. New York: Springer.

Sanday, P. (1981). The socio-cultural context of rape: A cross-cultural study. *Journal of Social Issues, 37*(4), 5–27.

Saunders, B., Villeponteaux, L., Lipovsky, J., Kilpatrick, D., & Veronen, L. (1992). Child sexual assault as a risk factor for mental disorders among women. *Journal of Interpersonal Violence, 7*(2), 189–204.

Schechter, S. (1982). *Women and male violence*. Boston: South End Press.

Schuyler, M. (1976). Battered wives: An emerging social problem. *Social Work, 21*, 488–491.

Shepard, M. (1991). Feminist practice principles for social work intervention in wife abuse. *Affilia, 6*(2), 87–93.

Sherman, L. W., & Berk, R. A. (1984). The specific deterrent effects of arrest for domestic assault. *American Sociological Review, 49,* 261–272.

Sonkin, D., Martin, D., & Walker, L. (1985). *The male batterer: A treatment approach.* New York: Springer.

Sousa, C. (1991). The dating violence intervention project. In B. Levy (Ed.), *Dating violence* (pp. 223–231). Seattle: Seal Press.

Straus, M. (1977). A sociological perspective on the prevention and treatment of wifebeating. In M. Roy (Ed.), *Battered women: A psychosociological study of domestic violence* (pp. 194–239). New York: Van Nostrand Reinhold.

Symonds, A. (Ed.). (1986, January). A step backwards for women? [Special issue]. *News for Women in Psychiatry, 4*(2).

Tavris, C. (1992). *The mismeasure of women.* New York: Simon & Schuster.

Torres, S. (1987). Hispanic-American battered women: Why consider cultural differences? *Response, 10*(3), 20–21.

U.S. Department of Justice, Bureau of Justice Statistics. (1986). *Crime statistics.* Washington, DC: Author.

U.S. Senate Committee on the Judiciary. (1992). Violence against women: The increase of rape in America 1990. *Response, 14*(2), 20–23.

Walker, L. (1984). *The battered woman syndrome.* New York: Springer.

Walker, L. (1992, February). *Feminist psychology and violence against women.* Paper presented at the National Conference of the Association for Women in Psychology, Long Beach, CA.

Walters, M. (1990, July/August). The codependent Cinderella who loves too much. . . fights back. *Networker,* pp. 60–65.

Wetzel, J. (1991). Universal mental health classification systems: Reclaiming women's experience. *Affilia, 6*(3), 8–31.

White, J., & Sorenson, S. (1992). Sociocultural view of sexual assault. *Journal of Social Issues, 48*(1), 187–195.

Wyatt, G. (1992). The sociocultural context of African American and white American women's rape. *Journal of Social Issues, 48*(1), 77–91.

18

A Feminist Life Span Perspective on Aging

Colette Browne

ike other industrialized nations, the population of the United States is aging. Nearly 33 million Americans were age 65 or older in 1990, and projections estimate that by the year 2025 this population will double in size to reach 66 million (American Association of Retired Persons [AARP], 1993). A critical variable in the study of aging and human development is gender (Bohan, 1993). This is especially true among older adults, the majority of whom are female. In 1992 there were 19.2 million older women and 13 million older men, or a ratio of 148 women for every 100 men (AARP, 1993). The sex ratio favoring women increases with age so that by the time adults are in their mid-eighties, there are nearly 100 women to every 42 men (U.S. Bureau of the Census, 1993c). By 2010 nearly half of all adult women will be at least 50 years of age (Allen, 1993a). Yet despite these unprecedented demographic developments and the fact that the needs of elders are often the needs of women (Forman, 1985; Hess, 1985; Markson, 1983), feminists were slow to address the concerns of older women (Gould, 1989; Hartman, 1990; Lewis & Butler, 1972; Rodeheaver, 1987). More recently, important contributions by feminist (Friedan, 1993; Greer, 1991; Steinem, 1992) and gerontological (Allen & Pifer, 1993; England, 1990; Gonyea, 1994; Hess, 1990; Hooyman & Kiyak, 1993; Quadagno & Harrington Meyer, 1990; Turner & Troll, 1994) scholars have critically broadened society's perspective on gender issues with an increased focus on the needs, opportunities, and challenges faced by midlife and older women in the United States. However, it can be argued that feminist contributions to gerontological literature, and gerontological contributions to feminist literature, remain in a state of infancy despite their great potential for improving women's lives.

The oppression of women has been the topic of serious debate by feminist scholars for more than 30 years. Feminists define gender as a sociocultural construct shaped by social structure and public policy (Hess, 1990). Gender inequality throughout the life cycle often results in women entering old age with far fewer resources than men. Feminists have focused much of their critique on understanding the relationships among gender, power, and privilege. Feminists also have turned their attention to how the experiences of ethnic, lesbian, never-married, and other marginalized women make them both similar and dissimilar to one another and diversity's subsequent challenge to feminist solidarity (Anzaldua, 1981; Caraway, 1991; hooks, 1984; Lorde, 1984). Sex may be biological but gender, like race and class, is a hierarchical system constructed by society, and not all women face the same challenges (because of the influences of racism, classism, and all other forms of oppression). As feminist legal scholar MacKinnon (1989) explained, "To look for the place of gender in everything [should not] reduce everything to gender" (p. xi).

Recent studies on women and aging have documented women's greater longevity compared with men (Verbrugge, 1989) and the fact that they generally end their years with stronger social supports and friendships than do men (Lewittes, 1989; Reinhardt & Fisher, 1989). However, women also face a number of problems throughout their lives that have profound consequences with each advancing year: the dual labor market; unmet social, economic, and health needs; physical and emotional assault; and unpaid caregiving duties (Abramovitz, 1992; Browne, 1994; Hooyman & Kiyak, 1993; Kingson & O'Grady-LeShane, 1993). Age discrimination, bias in pensions, demeaned physical appearance, and other gender inequalities exacerbate many women's problems as they age, leaving them vulnerable and financially, physically, and socially at risk (Davis, Grant, & Rowland, 1990; Hess, 1985, 1990; Minkler & Stone, 1985; Older Women's League, 1990). Projections into the 21st century suggest that the economic and health concerns of aging women (Hess, 1990; O'Grady-LeShane, 1990; Ozawa, 1993), and particularly older women of color (Axinn, 1989; Dressel, 1988; Jackson, 1985; Taeuber & Allen, 1993), will only increase, in part because of policies that continue to neglect the needs, choices, and realities of women's experiences.

This chapter begins with a description of the current and projected status of older women in America. First, the consequences for women of a lifetime of inequalities are presented, with a focus on income, caregiving, and health. Second, a feminist life span perspective on aging is introduced as a strategy that contributes to an analysis of women's problems within the context of social, economic, and political forces. Such a perspective makes women's diversity central to the discussion and acknowledges the interlocking of women's problems both with one another and with each stage in the life cycle (Anderson & Collins, 1992). Aging is thus viewed as a cumulative experience, with women's inequalities following them as they age, and as an experience shaped by gender, race, class, and other oppressions. Finally, this chapter offers a beginning critique of current and proposed social welfare strategies and suggests politically feasible policy directions applicable to social work practice.

LIFE STATUS OF OLDER WOMEN
Income
Women's retirement income is most often a result of wages, either based on their own work history or that of a spouse. This income reflects numerous gender-based experiences women face throughout their lives, including job discrimination and segregation; limited earnings, entitlements, and other supports in home and work life; inconsistent work patterns; the absence of social security or private pension credit for unpaid child and elder caregiving responsibilities; and age discrimination in employment, all of which lead to inadequate social security benefits (Davis et al., 1990; Moon, 1990). Scholars have noted that it is not just that poor young women grow into poor women, but that middle-aged women become poor in later life as a result of divorce, job segregation and discrimination, and years of unpaid caregiving duties (Quadagno & Harrington Meyer, 1990). This statement does not dispute the fact that some women have benefited from their role as dependent and that some older women are financially secure. However, the overall picture of older women's economic status is disheartening. Women are disproportionately represented among poor and near-poor people.

Older women are poorer than older men. The poverty rate for all elderly people is 15 percent—double that of the under-65 population. Although women constitute 58 percent of elders, they account for 74 percent of the poor aged (Taeuber & Allen, 1993). Moreover, nearly one-third of all older women had incomes within 150 percent of the poverty line (Malveaux, 1993), and 74 percent of the beneficiaries for old age assistance under the Supplemental Security Income (SSI) program are women (Taeuber & Allen, 1993). Poverty affects women for a number of interconnected reasons.

Marital status is a great determinant of poverty for women because it often is the main eligibility criteria for social security and pension benefits. In 1990 most older men were married and most older women were not. Nearly half of all widowed and divorced women 65 or older had an income below $7,500 (U.S. Bureau of the Census, 1991). Living arrangements, like marital status, also are related to income. Among elderly people who live alone, 77 percent are women, usually widows (U.S. House Select Committee on Aging, 1989), who are six times more likely to be poor than their male counterparts (Taeuber & Allen, 1993). Forecasts for the 21st century predict that unmarried women, primarily the oldest widows, will continue to be at financial risk compared with men and married couples. Of the unmarried women who receive pensions, half will receive less than $1,200 annually, compared with $4,000 annually for men (Ozawa, 1993).

Race is another determinant of poverty among older women. Throughout their lives women of color tend to be poorer than white women. The multiple influences of race, class, gender, and age are inextricably linked in American society and leave their mark on women's potential for economic survival in later life (Dressel, 1988; Gould, 1989; Taeuber & Allen, 1993). Unlike white women, a history of low earnings among black women appears to be more a function of poverty than is marital status (Malveaux, 1993). Although black women constitute 5 percent of the elderly population, they account for 16 percent of poor elders (U.S. Bureau of the Census, 1991). Alarmingly, among black elderly women living alone, 63 percent of those age 75 and older are poor (AARP, 1993). The poverty rate of Hispanic women is double the rate for white females (Malveaux, 1993), and for Asian and Pacific Island women over the age of 75, the rate is as high as 40 percent (Kim, 1983). Particularly vulnerable are the most recent immigrant Asian groups—Vietnamese, Hmomg, and Laotian—and Pacific Islander populations—Samoan and Tongan (U.S. Bureau of the Census, 1993a, 1993b).

In 1990 only a small percentage of older adults—16 percent of men and 9 percent of women—remained in the workforce (Taeuber & Allen, 1993). Whereas women's participation in the paid labor force has increased, their occupational profile continues to reflect job segregation and discrimination. Despite guarantees of the Fourteenth Amendment, Title VII of the federal Civil Rights Act of 1964, and the Equal Pay Act of 1963, women still face inequality in earnings, hiring, and promotions. Among women age 50 or older, 58 percent are employed in the sales, clerical, and retail businesses, usually with poor earnings and limited benefits (U.S. Department of Labor, 1990). Women earn less than men throughout their lives, and lower incomes continue in retirement because of wage-based public and private pensions. The additional dilemma of age discrimination is faced by middle-age and aging women who enter the job market late, only to find that their limited marketable experience and education leaves them markedly disadvantaged. Middle-age and older women of color are most at risk for this disadvantage (Taeuber & Allen, 1993).

The Social Security Act of 1935, together with its subsequent amendments, provides old age insurance (social security) for eligible workers and their families. As a result of social roles and expectations (and resultant choices), the dual labor market, work policies that are not family responsive, and the necessity to work, most men receive social security benefits as workers and most women, especially white women, receive social security benefits as dependents. However, recent figures reveal that the number of women age 62 years and older who receive dependent benefits has declined from 57 percent in 1960 to 39 percent in 1993 (U.S. Social Security Administration, 1993). In 1992 the average social security monthly benefit amount for retired workers was $735 for men and $562 for women. In contrast, a retired worker in the same year, usually a man, received $735 and the spousal benefit was $338 (U.S. Social Security Administration, 1993). Given women's traditional low wages, the increasing divorce rate, and the fact that survivor's benefits for widows have traditionally been higher than retirement benefits based on a woman's own work history (Ozawa, 1993), this trend will not result in improvements to the financial status of women. Social security paired with a private pension provides a more adequate retirement income than social security alone. Unfortunately, women tend to find private pensions nearly inaccessible because of their shorter work periods and consequent difficulty in meeting vesting requirements. Women can have pensions based on their marital status, but pensions based on another's work history are precarious at best (Abramovitz, 1992). Only half of men and one-fourth of women receive pensions. When women do receive a pension, their benefits are less than men's. In 1990 the combined mean monthly social security and pension income for male retirees was $1,160; this amount is 45 percent higher than the mean for women, which was $800 (Taeuber & Allen, 1993).

Caregiving

Caregiving has become a critical issue for Americans today, especially for the women who account for 75 percent of the nation's caregivers (Stone, Cafferata, & Sangl, 1986). Caring in America is frequently invisible, usually devalued, and generally assigned to women (Baines, Evans, & Neysmith, 1992). Three divergent trends affect how caregiving will be defined and practiced in U.S. society in the 21st century: (1) the increasing number of older adults, especially the oldest-old (those over age 85), (2) the changing American family (increasing number of single, blended, and other family patterns), and (3) the increasing number of women in the paid workforce. As England (1990) suggested, the expectations that "women can do it all are on a collision course" (p. 9) with the increasing number of dependent people and the declining number of available caregivers. These social and demographic changes have resulted in the public and private sectors asking who will take care of frail elders (Executive Office on Aging, State of Hawaii, 1993; Rivlin & Wiener, 1988). The availability and accessibility of long-term-care services provided to frail elders and other functionally impaired people is a critical issue for aging women because they are both the chief consumers of these services and the primary caregivers for frail elderly people. Caregiving may have its joys, but studies also document the startling consequences of caregiving on the emotional and physical well-being of the caregiver (George & Gwyther, 1986; Zarit, Reever, & Bach-Peterson, 1980). The years of no credit for caregiving in public or private pensions and the conceptualization of caregiving as the woman's domain, together with retirement and health care policies, make caregiving financially risky (Abramovitz, 1992; Baines et al., 1992; Browne, 1994; England, 1990), especially for those in low-paying jobs (Kingson & O'Grady-LeShane, 1993). Furthermore, according to the U.S. Congressional Budget Office (1988), the number of older women living alone will jump from 6.4 million to 17.7 million, a 179 percent increase, from 1983 to 2030. Older women living alone often have fewer resources, so who will their caregivers be? In the end, this shifting of the costs of long-term care to the family, that is, to women, can be expected to continue into the 21st century as long as public policies promote traditional gender role duties, neglect the protection of older women who live alone, ignore the needs of employees who are caregivers, and fail to adopt a government-funded long-term-care program.

The literature on caregiving generally neglects race and class influences. Discussions on the dichotomies between paid and unpaid work, and between the public and private spheres, ignore the fact that lower-class and economically disadvantaged ethnic minority women have always been expected to provide both paid and unpaid work and to work in both the public and private spheres for minimal salaries.

Health Issues

Because women have generally been neglected in research studies, far less is known about the health of aging women than that of aging men (Hooyman & Kiyak, 1993). However, recent studies have documented sex differences in physical health status among older adults (Verbrugge, 1984, 1989) and have begun to focus on gender-specific and gender-related health issues such as breast cancer and osteoporosis. An interesting paradox in the United States is the gender longevity gap—the fact that women, on average, report more illness and health care use than men and yet live seven years longer than men. The gender differences in health status, morbidity, and mortality rates have led researchers to investigate possible antecedents for such differences although none have been conclusive (Verbrugge, 1989; Waldron, 1976; Wingard, 1982). Native Americans and African Americans have shorter life expectancies and Japanese and Chinese Americans have longer life expectancies than white Americans (Hooyman & Kiyak, 1993). Studies suggest that mortality rates for both men and women have continued to decline, attributing such improvements to medical technology, wider access to medical care, improved public health measures, and the adoption of more positive lifestyle behaviors (Verbrugge, 1989). Although men have recently made greater gains than women in lengthening their life span (Sempos, Cooper, Kovar, & McMillen, 1988), women continue to live longer and will continue to make up the majority of the elderly population in the 21st century.

Mortality rates show that older men and women die from the same major problems even though their death rates differ. Heart disease, cancer, and cerebrovascular disease account for 75 percent of deaths in older males and females (Verbrugge, 1984). However, at older ages (past age 65) women's mortality rate for heart disease rises much more swiftly than men's and a larger proportion of women than men die from diabetes and atherosclerosis (Verbrugge, 1989). Black women age 65 to 74 die from cerebrovascular disease at twice the rate of white women (Manton, Patrick, & Johnson, 1987). Although the majority of older women are not disabled, white women suffer more from chronic illness and debilitating diseases than white men, and black women have more disability days compared with white women (Fahs, 1993).

After age 75, gender differences in patterns of illness and disability become even more striking. Seventy-five percent of nursing home residents are female, the majority of whom depend on Medicaid payment for care. This dependency is generally a result of three factors: (1) older men are likely to be married and their wives care for them, (2) women older than 75 have outlived their spouses and have few available resources for home-based care, and (3) women cannot afford private long-term-care services. Although longevity has its benefits, it is also true that the longer one lives the greater the chance that one will be poor and need long-term-care services. Any discussion of health care that neglects the economics of health care would be sadly incomplete. The organization of the present health care system and its emphasis on acute care, the institutional bias in Medicare and Medicaid, and the absence of a government-funded long-term-care program results in older adults spending 15 percent of their income on health care costs (U.S. Senate Special Committee on Aging, 1992). Because women tend to be poorer than men, every dollar spent on health care is a greater percentage of their income. Women's health needs differ from men's, and it is long-term care that is most needed but least funded by any social insurance programs.

In short, great diversity exists among women and yet some common themes emerge. Women come to retirement poorer than men because of a different work history shaped by the gender, and race, division of labor that relegates women to unpaid work in the home and poorly paid jobs in the workforce; the subsequent inaccessibility, inequality, and inadequacy of public and private pensions; the social role expectations and choices in caregiving; and the political decisions that have promoted or failed to correct the effects of age, race, and gender discrimination. Finally, whereas women were often neglected in research, more recent work documents their different health patterns and their different health, long-term care, and social welfare needs.

A FEMINIST LIFE SPAN PERSPECTIVE ON AGING

A feminist life span perspective on aging offers a standpoint for analyzing the usefulness of public and private policies for older women. Such a perspective integrates ideas from the literature on cohort influences and the life course (Riley, 1981, 1985; Riley & Riley, 1989) with the work of feminist gerontological scholars that emphasize aging as a life span issue (Gonyea, 1994; Gottlieb, 1989; Hess, 1985; Stoller & Gibson, 1994). The life span perspective on aging examines the developmental changes that occur across the life span in the biological, physiological, social, and psychological spheres. Central to this analysis is the acknowledgment of the forces behind one's social location, the sociohistorical period, and one's personal biography in shaping individual aging experiences (Stoller & Gibson, 1994). Feminism, on the other hand, is both a philosophical perspective, a way of visualizing and thinking about situations, and an evolving set of theories that attempt to explain the various phenomena of women's oppression (Van Den Bergh & Cooper, 1986). At its most elementary level feminism is a critique of patriarchy and sexual oppression, but it is also concerned with the oppression of all people (Caraway, 1991; P. H. Collins, 1989; DiNitto & McNeece, 1990).

The existence of multiple feminisms in the literature makes defining a feminist life span perspective for aging women a challenging task. Nevertheless, the writings of a number of feminist scholars have identified themes that guide the development of such a framework (Abramovitz, 1992; Anzaldua, 1981; Baines et al., 1992; Bricker-Jenkins & Hooyman, 1986; Browne, 1994, 1995; Caraway, 1991; B. G. Collins, 1986; P. H. Collins, 1989; Estes, Hernandez, & Hooyman, 1994; Gilligan, 1982; Gonyea, 1994; Gould, 1989; Gutierrez, 1990; Hess, 1985, 1990; hooks, 1984; Kolb Morris, 1993; Lorde, 1984; MacKinnon, 1989; Swigonski, 1993; Van Den Bergh & Cooper, 1986; Zinn, 1990). The themes these scholars address include women as an oppressed population; a life span approach to the sociopolitical study of women and aging as opposed to the pathologization of women; the recognition of strengths and personal power and the reconceptualization of power as opposed to victimization; the challenges of unity and solidarity; uniqueness and strengths within diversities; the celebration of differences and voices between men and women and among women; the need for holistic and ecological thinking; the personal as political; and the contributions of new visions in feminist theory and methodology.

The life span and feminist perspectives guide us toward the development of a feminist life span perspective on aging. Such a perspective, less a series of techniques than a philosophical base, provides a gender lens for recognizing older women's economic, health, and caregiving needs as outcomes of political, economic, and social forces that have essentially followed women throughout the life cycle. It is a perspective that

- begins with an acknowledgment of women's oppression and women's inequality to men.

- views women's oppression from a life span perspective as opposed to one of pathology.

- understands that one's status in life is determined not only by personal biography but by social, cultural, and political forces and structures. It sees a lifetime of inequities and recognizes that age only exacerbates most women's risk for poverty.

- hears the varied voices of women and is thus critical of a singular voice of women. It understands that women's inequality is shaped by the multiple intersections of race, class, age, ethnicity, and sexual orientation.

- understands that political and structural changes are needed to change women's lives and that a new paradigm is essential for caregiving, health care, and work.

- looks to new conceptualizations of power and empowerment, moving away from victimization to women's empowerment, self-responsibility, and strengths.

- is rooted in women's lives, and seeks a vision, not a fantasy. Although it hopes for unity, it courts solidarity, recognizing that there will be issues around which women's voices can converge, and times when race and class, not gender, may be the primary organizing force.

- embraces an ecological and holistic perspective and looks to linkages between the young and the old, between races, between men and women, and between the healthy and the frail. It also sees the linkages between social, political, and economic issues and their impact on the life chances of women: between caregiving across the life span and women's poor wages; between income and health care accessibility and adequacy; between the gender division of labor and poverty; between capitalism, patriarchy, and violence in the home; and between practice, policy, and research.

- finds fault with research methods that isolate variables from the context in which they occur. Feminist research views the social reality of a situation as the research agenda. A feminist life span perspective on aging advocates a methodology that incorporates a holistic view of women's lives and identifies strategies to change the status quo and improve women's lives.

Such a perspective can be useful in providing a method to critique present and proposed public policies.

CURRENT AND PROPOSED PUBLIC AND PRIVATE POLICIES
Social Security, Private Pensions, and Employment Policies
Feminists have sharply criticized the ideological underpinnings that have framed retirement and other pubic policies that are based on gender role stereotypes. Two values and beliefs have come under the most scrutiny: (1) that women are dependent and men are

independent (the breadwinners), as opposed to viewing marriage as an equal family unit; and (2) that women are natural nurturers, so caregiving is assigned to women and they receive no retirement work credits for this work. The Social Security Act of 1935 was designed to reward the typical upper- and middle-class family of the time in which the male was the breadwinner and his wife was his dependent. White, middle-class women generally followed gender role expectations by focusing their energies on the private as opposed to the public sphere and taking care of their families. Few middle-class women worked full-time out of the home, primarily because the financial burden of the family was firmly placed on the man's shoulders and care of children, the sick, and the aged were the responsibilities of the woman. Public policies directly or indirectly supported such gender role stereotypes by binding marital status to public or private pension benefits and investment capabilities via the income of a husband and by not crediting child care or elder care in either public or private pension plans (Abramovitz, 1992; Gottlieb, 1989). As Abramovitz cogently pointed out, women who followed such traditional definitions were generally rewarded financially more than women who were employed outside the home. For example, the present cohort of oldest-old (85 or older) married women typically benefit from their husband's more generous social security and private pension benefits. On the other hand, divorced older women must have been married for at least 10 years to collect benefits in their former husband's name, and their eligibility further depends on whether or not he is collecting benefits. Working class and ethnic women were never excluded from the demands of the public sphere, only the rewards.

Social Security. The divorce rate has risen, the number of women in the paid labor force has grown, and women's roles have changed since the enactment of the Social Security Act of 1935 (Rodeheaver, 1987). Although social security was never designed to be the sole retirement income of Americans, the majority of older women live only on social security, and the amount is not sufficient for health and financial well-being. If the future sees no changes in the premises underlying social security (women as dependent, men as breadwinners, no credit for caregiving) and if sex, race, and age discrimination continue, women's benefits will continue to be less than men's. Furthermore, old age assistance from the means-tested SSI program is more vulnerable to cuts than is social security, which affects more ethnic women (Torres-Gil, 1992).

As a result of these demographic changes, two issues have surfaced in the social security debate: equity and adequacy (Bandler,

1989). Vertical equity emphasizes workers' contributions over those who have been defined as noncontributory, such as dependents. Adequacy emphasizes provision of minimal benefits to retired workers, children and elderly wives of retired workers, elderly widows of insured workers, and children and widows of deceased workers. Reform strategies have striven to promote equity for working spouses and to ensure adequacy for the homemaker and the elderly widow (Burkhauser & Smeeding, 1994).

Achieving the balance, however, between ensuring adequacy and ensuring equity continues to plague policymakers, especially with the dual entitlement clause, which states that a dependent, usually a woman, must choose between receiving her pension on her own work history or receiving a benefit as a homemaker and spouse. Reform proposals have generally focused on marital earnings sharing to replace the dual entitlement clause. Marital earnings strategies would combine the couple's earnings during their marriage and divide them equally, with each spouse receiving a benefit based on 50 percent of the marital earnings plus any individual earnings before and after the marriage (Bandler, 1989). As Bandler stated, this strategy "recognizes marriage as an economic partnership, reduces benefit disparities between spouses, provides homemakers protection, and increases benefits for many divorced workers" (p. 309). Advocates for equity reform hope that the marital earnings strategy will provide a more just distribution of resources for working women and two-income couples. However, critics claim that such changes will help the upper-income two-income couple at the expense of the homemaker, cut benefits for one-income couples and divorced men, eliminate all family entitlements, cut many benefits for the young family, penalize low-benefit couples, and lower benefits for older adults (U.S. House Committee on Ways and Means, 1985). In contrast, those favoring adequacy reforms advocate preserving the financial security of the worker and family members, regardless of whether they are employed outside the home, and have focused on entitlement gaps and inadequate benefits. Critics of adequacy reform claim any changes will help the homemaker and elderly widower but not employed women. The debate continues about how to preserve adequacy for elderly widows, families, and low-benefit couples and equity for dual-income couples (see Kingson & O'Grady-LeShane, 1993; Sandell & Iams, 1994). A life span perspective acknowledges this dilemma and advocates a thorough evaluation of these and other proposals that aim to improve women's lives. Such a perspective can help policymakers conceive of older women as a diverse population and recognizes that any structural change to social security will have winners and losers.

One strategy is to target those who are in the most financial need of benefits. At the same time, feminists realize that targeting the poor has inherent political dilemmas. Unlike social security, there are no public welfare sacred cows, and targeting financially needy older women as recipients of social insurance programs will be a difficult tightrope for policymakers to walk.

To its credit, social security has adapted, albeit slowly, to demographic changes. Numerous amendments have liberalized its definitions of the family, increased flexibility in retirement ages, and increased benefits for divorced spouses. Social Security has a number of positive biases, including the fact that it is involuntary and inaccessible until retirement age. This inaccessibility eventually helps poor people in a paternalistic sort of way. Female workers also make greater use of the weighted, progressive benefit that helps those in lower wage brackets (Bandler, 1989). However, social security still does not lift women from the ranks of the poor. A different reform strategy to improve older women's economic status is to raise SSI payments to at least 100 percent of the poverty level for individuals and couples (U.S. House Select Committee on Aging, 1989).

Private Pensions. Private pensions are criticized for being inaccessible. Private pensions are necessary to meet the financial needs of older Americans, and yet as previously discussed, men's work histories and types of employment result in their receiving private pensions more often than women. The Employee Retirement Income Security Act (ERISA) of 1974 was aimed at stopping retirement funding abuse. However, the act did not make pensions mandatory, and it rarely protects the marginalized worker. Instead, protection is most often offered to long-term employees, full-time employees, well-paid employees, and employees for large industrial employers. Rarely do women and ethnic minorities fit this profile. Furthermore, ERISA covers only traditional and private pensions, not pensions from the state, county, and federal governments, where women are more often employed. Furthermore, the vesting requirements exceed the time most women remain in one job. The minimum vesting period is five to seven years, but the average woman works in one job only 4.3 years, and unlike social security, private pensions are not portable. Reform strategies have advocated amending ERISA to make it mandatory and involuntary like social security, including 401K plans as a supplement; reducing the vesting period to one year; requiring spousal consent to all options; and eliminating pension integration (U.S. House Select Committee on Aging, 1989).

Employment Policies. A number of proposed strategies aim to improve economic security for all women in later life. A feminist life span perspective on aging understands the life cycle nature of discrimination against women and the relationships between deindustrialization, a stagnant economy, and the poverty of women and people of color. Therefore, a critical reform strategy is to support the Equal Employment Opportunity Commission (EEOC) in making a greater commitment to investigate race, age, and gender discrimination. Class action suits and other legal mechanisms could result in better funding for affirmative action programs and an end to segregated employment. Employment policies should provide wage and job equity (job parity for full- and part-time workers and an increased minimum wage) as well as compensation equity (pension, health insurance, and family-responsive options). Small business should not be excluded from pension policy changes as women work primarily in small business. Caregiving credit should be given toward one's retirement in public and private pensions for both men and women. In addition to supporting such reform strategies, a feminist life span perspective on aging advocates the end to men's work patterns as the model for building retirement plans for women.

Caregiving, Health Care, and Long-Term-Care Policies

Caregiving has serious dilemmas for women (Browne, 1994) and raises ideological and programmatic issues for social workers, especially those who work with the aged: How can women not be exploited when there are not enough long-term-care services? A number of reform strategies have been suggested: a reexamination of eligibility rules for pensions to include caregiving credit; the reeducation of men and women to promote caregiving as a family and community responsibility; the expansion of community-based services; increased caregiver training and education; and support from employers for family-friendly, responsive services and benefits (Allen, 1993b; U.S. House Select Committee on Aging, 1988; Zarit, Reever, & Bach-Peterson, 1980). Such programs to help caregivers may, at first glance, appear gender neutral. However, social policies that appear gender neutral in intent are not gender neutral in impact (Abramovitz, 1992; England, 1990; Moon, 1990). As England (1990) argued, gender-neutral policies may influence choices already shaped by sex-role stereotypes, thus perpetuating gender inequities. In contrast, a feminist perspective on aging begins with the understanding that caregiving must be analyzed within a framework based on women's reduced status in a patriarchal society. Caring and caregiving are not the problem; rather, it is the assignment of caregiving to women and the rules that have ignored or punished women's contributions to family life (Browne, 1994). A new vision for caregiving demands that social workers advocate for a comprehensive universal health care plan and a national long-term-care policy to support all caregivers. A life span perspective, with its emphasis on empowerment and responsibility, also asks why women continue to maintain this role and to resist change. According to England (1990), caregiving raises contradictions and dilemmas that must be understood in light of women's commitment to this role and the power of social relations.

Advocates for health care and long-term-care reform have generally attacked the system for its lack of accessibility, its high costs, and its inequitable distribution (Hooyman & Kiyak, 1993; Zones, Estes, & Binney, 1987). Others have focused on evaluating alternatives to pay for health care for older adults (Executive Office on Aging, State of Hawaii, 1993; Rivlin & Wiener, 1988). Older adults generally rely on Medicare, private health insurance, and private savings to pay for their health care needs. Medicare pays 45 percent of health care costs and limited nursing home care for older adults (Hooyman & Kiyak, 1993). Medicaid, the state and federal funding medical insurance program for indigent people, accounts for 71 percent of government spending for nursing home and home care (Rivlin & Wiener, 1988). Older women often turn to Medicaid to pay for their long-term-care needs. The recent Spousal Impoverishment Plan helps married women (and men) to avoid having to spend all of their assets before being eligible for Medicaid. Although this plan aims to protect part of a spouse's income, health care costs, especially long-term-care costs, remain a major source of worry for many Americans.

The national debate on health care continues. A feminist life span perspective on aging advocates for universal health care coverage for all Americans that includes long-term care. Given the differences in longevity between men and women, the financial difficulty in attaining long-term care, and the nation's reliance on women's unpaid caregiving, health care reform is especially essential for women. Without a provision for long-term-care funding, Medicaid remains an unworkable de facto primary funding source for long-term care. Consequently, as Butler (1994) recently warned, "it is really women that new ageists are referring to when they talk about denying health care to the elderly" (p. 7).

THE 21ST CENTURY

Public policies have primarily been meliorative in their strategies and have experienced some success. Universal health care, and, to a more limited extent, long-term care, are on the nation's political agenda. An increasing number of women in the paid workforce are earning their own retirement benefits as well as increased attention from feminists to the contributions and needs of women of color. Society is becoming more aware of the strengths as well as the challenges of older women, in part because of the educational and political efforts of organizations such as the Older Women's League. Still, a look at the 21st century is disheartening without prospects for fundamental change. There is scant reason to be optimistic for the future of many young women.

First, the growth of the female-headed household is accelerating at an unprecedented rate, especially among young black women (Ozawa, 1993). Many are single women and single mothers who are economically at risk. Low pay continues to make life difficult and gender discrimination in employment continues. According to a recent report, 80 percent of women still occupy 5 percent of the nation's categories of jobs (U.S. Bureau of the Census, 1990). The move out of segregated employment is painstakingly slow, and retirement benefits continue to be built on wage-based formulas.

Second, the decline in manufacturing jobs and deindustrialization has led to the increasing use of part-time workers and leased employees (Zinn, 1990). Such workers usually have no benefits, and 70 percent of all part-time workers in this country are women. With deindustrialization comes downsizing, and age discrimination begins earlier for women than for men. The result is that women and minorities generally lose their jobs before white men.

Third, the business community, with some exceptions, has not taken a leadership role in promoting family-friendly options such as day care, elder care benefits, and family leave in the workplace (Tennstadt & Gonyea, 1994; Trzcinski, 1994). According to data from the U.S. Department of Labor (1993), only 5 percent of all full-time employees in medium and large businesses have access to child care benefits, 9 percent have flexible benefit plans, 3 percent have paid maternity leave, and only 1 percent have paid paternity leave. In small establishments, the percentages are even smaller (U.S. Department of Labor, 1991). The results of suggestions that business will embrace eldercare remain to be seen.

Fourth, by the year 2030, racial and ethnic groups are projected to represent 25 percent of the older population, up from 13 percent in 1990 (AARP, 1993). It remains to be seen whether social and economic resolutions between the classes, races, and generations will continue to evolve.

A feminist life span perspective on aging introduces a strategy in which to scrutinize, evaluate, and expose contradictions in the effectiveness of public and private policies to meet the needs of women. If justice means, as Kirp, Yudof, and Franks (1986) argued in their book *Gender Justice,* enhancing choices for individuals and securing a focus on process rather than on particular outcomes, then a feminist perspective on aging asks, in contrast, if meaningful choice can be made within a capitalist and patriarchal society. With its focus on the life cycle nature of women's oppression, this perspective is critical of any policy, program, or law that does not address the social and economic realities of women of any age in light of the nation's ills. Therefore, a feminist life span perspective on aging advocates for equity for women in their younger years in terms of decent jobs and wages, child support, and adequate government transfer programs (Ozawa, 1993). Feminists understand that women's later years are characterized by more dependency on public policy than are men's and that public policy changes to limit benefits will affect women disproportionately. Accordingly, there are dangers in the argument for making social security a means-tested program, for it will be more vulnerable to political and economic forces and will, in the end, affect women and disadvantaged minorities more than white men. Furthermore, the realization that both men's and women's lives are shaped, for good and bad, by social structure can increase linkages between the sexes with the understanding that both have unfair burdens placed on them. With its focus on diversity, this perspective acknowledges racial oppression in society and among feminists, with an aim away from race-blind theoretical formulations (Dressel, 1988) and toward social justice by structurally addressing the roots of all oppression (Abramovitz, 1994). Acknowledgment of the multiple experiences of women is central because it negates the portrayal of the aged as only a prosperous population.

Feminists often advocate for meliorative strategies because they appear more feasible and palatable than radical ones, but will they be successful? In *Women on the Front Lines* (1993), Allen and Pifer articulated the challenge as one of creating new policy initiatives that generally empower and integrate older women in our aging society. While one hopes that reform and integrationist strategies will address the needs of women, serious risks exist in asking a government that is insensitive to the needs of women to remedy the situation.

This chapter examined three areas of concern for aging women—income, caregiving, and health. A feminist life span perspective on aging calls for a new epistemology of gender and age that recognizes that women's problems relate to inequality. The perspective begins to question the basic premises that underlie public and private policies. Rather than ask whether employment policies can be made more responsive to the needs of women as caregivers, the perspective asks why the family is the responsibility of women. Can caregiving be incorporated into public policy without discrediting it? An epistemology of gender and age also redefines citizenship to conceive of caregiving and work as both a family and a societal responsibility and that values, both economically and in other ways, the contributions of both to the family and to the market. It advocates for policies that address these issues from a perspective that recognizes caregiving as an economic, work, and community concern.

A feminist life span perspective on aging raises new questions: Why do women have a better chance of receiving adequate benefits if their work history is similar to men's? Given that the average marriage last only seven years, should marriage continue to be an eligibility factor for pensions? Can we redefine health and well-being? Can we make women's health needs, throughout the life span, a priority research agenda? Thus, a feminist life span perspective on aging supports ameliorative reform to help older women today but also advocates a new vision for women in the 21st century that seeks answers to questions about gender and power relationships that are embedded in our social, cultural, and political fabric. In the end, a new discourse may start with this question: Can society regard women as if who they are and what they do matter?

REFERENCES

Abramovitz, M. (1992). *Regulating the lives of women.* Boston: South End Press.

Abramovitz, M. (1994). Is the social welfare system inherently sexist and racist? Yes. In H. Karger & J. Midgley (Eds.), *Controversial issues in social policy* (pp. 142–149, 153–156). Needham Heights, MA: Allyn & Bacon.

Allen, J. (1993a). The front lines. In J. Allen & A. F. Pifer (Eds.), *Women on the front lines: Meeting the challenge of an aging America* (pp. 1–10). Washington, DC: Urban Institute Press.

Allen, J. (1993b). Caring work and gender equity in an aging society. In J. Allen & A. F. Pifer (Eds.), *Women on the front lines: Meeting the challenge of an aging America* (pp. 221–239). Washington, DC: Urban Institute Press.

Allen, J., & Pifer, A. (Eds.). (1993). *Women on the front lines: Meeting the challenges of aging America.* Washington, DC: Urban Institute Press.

American Association of Retired Persons. (1993). *A profile of older Americans*. Washington, DC: Author.

Anderson, M. L., & Collins, P. H. (Eds.). (1992). *Race, class, and gender: An anthology*. Belmont, CA: Wadsworth.

Anzaldua, G. (1981). La Prieta. In C. Moraga & G. Anzaldua (Eds.), *This bridge called my back: Writings by radical women of color* (2nd ed., pp. 198–209). Watertown, MA: Persephone Press.

Axinn, J. (1989). Women and aging: Issues of adequacy and equity. In J. D. Garner & S. O. Mercer (Eds.), *Women as they age: Challenges, opportunities, and triumphs* (pp. 339–362). New York: Haworth Press.

Baines, C., Evans, P., & Neysmith, S. (1992). Confronting women's caring: Challenges for practice and policy. *Affilia, 7*(1), 21–44.

Bandler, J.T.D. (1989). Family protection and women's issues in social security. *Social Work, 34,* 307–311.

Bohan, J. (1993). Regarding gender: Essentialism, constructionism, and feminist psychology. *Psychology of Women Quarterly, 17,* 5–21.

Bricker-Jenkins, M., & Hooyman, N. (1986). *Not for women only: Social work practice with a feminist future*. Silver Spring, MD: National Association of Social Workers.

Browne, C. (1994). A vision for practice with older women. *Journal of Applied Social Sciences, 18*(1), 5–16.

Browne, C. (1995). Empowerment in social work practice with older women. *Social Work, 40,* 358–364.

Burkhauser, R. V., & Smeeding, T. M. (1994). *Policy brief: Social security reform: A budget neutral approach to reducing older women's disproportionate risk of poverty* (No. 2). Syracuse, NY: Syracuse University Maxwell School of Citizenship and Public Affairs/Center for Policy Research.

Butler, N. (1994). Dispelling ageism: The cross-cutting intervention. In R. B. Enright, Jr. (Ed.), *Perspectives in social gerontology* (pp. 3–10). Needham Heights, MA: Allyn & Bacon.

Caraway, N. (1991). *Segregated sisterhood*. Knoxville: University of Tennessee Press.

Civil Rights Act of 1964, P. L. 88-352, 78 Stat. 241.

Collins, B. G. (1986). Defining feminist social work. *Social Work, 31,* 214–219.

Collins, P. H. (1989). The social construction of Black feminist thought. *Signs, 14*(4), 745–773.

Davis, K., Grant, P., & Rowland, D. (1990). Alone and poor: The plight of elderly women. *Generations, 14*(3), 43–47.

DiNitto, D. M., McNeece, C. A. (1990). *Social work: Issues and opportunities in a challenging profession.* Englewood Cliffs, NJ: Prentice Hall.

Dressel, P. (1988). Gender, race, class: Beyond the feminization of poverty in later life. *Gerontologist, 28*(2), 177–180.

Employee Retirement Income Security Act of 1974, P.L. 93-406, 88 Stat. 829.

England, S. E. (1990). Family leave and gender justice. *Affilia, 5*(2), 8–24.

Equal Pay Act of 1963, P.L. 88-38, 77 Stat. 56.

Estes, C., Hernandez, G. G., & Hooyman, N. (1994, March). *Creating a new age for women: Advocacy for the next century.* Paper presented at the Annual Meeting of the American Society of Aging, San Francisco.

Executive Office on Aging, State of Hawaii. (1993). *Long-term care plan for the state of Hawaii.* Honolulu: Author.

Fahs, M. (1993). Preventive medical care: Targeting elderly women in an aging society. In J. Allen & A. Pifer (Eds.), *Women on the front lines: Meeting the challenges of an aging America* (pp. 105–131). Washington, DC: Urban Institute Press.

Forman, M. (1985). Social security is a women's issue. In B. Hess & E. Markson (Eds.), *Growing old in America: New perspectives on old age* (pp. 212–275). New Brunswick, NJ: Transaction.

Friedan, B. (1993). *Fountain of age.* New York: Simon & Schuster.

George, L., & Gwyther, L. (1986). Caregiver well-being: A multi-dimensional examination of family caregivers of demented adults. *Gerontologist, 26,* 449–456.

Gilligan, C. (1982). *In a different voice.* Cambridge, MA: Harvard University Press.

Gonyea, J. (1994). The paradox of the advantaged elder and the feminization of poverty. *Social Work, 39,* 35–41.

Gottlieb, N. (1989). Families, work, and the lives of old women. In J. D. Garner & S. O. Mercer (Eds.), *Women as they age: Challenges, opportunities, and triumphs* (pp. 217–244). New York: Haworth Press.

Gould, K. H. (1989). A minority-feminist perspective on women and aging. In J. D. Garner & S. O. Mercer (Eds.), *Women as they age: Challenges, opportunities, and triumphs* (pp. 195–216). New York: Haworth Press.

Greer, G. (1991). *The change: Women, aging, and menopause.* New York: Fawcett Columbine.

Gutierrez, L. (1990). Working with women of color. *Social Work, 35,* 149–154.

Hartman, A. (1990). Aging as a feminist issue [Editorial]. *Social Work, 35,* 387–388.

Hess, B. (1985). Aging policies and older women: The hidden agenda. In A. Rossi (Ed.), *Gender and the life course* (pp. 319–331). New York: Aldine de Gruyter.

Hess, B. (1990). The demographic parameters of gender and aging. *Generations, 14*(3), 12–16.

hooks, B. (1984). *Feminist theory: From margin to center.* Boston: South End Press.

Hooyman, N., & Kiyak, H. A. (1993). *Social gerontology* (3rd ed.). Needham Heights, MA: Allyn & Bacon.

Jackson, J. (1985). Poverty and minority status. In M. Haugh, A. Ford, & M. Sheafor (Eds.), *The physical and mental health of aging women* (pp. 166–181). New York: Springer.

Kim, P. K. (1983). Demography of the Asian-Pacific elderly: Selected problems and implications. In R. L. McNeely & J. L. Cohen (Eds.), *Aging in minority groups* (pp. 29–41). Beverly Hills, CA: Sage Publications.

Kingson, E. R., & O'Grady-LeShane, R. (1993). The effect of caregiving on women's Social Security benefits. *Gerontologist, 33*(2), 230–239.

Kirp, D. L., Yudof, M. C., & Franks, M. S. (1986). *Gender justice.* Chicago: University of Chicago Press.

Kolb Morris, J. (1993). Interacting oppressions: Teaching social work content on women of color. *Journal of Social Work Education, 29*(1), 99–110.

Lewis, M., & Butler, R. (1972). Why is feminism ignoring older women? *International Journal of Aging and Human Development, 3,* 223–232.

Lewittes, H. H. (1989). Just being friendly means a lot: Women, friendship, and aging. In L. Grau (Ed.), *Women in the later years* (pp. 139–160). New York: Harrington.

Lorde, A. (1984). *Sister outsider.* Trumansburg, NY: Crossing Press.

MacKinnon, C. (1989). *Toward a feminist theory of the state.* Cambridge, MA: Harvard University Press.

Malveaux, J. (1993). Race, poverty and women's aging. In J. Allen & A. Pifer (Eds.), *Women on the front lines: Meeting the challenges of aging America* (pp. 167–190). Washington, DC: Urban Institute Press.

Manton, K. G., Patrick, C. H., & Johnson, K. W. (1987). Health differentials between blacks and whites: Report of trends in mortality and morbidity. *Millbank Memorial Fund, 65*(Suppl.), 129–199.

Markson, E. (1983). *The older woman: Issues and prospects.* Lexington, MA: Lexington Press.

Minkler, M., & Stone, R. (1985). The feminization of poverty and older women. *Gerontologist, 25*(4), 351–357.

Moon, M. (1990). Public policies: Are they gender-neutral? *Generations, 14*(3), 59–63.

O'Grady-LeShane, R. (1990). Older women and poverty. *Social Work, 35,* 422–424.

Older Women's League. (1990). *Heading for hardship: 1990 Mother's Day report.* Washington, DC: Older Women's League.

Ozawa, M. N. (1993). Solitude in old age: Effects of female hardship on elderly women's lives. *Affilia, 8*(2), 136–156.

Quadagno, J., & Harrington Meyer, M. (1990). Gender and public policy. *Generations, 14*(3), 64–66.

Reinhardt, J., & Fisher, C. (1989). Kinship versus friendship: Social adaptation in married widowed elderly women. In L. Grau (Ed.), *Women in the later years* (pp. 191–212). New York: Harrington.

Riley, M. W. (1981). Health behaviors of older people: Toward a new paradigm. In D. L. Parron, F. Soloman, & J. Rodin (Eds.), *Health, behavior, and aging: Summary of a conference* (pp. 25–39). Washington, DC: National Academy Press.

Riley, M. W. (1985). Women, men and the lengthening life course. In A. S. Rossi (Ed.), *Gender and life course* (pp. 333–348). New York: Aldine de Gruyter.

Riley, M. W., & Riley, J. W. (1989). The lives of older people and changing social roles. *The Annals of the American Academy of Political and Social Sciences: The Quality of aging. Strategies for Interventions, 503,* 14–28.

Rivlin, A. M., & Wiener, J. (1988). *Caring for the disabled elderly: Who will pay?* Washington, DC: Brookings Institution.

Rodeheaver, D. (1987). When old age became a social problem, women were left behind. *Gerontologist, 27*(6), 741–746.

Sandell, S. H., & Iams, H. (1994). Caregiving and women's social security benefits: A comment on Kingson and O'Grady-LeShane. *Gerontologist, 34*(5), 680–684.

Sempos, C., Cooper, R., Kovar, M., & McMillen, M. (1988). Divergence of the recent trends in coronary mortality for the four major race-sex groups in the United States. *American Journal of Public Health, 78*(11), 1422–1426.

Social Security Act of 1935, ch. 531, 49 Stat. 620.

Steinem, G. (1992). *Revolution from within.* New York: Little, Brown.

Stoller, E. P., & Gibson, R. C. (Eds.). (1994). *Worlds of difference: Inequality in the aging experience.* Thousand Oaks, CA: Pine Forge Press.

Stone, R., Cafferata, G., & Sangl, S. (1986). *Caregivers of the elderly: A national profile.* Washington, DC: U.S. Department of Labor.

Swigonski, M. E. (1993). Feminist standpoint theory and the question of social work research. *Affilia, 8*(2), 171–183.

Taeuber, C., & Allen, J. (1993). Women in our aging society: The demographic outlook. In J. Allen & A. Pifer (Eds.), *Women on the front lines: Meeting the challenges of aging America* (pp. 11–45). Washington, DC: Urban Institute Press.

Tennstadt, S. L., & Gonyea, J. G. (1994). An agenda for eldercare research. *Research on Aging, 16*(1), 85–108.

Torres-Gil, F. (1992). *The new aging: Politics and change in America.* New York: Auburn House.

Trzcinski, R. (1994). Family and medical leave, contingent employment, and flexibility: A feminist critique of the U.S. approach to work and family policy. *Journal of Applied Social Sciences, 18*(1), 71–88.

Turner, B. F., & Troll, L. E. (1994). *Women growing older: Psychological perspectives.* Thousand Oaks, CA: Sage Publications.

U.S. Bureau of the Census. (1990). *Statistical abstract of the United States* (110th ed., pp. 390–391). Washington, DC: U.S. Government Printing Office.

U.S. Bureau of the Census. (1991). Poverty in the United States: 1990. In *Current population reports* (Series P-60, No. 175). Washington, DC: U.S. Government Printing Office.

U.S. Bureau of the Census. (1993a). *We the American Asians.* Washington, DC: U.S. Government Printing Office.

U.S. Bureau of the Census. (1993b). *We the American Pacific Islanders.* Washington, DC: U.S. Government Printing Office.

U.S. Bureau of the Census. (1993c). *We the American elderly.* Washington, DC: U.S. Government Printing Office.

U.S. Congressional Budget Office. (1988). *Changes in living arrangements of the elderly: 1960–2030.* Washington, DC: U.S. Government Printing Office.

U.S. Department of Labor. (1990). *Annual averaging.* Unpublished tabulations from the current population survey, 1989. Washington, DC: Author.

U.S. Department of Labor, Bureau of Labor Statistics. (1991, June 24). BLS reports on its first survey of employment benefits in small private establishments. *News.*

U.S. Department of Labor, Bureau of Labor Statistics. (1993, May). *Employee benefits in medium and large firms, 1991* (Bulletin 2422). Washington, DC: Author.

U.S. House Committee on Ways and Means, Subcommittee on Social Security. (1985). *Report on earnings sharings implementation study.* Washington, DC: U.S. Government Printing Office.

U.S. House Select Committee on Aging. (1988). *Exploding the myths: Caregiving in America.* Washington, DC: U.S. Government Printing Office.

U.S. House Select Committee on Aging. (1989). *The quality of life for older women: Older women living alone* (No. 100-693). Washington, DC: U.S. Government Printing Office.

U.S. Senate Special Committee on Aging. (1992). *Aging America: Trends and projections* (1991 ed.). Washington, DC: U.S. Government Printing Office.

U.S. Social Security Administration. (1993). *Facts about social security.* Washington, DC: Author.

Van Den Bergh, N., & Cooper, L. (1986). *Feminist visions for social work.* Silver Spring, MD: National Association of Social Workers.

Verbrugge, L. (1984). A health profile of older women with comparisons to older men. *Research on Aging, 6*(3), 291–322.

Verbrugge, L. (1989). Gender, aging, and health. In K. Markides (Ed.), *Aging and health* (pp. 23–78). Newbury Park, CA: Sage Publications.

Waldron, I. (1976). Why do women live longer than men? *Social Science and Medicine, 10,* 340–362.

Wingard, D. (1982). The sex differential in mortality rates: Demographic and behavioral factors. *American Journal of Epidemiology, 115*(2), 205–216.

Zarit, S., Reever, K., & Bach-Peterson, J. (1980). Relatives of the impaired elderly: Correlates of feelings of burden. *Gerontologist, 20,* 649–655.

Zinn, M. B. (1990). Family, feminism and race in America. *Gender and Society, 4*(1), 68–82.

Zones, J., Estes, C., & Binney, E. (1987). Gender, public policy, and the oldest old. *Ageing and Society, 7*(3), 275–302.

Index

Andersen, T., 26
Anderson, Carol, 22
Anderson, H., 27–29
Angier, N., 111
Aries, E., 47
Asian women, 333
Association for the Advancement of Feminism (Hong Kong), 187

B

Balch, Emily Greene, 159–160
Bandler, J.T.D., 341
Bateson, G., 26
Begum, H. A., 177
Behavior
    perceptions of normality and deviance in, 7–8
    reductionistic models of, 10
Belenky, M. F., 72, 233, 244
Benda, B. B., 239
Bennett, William, 227
Bennis, W. G., 77
Birch, E. L., 240–241
Blackwell agency, 79
Blum, L., 128, 132
Bombyk, M. J., 81
Boneparth, E., 152
Borderline personality disorder, 317, 318
Boyd, Neva, 46
Brace, Charles Loring, 215
Brettle, R. P., 299
Brienes, W., 222
Brodsky, A., 43
Brody, C. M., 43
Bruner, Edward, 26
Bureaucratic authority, 90–91
Burt, M. R., 236
Bush, George, 150
Butler, S., 43, 48

C

Cahalan, D., 261
Campbell, J., 322
Caregiving
    analysis of, 343–344
    for elderly, 334–335
    employee benefits for, 110–111
Caring
    ethics of, 134–135, 158
    ownership of, 135–138
    as social responsibility, 133–134
    war and ethics of, 166–168
Carroll, S. J., 150
Center for Latin American Social Work (CELATS) (Peru), 187–188
Chafetz, J., 146, 148
Chernesky, R. H., 81, 110
Child rearing
    effect of mother's personality on, 220–223
    poverty and faulty, 218–219
    scientific, 218, 219
    by working mothers, 220–222
Children
    homeless, 237–238
    as malleable creatures, 218
    moral contagion theory and, 214–215
Chin, A., 81
Chodorow, Nancy, 23
Christy, C. A., 148
Cisin, I., 261
Civil Rights Act of 1964, 333
Clark, C., 146
Clark, J., 146
Clark, W. B., 260
Clinchy, B. M., 72, 233
Clinton, Bill, 280, 281

Kirp, D. L., 346
Krauss, B. J., 287
Kravetz, D., 112

L

Labor force. *See* Work force
Laird, J., 21
Laotian women, 333
Leadership style
  description of preferred, 75
  gender and, 76–77
  male, 74–75
Learnfare, 226
Lee, J.A.B., 247, 248
Leen, C.L.S., 299
Lesbian families
  acceptance of, 285–287
  example of, 32–36
  overview of, 30–32
Lesbians
  civil rights issues and, 279
  coming out as issue facing,
    282–285
  current activism among,
    280–281
  demographics of, 279
  domestic violence among,
    288–289, 320–321
  ecological perspective in
    working with, 289
  HIV and AIDS among,
    287–288, 305
  needs of, 278
  policy implications for
    working with, 290–291
  program implications for
    working with, 291–292
  role in women's liberation
    movement, 279–280
  strengths perspective in
    working with, 290
Levinson, D., 314
Lewis, E., 42, 43–44, 65

Lewis, O., 224
Life span perspective, 337–339,
  344–347
Long-term care, 335, 344
Lowell, Josephine Shaw, 217
Lundberg, F., 221

M

Mackinnon, C. A., 197
Management. *See also* Feminist
  administration
  female qualities for, 71–73
  objectives of, 114
  styles of feminist versus
    nonfeminist, 80
  supportive versus directive,
    75, 76
Martin, P. Y., 91
Martinez-Brawley, E. E., 126
Masochistic personality
  disorder, 318
Maternal deprivation theory,
  221–223
Maternity benefits, 110–111
McChesney, K. Y., 239–241,
  243
McGoldrick, Monica, 22–24, 27
McIntyre, J. R., 265
Medicaid, 336, 337
Medicare, 337
Membership assistance programs (MAPs), 112,
  114, 120
Men. *See also* Gay men
  alcohol use and abuse
    among, 260
  coming-out process among
    homosexual, 284
  disaffiliation of homeless,
    235
Mental health issues
  emphasis on prevention,
    175–176

relationship between personality of mother and mental health of child, 222–223
social development and, 176
stigma and, 176–177
worldwide female, 177–178
Mental hygiene movement, 219
Mental illness
among homeless women, 235, 241
stigma regarding, 176–177
Mexican Human Rights Academy, 183
Middleman, R. R., 49
Military issues
arms proliferation and, 161–163
death and, 161
federal spending and, 160–161
Miller, Jean Baker, 23
Moral contagion theory, 213–215
Mortality rates
for alcoholic women, 264
male versus female, 336–337
Mothers
child rearing and effect of personality of, 220–223
lesbians as, 286–287
post–World War II image of, 221
Moynihan, D. P., 224–225

National Association of Social Workers (NASW), 154, 158
National Institute on Drug Abuse (NIDA), 259, 260
New Haven Home Recovery (Connecticut), 246–247
New York City Fire Department, 115–120

Nightingale, Florence, 111
Noddings, N., 134, 138, 165–167
Norwegian Housewives Association, 184–185
Nuclear threat
arms proliferation and, 161–163
feminism and, 159
strategies to prevent, 163–165

Occupational social work
feminist approach to, 112–120
future outlook for, 120–122
history of, 111–112
Organizational structure
gender and, 78–79
isolation in hierarchical, 113
preferred, 77–78
Our Sister's Place (Hartford, Connecticut), 247
Owen, D., 147

Pacific Island women, 333
Palley, M. L., 149
Papell, C. P., 49, 55
Peace
feminist ethical principles and issues related to, 159, 165–168
promotion of, 158–160
social work and, 168–170
Peace camps, 159
Pearce, J., 27
Pensions, 334, 335, 342
Personal is political
clients with HIV and AIDS and, 304–305, 307
political participation and, 150–151

Physicians, 111
Pifer, A., 346
Political participation
  access to existing political
    structure and, 147–148
  feminist theory and, 148–151
  gender stratification and,
    145–146, 151
  model to promote female,
    151–152
  social work and, 154
  socialization, discrimination,
    and, 146–147
  strategies for, 153
  women and, 143–145
Politics
  feminist agenda for 21st
    century in, 154–155
  representation of women in,
    144–145
  roles for women in, 152–153
Postmodern era, 26–28
Posttraumatic stress disorder,
  322
Poverty
  among elderly, 332, 333
  conservative theories of, 227
  culture of, 224–225
  extent of female worldwide,
    177
  genetic transmission theory
    of, 215–217
  homelessness and feminiza-
    tion of, 239–240
  mainstream theories of,
    211–213
  marital status and, 333
  moral contagion theory of,
    213–215
  psychological internalization
    theory of, 217–224
  social policy and, 225–228
  underclass theory of, 212, 225

Power
  dynamics in therapeutic
    relationship of, 8
  female versus male view of,
    73
  homelessness and, 232–233
  personal empowerment
    versus, 129
  political, 149
Powerlessness
  acceptance of, 269
  among substance-dependent
    women, 262
Praxis, 45, 57–58
Psychological internalization,
  217–224
Psychosocial spectrum,
  179, 180
Psychotherapy
  male-directed, 6–7
  value-free, 11
Purcell, K., 114

Q, R

Quayle, Dan, 147
Racism. *See also* Discrimination
  conflict stemming from, 61
  in early group work practice,
    46
Rainwater, L., 132
Rankin, Jeannette, 160
Rape
  intervention for perpetrators
    of, 319–320, 322–324
  study of societies prone to,
    314
  varying perceptions of, 315
Rappaport, C., 238
Reductionistic models, 10
Renaming, 244, 288–289
Renzetti, C. M., 146
Reynolds, Bertha, 4
Rich, Adrienne, 249, 278

Richmond, Mary, 4
Ridgeway, C. L., 48
Roberts, J., 27
Rockefeller Foundation, 219
Roe v. Wade, political process
    and, 152
Role change, 149
Role equity, 149
Roosevelt, Theodore, 216
Rosener, J. B., 77, 84
Roth, L., 238
Rothman, B., 49, 55
Rothschild, J., 72
Ruddick, S., 167
Rural women
    alternative perspectives on
        work of, 128–132
    caring and, 134–135
    caring as social responsibility
        and, 133–134
    employment opportunities
        for, 126–128
    ownership of caring and,
        135–138
Russell, B. G., 235
Ryan White Comprehensive
    AIDS Resources Emer-
    gency Act, 306
Ryland, Gladys, 45

S

Sagan, C., 162
Sanday, P., 314
Save the Children–USA
    (Bangladesh), 185
Schell, J., 162–163
Scientific mothering, 218, 219
Self-abuse, 241
Self-assessment, 200
Self-defeating personality
    disorder, 7–8, 317, 318
Self-disclosure, 9
Self-help groups, 60

Sex-role socialization, 23,
    263–264
Sexual harassment, 8–9, 110
Sexual reproduction, 226–227.
Shadow work, 137
Shilts, R., 295
Siegel, K., 287
Sivard, R. L., 161, 162
Smith, A. J., 303
Social change
    within service organizations,
        100
    sexual violence to women
        and, 314–315
Social construction, 27
Social Darwinism, 211, 215, 216
Social security, 340–342
Social Security Act of 1935,
    334, 340
Social status, 177–178
Social therapy, 322
Social wage, 131–133
Social work. *See also* Feminist
    social work
    implications of political
        participation of women
        for, 154
    in workplace, 111–120. *See
        also* Workplace
Social work education, 14
Social workers
    overview of early feminist,
        4–5
    as peacemakers, 168–170
Society for the Prevention of
    Cruelty to Children, 214
Socrates, 105
Soper, K., 166
Star Wars, 164
Sterilization, 217, 226
Stockholm syndrome, 318
Stolz, B. A., 121
Stoper, E., 129, 152

About the Editor

Nan Van Den Bergh, PhD, BCSW, LCSW, is director of the doctoral program at the School of Social Work, Tulane University, New Orleans. Previously, she served as director of the Employee Assistance Program at the University of California at Los Angeles and was a tenured faculty member in the Department of Social Work Education at California State University, Fresno. Dr. Van Den Bergh has served as a social work educator, practitioner, researcher, administrator, and community organizer. She began her involvement in feminist issues in the early 1970s and has used a feminist analysis in many purviews (for example, social work practice, occupational social work, and addictions). She has edited two other books using a feminist analysis: *Feminist Visions for Social Work* and *Feminist Perspectives on Addictions*. In addition to this book, she is also editing *Employee Assistance Practice in the Twenty-first Century*. Her most current research activities have focused on workplace discrimination and harassment experienced by members of sexual minorities as well as addictions within the lesbian/gay/bisexual/transsexual community.

About the Contributors

Ann A. Abbott, PhD, ACSW, is associate professor and associate dean at the School of Social Work, Rutgers University, Camden, New Jersey. Currently, she is a faculty fellow with the Center for Substance Abuse Prevention (CSAP) and the Substance Abuse and Mental Health Services Administration (SAMHSA). She has a bachelor's degree in psychology from St. Norbert College and master's and doctoral degrees in social work and social research from Bryn Mawr College, Graduate School of Social Work and Social Research. Dr. Abbott is president of the National Association of Social Workers (NASW). From 1989 to 1992 she served on the NASW Book Committee and from 1991 to 1992 on the editorial board of *Social Work Research & Abstracts.*

Mimi Abramovitz, DSW, is professor, School of Social Work, Hunter College, City University of New York, and author of *Regulating the Lives of Women: Social Welfare Policy from Colonial Times to the Present* now its fourth printing. She received her master's and doctoral degrees in social work from Columbia University. She is currently writing a book about women and welfare for Monthly Review Press and conducting research on the history of activism among low-income women in the United States, paying special attention to the claims they make on the welfare state.

Sheila H. Akabas, PhD, is professor, School of Social Work, Columbia University, New York, where she chairs the World of Work Field of Practice and directs the school's Center for Social Policy and Practice in the Workplace. She is coeditor with Paul Kurzman of *Work and Well-Being: The Occupational Social Work Advantage.* She has a long-standing interest in issues concerning women and work and served as the director of an organizational development and training program designed to improve gender integration in the New York City Fire Department.

Colette Browne, Dr PH, is associate professor of social work, School of Social Work , University of Hawaii, Honolulu; chair of the gerontology concentration; and faculty affiliate at the university's Center on Aging. Her research and scholarly interests are ethnogerontology, women and aging, and feminist theory.

Stephanie Brzuzy, PhD, is a lecturer in the College of Social Work at Ohio State University. Her background includes direct services in research and policy positions at the state level as well as in Washington, D.C. She is currently involved in research related to health care policy and women's issues.

Roslyn H. Chernesky, DSW, is professor, Graduate School of Social Service, Fordham University, New York. She chairs the administration practice area and teaches in both the master's and doctoral programs. She has been writing about women and administration since the 1970s. Other recent publications deal with the field of aging and foundation funding.

June Clark, MSW, is instructor of human services, Ottawa University (Arizona Center), Phoenix. She is currently working toward the completion of her doctorate in social work at Arizona State University and plans to focus on prison policies and programs affecting women in Arizona's state prisons. She is a mayoral appointee to the Phoenix Women's Commission.

Charles Garvin, PhD, is professor of social work, School of Social Work, University of Michigan at Ann Arbor, and director of the school's joint doctoral program in social work and social science. His research interests are group processes, gender and cultural diversity issues in groups, and services to people with serious mental illness. He has published extensively on group processes and on interpersonal practice in social work.

Cheryl Hyde, MSW, PhD, is assistant professor of human behavior in the social environment, School of Social Work, Boston University, where she also coordinates the sequence on racism and oppression. Her areas of interest include multiculturalism in social work education and praxis, organizational culture and transformation, feminist and progressive models of social change, the women's movement, and the New Right. She is the editor of *The Journal of Progressive Human Services.*

Alice K. Johnson, MSW, PhD, is assistant professor, Mandel School of Applied Social Sciences, Case Western Reserve University, Cleveland. Her research focuses on homelessness, especially homeless women and children, and the development of shelter-based services. Currently, she is completing a study of formerly homeless families and a book on homeless welfare and working poor families. Since 1991, she has been involved in research and child welfare training in Romania.

Mary Ann Kuszelewicz, ACSW, is a medical social worker at Tulane University Medical Center and a doctoral student at the School of Social Work, Tulane University, New Orleans. She is also a research assistant for the Tulane School of Social Work Institute for Research and Training in human immunodeficiency virus (HIV) and acquired immune deficiency syndrome (AIDS) counseling. Her main areas of interest include AIDS and women, social work practice with lesbians, feminist theory, and feminist spirituality.

Joan Laird, MS, is professor, Smith College School for Social Work, Northampton, Massachusetts. Coauthor with Ann Hartman of *Family-Centered Social Work Practice,* she has published extensively in the fields of social work and family therapy on family, gender, sexual orientation, and cultural themes. Most recently, she edited *Revisioning Social Work Education: A Social Constructionist Approach.*

Helen Land, MSW, PhD, is associate professor, School of Social Work, University of Southern California, Los Angeles. She has published extensively in the areas of clinical social work theory and practice and is the author of *AIDS: A Complete Guide to Psychosocial Intervention.* She currently chairs the clinical practice symposium of the Council on Social Work Education (CSWE).

Barrie Levy, LCSW, is a psychotherapist, consultant, and trainer and teaches at the School of Social Welfare, University of California at Los Angeles. She has published four books and several articles on domestic and sexual violence and has been involved in the movement against violence against women for 20 years.

Eileen F. Levy, PhD, is associate professor, School of Social Work and Jewish Studies Program, San Francisco State University. Her research and publications have focused on social work practice with lesbian clients, primarily in the area of lesbian parenting. She has given several workshops for social work educators on integrating lesbian and gay content throughout the curriculum. She serves on the editorial boards of the *Journal of Gay and Lesbian Psychotherapy* and the *Journal of Gay and Lesbian Social Services*. She has been a member of the CSWE Commission on Lesbian Women and Gay Men since 1990.

Edith A. Lewis, MSW, PhD, is associate professor of social work and women's studies at the University of Michigan, Ann Arbor. She also serves as codirector of the Program in Conflict Management Alternatives at the university. Her research has focused on culturally competent social work practice with women and families. Additionally, she has interest and expertise in the area of multicultural teaching and managing conflict within diverse organizations and communities.

Emilia E. Martinez-Brawley, MSW, EdD, is dean and professor at the School of Social Work, Arizona State University, Tempe. She has extensive involvement in research on rural areas, both nationally and internationally. She is the author of several books, among them *Transferring Technology in the Personal Social Services; Perspectives on the Small Community: Humanistic Views for Practitioners; Rural Social and Community Work in the U.S. and Great Britain; Seven Decades of Rural Social Work;* and *Pioneer Efforts in Rural Social Work: First Hand Views Since 1908.* Her current research focuses on locality-based and community-oriented rural services in the United States, the United Kingdom, Spain, and other European countries. She has written several articles on women and social work in rural areas.

Jane Miller, MSSA, LSW, is a feminist therapist working in a lesbian and gay psychotherapy practice in Cleveland. She served a two-year term as a member of NASW's Committee on Lesbian and Gay Issues (1989–1991). She is a frequent guest lecturer at local universities and community organizations. She also serves on the editorial board of the *Journal of Gay and Lesbian Psychotherapy.* Her areas of expertise include lesbian and gay issues, AIDS and women, feminist theory and practice, and social activism.

Beth Glover Reed, holds a joint appointment in social work and women's studies at the University of Michigan, Ann Arbor. Her research interests center on the ways that race, ethnicity, and gender operate within social systems of various sizes, especially within small groups, human services organizations, and other types of complex organizations. She also focuses on prevention and social change theory and interventions and has published extensively on issues for women who have problems with alcohol and other drugs.

Rosalie Richards, MSW, is an Episcopal priest who has served in bilingual inner-city churches in New York and Connecticut. In 1989 she began direct work with homeless families and helped develop New Haven Home Recovery, an agency that provides transitional housing, advocacy, and other support services to homeless families and to families headed by an HIV-positive mother. She is presently a doctoral student at the University of Texas School of Public Health in Houston, where she is studying ethnic and religious violence prevention on a societal level, education as a variable in health outcomes, and spirituality as a variable in health choices.

Elizabeth A. Segal, PhD, is associate professor, College of Social Work, Ohio State University. She teaches social welfare policy, research methods, child welfare, and statistics courses at both the graduate and undergraduate levels. She is currently involved in research on welfare reform initiatives and their impact on poor women and children.

Zulema E. Suarez, MSW, PhD, is assistant professor of social work, School of Social Work, University of Michigan, Ann Arbor, where she teaches culturally competent social work practice. Zulema writes about social work practice with ethnically diverse populations and has done research on Latino access to health care in the United States. She is embarking on a collaborative qualitative research study of migrant farmworker women.

Dorothy Van Soest, DSW, MSW, is associate dean, School of Social Work, University of Texas at Austin. She is past chair of NASW's Peace and Social Justice Committee. She wrote *Incorporating Peace and Social Justice into the Social Work Curriculum,* co-authored *Empowerment of People for Peace,* and has written several articles related to peace and social justice issues.

Janice Wood Wetzel, MSW, PhD, is dean of Adelphi University School of Social Work, Garden City, New York. Concerned with the relationship between women's human rights and mental health from a global perspective, she has written numerous articles on the subject, as well as two books: *Clinical Handbook of Depression* (1991) and *The World of Women: In Pursuit of Human Rights* (1993). Dr. Wetzel is an NGO ECOSOC Representative to the United Nations for the International

Association of Schools of Social Work. She is the coordinator of their International Symposium on Violence Against Women, which was organized in preparation for the Fourth World Conference on Women to be held in Beijing, China in September 1995.

Paz Méndez-Bonito Zorita, MSSA, PhD, is assistant professor of social work at Arizona State University, Tempe. She received her master's degree in social work and her doctorate in social welfare from Case Western Reserve University, Cleveland. She has published on the Latino family and has done research on financial management in poverty-stricken households. She was a practicing social worker for many years in a Latino neighborhood in Cleveland. She has been a Fulbright scholar and has lectured in Spain on family counseling, voluntarism, and cultural pluralism.

Feminist Practice in the 21st Century

Designed by Anne Masters Design.

Composed by Sheila Holzberger, Wolf Publications, Inc., in Futura,
Futura Condensed, and Galliard.

Printed by Victor Graphics, Inc., on 60# Windsor Offset.